BELGIUM
AND
LUXEMBOURG

FODOR'S TRAVEL PUBLICATIONS

are compiled, researched and edited by an international team of travel writers, field correspondents and editors. The series, which now almost covers the globe, was founded by Eugene Fodor in 1936.

OFFICES
New York & London

Fodor's Belgium & Luxembourg:

Area Editor: Nicolas Stevenson
Editorial Contributors: Robert Brown, Frances Howell, Tom Szentgyorgyi
Editor: Richard Moore
Maps: C. W. Bacon, Jeremy Ford, Bryan Woodfield
Drawings: Elizabeth Haines

FODOR'S

BELGIUM
AND
LUXEMBOURG
1988

Fodor's Travel Publications, Inc.
New York & London

ISBN 0-679-01471-3
ISBN 0-340-41786-2 (Hodder and Stoughton edition)

MANUFACTURED IN THE UNITED STATES OF AMERICA
10 9 8 7 6 5 4 3 2 1

CONTENTS

FOREWORD

Belgium and Luxembourg are among the smallest countries on the continent of Europe, yet there can be few areas of comparable size in the world where so much can be seen with so little expenditure of time and travel. You can go through centuries in a matter of hours; from prehistoric relics to visionary town-planning, from placid farmlands to throbbing powerhouses of technological progress, from traces of an ancient empire to modern European co-existence.

Belgium possesses one of Europe's largest ports, Antwerp. It has cities fabulously endowed with artistic treasures, and its capital, Brussels, also capital of the EEC and headquarters of NATO, is one of the busiest spots on the continent and offers some of the finest food in the world. Sadly, the vast influx of expense-account bureaucrats has turned it into one of Europe's more expensive cities.

Belgium is a minor United Nations all by itself, in that it has three distinct cultural divisions, the Walloons (French-speaking), the Flemish (Dutch-speaking), and a much smaller proportion of German people speaking German. The rivalries between the linguistic groups form a constant counterpoint to Belgian life.

This is the country of robust living, of joyous fun-fairs, uninhibited religious processions, and brassy nightclubs. Belgium also has two excellent holiday areas to offer; on its endless string of popular beaches, from De Panne through Oostende to Knokke-Heist, and in the pastoral, restful valleys of the Ardennes hills.

The rule of contrast so prevalent throughout Belgium applies also to the Grand Duchy of Luxembourg. It is industrially important out of all proportion to its geographic size, but none the less it remains for the visitor one of the last miniature countries of romantic fiction. Although boasting mighty steel foundries and modern farms, it exudes a medieval atmosphere that makes you feel you have stepped into a different world, full of castles, turrets, and moats. This, too, is a country of parades and processions, of good cheer and a hearty capacity to absorb beer and Moselle wine.

We wish to offer our sincere gratitude to all those who helped us in the preparation of the book. Our particular thanks go to the Commissioners of Tourism in Belgium, who have extended all possible help and courtesy through their organizations; to M. Pierre Claus, Director of the Belgian National Tourist Office in London, and to Pauline Owen of the London office for their constant help and advice. Also to our Area Editor, Nicolas Stevenson for his enthusiasm and knowledge of both Belgium and Luxembourg.

We are equally grateful to Mr. Georges Hausemer, Director of the Luxembourg National Tourist Office, for the advice and aid rendered us on his country. Mr. J. Uhres, secretary of the same organization, was also extremely helpful. Our thanks go, also, to M. André Claude, Government Counsellor of the Information and Press Service, who has been a constant source of information and advice over the years.

While every care has been taken to ensure the accuracy of the information contained in this guide, the publishers cannot accept responsibility for any errors which may appear.

All prices quoted in this guide are based on those available to us at the time of writing. In a world of rapid change, however, the possibility of inaccurate or out-of-date information can never be totally eliminated. We trust, therefore, that you will take prices quoted as indicators only, and will double-check to be sure of the latest figures.

Similarly, be sure to check all opening times of museums and galleries. We have found that such times are liable to change without notice, and you could easily make a trip only to find a locked door.

When a hotel closes or a restaurant produces a disappointing meal, let us know, and we will investigate the complaint. We are always ready to revise our entries for the following year's edition should the facts warrant it.

Send your letters to the editors of Fodor's Travel Publications, 201 E 50th Street, New York, N.Y. 10022. European readers may prefer to write to Fodor's Travel Guides, 9–10 Market Place, London W1N 7AG, England.

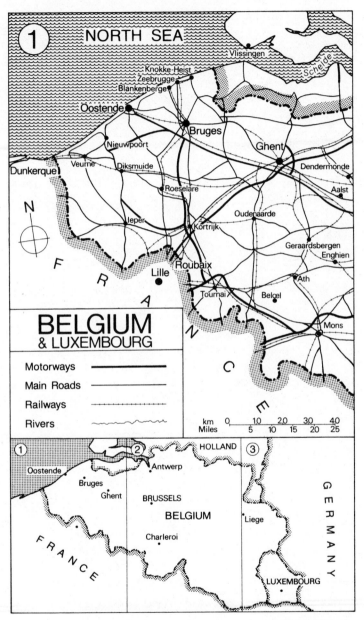

BELGIUM
& LUXEMBOURG

Motorways
Main Roads
Railways
Rivers

km 0   10   20   30   40
Miles   5   10   15   20   25

NORTH SEA

Vlissingen
Schelde
Knokke-Heist
Zeebrugge
Blankenberge
Oostende
Bruges
Ghent
Dendermonde
Nieuwpoort
Aalst
Veurne
Diksmuide
Dunkerque
Roeselare
Oudenaarde
Ieper
Kortrijk
Geraardsbergen
Enghien
Roubaix
Ath
Lille
Tournai
Beloel
Mons
F R A N C E

① ② HOLLAND ③
Oostende
Antwerp
Bruges
Ghent
BRUSSELS
BELGIUM
Liege
GERMANY
Charleroi
FRANCE
LUXEMBOURG

(see next two pages)

BELGIUM & LUXEMBOURG

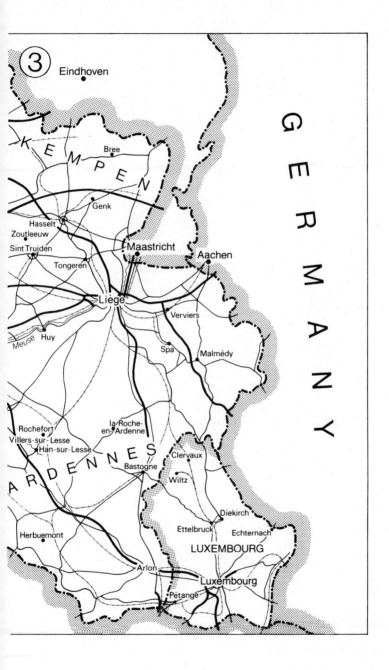

FACTS AT YOUR FINGERTIPS

 SOURCES OF INFORMATION. Unless you travel on a packaged tour, with a fixed itinerary and schedule which you can't modify, it's most unlikely that you will follow unchanged any detailed plans you make in advance. Nevertheless, it is advantageous to rough out your trip. This gives you an opportunity to decide how much you can comfortably cover in the time at your disposal. If you travel in the peak season, you will have to make reservations. Finally, poring over the folders any travel agency will give you in profusion is as much fun as the winter gallop through the seed catalogs. The best places to start your search are the National Tourist Offices:

United States: Belgian National Tourist Office, 745 Fifth Ave., New York, N.Y. 10151 (tel. 212–758–8130); Luxembourg, 801 2nd Ave., New York, N.Y. 10017 (tel. 212–370–9850).

United Kingdom: Belgian National Tourist Office, 38 Dover St., London W1 (tel. 499 5379); Luxembourg, 36 Piccadilly, London W1 (tel. 434–2800).

 TRAVEL AGENTS. When you have decided where you want to go, your next step is to consult a good travel agent. If you haven't one, the American Society of Travel Agents, 4400 MacArthur Blvd. N.W., Washington D.C. 20007; and ASTA West Coast, 4420 Hotel Circle Court, Suite 230, San Diego, CA 92108; or the Association of British Travel Agents, 50–57 Newman St., London WIP 4AH, will advise you. Whether you select Maupintour, American Express, Thomas Cook or a smaller organization is a matter of preference. Most of them have branch offices or correspondents in the larger European cities.

There are good reasons why you should engage a reliable travel agent. Travel abroad today, although it is steadily becoming easier and more comfortable, is also growing more complex in its details. As the choice of things to do, places to visit, ways of getting there, increases, so does the problem of *knowing* about all these questions. A reputable, experienced travel agent is a specialist in details, and you should inquire in your community to find out which organization has the finest reputation.

If you wish him merely to book you on a package tour, reserve your transportation and even your first overnight hotel accommodation, his services should cost you nothing. Most carriers and tour operators grant him a fixed commission for saving them the expense of offices in every town and city.

If, on the other hand, you wish him to plan for you an individual itinerary and make all the arrangements down to hotel reservations and transfers to and from rail and air terminals, you are drawing upon his skill and knowledge and thus he will make a service charge on the total cost of your planned itinerary. This charge may amount to 10 or 15%, but it will more than likely *save* you money on balance. A good travel agent can help you avoid costly mistakes due to inexperience. He can help you take advantage of special reductions in rail fares and the like that you would not otherwise know about. Most important, he can save you *time* by making it unnecessary for you to waste precious days abroad trying to get tickets and reservations.

1

PACKAGE TOURS. If you wish for a fair degree of certainty as to what your trip to Belgium and Luxembourg will cost you, there is no substitute for the package tour. Apart from money for shopping, extra evening entertainment, drinks and snacks along the way, all the basic costs of your trip—transport, hotels, most food—may already have been covered. Of course, when booking a package tour it is always wise to check with your travel agent on the extent of the "package". Some really are inclusive—down to tips and taxis, nightclubs and theaters; others cover all your transportation, accommodation and meals but leave you to pay on the spot for trips, excursions, etc.

Here are a few of the tours available from the U.S. and the U.K. at time of going to press:

From the U.S.— A good many tours are available, though most lump Belgium and Luxembourg together with one or more of their neighbors (Holland, Germany, Switzerland and France) to round the package out.

Cosmos/Globus Gateway (92–25 Queens Blvd., Rego Park, N.Y. 11374) includes Belgium and Luxembourg in its "Europe Top Cities" tour, 12 days from $475, taking in London, parts of France, Switzerland, Austria, and Italy. A 7-day "Best of Switzerland and Paris" tour also includes both, with prices starting at $308.

Maupintour (1515 St. Andrews Dr., Lawrence, KS 66044) gives you Belgium, but not Luxembourg, in their "Middle Europe Leisurely" tour. (They include Switzerland, Holland and Germany to make up for it, though.) It runs 15 days, and costs approximately $2700.

Floating Through Europe, 271 Madison Ave., New York, NY 10016 (212-685–5600), offers a "Hidden Treasures" tour of Belgium, six-night river and canal cruises in a comfortable barge with a premium on gourmet food and drink and Belgium's beautiful out-of-the-way places. Prices run from about $1500 per person, and include all accommodations and meals, and sightseeing charges. There is a small additional charge for single cabins.

Other tours of the region are available from *American Express* (Travel Division, 822 Lexington Ave., New York, N.Y. 10021), and *Travcoa* (875 N. Michigan Ave., Ste. 3732, Chicago, IL 60611).

From the U.K.— The *Belgium Travel Service Ltd.,* Bridge House, Ware, Herts. SG12 9DG (tel. 0920–61171), has a large selection of tours, some of which enable the visitor to experience first-hand Belgium's more noteworthy festivals, such as the Oostende Carnival (3 and 4 days from around £70 to £110); or the Diksmuide Beer Festival (3 and 4 days from around £75 to £120).

Prospect Art Tours Ltd., 10 Barley Mow Passage, London W4 (tel. 01–995–2163/4) have a 4-day Art Treasures tour of Flanders with accompanying guest lecturer which explores the sights of Bruges, Ghent, Antwerp and Brussels; this only runs a few times a year, however. Tours from around £210, and up, for 4 days.

TRAVEL FOR THE HANDICAPPED. For a complete list of tour operators who handle travel for the handicapped, write to the Society for the Advancement of Travel for the Handicapped, 26 Court St., Brooklyn, N.Y. 11242 or the Travel Information Center, Moss Rehabilitation Hospital, 12th St. and Tabor Rd., Philadelphia, PA 19141. In Britain, the Royal Association for Disability and Rehabilitation, 25 Mortimer St., London W1N 8AB. *Access to the World* by Louise Weiss (available from Facts On File, 460 Park Ave. South, New York, N.Y. 10016; $14.95) is an outstanding general guide and reference work for handicapped travelers.

TRAVEL INSURANCE. Travel insurance can cover everything from health and accident costs, to lost baggage and trip cancellation. Sometimes they can all be obtained with one blanket policy; other times they overlap with existing coverage you might have for health and/or home; still other times it is best to buy policies that are tailored to very specific needs. But, insurance is available from many sources and many travelers unwittingly end up with redundant coverage. Before purchasing separate travel insurance of any kind, be sure to check your regular policies carefully.

Generally, it is best to take care of your insurance needs *before* embarking on your trip. You'll pay more for less coverage—and have less chance to read the fine print—if you wait until the last minute and make your purchases from, say, an airport vending machine or insurance company counter. Best of all, if you have a regular insurance agent, he is the person to consult first. Flight insurance, often included in the price of the ticket when the fare is paid via American Express, Visa or certain other major credit cards, is also often included in package policies providing accident coverage as well. These policies are available from most tour operators and insurance companies. While it is a good idea to have health and accident insurance when traveling, be careful not to spend money to duplicate coverage you may already have . . . or to neglect some eventuality which could end up costing a small fortune. For example, basic Blue Cross Blue Shield policies cover health costs incurred while traveling. They will not, however, cover the cost of emergency transportation, which can often add up to several thousand dollars. Emergency transportation *is* covered, in part at least, by many major medical policies such as those underwritten by Prudential, Metropolitan and New York Life. Again, we can't urge too strongly that you check any policy carefully before buying. Another important example: most insurance issued specifically for travel does not cover pre-existing conditions, such as a heart problem.

Several organizations offer coverage designed to supplement existing health insurance and to help defray costs not covered by many standard policies, such as emergency transportation. Some of the more prominent are:

Travel Assistance International, the American arm of Europ Assistance, offers a comprehensive program providing medical and personal emergency services and offering immediate, on-the-spot medical, personal and financial help. Trip protection ranges from $35 for an individual for up to eight days to $220 for an entire family for a year. Full details from travel agents or insurance brokers, or from Europ Assistance Worldwide Services, Inc., 1333 F St., N.W., Washington, D.C. 20004 (800–821–2828). In the U.K., contact Europ Assistance Ltd., 252 High St., Croydon, Surrey (01–680 1234).

Carefree Travel Insurance, c/o ARM Coverage Inc. 120 Mineola Blvd., Box 310, Mineola N.Y. 11510, (516–294–0220) offers insurance, legal and financial assistance, and medical evacuation arranged through Inter-Claim. Carefree coverage is available from many travel agents.

International SOS Assistance Inc., P.O. Box 11568, Philadelphia, PA 19116, has fees from $15 a person for seven days, to $195 for a year (tel. 800–523–8930).

IAMAT (International Association for Medical Assistance to Travelers), 417 Center St. Lewiston, N.Y. 14092 in the U.S. (tel. 716–754–4883) or 188 Nicklin Road, Guelph, Ontario N1H 7L5 in Canada (tel. 519–836–0102).

The British Insurance Association, Aldermary House, Queen St., London EC4 (tel. 01–248 4477), will give comprehensive advice on all aspects of vacation travel insurance from the U.K.

Loss of baggage is another frequent inconvenience to travelers. It is possible, though often complicated, to insure your luggage against loss through theft or negligence. Insurance companies are reluctant to sell such coverage alone, however, since it is often a losing proposition for them. Instead, this type of coverage is usually included as part of a package that also covers accidents or health. Remuneration is often determined by weight, regardless of the value of the specific contents of the luggage. Should you lose your luggage or some other personal possession, it is essential to report it to the local police immediately. Without documentation of such a report, your insurance company might be very stingy. Also, before buying baggage insurance, check your home-owners policy. Some such policies offer "off-premises theft" coverage, including the loss of luggage while traveling.

The last major area of traveler's insurance is trip cancellation coverage. This is especially important to travelers on APEX or charter flights. Should you get sick abroad, or for some other reason be unable to continue your trip, you may be stuck having to buy a new one-way fare home, plus paying for the charter you're not using. You can guard against this with "trip cancellation insurance," usually available from travel agents. Most of these policies will also cover last minute cancellations.

 WHEN TO GO. The main tourist season in Belgium and Luxembourg runs from about the beginning of May to the end of September; the peak comes in July and August. This is when the weather is best and it is when most British and Americans take their vacations. However, these two countries do not stage as many big festivals designed largely for foreigners as various other countries put on in the peak travel months. Therefore, if you are making an extended tour of Europe, you may, without missing much, go to the standard spectacles in some of the other countries, and explore Belgium and Luxembourg in the earlier or latter part of your vacation. The most charming features of these countries are just as lovely in May, June, and September as in July and August: the old buildings and canals of Belgian Flanders and the lovely scenery of the hills of Luxembourg and Belgium's Ardennes.

Climate. Temperatures are moderate so you need not prepare yourself for excessive heat or cold. It does drizzle frequently, however, so take a raincoat with you. Average afternoon temperatures in degrees Fahrenheit and centigrade:

Brussels	Jan.	Feb.	Mar.	Apr.	May	June	July	Aug.	Sept.	Oct.	Nov.	Dec.
F°	42	43	49	56	65	70	73	72	67	58	47	42
C°	6	6	9	13	18	21	23	22	19	14	8	6

Off-season travel. This has become more popular in recent years as tourists have come to appreciate the advantages of avoiding the crowded periods. Transatlantic sea and air fares are cheaper, and so are hotel rates. Even where prices remain the same, available accommodations are better; the choicest rooms in the hotels, the best tables in the restaurants have not been pre-empted, nor are train compartments packed full.

 SEASONAL EVENTS. The Belgians love a party, and carnivals, festivals, all kinds of wingding come naturally to them. A great many of these are saturated with folklore and legend—not dreamed up as tourist catching gimmicks—and all the more fun for that. As many of them are tied to the feasts of the church calendar, their dates vary from year to year and will need checking with the National Tourist office.

January. Brussels International Motor Show (Jan. or Feb.).

February. Hasselt annual fair, and election of Carnival Prince Eugen during the carnival, five days before Shrove Tuesday. World-famous Binche Carnival on Shrove Tuesday—there's also a good procession at Tournai on the same day. On Shrove Sunday, Aalst holds a procession with traditional cortège, and on the following Sunday Geraardsbergen holds its curious Cracknel Festival. (NB When Easter is later, these Shrovetide festivals take place in early March.) Carnival Processions at Blankenberge and Heist. Malmédy Festival when harlequins, jesters and *haguettes* (long arms) run about the streets for four days frolicking with the passers-by.

March. Early March, Oostende stages its masked ball of the "Rat Mort," a stupendous affair involving the whole town. Later in the month its traditional carnival cortège takes place. La Louvière 2 day carnival. Stavelot mid-Lent Sunday Festival.

April. Brussels music season in full swing. Every 5 years (ending in a 5 or an 0) Ghent holds its world-famous Floralities Gentoises, a massive flower show. Mid-April, La Roche (Ardennes) stages the Courses du Côte, an exciting international road circuit in hilly countryside for cars, motorcycles and sidecars. The arrival of spring is celebrated in April with a vast Flower Market at Koksijde, usually on Easter Sunday. Holy Week procession, Veurne. Procession in honor of St. Ursmer at Binche. Late April–early May, 2 weeks Brussels International Samples Fair.

May. Queen Elisabeth Musical Competition, a prestige prize open to young artists of all nationalities. 1st May, Play of St. Evermeire, only mystery play still performed in Belgium, presented at Rutten; and there's a good Festival Fair at Genk. 8th May, commemorations of *Vindictive's* exploit in World War 1 and Germany's capitulation in World War 2. Second Sunday (even years only) Procession of the Cats in Ypres. Vast apple and cherry orchards in bloom around St. Truiden. Procession in honor of St. Dymphne at Geel. Youth Festival at Neerpelt. Sunday before Ascension, flower festival in Mechelen.

Ascension Day Procession of the Holy Blood at Bruges. End of May to early June, Antique Fair of Flanders at restored St. Peter's Abbey. International Rowing regattas at Ghent's Aquatic Stadium. End of May, farmers' pilgrimage to Onze Lieve Vrouw van Hanswijk (Mechelen). Traditional military marches at Walcourt and Thuin. Grand Prix at Chimay for racing cars and motorcycles. End of month, Liège International Fair. First Sunday after Whitsun, St. George kills the dragon in Mons. 10 days after Whitsun, Corpus Christi Procession of Liège dating from 1246.

June. Early June, Pilgrimage to St. Guidon at Anderlecht. Early June–July, Tree Festivities in Leuven. Military marches at Florennes and Morialmé. Mid-June until end of August, Mechelen Carillon concerts (each Monday at 8.30 P.M.). Each Sunday from mid-June until August, sculpture and light shows using latest laser techniques at Bouverie Park in Liège. Giants' Sortie at Koksijde. Traditional Ommegang procession at Oostende, with Blessing of the Sea. Last Sunday of the month, Procession of St. John at Nieuwpoort. End of month, shrimp-catching contest on horseback and Shrimp Pageant at Oostduinkerke. End of June–early July, "International Musical Encounters" at Château de Chimay.

July. Summer Festivals at Oostende and Knokke throughout July and August. International Folk Dancing Festival at Yvoir. St. Hubert Music Festival. Procession of St. Begge in Andenne, first Sunday after July 7 every year. Foire du Midi in Brussels begins on 15th July. Second Sunday, Chevaliers de la Tour lead carnival processions in Tournai. St. Truiden's Cherry Festival with Folklore and Carnival Procession. Grand Féerie de Namur festivities throughout month. Last Sunday, Procession of Penitents at Veurne. Temse Water Festival on River Schelde (alternate years).

August. First Sunday, Flemish Painting Pageant at Koksijde. Seafarers Day at Oostende. Grand Prix de Belgique motorcycle races on Citadel circuit at Yvoir. Military marches at Ham-sur-Heure and Jumet. 15th August, Naval Cortège and Blessing of the Sea at Knokke-Heist. Reiefeest Son et Lumière events on floodlit canals of Bruges—historic events enacted for several days by hundreds of costumed players and musicians. King Albert Commemoration Day just outside Nieuwpoort. 4th Sunday, cortège at Ath; 2-day celebrations include David slaying Goliath.

Every 5 years at Bruges: *Sanguis Christi*, a modern passion play based on the story of the Holy Blood, performed before the Belfry (years ending in 2 or 7); and Feast of the Golden Tree, re-enacting the wedding procession of Charles the Bold and his bride, Margaret of York (years ending in 0 or 5). Stavelot Chamber Music Festival, in Abbey refectory. End of month, Flower Corso at Knokke.

September. In Brussels, Manneken Pis dons uniform of the Welsh Guards to commemorate the city's liberation on 3rd Sept 1944. First Sunday, Plague Procession, nearly a thousand-years-old, at Tournai; hunters festival at St. Hubert. 2nd Sunday, Bouillon parade of ancient costumes. Folklore Procession, with amusing Knights of Flamiche, at Dinant. Liège Festival, which includes international competition for String Quartets..Wieze Beer Festival begins at the end of the month.

October. Procession of Pilgrims at Lier. 27th October, Brussels Manneken Pis wears American sailor's uniform to commemorate U.S. Navy Day.

November. 20th November, students rule the city of Brussels on the day of their patron saint.

December. Lovers' Fair at Arlon with giant matchmaker. Nut Fair at Bastogne, ancient marriage market. Xmas Day, "Republic of Outremeuse" stages Feast of the Nativity in Liège.

PASSPORTS. Generally there is some delay so apply several months in advance. **U.S. residents** must apply in person to the US Passport Agency in Boston, Chicago, Honolulu, Houston, Los Angeles, Miami, New Orleans, New York, Philadelphia, San Francisco, Seattle, Stamford (Conn.), or Washington, D.C., or to their local county courthouse. In some areas selected post offices are also able to handle passport applications. If your latest passport was issued within the past eight years use this to apply by mail. (Ask for Form DSP-82.) You will need: 1) Proof of citizenship, such as a birth certificate; 2) two identical photographs two inches square, in either black and white or color, on non-glossy paper and taken within the past six months; 3) $35 for the passport itself plus a $7 processing fee if you are applying in person (no processing fee when applying by mail) for those 18 years and older, or if you are under 18, $20 for the passport plus a $7 processing fee if you are applying in person (again, no extra fee when applying by mail). Adult passports are valid for 10 years, others for five years; 4) proof of identity that includes a photo and signature, such as a driver's license, previous passport or any governmental ID card, or a copy of an income tax return. When you receive your passport, write down its number, date and place of issue separately; if it is later lost or stolen, notify either the nearest American Consul or the Passport Office, Department of State, 1425 K St. NW, Washington DC 20524, as well as the local police.

British subjects must apply for passports on special forms obtainable from your travel agency or a main Post Office. The application should be sent to the Passport Office for your area (as indicated on the guidance form) or taken personally to your travel agent. Apply at least 5 weeks before the passport is required. The regional Passport Offices are located in London, Liverpool, Peterborough, Glasgow, and Newport (Gwent). The application must be countersigned by your bank manager or a solicitor, barrister, doctor, clergyman or Justice of the Peace who knows you personally. You will need two photos. Fee £15.

British Visitor's Passport. This simplified form of passport has advantages for the once-in-a-while tourist to Belgium and most other European countries. Valid for one year and not renewable, it costs £7.50. Application must be made in person at a main Post Office and two passport photographs are required.

Visas. Not required by either country for nationals of the United Kingdom, United States, Ireland, Canada, Australia or New Zealand. Visas are required from nationals of these countries, however, if a stay of more than three months is to be made in Belgium or Luxembourg.

Health Certificates. Not required for entry to Belgium and Luxembourg. Neither the United States nor Canada requires a certificate of vaccination prior to re-entry. Check with your local or state Public Health authorities as to any recent changes in requirements.

MONEY. In Luxembourg and Belgium the monetary unit is the franc. Technically, 100 centimes equal one franc, but inflation has all but eliminated the smaller unit from everyday use. In Luxembourg, Belgian money is legal tender, but the reverse is not true. This otherwise good currency having no official rating outside the Grand Duchy, you are advised to change your remaining banknotes before leaving the country.

Belgium issues notes in denominations of 50, 100, 500, 1,000 and 5,000 francs. Luxembourg issues notes in denominations of 50 and 100 francs. Belgian coins are issued in denominations of 1, 5, 10 and 20 francs, and 50 centimes with 50 and 100 franc pieces for numismatists. It is worthwhile making sure that you always have a few 5 franc pieces on you, as these are useful for small tips and phone calls. Both the new Belgian and Luxembourg 20 franc coins resemble the French 10 franc coin in weight and color, for which they may be mistaken.

At the time of writing the rates of exchange were fluctuating around BF40 to the U.S. dollar and BF60 to the pound sterling; but do check for the latest rates.

Travelers' Checks. Travelers' checks and credit cards are probably still the safest and simplest ways to carry money. There are eight brands of travelers checks. The best known are American Express, Bank of America, Barclays and Thomas Cook's. Most companies charge a commission for their services. Barclays charge no commission in the United States.

Important. Avoid exchanging money on weekends or at hotels and restaurants. You'll pay a big premium for the convenience. Wait for the banks to open. Also, always keep a written record of the check numbers in a place other than that where you carry the checks, or give the numbers to a companion or friend. In the event the checks are lost or stolen this will greatly facilitate obtaining replacement checks.

Credit Cards. Credit Cards are now an integral part of the Western Financial Way of Life, and, in theory at least, are accepted all over Europe. But, while the use of credit cards can smooth the traveler's path considerably, they should not be thought of as a universal answer to every problem.

Firstly, there is a growing resistance in Europe to the use of credit cards, or rather to the percentage which the credit card organizations demand from establishments taking part in their schemes. If you intend to use your credit cards in Europe, you would be well advised to get one of the directories that the companies put out, listing the firms that will accept their particular cards. Without keeping a sharp lookout for those little signs on the windows, you might find yourself in an embarrassing position. You will find that one of the most widely accepted cards in Europe is Visa.

Another point that should be watched with those useful pieces of plastic is the problem of the rate at which your purchase may be converted into your home currency. We have ourselves had two purchases made on the same day in the same place charged ultimately at two totally different rates of exchange. If you want to be certain of the rate at which you will pay, insist on the establishment entering the current rate onto your credit card charge at the time you sign it—this will prevent the management from holding your charge until a more favorable rate (to them) comes along, something which could cost you more dollars than you counted on. (On the other hand, should the dollar or pound be revalued upward before your charge is entered, you could gain a little.)

We would advise you, also, to check your monthly statement very carefully indeed against the counterfoils you got at the time of your purchase. It has become increasingly common for shops, hotels or restaurants to change the amounts on the original you signed, if they find they have made an error in the original bill. Sometimes, also, unscrupulous employees make this kind of change to their own advantage. The onus is on you to report the change to the credit card firm and insist on sorting the problem out. Remember that they are making a handsome profit out of providing you with this convenience. There is no reason for you to swell their turnover unnecessarily.

Exchange Information. As keeping abreast of fluctuating currency can be confusing—and not doing so can be costly!—a little expert advice always comes in handy. Ruesch International, 1140 19th St., N.W., Washington D.C. 20036, a company specializing in foreign exchange, has put out a brochure that answers many questions on the thorny subject of foreign exchange. They also have available a foreign currency guide for 24 countries with much relevant information. For copies of the free brochure send them a self-addressed, stamped business envelope.

 WHAT TO TAKE. Travel light: If you plan to fly the transatlantic route to Europe, airline baggage allowances are now based on size rather than weight. Economy class passengers may take free two pieces of baggage provided that the sum of their dimensions is not over 3.15 m. (124 in.) and neither one singly is over 1.58 m. (62 in.)—height, width and length. For First Class, the allowance is two pieces up to 1.58 m. (62 in.) each, total 3.15 m. (124 in.). The penalties for oversize are severe; to Western Europe around $54 per piece.

Outside this route the old weight allowance still holds good. Moreover, most bus lines and some of the crack international trains limit the weight, usually 25 kg. (55 lb.) or bulk of your luggage. The principle is not to take more than you can carry yourself (unless you travel by car). Motorists will find it advisable to be frugal as well. You should limit your luggage to what can be locked into the trunk or boot of your car when making daytime stops.

Clothing. At the head of your list should be a raincoat. It rarely rains hard in the Low Countries but it drizzles a lot, all year round, and a clear blue sky in the morning is no guarantee that it won't be raining half an hour later. No one ever goes out for more than an hour without a raincoat, no matter what the sky looks like. Better follow suit. Otherwise, wear just what you would wear at home. If you plan to go to expensive restaurants or nightclubs, bring a long skirt or dress. Many of the streets in the older parts of Belgian towns still have cobblestones. For that reason, and as a protection against "museum ache", a comfortable pair of walking shoes is essential.

GETTING THERE BY AIR FROM NORTH AMERICA. As one of the most popular jumping off points for European travelers, Belgium enjoys excellent service by the major carriers as well as by charter companies and tour packagers. Direct flights from the U.S. are frequently the cheapest of those going anywhere on the Continent, while certain economy fares have in the past allowed stop-overs of up to 72 hours in certain other cities en route. Belgium is also easily reached via connecting flights from most European capitals.

Although there are some daytime flights, most service tends to depart from east-coast cities in evening hours in order to arrive early the next morning; flights from more westerly points are timed accordingly. (The one problem with this arrangement is that most hotels will not allow you to check in before noon or 1 P.M. and that can leave you exhausted with no place to nap or unwind for several hours.)

Air fares, however, are in a constant state of flux, and our best advice is to consult a travel agent and let him or her make your reservations for you. Agents are familiar with the latest changes in fare structures as well as with the rules governing various discount plans. Among those rules: booking (usually) 21 days in advance, minimum stay requirements, maximum stay, the amount that (sometimes) must be paid in advance for land arrangements. Lowest prices overall will, of course, be during the off-season period between November and March (with the exception of Christmas and New Year holidays).

Generally, on regularly scheduled flights, you have the option, in descending order of cost, of First Class, Club, Business Class or APEX (Advance Purchase Excursion). Budget tickets, in which you choose the week you wish to fly but give the airline the option of determining on which flight, are also sometimes available. Budget travelers with fixed schedules will want to meet the requirements for APEX. The less tied to a timetable you are, of course, the more you can save. At press time (mid-'87) fares from New York to Brussels were: First Class $3030 round trip, Apex $659 round trip, plus $23 security charge for both.

If you have the flexibility, you *can* sometimes benefit from last-minute sales tour operators have in order to fill a plane; if in the U.S., check the *New York Sunday Times* travel pages for such advertisements, but do try to find out whether the tour operator is reputable and whether you are tied to a precise round trip or whether you will have to wait until the operator has a spare seat in order to return.

To Luxembourg. Luxembourg is best reached via London, Paris, Brussels, Frankfurt or Amsterdam—and then on via Luxair. Alternatively, you can use the grandaddy of all budget airlines, Icelandair, which will take you to Luxembourg from Chicago, Detroit, Orlando, Washington and New York, via Iceland.

GETTING THERE BY SEA FROM NORTH AMERICA. The options for traveling by boat across the Atlantic reduce each year. In the past, sea-lovers had a choice between ocean liners—the number of these in regular service on trans-Atlantic routes has now diminished to one: Cunard's Queen Elizabeth II—and freighters. The possibilities in the latter category have dwindled almost as drastically. The few cargo ships making the trip and accepting passengers are booked several years ahead.

Nonetheless, the persistent *can* be rewarded with passage on the rare freighter offering relatively comfortable one-class accommodations for a maximum of 12 people. What they lack in the way of entertainment and refinement these ships make up for by way of informality, relaxation and cost (though flying is almost always cheaper). For details, and to help you choose from the lines available, consult *Air Marine Travel Service*, 501 Madison Avenue, New York, N.Y. 10022, publisher of the *Trip Log Quick Reference Freighter Guide*.

Cunard has had ships on the North Atlantic route since 1839. The company's flagship *QE2* now maintains regular service from April to October between New York, Cherbourg, France and Southampton, England. There are no liner services direct to Belgium or (of course!) Luxembourg. Fares are subject to change, but are always cheaper off-season than during the peak summer months. Among special promotions are air-sea combination tickets, with Cunard providing service in one direction on the *QE2* and in the other by jet. Other tour programs and special land arrangements can be made through Cunard, 555 Fifth Avenue, New York, N.Y. 10017.

GETTING THERE BY AIR FROM BRITAIN. Belgium is not as well served by air from Britain as some other European countries. From London (Heathrow) to Brussels *Sabena*—the Belgian National Airline—and *British Airways* operate a pooled service of at least five flights each way a day, with a flying time of 55 minutes. Brussels is also served by four *British Caledonian* flights a day from London (Gatwick). There are relatively few flights available from other parts of the country. From Birmingham, *British Midland* run two flights a day to the Belgian capital, from Manchester there are four flights on most days by British Airways/Sabena to Brussels. Belgium's second city and major port, Antwerp, has a direct service of five flights on weekdays by British Caledonian from London (Gatwick) airport.

Fares are relatively high to Brussels, ranging from around £190 roundtrip in Club, down to around £77 for an excursion roundtrip fare which requires the flight to be booked in advance and a Saturday night to be spent abroad. Discounted tickets are not available to Belgian destinations.

Virgin Atlantic fly daily from London (Gatwick) to Maastricht, only a few miles from the Belgian border in Limburg. Roundtrip fare is around £70, bookable any time, with no restrictions. From here there are good train services to Liège. Reservations can be made through Virgin Atlantic, 166 West 32nd Street, New York, or in UK phone 0293–38222 for latest fare information. Good connections are available from their flights coming from the US.

To Luxembourg, *Luxair* flies from London (Heathrow) to Luxembourg direct, and the fares are similar to those for Belgium, with a special excursion fare of around £130.

GETTING THERE BY TRAIN FROM BRITAIN. Belgian Marine, known by its initials R.T.M., has now combined forces with Townsend Thoresen to operate a Jetfoil service from Dover (Western Docks) to Oostende which has helped cut the overall traveling time between the British and Belgian capitals to a mere 4 hours 52 minutes for the fastest journey! There are a minimum of four rail-connected Jetfoil services each way. The most convenient morning departure leaves London (Victoria) at 8.15 and you pull into Brussels just after 2. The last service of the day leaves Victoria at four in the afternoon to arrive in Brussels just after 10. The journey is in three stages, by rail from London to Dover Western Docks, where there is a simple transfer via the new floating terminal to board the Jetfoil for the 100-minute crossing to Oostende. There you transfer to the waiting trains for the last leg of the journey to Brussels or Antwerp. The Jetfoil service has proved very popular and a supplement is charged for its use. Due to the limited space on board it is essential to reserve seats in advance.

The Channel crossing can still be made by traditional ferries and there are two daytime sailings both with train connections from London. The first boat train leaves London Victoria at 9.15 in the morning and you reach Brussels just before 6. There is also a lunch-time service which gets to Brussels by 10 in the evening. It is possible to travel overnight on this route but it is not recommended. The most practical and comfortable method of traveling to Brussels overnight is to use the service via the Hook of Holland. Travel by train from London (Liverpool Street) to Harwich then take the night boat to the Hook. The longer crossing means it is possible to get a decent night's sleep. From the Hook of Holland there is a connection to Rotterdam where you catch one of the new EuroCity or InterCity expresses which has you in Brussels by 10.30 A.M. at the latest.

To Luxembourg. The best service for this route is to leave Victoria at 8.15 A.M., travel via Dover and Jetfoil to Oostende, train to Brussels, cross-platform change at the Gare du Midi to the express for Luxembourg, arriving just after 5 P.M. Excellent connections for Paris, Germany and Switzerland.

GETTING THERE BY CAR FROM BRITAIN. Motorists are spoilt for choice when it comes to traveling to Belgium. The entire Benelux region is easily accessible in a day from London and the southeast. There are several companies which operate sailings direct to the Belgian ports of Oostende and Zeebrugge (see table). The greatest frequency of sailings is from the south coast ports and during the summer months from Dover there are up to six sailings daily to Zeebrugge, and seven to Oostende by the Townsend Thoresen/RTM consortium. The travel time on these routes is upward of three and a half hours depending on the crossing you choose.

Belgium can also be reached quickly from the French ports of Dunkerque and Calais. The former—though not particularly attractive—is only a few minutes' drive from the Belgian border near the resort of de Panne, and is served by Sally Line from Ramsgate. The port of Calais has the advantage of the hovercraft link from Dover operated by Hoverspeed. This whips you across the Channel in a mere 35 minutes. From Calais there is a slightly longer drive along the northern coast of France (or via the toll-free autoroute through Lille) but the total traveling time is much less than by the conventional ferries direct to Belgium.

There are no direct sailings from the south of England which allow a good night's sleep on board ship. Crossings are too short for more than just a nap, and these days most operators no longer even have cabins on most of their ferries. If you do want to make an overnight crossing and have a cabin therefore, a good bet is the Olau Line sailing from Sheerness to Vlissingen in the southwestern corner of the Netherlands. From Vlissingen you can take either the local ferry across the mouth of the Scheldt and land on the coast 18 km. (11 miles) from Knokke, or if your destination is deeper in Belgium drive round on the motorway, turning off for Antwerp at Hoogerheide.

Fares vary widely on the cross-channel routes to Belgium, not so much between the companies or routes but according to the season and time of day. A peak summer sailing from Dover to Oostende (Thoresen/RTM) for a "standard" 4.5m car and two adults works out at around £90—one way. For a crossing to Dunkirk the cost is around £80 one way. However, early or late season sailings offer great savings. The cost of the return trip from Dover to Zeebrugge can be greatly reduced by using an early morning sailing; or cut to around £90 return by taking a bargain Five Day Mini-Break, available throughout the year.

GETTING THERE BY BUS FROM BRITAIN. Brussels has a really excellent coach service from London. In fact this coach service is in many ways superior to the combination of rail/ferry or rail/Jetfoil. The hovercraft company Hoverspeed operate, as part of the International Express network, a service called *City Sprint* from London (Victoria Coach Station) which connects the two capitals in a mere 6¼ hours. Throughout the year there is one daily departure, which leaves at 9.30 A.M. in summer. There are also two City Sprint coaches a day from London to Antwerp. Fares are attractively low at £21 single to both Brussels and Antwerp. Students under 26 get a slightly reduced fare. For further details contact Hoverspeed Ltd., Freepost, Maybrook House, Dover, Kent CT17 9BR or telephone 0304–214514. In addition Eurolines, also part of International Express—a grouping of reliable bus operators—run a service to Brussels, nightly in summer. These leave London's Victoria coach station at 7.30 in the evening and arrive in Brussels at 7 the following morning. The Channel crossing from Dover to Zeebrugge is by conventional ferry. Details can be obtained from British Rail Travel in New York (tel. 212–599 5400). In London the International Express timetable can be obtained from International Express, The Coach Travel Center, 13 Regent Street, London, SW1Y 4LR (tel. 01–439 9368).

FERRY SERVICES FROM THE U.K. FOR BELGIUM					
TO	**BELGIUM**		**FRANCE**		**HOLLAND**
	Zeebrugge	Ostend	Dunkirk	Calais	Vlissingen
From					
Hull	N				
Felixtowe	T				
Sheerness					O
Ramsgate			SV		
Dover	T	TR		T B H	
Operators: N = North Sea Ferries; B = British Ferries; O = Olau line; T = Townsend Thoresen; TR = Thoresen/RTM; SV = Sally Viking; H = Hoverspeed.					

GETTING AROUND BY TRAIN. Belgium's once less-than-entirely-reliable train service has lately undergone drastic reorganization and rationalization and now boasts a well-thought out network of fast and frequent Inter City (IC) trains connecting all main towns and cities. These premier services are in turn backed up by a new system of Inter Regional trains calling at smaller towns and connecting them with the IC and international networks. In addition, a new easy-to-read timetable, listing 1,001 IC connections, where you have to change (if necessary) and journey times, has been brought out. It is available from any Belgian Railways' office. The lot of the rail traveler in Belgium, in short, has been greatly improved.

Fares. For visitors intending to do a lot of rail travel the best buys are the *Tourrail Ticket* and the all-line rail rover—*Abonnement réseau.* The Tourrail ticket is probably the most useful. The ticket can be bought to give unlimited travel on either 5 or 8 days out of a period of 16. When you buy the ticket state the date on which the 16 days begin and then, as you go along, validate the ticket for the days on which you wish to travel—they don't have to be consecutive. The ticket can be bought from mid-March to end-September costing BF 2,400 for 5 days and BF 3,100 for 8 days in first class, and BF 1,550 for 5 days and BF 2,070 for 8 days in second class. A 5-day Benelux Tourrail Ticket, good for Belgium, Luxembourg and Holland, is also available for BF 3,830 in first class and BF 2,560 in second class.

For rail travel within Belgium there is an all-line railrover ticket valid for 16 days which costs BF 4,420 in first class and BF 2,940 in second. Please note that supplements when required still have to be paid. Belgian Railways operate a wide range of day excursions to places of interest under the heading of *"Un beau jour à . . . "*—a beautiful day at . . . These are good value for money, so check at the local tourist information office or railway station when you get there. If you have a railcard you travel at a reduced rate.

For those who love the fresh air Belgian Railways have bicycles for hire at 48 of their stations—at reduced rates for rail travelers. One of the good points of the scheme is that you do not have to return the cycles to the station you hired them from. Ask for the special map and brochure, *Train + Vélo.*

Luxembourg is well served by its *Chemins de Fer Luxembourgeois* and by through trains with neighboring Belgium, France, Germany—and beyond. Rover tickets (second class only) are available for buses and trains for 197 fr.L. for a day, 569 fr.L. for a week, or 1,513 fr.L for a month. For advance information, write: *C.F.L.,* 9 pl. de la Gare, B. P. 1803, 1018 Luxembourg; or: Office National du Tourisme, 36–37 Piccadilly, London WI, or 801 Second Avenue, New York, N.Y. 10017.

 GETTING AROUND BY BUS. There is an extensive and reliable network of local and regional bus services throughout Belgium and Luxembourg. Full details can be obtained from most rail stations and all tourist offices. Europabus (combined with Belgian State Railways) operates a number of tours lasting from half-a-day up to 10 days. Particulars from travel agents.

 GETTING AROUND BY CAR. In Belgium. The system of express highways includes the Wallonie (E41), the Brussels-Paris (E10), the Brussels-Liège (E5), and the Antwerp-Lille (E3). A few roads in country districts may be cobbled and narrow. The hilly nature of southern Belgium means, of course, more curves and slower average speeds. In Brussels the traffic growth is a continuous challenge. The system of over- and underpasses is being extended; and, with more paying car parks, the tolerance of street parking is growing less.

Except in the Ardennes and on the motor highways (A-roads), there's hardly a mile of principal roadway in Belgium without a gasoline station. Main highways are patroled by Touring Secours (Wegenhulp), who are expert mechanics. They attend to the needs of foreign drivers just as willingly as to their paying members. Their tool-carrying vehicles are painted yellow, and their uniforms resemble those of the British AA patrols, which actually served as a model for this organization.

In Luxembourg the roads are excellent, but occasionally narrow, and the hilly nature of the country means more curves and slower speeds than usual. The Automobile Club of Luxembourg assures permanent road service and other assistance or advice motorists may need.

Car documents. As with the majority of Western European countries, neither Belgium nor Luxembourg requires from private motorists international documents: your national driving licence and your vehicle registration certificate will do. Nationals of all EEC countries are automatically covered for third party insurance, but would be well advised to have Green Card comprehensive insurance from their own insurance company. Drivers from non-EEC countries are obliged to have a Green Card. All drivers must have a nationality plate indicating their car's country of origin. Once you have entered the Benelux countries, there are few formalities.

Fuel. In Belgium gasoline (petrol) costs about BF 30 per liter for super grade, but shopping around often results in discounts of up to 10%. In Luxembourg the cost is less, around 26 fr. L.

Winter Road Conditions. Dial 991 or 971.

Highway Code. Belgium: The storming out from a side street—providing it lies to the right of the flow of traffic—is **legal** *(priorité à droite)*. Street-cars, however, continue to have priority over all traffic. All this is a bit confusing; the best advice we can give you is to drive slowly in built-up areas and watch the side streets to your right. Absolute priority on the highways is indicated by the usual black arrow in a red triangle—nevertheless, use your horn generously when approaching a T-road or a crossing. When entering a first class road from a secondary one, an inverted red-framed white triangle warns you to slow down. Speed limits are posted where applicable, but a limit of 60 k.p.h. (37 m.p.h.) operates in Brussels, and all urban districts. On motorways a *minimum* speed of 70 k.p.h. (43 m.p.h.) is required, and there is a maximum limit of 120 k.p.h. (74 m.p.h.) on all roads of less than four lanes.

Tire mouldings must not be less than 1 mm. deep over the whole surface in contact with the road.

Dipped lights must be used in all areas when driving between nightfall and dawn, as well as in unfavorable weather conditions.

Seat belts must be worn by driver and front passenger at all times. If possible, no children under 12 years old in the front seat.

Red triangle for use following breakdown or accident is obligatory, and the car and car driver's identification papers must be carried in the car.

The Luxembourg highway code differs in some important ways from the Belgian. The use of horns, for instance, is reserved for cases of *imminent danger*. The speed limit is fixed at 60 k.p.h. (37 m.p.h.) in built-up areas, 90 k.p.h. (55 m.p.h.) outside the agglomerations. A parking disc (available free in many stores and banks) properly displayed is required for blue zones in the Luxembourg City town center and railway areas, Esch-sur-Alzette, Dudelange, Remich and Wiltz. This is supplemented by parking meters and a system of ticket dispensers which allows motorists to buy half-hour parking periods for a few francs. Spending the night in a vehicle or trailer on the roadside is prohibited.

Automobile Clubs. In Belgium (all in Brussels): Royal Automobile Club de Belgique, Rue d'Arlon 53 (tel. 230 0810); Touring Club de Belgique, Rue de la Loi 44 (tel. 233 2211).

British AA and RAC port representatives assist members at the Oostende and Zeebrugge marine piers.

In Luxembourg: Automobile Club du Grand Duché de Luxembourg, Rte. de Longwy 13, Luxembourg-Helfenterbruck.

Car Hire: In Belgium. A stock of cars, Volkswagen and Porsche, with U.S. specifications is kept expressly for delivery to American and British tourists, by Avis, Rue Américaine 145, Brussels (tel. 537 1280) and Brussels Airport. (Avis is also at Antwerp, Charleroi, Coutrai, Liège, Mons and Oostende.) The firm will also take care of the home shipment of your car. Other car-hire firms are Hertz, Blvd. Maurice Lemonnier 8, Brussels (tel. 513 2970) and Brussels Airport; and ABC Rent-a-car, Rue d'Anderlecht 133, Brussels (tel. 513 1954). The daily rate for the smallest car is from BF 800.

If you arrive in Belgium by train, you can arrange through the Belgian Railways to have a self-drive Volkswagen meet you at the following stations: Antwerp, Brussels, Dinant, Ghent, Liège, Mons, Namur, Oostende. A deposit of BF 5,000 is required. Rental for the first day is about BF 400, including 50 free kilometers (31 miles). If you arrive in Brussels via Sabena Airlines, you may arrange (at the time of purchasing your ticket) to have a self-drive car meet you at the airport. Cars with or without chauffeur may also be hired from garages in the large towns.

In Luxembourg. Volkswagen rentals and arrangements, Rte. de Thionville 88. Avis, Rue Duchscher 13. Hertz, Ave. de Liberté 25. Both in Luxembourg City.

Kilometers Into Miles. This simple chart will help you to convert to both miles and kilometers. If you want to convert from miles into kilometers read from the center column to the right, if from kilometers into miles, from the center column to the left. Example: 5 miles = 8.0 kilometers, 5 kilometers = 3.1 miles.

Miles		Kilometers	Miles		Kilometers
0.6	1	1.6	37.3	60	96.6
1.2	2	3.2	43.5	70	112.3
1.9	3	4.8	49.7	80	128.7
2.5	4	6.3	55.9	90	144.8
3.1	5	8.0	62.1	100	160.9
3.7	6	9.6	124.3	200	321.9
4.3	7	11.3	186.4	300	482.8
5.0	8	12.9	248.5	400	643.7
5.6	9	14.5	310.7	500	804.7
6.2	10	16.1	372.8	600	965.6
12.4	20	32.2	434.9	700	1,126.5
18.6	30	48.3	497.1	800	1,287.5
24.8	40	64.4	559.2	900	1,448.4
31.0	50	80.5	621.4	1,000	1,609.3

HITCH-HIKING. Hitch-hiking is permitted in Belgium and Luxembourg, though it is not encouraged and lifts are often difficult to come by. Hitching is not allowed on motorways, but you can wait on the approach road. During the summer there are a lot of students plying the Oostende–Brussels–Liège–German border route, and you will often have to wait for hours.

COSTS. We deal with Hotel and Restaurant costs below, in the relevant sections. Here are a few general facts to help you estimate what your visit might run out at. Belgium, with its larger cities, greater amenities and reputation for gourmet dining, is obviously more expensive than Luxembourg. Luxembourg has limited rising costs more effectively than its larger neighbors. 2½% for 1988 is likely to be accurate. Finding a bargain vacation spot in the Grand Duchy is less a problem of geography than of selection, due to its compact size. In the capital city itself, it is possible to make a week's vacation on 6,000 fr.L. per person, or to spend that much in a day—and half of that if you are camping or hostelling.

Sample Costs. In Belgium: train travel works out at around BF 6 a mile; a cup of coffee in a cafe will cost you BF 50; a glass of beer in a cafe BF 60, and a glass of wine BF 100; 2 theater tickets will average out at BF 800, and 2 movie tickets BF 400; a normal bus ride will be about BF 40; a local telephone call is BF 10.

In Luxembourg: a bottle of wine about 140 fr.L.; glass of gin 100 fr.L.; of whisky 120 fr.L.; a pair of average opera tickets 600 fr.L., two seats for a movie 300 fr.L.

HOTELS. Belgium. Almost without exception, Belgian hotels are clean and managed to a high standard. In the big cities, the more expensive ones have a wide range of amenities—from swimming pools to discos—however, they can be *very* expensive. In the resorts, hotels often provide amenities at more reasonable rates. The country, family-run establishments in more out-of-the-way spots, such as the Ardennes, can be surprisingly inexpensive, especially if you are visiting them out of season—but check in advance, as many country hotels close in the off periods.

Hotel prices are all inclusive and are listed in each room. Our hotel grading system is divided into four categories. All prices are for two people in a double room. Deluxe (L) BF 3,700 upwards; Expensive (E) BF 2,600–3,700; Moderate (M) BF 1,600–2,600; and Inexpensive (I) BF 1,600 or less. Most towns levy a small visitor's charge which comes on your hotel bill. Weekends, particularly during summer in the cities, vacant rooms are sometimes offered at half price.

Pensions. A single room with bath or shower and full board will run from BF 900 to 1,100 in Brussels, a double from BF 1,400 to 1,600. In other places, charges are from BF 500 to 700 single, 900 to 1,050 double. These terms are often available only for a minimum stay of 3 days.

Luxembourg. The following gradings are for double rooms, with bath, occupied by two people. Rooms without bath run around 15 to 40% less; single rooms about 25% less. In Luxembourg City—Luxury (L), 3,300–7,000 fr.L.; Expensive (E), 2,200–3,300; Moderate (M), 1,200–2,200; Inexpensive (I), 900–1,200. In the rest of the country—(L), 2,200–3,500; (E), 1,600–2,200; (M), 1,000–1,600; (I), 550–1,000.

Some hotels offer a Gourmet Weekend package—four main meals and accommodation for prices ranging from 2,000 fr.L to 5,000 fr.L. depending on the hotel, for the 2-day stay. Some offer 5 days at 4,000–9,000 fr.L. and a few will take you for a month at full board for about 28,000 fr.L. Offers are varied and complex. The ONT leaflets *Pouponné au Grand-Duché (Bargain Rate Hotels & Inns)* help with these and low-season proposals. Ask also about special sites, events and reduced prices for pre-teens. Many hotels welcome the handicapped.

Pensions. A single room with bath or shower and full board will cost from 1,800 francs upward in Luxembourg City, from 1,300 up in other places. Pensions offer half-pension (room, breakfast and one other meal) at about 8% less, and prices out of high season are about 10% less. Longer stays than the 3-day minimum usually reduce prices. Arrange with the proprietor. Write the National Tourism Office, P.O. Box 1001, Luxembourg for details of year-round special offers.

YOUTH HOSTELS. Of late years, encouraged particularly by the extension of the Youth Hostel system, foreign visitors to the two countries, especially those under 25, have been participating in increasing numbers in the cheapest and ruggedest form of traveling, formerly confined pretty much to natives. This means moving about the country on bicycles, in boats or on foot, or hitch-hiking (German or Scandinavian number plates are the best bet). If you elect to travel in bourgeois fashion by train or bus, you can often get reduced rates through the Youth Hostel organizations.

In Belgium hostels are numerous and inexpensive, but locker space is often inadequate. For information write to Fédération Belge des Auberges de la Jeunesse, Rue Van Oost 52, 1030 Brussels (tel. 215 3100).

Luxembourg has many hostels. Plentiful and rewarding, they are often parts of ancient fortresses and castles. You will find them at Echternach, Hollenfels, Luxembourg City, Vianden, and a number of other places. Full particulars can be had from Centrale des Auberges de Jeunesse, Place d'Armes 18, Luxembourg.

It is also possible to get information in England and the United States at the following addresses; American Youth Hostels, Inc., PO Box 37613, Washington, D.C. 20013; Camping and Caravan Club Ltd., 11 Lower Grosvenor Pl., London SW1; Youth Hostels Association International Travel Bureau, 14 Southampton St., London WC2; Cyclists' Touring Club, 69 Meadrow, Godalming, Surrey.

CAMPING AND CARAVANING. In both Belgium and Luxembourg this is well organized, with both authorized campsites and other facilities. Information from the Tourist Offices in Belgium and Luxembourg.

For Belgium from the Royal Camping and Caravaning Club of Belgium, Rue Madeleine 31, B-1000 Brussels (tel. 513 1287). For Luxembourg, consult the Fédération Luxembourgeoise de Camping et de Caravaning, 174 Rue de Soleuvre, Belvaux. An excellent and very detailed list of camping and caravan sites is issued by the National Tourist Office of each country.

Luxembourg. The Grand Duchy is probably the best organized country in Europe for camping. Specially arranged camping grounds with full amenities abound. There are some 120 sites, with a great choice of terrain and view.

FOR STUDENTS. There are several sources of youth information in Brussels. Infor-Jeunes covers north and west Brussels from Boulevard de Smet de Naeyer 145 (tel. 426 3333). For south and east Brussels go to rue de France 7 (Gare du Midi) or call 522 5866. Acotra, rue de la Montagne 38 (tel. 513 4480) will help in finding cheap accommodations. SOS Jeunes, rue Mercelis 27 (tel. 512 9020) is more of a "crisis line" but can be a useful source of information.

Information in Britain can be obtained from the National Union of Students, 3 Endsleigh St., London WC1.

Student package tours of Europe are organized by several American companies including Arista Student Travel, 11 E. 44th St., New York, NY 10017 (tel. 212–687–5121). Bailey Travel Service, 123 E. Market St., York, PA 17401 (tel. 717–854–5511); Harwood Tours and Travel, 2428 Guadalupe St., Austin, TX 78705 (tel. 512–478–9343).

 RESTAURANTS. Belgian restaurants serve good food in lavish proportions. Chips appear at practically every course and chefs can never be accused of being mean in their use of cream and butter. We have graded restaurants in three categories: Expensive (E) BF 1,600 upward (one person); Moderate (M) BF 850–1,600; Inexpensive (I) BF 400–850. Many restaurants have special tourist menus with set meals. These comprise *hors d' oeuvres,* main course and dessert, and usually cost between BF 550 and 850.

Restaurants in Brussels will charge towards the top of each of our gradings. Indeed, the luxury restaurants in Brussels are sky-high and could easily set you back 5,000 francs for two. For Belgian cuisine, see the *Food and Drink* chapter.

Luxembourg. Restaurant prices in Luxembourg run much the same as in Belgium, though don't ever quite get so stratospheric. In Luxembourg City they run: Expensive (E) 1,200–3,000 fr.L.; Moderate (M) 700–1,200; Inexpensive (I) 250–700. In the rest of the country the rates are, naturally, less. (E) 1,000–2,000; (M) 700–1,000; (I) 250–700.

 TIPPING. In Belgium hotels and restaurants will usually add up to 16% to the bill; frequently people will give a bit more than the required sum. Café waiters in Belgium expect about 15%, but you should ask whether the price they name includes the tip ("avec ou sans service?"). Porters in railway stations have a fixed price per suitcase. Minimum around BF 35. In Luxembourg hotels and restaurants, taxes and service charges are included in the charge. Taxis in both countries are very expensive. In Luxembourg, taxi drivers expect a tip, but in Belgium it is included in the fare.

 CLOSING TIMES. Legal holidays **in Belgium** are: New Year's Day (Jan. 1), Easter Monday, May Day (May 1), Ascension Day, Whit Monday, National Holiday (July 21), Assumption Day (Aug. 15), All Saints Day (Nov. 1), Armistice Day (Nov. 11), King's Birthday (schools, Nov. 15), Christmas Holidays (Dec. 25, 26); **in Luxembourg:** same, but National Holiday June 23, and Nov. 11 and 15 are not holidays. Most museums are closed on Mondays.

The Belgian shopkeeper spends most of his life in his shop and usually lives in the same building where it is located. Grocers, butchers, and bakers may open as early as 7 and close between 7 and 8 P.M. In provincial towns there is a 2-hour lunch break between 12–2. The large department stores and shops in larger towns are open weekdays from 9–6, in some cases staying open in the evening one day a week (usually Wednesdays); and a number of supermarkets are open 9–9 daily. Shopping centers usually make it a condition that the shops stay open from 9–9, six days a week. In holiday resorts on the coast and in the Ardennes, tradesmen keep open until 9 or 10 P.M. On Sundays bakers, butchers, grocers, fruit dealers, etc., keep open in the morning from 8–12; patisseries and flower shops the whole day. Belgian law limits employees' working hours to 40 hours per week, but since these are small family businesses, the authorities cannot interfere if they prefer to keep open—and the public has yet to complain. To prevent unfair competition the Government has imposed a compulsory closing day once a week—of the shopkeepers' choice.

In general, the same hours are observed in Luxembourg. On Monday mornings nearly everything is closed. Most museums close for the 12–2 lunch break.

CARILLONS. One of the oustanding features of Belgium are the carillons, which usually play automatically on the hour and half-hour; a few also play every quarter-hour. Chief places to hear the carillons are: Aalst (belfry), Antwerp (Notre Dame Cathedral), Oudenaarde (St. Walburga's Church), Binche (belfry), Bruges (belfry), Charleroi (belfry), Courtrai (St. Martin's Church), Ghent (belfry), Huy (Notre Dame), Liège (St. Paul's Cathedral), Lier (St. Gummaris), Mechelen (St. Rombaut's Cathedral), Dendermonde (Town Hall), Tongeren (Notre Dame), Tournai (belfry). For times of the principal concerts given by the carilloneurs at Bruges, Ghent and Mechelen, see the Practical Information sections for these cities.

BEGUINAGES. These distinctive communities, less secluded than convents, were started in the 13th century for either the widows of knights killed in the Crusades or unmarried sisters or daughters of such families. They did not wish to become nuns but spent their time in doing good works and tending the sick. Once they flourished in many countries including Britain, and there are still a few left in Belgium. These women are known as "beguines," and the buildings as "beguinages." The most characteristic are in Flanders (in Flemish called *begijnhof*). The most important ones are located in: Bruges, Courtrai, Diest, Ghent, Lier; others in: Aalst, Antwerp, Brussels (Anderlecht), Dendermonde, Dixmude, Leuven, Mechelen, Tongeren, etc.

SPAS AND CASINOS. Spa, which has given its name to similar establishments around the world, produces a well known mineral water of high iron content. The waters of The Queen's Spring are particularly beneficial for all forms of arthritis, and various mud, turf, and carbonized water baths are also available. Chaudfontaine possesses the only warm springs in Belgium. Oostende offers mineral waters and thermal baths.

Oostende's casino, Europe's biggest, is open all year round, usually from 2 P.M. onwards. The casino at Blankenberge is open from 11 A.M. on Sundays and from 2 P.M. on weekdays; at Dinant, daily from 3 P.M., Sundays one hour earlier; Knokke-Heist opens at 4 P.M. on Sundays; Namur, weekdays at 2 P.M., Sundays and holidays at noon; Spa, 4 P.M. on weekdays, one hour earlier on Sundays; Chaudfontaine, 3.30 P.M. daily. Middelkerke, near Oostende, has a small casino (in season 4 P.M. daily—weekends only in winter). All these casinos open year round. For information on admission, etc., apply directly to the casinos; formalities are simple, membership fees reasonable.

The Casino de Jeux du Luxembourg adds variety programs and gourmet dining to its games at Mondorf-les-Bains, an old and established thermal complex which now specializes in physical rehabilitation and other health treatments.

BELGIAN PLACE NAMES. You may see *Antwerpen* (Dutch) and *Anvers* (French) on signs posted along the highway, even though both names refer to the same city, *Antwerp*. This is because roadsigns normally reflect the language spoken by the people living nearby, even though the city in question may be located in the other language area—or even in another country. We give, first, the local version of certain towns, and, second, what the other language-group calls them.

Local version	Alternative version	Local version	Alternative version
Aachen (W. Ger.)	Aix–la–Chappelle/ Aken	Lille (Fra.)	Rijssel
Aalst	Alost	Lincent	Lijsem
Antwerpen	Anvers/Antwerp	Mechelen	Malines
Beauvechain	Bevekom	Mons	Bergen
Braine l'Alleud	Eigenbrakel	Mouscron	Moeskroen
Braine– le–Château	Kasteelbrakel	Namur	Namen
		Nieuwpoort	Nieuport
		Nivelles	Nijvel
Braine–Le–Comte	's-Gravenbrakel	Oostende	Ostende
Brugge	Bruges	Paris (Fra.)	Parijs
Bruxelles	Brussel(s)	Ronse	Renaix
Comines	Komen	Roeselare	Roulers
De Haan	Le Coq	Scherpenheuvel	Montaigu
Dendermonde	Termonde	Sint–Genesius– Rode	Rhode–Saint– Genèse
Diksmuide	Dixmude		
Dottignies	Dottenijse	Sint–Niklaas	Saint–Nicolas
Dunkerque (Fra.)	Duinkerken	Sint–Stevens– Woluwe	Woluwé–Saint– Etienne
Enghien	Edingen		
Flobecq	Vloesberg	Sint–Truiden	Saint–Trond
Geraardsbergen	Grammont	Soignies	Zinnik
Genappe	Genepiën	Temse	Tamise
Grez Doiceau	Graven	Tienen	Tirlemont
Hannut	Hannuit	Tongeren	Tongres
Huy	Hoei	Tournai	Doornik
Ieper	Ypres	Tubize	Tubeke
Ixelles	Elsene	Veurne	Furnes
Jodoigne	Geldenaken	Visé	Wezet
Kelmis	La Calamine	Voeren	Fourons
Kluisberg	Mont de l'Enclus	Waremme	Borgworm
Koksijde	Coxyde	Warneton	Waasten
Kortrijk	Courtrai	Woluwé–Saint– Lambert	Sint–Lambrechts– Woluwe
La Hulpe	Terhulpen		
Leuven	Louvain	Woluwé–Saint– Pierre	Sint–Peters– Woluwe
Liège	Luik/Lüttig		
Lier	Lierre	Zoutleeuw	Léau

CUSTOMS ON RETURNING HOME. If you propose to take on your holiday any *foreign-made* articles, such as cameras, binoculars, expensive timepieces and the like, it is wise to put with your travel documents the receipt from the retailer or some other evidence that the item was bought in your home country. If you bought the article on a previous holiday abroad and have already paid duty on it, carry with you the receipt for this. Otherwise, on returning home, you may be charged duty (for British residents, Value Added Tax as well). In other words, unless you can prove prior possession, foreign-made articles are dutiable *each time* they enter the U.S. The details below are correct as we go to press. It would be wise to check in case of change.

U.S. residents may bring in $400 worth of foreign merchandise as gifts or for personal use without having to pay duty, provided they have been out of the country more than 48 hours and provided they have not claimed a similar exemption within the previous 30 days. Every member of a family is entitled to the same exemption, regardless of age, and the exemptions can be pooled. For the next $1,000 worth of goods, inspectors will assess a flat 10% duty, based on the price actually paid, so it is a good idea to keep your receipts.

Included in the $400 allowance for travelers over the age of 21 are one liter of alcohol, 100 cigars (non-Cuban) and 200 cigarettes. Any amount in excess of those limits will be taxed at the port of entry, and may additionally be taxed in the traveler's home state. Only one bottle of perfume trademarked in the U.S. may be brought in. There is no duty on antiques or art over 100 years old, though you may be called upon to provide verification of the item's age. Write to U.S. Customs Service, Washington, D.C. 20229 for information regarding importation of automobiles and/or motorcycles. You may not bring home meats, fruits, plants, soil or other agricultural items.

Gifts valued at under $50 may be mailed to friends or relatives at home, but not more than one per day (of receipt) to any one addressee. These gifts must not include perfumes costing more than $5, tobacco or liquor.

If you are traveling with such foreign made articles as cameras, watches or binoculars that were purchased at home, it is best either to carry the receipt for them with you or to register them with U.S. Customs prior to departing. This will save much time (and potentially aggravation) upon your return.

Military personnel returning from abroad should check with the nearest American Embassy for special regulations pertaining to them.

Canadian Customs. In addition to personal effects, the following articles may be brought in duty free: a maximum of 50 cigars, 200 cigarettes, 2 pounds of tobacco and 40 ounces of liquor, provided these are declared in writing to customs on arrival and accompany the traveler in hand or checked-through baggage. These are included in the basic exemption of $300 a year. Personal gifts should be mailed as "Unsolicited Gift—Value Under $40". Canadian customs regulations are strictly enforced; you are recommended to check what your allowances are and to make sure you have kept receipts for whatever you have bought abroad. For details ask for the Canada Customs brochure, "I Declare."

British Customs. There are two levels of duty free allowance for people entering the U.K.; one, for goods bought outside the EEC or for goods bought in a duty free shop within the EEC; two, for goods bought in an EEC country but not in a duty free shop.

In the first category you may import duty free: 200 cigarettes or 100 cigarillos or 50 cigars or 250 grammes of tobacco (*Note* if you live outside Europe, these allowances are doubled); plus one liter of alcoholic drinks over 22% vol. (8.8% proof) or two liters of alcoholic drinks not over 22% vol. or fortified or sparkling wine; plus two liters of still table wine; plus 50 grammes of perfume; plus nine fluid ounces of toilet water; plus other goods to the value of £32.

In the second category you may import duty free: 300 cigarettes or 150 cigarillos or 75 cigars or 400 grammes of tobacco; plus 1½ liters of alcoholic drinks over 22% vol. (8.8% proof) or three liters of alcoholic drinks not over 22% vol. or fortified or sparkling wine; plus four liters of still table wine; plus 75 grammes of perfume; plus 13 fluid ounces of toilet water; plus other goods to the value of £250 (*Note* though it is not classified as an alcoholic drink by EEC countries for Customs' purposes and is thus considered part of the "other goods" allowance, you may not import more than 50 liters of beer).

In addition, no animals or pets of any kind may be brought in to the U.K. The penalties for doing so are severe and are strictly enforced.

DUTY FREE is not what it once was. You may not be paying tax on your bottle of whiskey or perfume, but you are certainly contributing to somebody's profits. Duty free shops are big business these days and mark ups are often around 100 to 200%. So don't be seduced by the idea that because it's duty free it's a bargain. Very often prices are not much different from your local discount store and in the case of perfume and jewelry they can be even higher.

As a general rule of thumb, duty free stores on the ground offer better value than buying in the air or on board ship. Also, if you buy duty free goods on a plane, remember that the range is likely to be limited and that if you are paying in a different currency to that of the airline, their rate of exchange will bear only a passing resemblance to the official one.

BELGIUM AND THE BELGIANS

Quest for the Real Belgium

by
NICOLAS STEVENSON

Belgium is a complex secret, shared by only a few. Coming to terms with the attitudes and lifestyles of Europe's most schizophrenic country appears altogether too daunting for the majority of casual observers. Charitably, they concede that Belgium is not unpleasant, if rather bland. More often than not, however, they simply write off the country and its people as boring.

This negative viewpoint tends to be reinforced by Belgium's current international image. In the worlds of politics, business and finance, "going to Belgium" contains little prospect of cultural or spiritual enlightenment. It symbolizes a pilgrimage to those modern shrines of faceless bureaucracy—the European Community, NATO and the European headquarters of a string of multinational companies. Today, Belgium finds itself slotted into a tightly-packed schedule of jet-lagged intercontinental meetings: like a giant office block elevated to the status of a sovereign state.

Behind the corporate facade, however, lies the real Belgium. It is a country where modern living is combined with a powerful sense of

23

tradition. Families still count; the events of 1302, 1585, 1830 or 1914 are firmly rooted in the popular consciousness and can still spark the emotions; and a deep-seated cultural awareness keeps modern artists in touch with their heritage. The idiosyncracies of a thousand years of European culture have left their mark on the ten million or so individuals that inhabit the Kingdom of Belgium. No such complex patchwork can possibly be dismissed as boring.

The problem you, the discerning visitor, will face, however, is making contact with this more personal side of Belgian life. The country makes few concessions to the style of mass tourism so well developed round the Mediterranean. You'll find no barbecue boat-trips to bodegas here; no ready-made displays of "native culture." This is a post-industrial, highly developed society. The standard of living probably exceeds that of your own country. The obvious signs of a "tourist industry," such as the well-established resorts on the coast and the kitsch souvenirs of Manneken-Pis round the Grand' Place in Brussels offer a wholly misleading picture of Belgian life: commercialism divorced from tradition.

No one should be content with such a superficial stereotype: yet it is still the prevailing impression of Belgium abroad. Cracking the facade, getting inside the Belgian enigma requires more than a day-trip to Oostende or a stroll along the avenue Louise from your luxury downtown hotel. It's not easy. In the beginning you'll be on your own. But it's worth making the effort to force your way through.

The Language Barrier

Breaking the social and linguistic code is crucial. You can read in the reference books that Belgium's official languages are Dutch, French and German. This might seem to suggest a similar outlook on life to that in Switzerland, where German, French and Italian are all officially recognized. But the contrast is fundamental. The Swiss have had six centuries of independence in which to develop a sense of national consciousness that transcends cultural and linguistic barriers. The Belgians, on the other hand, are still divided on whether any distinctively Belgian national identity has emerged since their independence from the Netherlands in 1830; and most wouldn't want to subscribe to it if it had.

As a result, Belgians of whatever class or language-group feel a regular need to assert a personal stake in their own cultural and linguistic community: a sort of confirmation of their faith in their diversity. Often this can be an apparently trivial act. The people you see heartily downing beer at the bar of the Graaf van Egmont or sipping their wine on the terrace of the Cafe du Centre do not do so simply because they prefer a particular beverage. They are making an overt, if subdued statement about themselves and their commitment to a particular way of life. In the daily newspapers, at schools and colleges, in art exhibitions and at theatrical and musical performances, the statements are sometimes obvious, sometimes less clearly defined. But they are always there. Every Belgian is prepared to take a stand, to resist the threat of a cultural blueprint being imposed from above. So uncomprehending comments like, "I can't understand why it hasn't been split between Holland and France," don't go down very well.

Belgium is not an amalgam of French and Dutch culture: that would be far too simple. One of the main reasons for its not having been absorbed by its larger neighbors is its strongly Catholic history and the impact this has had on present-day thinking. In true Belgian style, this does not lead to harmony. There is still a considerable degree of tension between Catholics and anti-clericals, to add to the better known linguistic divisions. In a country where public attitudes (and the laws) on issues like divorce, contraception and abortion tend to be framed with one eye on Papal pronouncements, young free-thinkers avoid being seen at the social functions of Catholic high-schools, while Catholic youngsters are told to keep away from massed gatherings of Socialists and Liberals. Apart from schools, the country's universities, clinics and labor unions are all split along religious/secular lines. Even apparently mundane organizations like mutual health insurance funds are divided according to the religious orientation of their membership.

Compromise as a Way of Life

On many issues, as much divides a Dutch-speaking anticlerical Socialist from a Dutch-speaking Catholic Christian Democrat as divides the two main linguistic groups. These cross-cutting tensions underlie Belgian politics, and account for much of its apparent instability. Although there are three broad ideological "families" (Socialists, broadly centrist Christian Democrats and rightwing secular Liberals) each now contains two separate regional parties—which can fall out with each other on a cultural or regional economic issue and bring yet another coalition to submit its resignation to the King. But the Belgians wouldn't want things any other way. Like the Italians, they are adept at getting on with life in the absence of a "strong" government. It probably represents their last line of defense in the struggle against creeping uniformity.

Their response to potentially divisive social and political issues is not to try to force through one particular partisan solution; rather it is to seek the least offensive compromise. Although long considered a thoroughly English virtue, *compromis à la belge* is fundamental to the way of life in Belgium. Take the law, for example. One-armed bandits and other forms of smalltime gaming are illegal. Yet an elaborate system exists to tax the profits from these (theoretically) non-existent money-spinners. At the same time, Belgian tax inspectors work on the not unreasonable assumption that since personal tax evasion is endemic and virtually unstoppable, it is better to settle for a "reasonable" amount, rather than risk total non-compliance by demanding the theoretical maximum.

North vs. South

This spirit of compromise underlies the relations between the country's two main socio-linguistic groups, the Dutch-speaking Flemings *(de Vlamingen* to themselves, *les Flamands* to their southern counterparts) and the French-speaking Walloons (who call themselves *les Wallons,* and are *de Walen* to their northern neighbors). It also needs to be said that much of the supposed antagonism between the communities is not shared at personal level: many business and social connections cross the language line. Nonetheless the country's somewhat fragile consensus rests on the unwillingness of either side to press home its political advantages over the other.

The Flemings, who are in any case in a majority, know that after thirty years of rapid—free-enterprise-based—industrial development they hold most of the economic cards; so, although they hate to admit it publicly, it's little skin off their noses if they have to speak French to get what they want from the Brussels bureaucracy. At the same time, the French-speakers realise that the bulk of tax revenue comes from the North; so they can't opt for wholly interventionist industrial policies in the former steel heartlands of Wallonia or try to exclude the minority Flemish community from the capital's government.

This central issue—of Brussels and its government and boundaries—exemplifies the Belgian political system at work. A typically ingenious solution was proposed in the mid-'70s, for example, to the thorny problem of administering the (again, theoretically non-existent) French-speakers of the capital's outer—hence solely Dutch-speaking—suburbs. This involved giving them all pseudo-addresses in the central urban area, which is officially bilingual. As it was, nothing came of the proposal: the necessary quid pro quo, parity representation for the city's Flemish community was not forthcoming.

As a result, the Brussels dispute still rumbles on, apparently threatening to divide the communities still further. Yet in a curiously paradoxical Belgian way, it holds the country together. The Flemish community will not let a city within its territory, containing 300,000 fellow Flemings, fall under Walloon domination. But it cannot be denied that Brussels is fundamentally a French-speaking city, with most of its cultural antennae tuned in to Wallonia. The two communities are inextricably locked together by their desire to keep a grip on the capital. The stories of rampant separatism and impending "breakup of the Belgian state" so often aired in the foreign press obviously fail to take this into account. In any case, a glance at the route of the Brussels-Liège railroad would suggest the nightmare complexity of trying to split what is still essentially one country into two. Belgium will continue as a single national entity for as long as the ability to compromise exists.

The Other Side of the Coin

The whole ethos of fudging the issue, agreeing to differ and turning blind eyes can lead, however, to some bad, or at least inadequate or hopelessly late decisions. Much valuable architecture has been lost as a result of the politicians' failure to put sensible curbs on the redevelopers' insatiable appetite for land. And the Belgians' low driving standards—the result of not having introduced actual road tests until the early '70s—are the butt of many a joke. But nowhere has the failure of the country to grasp the nettle been more apparent than the economy. Belgium failed miserably to react to either of the oil-shocks, and the country went on spending as if the boom era of the '60s were just around the corner again. The price is only being paid now. Closed steelworks, shipyards and factories are just some of the outward signs of the painful process of adjustment that is now belatedly under way. It is wrong to seek comfort in misfortune, but the economic difficulties and their attendant devaluations have at least made Belgium a slightly less costly place to visit.

Understanding the system, therefore, is the first essential you need in your quest for the real Belgium. Formalities are there to be respected: but basics are what count. Always have copious identity documents about your person (and your car) when you deal with petty functionaries, in which Belgium abounds. Always go out of your way to put your coats and bags in the inevitable cloak-room at the entrances to public buildings and museums. Always tip the attendant. Tip cinema usherettes too, as you enter, and night-club bouncers when you leave. Be suitably humble with railroad and tram conductors, customs men and traffic police.

You may never know when you'll need them. If you're being given a bad deal, they will go out of their way to help you. If you've "overlooked" the speed restriction sign, and your attitude is one of awed contrition, you'll be let off. Play the shopping game the Belgian way, and you'll find that most articles, particularly antiques, have a negotiable price: more negotiable still if you offer cash and the taxman isn't looking. Rules will be bent to suit you, a "fully-booked" show will find it has just one or two seats, and bureaucratic obstacle courses—like reclaiming Value-Added Tax when you come to leave—will become pleasant social occasions. But it depends very much whether you've gone out of your way not to offend the official or the shopkeeper's dignity. And, of course, whether you used the right language.

This structure of semi-bureaucratic formality often seems to have spilled over in to Belgians' social lives. Hands are there to be shaken. "Good morning" and "see you tomorrow" are said religiously. At a formal level, everything is very friendly: but making personal contact is still not easy for the outsider. Invitations to a Belgian's home are rare, and are never handed out lightly. This can sometimes prove distressing to the English or North American visitor, used to fairly casual invitations to dinner from convivial new acquaintances. If you do receive one it really shows you've made it: so don't cancel at the last minute, and don't assume that when your host says "drop round for a bite" he's inviting you to some informal snack. Belgians take their food seriously. Otherwise, "casual" socializing tends to be confined to organized after-work drinks in favored bars, organized outings to the coast or the Ardennes, and staunch, organized support for the inevitable office soccer team. Spontaneity is definitely not the name of the game.

Of Bicycles and Banks

So how do you catch the individual, unofficial Belgian on his home ground? Here, another element of the Belgian character tends to work to your advantage. In keeping with his assertive individualism, every

Belgian is an enthusiast about something. Some sport, pastime, artform or topical subject is dear to his heart; if you share that passion, you will be able to establish an enviable rapport. If, for example, you are (or were) a bicycle-racing fan, you'll have no trouble making contact. Seat yourself in an appropriate bar (virtually every one outside the coastal resorts has some sort of sporting affiliation) and ask one of the "regulars" who'll win the Tour de France, the Paris-Roubaix, the Giro d'Italia or the Ronde van Vlaanderen this year. You won't lack for conversation. Should your knowledge of the sport extend to the relative merits of the current, or past, masters of the track and road (or should you reveal some of your own past glories), you'll be sure to be treated as an honored guest. And you'll get to know more of what makes Belgians tick than you ever will from a guided bus-tour. Soccer, basketball (which is extremely popular) and more eclectic sports like pigeon-racing and bar-room games can also act as icebreakers in your attempts to get a feel for the true way of life.

Culture too is a consuming passion: so catching the Belgians at their cultural rites is important. Luckily for you, art is a participative rather than just a spectator event in Belgium. First, get away from the neon-lit Euroculture of Brussels: there is a wide range of cultural activities in the capital, of course, but your chances of meeting like-minded Belgians in a relatively informal atmosphere are slim. The most likely encounter will be with an English or North American accountant or bureaucrat: surely not what getting to know another country is all about. Take a day trip to Leuven or Liège. Spend a week-end in Dinant or Ghent, or an evening in Mons or Antwerp.

The best events can be found in the least likely locations. Belgian banks, for example, often host superb art exhibitions in their imposing premises. If you happen to time your visit to coincide with a Friday "Opening Night," you'll be treated to a free drink, a speech of welcome and appreciation by a prominent local art-critic, writer or public figure, and a chance to meet the artist in person.

Belgium has a large number of cultural centers, where libraries are combined with galleries and small theaters. Town halls, museums and schools also host cultural events. Track down a concert or poetry reading in one of the better-known cities, and in all probability you'll find yourself in a splendid palazzo (like Antwerp's International Cultural Center, the former Royal Palace) left over by the Spanish or Austrian empires. Over the interval coffee, you'll probably find a kindred spirit who'll tell you all the history you need to know.

In general, it's worth seeking out the smaller museums, and the one-off exhibitions where the curator or maybe the artist will be happy to show off their treasures. The Horta House in Brussels (which has a gallery attached) and the Smidt van Gelder museum in Antwerp both have an intimate quality lacking in some of the larger institutions. In smaller towns, visits to lesser-known collections are all the more rewarding for the warmth of the welcome. And the romantic atmosphere of the Verhaeren museum at Sint Amands aan de Schelde and of the ecclesiastical treasures of Tongeren add to the experience of seeing the exhibits themselves, and make the detour from the usual tourist track that much more worthwhile.

The "culture" connection need not confine you to highbrow art events, however. Everything from jazz and rock, to alternative feminist cinema and radical puppet theater has its own group of dedicated followers. Usually the contact point will be a bar, sometimes a labor-union hall or a rather more left-wing version of the cultural center. If you're staying at an up-market hotel, the reception may even deny that such entertainment exists: but it's out there. Finding it requires the simple expedient of lighting on a suitable bar or cafe and seeing what sort of posters are pinned up in the hallway or above the pinball machine. Whether they are advertising madrigals or big-band music, modern sculpture or medieval ecclesiastical carving, you'll find the elusive starting point of the route that leads to the discovery of the real Belgium.

The Good Life?

Will you like what you find? The answer to this question probably reveals more about you and your attitude to modern life than it does about Belgium itself. Informed critics of Belgium—and there are some who speak sympathetically from experience, rather than condemn from a position of ignorance—generally complain that the life-style is un-comfortably "bourgeois." And they don't just refer to the preponder-ance of heavy Louis-XV furniture or the quaintly-framed "drive safely" photographs of wife and family in the front of Belgian cars.

More than any other developed country in Europe, except, perhaps, Switzerland, Belgian thinking is permeated by a strong sense of materi-alism. Wanting to be wealthy is the driving force of Belgian life. In Britain, no amount of wealth will change your social class; in the Netherlands and Scandinavia, everyone seems concerned with the nonfinancial quality of life; in Germany and France, discretion and a more efficient taxation system seem to limit the urge to conspicuous affluence. In Belgium, however, possession of property is still the mea-suring-rod by which to judge your success.

Many social values appear not to have changed in essence since the last century. Most young men still dream of owning their own factories, a large German or American car, and a large urban apartment and a country cottage in which to bring up their large families. Add this to the continuing active role of the church in daily life, and it's easy to see why many Belgians hold the country up as a bastion of traditional western ideals.

The critics' view maintains that an enviable level of economic devel-opment and a concentration on solving linguistic rather than social problems has slowed the pace of evolution to a point where Belgium is unable to come to terms with the current social and economic forces of change at work throughout Europe. As an example, they would cite the prevailing Belgian attitude to the role of women in society. Most parents still think it best that daughters leave the family home to enter straight into married life: there's little talk of "liberation" away from the big cities. Similarly, tolerance of ethnic minorities—the guestwork-ers from Turkey and North Africa—is far from wide-ranging: bars in Antwerp and Brussels still have hateful notices on their doors proclaiming, "Interdit aux chiens et aux nord-africains." Perhaps the effort of being Belgian has stunted the growth of more enlightened ideas.

Yet the Belgian quest for good living does have wholly positive effects. Belgian shops still offer those touches of service—like polite assistants and gift-wrapping—that have largely died out elsewhere in Europe. (Oddly enough though, shops, like the rest of the financial system, make heavy weather of handling personal checks.) And the variety of quality goods on display is astounding. Belgian supermarkets, for example, stock a range of food products unrivalled in Europe. Their customers demand a far broader range of international delicacies (including American stalwarts like cranberries) than their more chauvinistic French or English counterparts. The cooking in Belgian restaurants offers similar variety, and is of a universally high standard. And don't be afraid of being served up horesemeat as a cheap substitute for steak: Belgians eat it from choice, not for reasons of poverty.

The free-spending economy offers visitors other less fattening benefits. The Belgian taste for automobiles is insatiable, and the country has a deluxe road system to match; the dense network of brightly-lit freeways was visible from the moon. Telephones and telex work impeccably; the postal service is prompt; and the highest ratio of law-enforcers to citizens in Europe helps keep property—and persons—safe from the crime wave that has flooded over the rest of the continent.

Creativity and Culture

It is probably in the field of the arts, however, that Belgium's "bourgeois" way of life makes its greatest contribution to Europe's well-being. You may not be impressed with the Belgians' taste for furniture, but when it comes to serious works of art you have to admit that five centuries of collecting have rubbed off into daily life. The old concept of patronage is alive and well. Perhaps it is a tax-dodge: but wasn't it always the patrician's duty to use his wealth to support the arts? And a picture or an antique ornament is, after all, a more pleasant "hedge" than a few kilos of gold bullion or some bearer bonds in the safe under the bed.

As a result, young artists and poets flourish. New art-forms are being developed. Galleries and exhibitions thrive, and attract an enthusiastic public. The works are almost always up for sale. You may be shocked at the prices: but the artists know what the market will bear. The purchasers are keen private individuals, not philanthropic bureaucrats. As a result, the dead hand of "Ministry of Culture" thinking does not inhibit the creativity of the country's artists and writers. They in their turn acknowledge their cultural roots, going back through Magritte and Ensor, Verhaeren and Gezelle to the Golden Age of the late 16th century and beyond. In the area of artistic self-expression, Belgians certainly know just who they are, where they came from, and where they are going.

In other areas too, like their aggressive presence on the international business scene, the Belgians seem able to combine the best elements of conservatism and modernism. Commercialism does reign supreme: but it is never divorced from tradition. Since the days of the medieval

traders, the people of this part of the world have been buying, processing, transporting and selling the necessities of civilized life. With their
profits, they have adorned one of the richest cultural storehouses in the
world: the fact that some of its finest treasures are in the Prado in
Madrid or London's National Gallery says far more about the troubled
political fortunes of the Low Countries than their inhabitants' creative
genius. For better or worse, the Belgians intend to stick to the mercantile ethos of their forebears: they see little reason to change.

So, when you get past the stage of superficial generalizations and of
cheap souvenirs, when you come into contact with the real face of
Belgian society and begin to understand what keeps this most improbable country in existence, you may still not be able to love it. But at least
you will be forced to admit that Belgium cannot be described with a
single adjective—baffling, boring, brilliant or bourgeois—without your
own attitude to life being questioned too.

BELGIAN HISTORY

Perennial Victim of Power Politics

A glance at the map will show you the importance of the Low Countries. Glistening with the estuaries of international waterways (Rhine, Scheldt and Meuse), they are the obvious trans-shipment point for goods and passengers seeking to avoid longer sea routes through the Baltic and the Mediterranean.

With few natural defenses against Europe's successive generations of warring armies, the Low Countries—especially that part of them that is now Belgium—have provided a perennial battlefield. Domination of the ports has been a goal of power politics in the rival empire-building of the French, the Spanish, the Austrians, the Dutch and the Germans. England's wool trade with Flanders, and her free access to the ports of the Low Countries have been undercurrents of history for many centuries. Today, NATO's plans for the defense of Western Europe still call for unrestricted access to these strategic ports.

As pawns on an international chessboard, therefore, the Belgians' character has been moulded by a tradition of alien occupation. The successive occupations by Rome, Burgundy, Spain, Austria, France, the Netherlands, and the recent incursions by Imperial and Nazi Germany have all left their mark. Belgians have become skilled during many centuries at feigning conformity, while preserving an inner independence: regulations, taxes and rationing systems imposed by alien governors are there to be avoided. The fact that something of the same ethos still prevails after more than 40 invasion-free years is wholly understandable.

From Roman Times to the Middle Ages

The Gaul of the Belgae tribes was primitive, but already productive, when Julius Caesar pushed his conquest to the North Sea. When Mark Antony reminded the Romans, at Caesar's funeral, of "the day he overcame the Nervi," he was speaking of a battle fought against the Belgians on Belgian soil. The matrons of Rome learned to prize the Menapian cloth made in the Flemish coastal district; and, for nearly five centuries, Belgian Gaul had the protection of the *pax romana*. Great roads were built, radiating from Bavay (a few miles south of the French border, near Mons), itself joined to Cologne by the Via Agrippa, passing through Tongeren and Maastricht. Other roads passed through Tournai, linked Arlon with Trier (West Germany) and, in what is now Dutch territory, joined Leiden with the Rhine at Utrecht.

When the last Roman legion was withdrawn, in the first half of the 5th century, Belgian Gaul became part of the Frankish kingdom of the Merovingian kings, established from Tournai and stretching from the Weser to the Pyrenees. This, however, did not hold together; and two centuries later Belgium herself became a nursery of kings, and knew a period of early splendor.

Towards the end of the 7th century, the astute Hesbaye family of Pepin reunited the kingdom and, through the victories of Charles Martel, pushed it farther eastward. With the Pope's consent, Pepin the Short was crowned King of the Franks at Soissons in 751; and in the year 800 his son, known to history as Charlemagne, was invested by Pope Leo III as Emperor of the West. His vast domain extended from Jutland to Naples and from the Ebro to the Oder.

The emperor's agricultural reforms were put into thriving practice on his Belgian personal domains at Herstal and Jupille. Roads were built and waterways put into use, notably the Scheldt up to and beyond Tournai. Charlemagne, apart from his military victories, was a great organizer and civilizing influence; but his administrative feats did not long outlive him. After his death in 814 the Carolingian empire started to disintegrate under the rule of his son, Louis the Pious, and the Treaty of Verdun in 843 divided the empire in three. A boundary along the Scheldt separated Flanders, faithful to France, from Belgium's southern (Walloon) provinces, which belonged to Lotharingia. This meant strength for Flanders, comparative feebleness for the south.

In the northern half, Baldwin Iron-Arm, by his resistance to the Norse invasions, established himself as the first Count of Flanders, in 862. The confines of Flanders were enlarged south of the Scheldt, into France and the Netherlands. By the middle of the 11th century Robert I, with his sister married to William the Conqueror of England and one of his daughters to the King of Denmark, was becoming too strong a vassal for France.

Meantime the southern kingdom had had trouble with its own nobility. Its northern Duchy of Lothier, which covered what is now southern Belgium, became involved in quarrels between the empire and the papacy. With Godefroy de Bouillon's absorption in the First Crusade, the ducal authority dwindled. The duchy became little more than a collection of feudal domains, themselves a prey to a series of masterful prince-bishops of Liège.

Against this background, commerce was growing and with it came the rise of the towns. Even the supreme power of the Counts of Flanders began to wane. By the time (1256) Black Margot, as reigning countess, had set all Europe by the ears to determine which of her families was legitimate, the city of Bruges had already secured the English cloth monopoly. Most of the towns date from this period for apart from Tongeren and Tournai, the Norsemen's ravages had left little trace of earlier settlements. The cities demanded privileges. Under loose princely supervision, they became states within the state, their citizens enfranchised from feudal serfdom, assuming their own responsibilities in education, justice, administration, even defence. Strong local patriotisms sprang up, trade and manufacture were regulated by guilds, rich merchants spent fortunes on public buildings and endowments. Liège prospered with its iron forges and its already flourishing arms manufacture. Bruges, with its fine port on the now vanished Zwin, became the central clearing house of Europe's trade, enriched by the counting-houses of German and Lombard bankers. The other "Members of Flanders," Ghent and Ypres (Ieper), grew wealthy on fine cloth made from English wool. As a result, these prosperous and proud communities developed an autonomy unheard of at the time elsewhere in Europe.

Battles and Revolts

France was naturally alarmed. Philip the Fair, having made a truce with Edward I of England, was emboldened to "confiscate" Flanders. The answer was the "Matines of Bruges," when Pieter de Coninck, a master-weaver, led the Men of the Claw in the merciless butchering of the Men of the Lily, whose French tongues boggled at a Flemish password. The commons of Flanders rallied and, on July 11 1302, routed the might of French chivalry near Kortrijk in the battle of the Golden Spurs; to this day, the anniversary is celebrated as the Flemings' finest hour. Their triumph was short-lived, however, and resistance was wiped out by 1328, except that periodic revolts (1338–45 and 1379–85) took place against the victimization of Flanders by both France and England during the Hundred Years' War. The result was a strengthened friendship between Flanders and England, cemented by Edward III's sojourn in Ghent, where John of Gaunt was born.

The spirit of the trading cities was still strong, and was the background to the next great period, the ascendancy of the four Dukes of Burgundy. The first two dukes meddled little in Flemish affairs, but the long reign of Philip the Good (1419–67) was the Low Countries' cultural high-point under the Burgundians. Allying himself with the victorious Henry V of England and out-intriguing his brother-in-law, Duke Humphrey of Gloucester, Philip gained ascendancy over Hainaut. He bought the lordships of Namur and Luxembourg and, for lack of an entitled rival, was proclaimed heir to the Duchies of Limburg and Brabant and the Marquisate of Antwerp. With his domains stretching into Holland as far as Texel, he was nicknamed Grand Duke of the West, and he united his nobles and princelings in the Order of the Golden Fleece.

His fabulous reign is the period of the Van Eycks and Hans Memling in painting, of the architects Jan van Ruysbroek and Mathieu de Layens, of the De Limbourg brothers in miniature-painting and of sculptors such as Claus Sluter and the Borremans. Politically there were troubles—firmly dealt with—between Philip and the communes of Ghent and Bruges: and there was strife which led to the sacking of Dinant and the razing to the ground of Liège. When Philip died, his son, Charles the Bold, was too keen a soldier and too impatient a politician to hold the situation Philip had so pertinaciously built up. His death at the siege of Nancy (1477) left his 19-year-old daughter, Mary of Burgundy, to face a revolt of the communes and the intrigues of Louis XI, the "eternal spider," to bring Burgundy under the French crown. A statesman-like marriage with Maximilian, son of Frederick III of Austria, the defeat of the French at Guinegatte and the birth of a son, Philip, and a daughter, Margaret, seemed to consolidate the Duchy of Burgundy, when Mary's sudden death in 1482 removed the linch-pin.

The independently minded Flemish cities refused to accept Maximilian as sole regent. In late 1482, in a move designed to secure good relations with France, the cities pushed the compliant regency council into accepting the Peace of Arras, which gave away Burgundian lands in Artois—and in the heart of Burgundy itself—to Louis XI. Maximilian, however, was determined not to preside over the piecemeal loss of his son's territories, and so set out to break the power of the cities.

After Louis' death in 1483, the tide turned in the Austrian's favor. The next nine years saw sporadic fighting, during which Maximilian's German mercenaries laid regular siege to Ghent, Bruges and Ypres: in 1492, the cities had to seek terms, and they assented to the Peace of Cadzand. It was the beginning of the end of their independence.

In 1494, Maximilian's son, Philip, took control of the Austro-Burgundian lands in the Low Countries when his father was called to Vienna to take up the imperial throne on the death of Frederick III. Philip was soon married, at his father's behest, to Juana, the daughter of Ferdinand and Isabella, the joint sovereigns of the emerging world power—Spain. The wedding was solemnized in Lier in November 1496. Little did they realise it was to change the face of Europe.

Philip and Juana's son Charles was born on February 4, 1500 in Ghent. But the young baby soon left Flanders for Spain, because by 1502, a series of deaths within the royal family had left Juana heiress-presumptive to the throne. In 1506, however, Philip died and Juana was declared insane: leaving an aging Ferdinand king in Spain, Maximilian Emperor in Vienna and the six-year-old Charles—nominally archduke of the Low Countries under the regency of Margaret of Austria—as their heir.

Over the next twenty years, however, these diverse responsibilities all devolved onto the young prince. By the time he was crowned emperor

of Austria in 1530, Charles V—known as Keizer Karel, Charles-Quint
or Carlos Quinto depending on which part of his vast domains his
subjects were in—ruled an empire that stretched from the fringes of
Turkey's realms in central Europe to Spain's recently founded outposts
in the New World. And he set about consolidating Habsburg rule with
a thoroughness worthy of his grandfather.

The Spanish Ascendancy—1530–1650

The next hundred years saw the golden age of the southern Low
Countries, as strong government, the expanding Spanish world empire,
and a well-established tradition of commerce combined to create
Europe's richest trading center. As Venice's star waned, so Antwerp's
rose: the counting houses of Amberis (as the English then called it)
financed the spice trade and the colonization of the Americas, forged
new trade routes to the East and oversaw the shipping of Flemish cloth
throughout the civilized world. Flemish seafarers and geographers,
such as Mercator, helped redraw the way that Europe looked at the
world—literally. But just as the mercantile revolution flourished, so too
did calls for social, political and above all religious reform.

From the outset, Charles' centralizing, ruthless style of government
had run afoul of the long-standing tradition of municipal autonomy;
added to this, conflict was now brewing between the traditionally-
privileged landowning aristocracy and the rapidly rising merchant
class of the cities. Into this explosive mixture, there were added the
increasing tax burdens required to finance a policy of military confron-
tation against France, the increasingly arbitrary style of the imperial
bureaucracy, and most important, the suspicion that the Low Countries' tradition of social and religious tolerance might be abruptly ter-
minated. Dissent mounted.

Charles V retired to a monastery in southern Spain in 1555. His
Spanish-educated son, Philip II, became King of Spain and archduke
of the Low Countries. In 1560, he decided to crack down on the
subversive political and religious ideas that had taken root throughout
the 17 provinces of the Spanish Netherlands. The threat of the Inquisition was too much for the Low Countries to bear: by the mid-1560s,
the whole area was in open revolt. In 1567, the Duke of Alba began
a military campaign designed to break the Netherlands resistance:
despite the military superiority of Spanish troops, Philip's inadequacy
in the fields of sea-faring and international finance sapped the imperial
war effort. The conflict dragged on.

In the late 1570s, the Italian general Alessandro Farnese (backed by
cash confiscated from Spanish nobles and plundered from the Incas)
succeeded in splitting the Low Countries' resistance. In January 1579,
Hainaut, Artois and Douai sought surrender terms. Other parts of the
more pro-Catholic south followed suit. The northern provinces and the
Flemish cities struggled on. The leading intellectuals and artists faced
an agonizing choice: to stay in the rich, but illiberal, Spanish empire,
or take their chances in the nascent independent state—the republic of
the seven undefeated United Provinces—centered round the trading
cities of North and South Holland. With the surrender of Antwerp in

1585, a cultural and religious iron curtain fell across the now divided Low Countries.

The final years of the Golden Age—the period of Rubens, Jordaens, Van Dyck and Brouwer—were, in fact, the last gasp for the Spanish Netherlands. By the 1640s, the Dutch republic had ploughed its massive trading profits back into a powerful navy—that even matched the might of England's own short-lived mercantile republic on the high seas. The United Provinces used their new-found power to exact a terrible vengeance on their former colonial masters: the Schelde was totally closed to international commerce, and within a few years, grass grew in the streets of Antwerp. At the same time, the French were not slow in seizing large tracts of territory along the southern border of the Spanish Netherlands. From their zenith as the hub of a world trading empire in 1540, Spain's northern provinces had become an economic and cultural backwater by the middle of the 17th century.

Obscurity and Decline—1650–1830

The period of obscurity was to last into the early years of the 18th century, when French intrigues secured the Spanish throne for a grandson of Louis XIV. The threat to the security of the United Provinces and to England was clear. The two protestant powers formed an alliance; which, under the brilliant military leadership of the Duke of Marlborough, made the French realize—at the battles of Ramillies, Oudenaarde and Malplaquet—that their power-play in the Low Countries was not worth the effort.

In 1713, the war-scarred Spanish provinces were handed over to authentic Austrian Habsburg rulers. Like their Spanish cousins, however, they did little to reawaken the country's social or economic vitality. In 1745, a Franco-Irish force outmaneuvered an Anglo-Austrian-Dutch defending force, and effectively became masters of the Belgian provinces (as they were beginning to be called). But they were in such a bad state of economic decline that the French duly handed them back to Austria.

In the later years of the 18th century, the emperor Joseph II attempted to institute a number of reforms to drag the provinces into the modern world. The irony of his move was that while the *ancien régime* in France provoked revolution by its stubborn refusal to change, the shop-keepers, peasants and landowners of the Austrian Netherlands were provoked into revolt by the threat to their traditional religious order and their dislike of modern government.

The rejection of Austrian-imposed reformism was fired by a growing sense of *l'ésprit national* among a growing band of city-dwellers in Brussels as well as by the innate conservatism of the peasants. They began to talk of themselves as Belgian: but while it was easy to agree what they were not—secular revolutionaries in the French mold, or Austrian paternalists—they were not really sure what they stood for, other than a refusal to change and a wish to be left alone. The first Brabançonne revolution took place against the backdrop of far more momentous events further south: and though the Austrians were able to regain control of their provinces by the end of 1790, they (and the reactionary Belgian revolution) were soon swept aside by an altogether more potent force—revolutionary France.

A minority of the province's citizens endorsed the radical ideal of *liberté, égalité, fraternité* but two attempts to imitate the French Revolution, in Brussels and Liège, failed ingloriously for lack of popular support. Five regiments of Belgian volunteers were formed to aid the Austro-Prussian support of the French monarchy against the new Republic, and there was a Belgian Legion on the opposing side under General Dumouriez, who crushed the coalition at Jemappes. Belgium changed hands several times and was annexed to France in 1795 at the price of a Peasants' Revolt against compulsory military service and a firm refusal by the English to allow the French to make full use of the Flemish ports.

After Bonaparte's first exile, the powers decided the fate of Belgium. Most of the former Austrian territory was to be integrated into the newly-formed Kingdom of the Netherlands. The exception was Eupen-Malmédy, which came under Prussian administration. The Congress of Vienna was busy approving this when news came of Bonaparte's return. His romantic march northward was halted only a dozen miles short of Brussels and, when the battle of Waterloo had been fought, the Congress's plans were put into action. At a stroke, the Netherlands were "reunited" after over 200 years. The shock of reunification was too much to bear. The Bishop of Ghent at once led an outcry against the liberty of conscience to which William I of Orange was committed, and the king rather provocatively adopted various anti-Catholic measures and others appearing to favor Dutch-speakers over French-speakers. *L'ésprit national* reasserted itself. Despite early efforts to industrialize the Kingdom, North–South relations went from bad to worse. Attempts by the Dutch to quell riots in Brussels (September 1830) were abandoned after some bloodshed, a provisional government was formed and a National Congress elected. French intrigues secured the election as king of the second son of King Louis-Philippe, but British opposition was so strong that the final choice fell on Prince Leopold of Saxe-Coburg-Saalfeld, an uncle of Queen Victoria. He took the oath of allegiance to the constitution on July 21 1831: now the occasion for Belgium's national day—a fact of which most Belgians are ignorant.

1831–1951—Flanders' Struggle for Equality

For the next 80 years, the Belgians trusted to their neutrality, and a British guarantee of territorial integrity, to protect them from the vicissitudes of European power politics. In the 1840s, the new state followed Britain in another important respect. Belgium staged its own industrial revolution based on coal, steel, textiles, glassmaking and shipbuilding. The concentration of many of the natural resources required for these industries in the south of the country helped to consolidate the post-1830 dominance of the French-speaking section of the community.

In the latter years of the 19th century, the Dutch speakers found themselves second-class citizens in their own country. Tied to a declining rural economy, excluded from power by the ruling elite in Brussels and cut off from their cultural roots by the Belgium-Netherlands frontier and a rigorous French-language education policy, they regarded the Belgian state as an oppressive alien force.

Meanwhile, Belgium reached the zenith of its development as a French-speaking state in the British mold with the acquisition of a colony in the Congo basin in central Africa. With a little place in the sun secured, Belgium's shortsighted politicians of the first decade of this century were sure that the gathering clouds on their horizon— Flemish discontent, a growing workers' movement, and, most disturbingly, German expansionism—would all evaporate of their own accord or be scared away by the rattle of a British saber.

They were rudely awakened in the summer of 1914. Stout resistance by "brave little Belgium" in the face of the lightning German advance saved the Belgians' dignity—but little else. The whole country was occupied, save for that small section between De Panne and the French frontier near Armentières where—for four long years—the old concept of warfare was transformed into a nightmare mechanical exercise of scientific destruction.

Playing host to an army of occupation and the horrors of the Great War was bound to leave its scars; political and social as well as physical and economic. Part of the Flemish community had looked on the Germans as liberators from years of Walloon oppression, and collaborated openly. Another part believed that by its sacrifices in the trenches of West Flanders it would win fair representation in the post-war government of Belgium: both groups were disappointed.

The German occupation became steadily more onerous and unpopular, while the eventual allied victory unleashed a wave of anti-Flemish feeling against even those citizens who had remained loyal to the Belgian state. "After the war, no one will speak Flemish any more," ran the cry. The ultimate expression of Walloon supremacy was the Franco-Belgian treaty of 1919, which ended Belgium's tradition of neutrality.

The inter-war period saw fundamental economic changes, however, that were already leading to the erosion of the French-speakers' power. The southern coalfields were badly damaged during the war, and never really recovered. Iron ore in Luxembourg started to run out, and the economics of steel making, textiles and glass manufacture all began to look sick during the Great Depression.

In the north, however, scientific farming methods boosted agricultural productivity, and new light industries sprang up round the port of Antwerp. The higher Flemish birth-rate began to make itself felt in the legislature. By the late-1930s, a newly assertive Flemish majority had forced the country back into neutrality and won the battle for Dutch as the language of administration, education and justice in Flanders.

The 1940–45 period saw a second German occupation; and once again, some sections of the Belgian population threw in their lot with the Germans, while others conducted a heroic clandestine resistance or fought with allied forces abroad. Where the two wars differed, however, was in the role of the King.

In 1914, Albert, the Soldier-King, had stood firm in the front line with his troops as they defended the tiny north-western corner of Belgian territory. In 1940, however, Leopold III thought it best to preside over the surrender of his forces and, against the advice of his ministers, to remain in Belgium to try to mitigate the severity of the occupation. Was it open encouragement of collaboration? Or was it a brave act of solidarity with his people? The question can still provoke a heated discussion today.

Whatever Leopold's motives, the closing days of the war found him a prisoner in Germany. A regent was appointed in his place. In 1949/50, however, it was felt to be opportune for Leopold to return to the throne, and a referendum narrowly confirmed his position as head of state. Wallonia, however, voted heavily against his return: protests became more violent, and secession, followed by some sort of association with the French Republic, was seriously canvassed in the southern cities. In 1951, Leopold wisely used his newly-regained sovereign power to abdicate in favor of his son Baudouin.

After 1951—the Capital of Europe

The accession of Baudouin, coming as it did at a time of European renewal and conciliation marked a new beginning. The concept of a bicultural Belgium, with power shared between the regions, began to take root. At the same time, closer ties with other countries, through the Benelux union and later NATO and the European Community, led to a massive build-up of incoming investment and stimulated economic growth.

A more international vocation has also helped to heal the wounds left by the occupation and soothe the bitterness aroused by the *question royale*. Above all, the creation of the European Community has provided a framework within which Flemings and Walloons can gradually become "closer"—both in terms of economic relations and cultural links—to their fellow Dutch or French speakers, without implying any distrust of the Belgian state.

So it is that Brussels, the administrative center of the Low Countries for so many centuries, and now host to the European Community and NATO's headquarters, has emerged as the "Capital of Europe." A true seat of power, it has always adapted itself to the dictates of successive waves of archdukes, regents, kings and commissioners—and their inevitable bureaucracies.

Writing in 1567, the Florentine Ludovico Guicciardini found Brussels one of Europe's most agreeable capitals: "There are," he wrote, "many fine residences of leading men who come to discuss their affairs and take part in government at the court of the king or the governor." As the ministers, diplomats, lobbyists and journalists from all over Europe—and elsewhere—gather to discuss new policies for agriculture, industry or trade, or Europe's defenses, they are the unwitting successors to a tradition stretching back over five hundred years. Belgium, while itself far from powerful, is always the stage on which Europe's great events take place.

A GLIMPSE OF THE ARTS

A Creative Melting Pot

by
PAUL STRATHERN

Paul Strathern is a freelance travel writer and prize-winning novelist. He has written over a dozen books on a wide variety of subjects, including several travel books on Europe based on 25 years' experience.

Since the Belgian nation is only just over 150 years old, it is not surprising that there is little strictly Belgian national culture as such. Compared to the Italian, French, German, Spanish and English contributions to the European scene, the Belgians have played a relatively small role. In the main Belgium has tended to absorb, rather than to originate influences. The main reasons for this are its geographical position sandwiched between Germany and France, and its history of conquests by almost every major European power. As a result the Belgians have always retained a refreshingly international outlook, though sometimes this has been at the expense of any rich ground of deeply-rooted provincialism. Yet despite these drawbacks the Belgian contribution to the European cultural scene has been significant and

41

distinctive, and in at least one sphere—that of Flemish painting—it certainly holds its own amongst its larger peers.

Origins and the Romanesque Period

Prior to 500 B.C. the territory now occupied by Belgium was inhabited by Celtic tribes, one of which was known as the Belgae. Dolmens (stone tombs) dating from this pre-historic period can be seen around Weris in the Ourthe Valley (outside Liège). There is also a fine monumental stone menhir at Hollain south of Tournai.

In 58 B.C. this territory was conquered by Julius Caesar and became one of the border provinces of the Roman Empire. A collection of remains and artefacts from this period can be seen in the Gallo-Roman Provincial Museum at Tongeren. This is traditionally the oldest town in Belgium and was founded in 57 B.C. by Julius Caesar himself, though today its central square contains a monument to his main local adversary Ambiorix, chief of the Eburones, who put the Roman legions under Sabinus to flight in 54 B.C. The monument, by Jules Bertin, was erected in 1866.

When the Romans left, the entire area of the Low Countries soon became subject to frequent Viking raids. These went on until well into the 10th century and account for why little remains from this period. After this, Romanesque culture began percolating into Belgium, by way of the Rhineland—picking up a certain amount of Germanic influence en route. In Belgium there were two main Romanesque styles. The earlier Meuse-Romanesque—with simple, square-pillared churches, wood vaulting and solid towers—lasted until the middle of the 12th century. The best example of this period is the Convent Church of St. Gertrude in Nivelles, which was begun around 1000—though much of it has been reconstructed. Also reconstructed (in 1755) is the church of St. Jean in Liège, which was built in 990 by Bishop Notger and modelled on the Imperial Chapel just across the German border at Aachen (Aix).

The later Schelde-Romanesque period lasted until the middle of the 13th century and produced an altogether richer style. The churches of this period tend to have more elaborate naves, rounded pillars and central towers. A prime example is the splendid nave of Tournai Cathedral. Another typical work of this period is the Collegiate Church at Soignies (Zinnik) 13 km. (8 miles) north-east of Mons, which was built between 965 and 1150, almost certainly to replace an earlier monastery destroyed by the Viking invaders.

Another effect of Rhineland influence was the establishment of goldsmiths and ironworkers in the Meuse valley in the 12th century. The work of these craftsmen soon achieved such renown that it was in demand all over Europe (examples even reaching Constantinople). The celebrated bronze font supported by ten bulls in the Church of St. Barthélemy in Liège, and the reliquary of Pope Alexander in the Musées Royaux d'Art et d'Histoire in Brussels are typical examples of this work. In the treasury of the Convent of Notre Dame in Namur there are a number of reliquaries by Hugo of Oignies, one of the greatest goldsmiths of this period.

Dating from this, and earlier periods, are several spectacular examples of book illustration. The best of these are to be found near Spa in the independent Benedictine Abbey of Stavelot (which was founded in the 7th century) and at the Premonstratensian Abbey of Park (on the outskirts of Leuven).

Gothic

The advent of the 13th century saw an increasing French influence on Belgian architecture. This was the beginning of the Gothic era. Whereas churches had previously been built by masons and craftsmen, their design now became the work of fully-fledged architects. The discovery of new techniques brought about the introduction of the pointed spire, and cross-ribbed interior arches supported by outer buttresses and arches. Gothic structures are characterized by a strong outer shell which bears the weight of the building, thus providing opportunity for much intricacy and imaginative flourish in the interior design. There were three main Gothic periods in the Low Countries. The Early Gothic of the 13th century evolved into the High Gothic of the 14th century, which culminated in the increasing complexity and richness of decoration which characterized the great period of Flamboyant Gothic in the 15th and 16th centuries. These styles also evolved their own Belgian regional variations, such as Scheldt Gothic, Limburg Gothic and Brabant Gothic.

The transition from the Romanesque to the Gothic periods is embodied in the great cathedral at Tournai. This was begun in 1140, but not completed until the end of the 13th century. Its five towers are a blend of German Romanesque and French Gothic dating from the 11th–12th centuries, but the extended choir is typically French Early Gothic. Amongst the finest examples of pure Early Gothic are the churches of St. Niklaas at Ghent and St. Walburga at Veurne. In medieval Bruges there is also the Cathedral and the Onze Lieve Vrouwkerk (Church of Our Lady) which contains the magnificent Virgin and Child by Michelangelo.

One of the finest examples of the High Gothic style is the Basilica of Our Lady (St. Martinus Basiliek) at Halle, a typical example of the Brabant Gothic variation showing considerable French influence, whose interior contains some fine sculptural decoration from the period. But the imposing Collegiate Church of Notre Dame at Huy, with its magnificent treasury, is generally considered Belgium's most impressive building from this period.

Flamboyant Gothic reaches its greatest imaginative flights in the magnificent cathedrals at Ghent, Antwerp and Mechelen. The sheer size of the Cathedral of Our Lady at Antwerp exhibits many of the great advances made by these medieval architects. The carillon north tower is over 400 ft. high; and its impressive interior contains two superb Rubens, *The Raising of the Cross* and the *Assumption* on the altar. The tower of St Rombout at Mechelen is over 300 ft. (though it was initially designed to reach more than 550 ft., which would have made it the tallest in Christendom). Its carillon dates from the 15th–16th centuries and has 49 bells, while the interior contains Van Dyck's magnificent *Crucifixion.* Other fine examples from this period are the Collegiate Church at Mons and St Jacques at Liège.

With the advent of medieval prosperity, the rich burghers and the guilds began erecting many superb secular buildings in the Gothic style—all expressing a new-found spirit of freedom, commercial enterprise and civic pride. There are belfries (carillons), cloth halls and town halls (Hôtels de Ville) all over Belgium dating from this period. The 13th-century Cloth Hall at Ieper (Ypres), though now largely rebuilt, is generally considered the most impressive of the early secular Gothic. 14th-century examples include the Cloth Hall at Leuven and the Town Hall at Bruges. Though the greatest flowering came in the 15th and 16th centuries with the erection of the Town Halls at Brussels, Leuven and Ghent. Typical features of these buildings include the sumptuous decoration and the impressive front steps (for the reading of proclamations to the assembled townsfolk).

The decorative work incorporated in these Gothic masterpieces encouraged the talents of a whole range of craftsmen. Notable among these were the book illustrators and the miniaturists. It was from this rich ground that Flemish painting came into being. The first great artists of this school were the Van Eyck brothers who worked in the early 15th century. The famous Italian biographer Vasari even claimed that Jan Van Eyck was the inventor of oil painting. One of the greatest works by the brothers Van Eyck is the polyptych altar at St. Bavon in Ghent. When open, this shows the *Adoration of the Mystic Lamb,* and when closed the doors reveal a portrait of the donor and his wife. This masterpiece includes landscape painting of a hitherto unknown realism which was to have much influence on later artists. The other great artist of this period, Hans Memling, was in fact born in Germany, though during the last half of the 15th century he worked in Bruges, where many of his masterpieces can be seen in the Groeninge Museum. However, the painter from this period who often appeals most to the 20th-century imagination is the Dutchman, Hieronymus Bosch (1450–1516), whose grotesque dream-like scenes such as *The Last Judgement* and *The Garden of Earthly Delights* are typical of the medieval mind. Examples of his earlier works can be seen in the Musée d'Art Ancien in Brussels and his *Last Judgement* is in the Groeninge Museum in Bruges.

The Renaissance

It was some time before the effects of the Renaissance began to be felt in Belgium. Not until the mid-16th century did a reaction set in against the extravagant splendors of Gothic in favor of the more balanced humanistic proportions which characterize the Renaissance. The new architectural ideas arriving from Italy first took on local form in the shape of the Antwerp Town Hall, which was the work of Cornelius Floris (1514–75). However, the effects of the Renaissance are mainly to be seen in domestic architecture, where brick and stone began to take the place of wood as the main building material. Though the local style remained largely unchanged—with its typical gables and leaded windows.

It was in the fields of painting and sculpture that the Renaissance produced its most significant influence. The greatest Flemish artist of the period was undoubtedly Pieter Breughel (1525–69), another Dutchman, who is best known for his depiction of the peasant life of the times set in landscapes of richly authentic detail. Most of his best known works are now in Vienna, but several fine examples are on show in Brussels in the Musée d'Art Ancien. Here you can also see works by his celebrated son Pieter Breughel the Younger.

Another great painter, the German Albrecht Dürer (1471–1528), had a considerable effect on local Belgian artists when he visited Antwerp, where he was received with much pomp. During his stay in Belgium he drew many portraits of contemporary artists. However, perhaps the most important Renaissance visitor to Belgium was the great Dutch scholar Erasmus (1466–1536). After a long sojourn in England, he settled in Leuven (Louvain) in 1516 where he founded the Collegium Trilingue for the study of Hebrew, Greek and Latin. At this time he was at the height of his fame and conducting correspondence with many of the great minds of Europe. His humanistic influence permeated the cultural sphere.

Though perhaps the main reason why the Renaissance did not produce such widespread concrete cultural and artistic achievements in Belgium as elsewhere was due to the Spanish occupation of Antwerp in 1585. This caused many of the rich burghers, who might well have patronized an artistic revival, to flee for safety to Holland.

The Age of Baroque and Belgian Genius

If the Renaissance had comparatively little direct effect on Belgian culture, this was more than compensated by the influence of the Baroque. This style also originated in Italy, and quickly spread throughout Europe—largely as a Catholic reaction to the more puritan simplicity of Protestant influence. The Baroque style was particularly encouraged by the Jesuits, and one of its earliest architectural examples in Belgium, the church of St. Carolus Borromeüs in Antwerp, was in fact built by the Jesuit architect Pieter Huyssens in 1615–21. Another well-known Belgian architect of this period was Wenceslas Coeberger, who was also a painter, engraver and engineer. Of his many architectural works perhaps the finest example is the pilgrimage church at Scherpenheuvel. In many cases Baroque frontages were added to buildings of earlier styles—such as that on the abbey at Park outside Leuven. Later the excesses of the baroque style gave way to the more refined elegance of the French Rococo style, which can be seen in the Town Hall (Hôtel de Ville) at Lier (1741) which was the work of the celebrated Antwerp architect Bauerscheit the Younger.

However, it is in the field of painting that the Baroque style reached its apotheosis in Belgium. And here the undisputed master is Peter Paul Rubens (1577–1640), who for many epitomizes the Belgian spirit in art. The sheer sensuousness of his fleshy nudes and the flamboyant composition of his great masterpieces are without equal in the entire history of European art. A Rubens is always unmistakably recognizable as such.

This most Belgian of all artists was in fact born in Germany, though his parents were Flemish, being in exile at the time. It was not until he was ten years old that Rubens arrived in Antwerp, the city which was eventually to be his home and the scene of his greatest triumphs. From 1600–8 Rubens traveled in Italy, where he was particularly influenced by the works of Michelangelo and Caravaggio. It was this combination of Italian discipline, refinement and technique, allied with his innately sensuous grandiose disposition, which formed Rubens' uniquely Baroque vision. Soon after returning from Italy to Antwerp, Rubens painted his greatest early masterpiece—the triptych containing the *Raising of the Cross* and the *Descent* which are now in Antwerp Cathedral. Other great works, such as the *Baptism of Christ* and *Virgin with a Parrot* can be seen in Antwerp at the Royal Museum of Fine Arts (Koninklijk Museum van Schone Kunsten). Rubens specialized in vast paintings on religious subjects, often returning to the same theme. One of his favorites was the *Adoration of the Magi,* of which he painted three large masterpieces—the earliest (1615) is in Brussels, another (1619) hangs in the church of St. Jan at Mechelen, and the third (1624) is in Antwerp.

As his fame spread far and wide, Rubens began to receive an increasing number of ambitious well-paid commissions. Soon becoming a rich man, he set himself up in a grand house in Antwerp where he lived in style, working on several large paintings at a time, along with many assistants and pupils. Only the gate in the courtyard of this building, together with a garden pavilion, are still standing—though a visit to the Rubens House, which stands on the original site, gives a good idea of the sumptuous lifestyle of the painter and his busy studio. The largest collections of Rubens' work are to be seen at the museum in Antwerp, and also at the Musée d'Art Ancien in Brussels, both of which have rooms entirely devoted to his work from all periods of his life.

Rubens' most famous pupil was a native of Antwerp, Anthony Van Dyck (1599–1641), who was eventually to achieve almost equal renown. As a result of an early trip to Italy, when he stayed in Venice and Genoa, Van Dyck's style benefited from a lasting and profound Italian influence. His paintings are more restrained and less grandiose than those of Rubens, achieving a delicacy of technique and insight which made him a far greater portrait painter than his master. Indeed, connoisseurs now consider Van Dyck to have been one of the greatest of all portrait painters, rivaling even Velazquez. One of Van Dyck's first early portraits was that of a Genoese Lady and her daughter, which he painted in Italy. This can now be seen in the Musée d'Art Ancien in Brussels, along with ten other fine portraits. Like his master, Van Dyck also painted religious subjects. Two excellent examples of these are his *Raising of the Cross* in the Onze Lieve Vrouwkerk (Church of Our Lady) at Kortrijk (Courtai), and the magnificent *Crucifixion* painted in 1627, which hangs in the Cathedral Church of St. Rombout at Mechelen. In 1632 Van Dyck traveled to London, where he became portrait painter to the court and was eventually knighted by Charles I.

The works of the painter Jacob Jordaens (1593–1678) are unfortunately overshadowed by those of his two more celebrated contemporaries. Had he lived under other circumstances he would undoubtedly be more widely known. His exaggerated style is more akin to that of Rubens, and his painting shows little Italian influence. An entire room in the Musée d'Art Ancien in Brussels is devoted to his work, and it is here that you can see his great *Allegory of Fecundity* which is considered by many as the quintessential masterpiece of Flemish Baroque.

18th and 19th Centuries

The 18th century was a time of change, culminating in the traumatic events of the French Revolution and the Napoleonic conquests which were to change the face of Europe. Though the fashion for Baroque and Rococo lasted longer in Belgium than elsewhere, a reaction eventually set in favoring the clear lines and more mathematical proportions of Neo-Classicism, a predominantly French influence. The finest architectural example of this style is to be found in the Town Hall (Hôtel de Ville) at Verviers, which was the work of Renoz in 1779. The effects of Classicism are also noticeable in the plan for the Upper Town of Brussels by Guimard, and the reconstruction of the Place Royale which was laid out in the elegant proportions of the Louis XVI style.

The advent of Belgian independence in 1830 saw the undertaking of several ambitious architectural projects in Brussels, notably the National Bank (Banque Nationale), which was built between 1859–64 (though the present facade was added in 1952.) The greatest of all these projects was undoubtedly the building of the huge Law Courts (Palais de Justice) between 1866–83 on the hilltop dominating the center of the city which had once been the site of the city's medieval gallows. This monstrous edifice with its 300 ft. high dome was the work of Joseph Poelaert and occupies an area greater than St. Peter's in Rome. In pleasant contrast to such crude monumentalism is the refined elegance of the Galeries St. Hubert, the work of Cluysmaer.

The expansion of Brussels at the end of the 19th century gave great scope for the architectural experiments of the *Art Nouveau* movement. Indeed, the first *art nouveau* building on the continent was Victor Horta's house, built in 1896 and now preserved as a museum. Other examples of Horta's work include the Palais des Beaux Art and the Central Station. The bold ideas and imaginative use of materials which characterized *art nouveau* are also seen to excellent effect in the Stoclet Palace which was designed by Josef Hoffman and contains frescos by the Austrian artist Gustav Klimt.

In the field of the arts, the transformation from Baroque to Classicism is seen in the work of the Frenchman Jacques-Louis David (1748–1825), best known for his paintings of the French Revolution. David, who was court painter to Napoleon, lived for many years in Brussels and examples of his work can be seen in Musée d'Art Ancien in Brussels, which contains his celebrated *Murder of Marat*.

Also worthy of note is the graphic artist and engraver Félicien Rops (1833–98) whose work was heavily influenced by the "Poor People's Pictures" school started by Courbet. Rops was a native of Namur, where there is now a museum devoted entirely to his works.

Another sometime member of the "Poor People's Pictures" school was the great Dutch artist Vincent Van Gogh (1853–90), who spent a formative period of his life in the depressed mining district of the Borinage, where he drew and painted many compassionate scenes of local life. His moving *Potato Pickers* which dates from this period can be seen in the Museum of Fine Arts (Museum voor Schone Kunsten) in Antwerp.

The work of the eccentric James Ensor (1860–1949) can best be described as nightmare-impressionistic. Though sadly neglected at present, Ensor was undoubtedly a painter of European stature—who lived in a strange fantasy world at his house in Oostende, from which he seldom stirred. This house is now open to the public and contains several of his weird masterpieces, further examples of which can be seen in the Museum of Fine Arts at Oostende.

20th Century

The coming of the 20th century and the First World War saw widespread devastation in Belgium, particularly in the southwestern border region of Flanders. Unfortunately, the consequent rebuilding was not noted for any great modernistic works. As in so many countries, uniformity followed by the unimaginative use of slab concrete have tended to characterize 20th-century architecture in Belgium— with the result that there are few modern buildings of character.

The staging of the 1958 World Fair in Brussels saw the construction of the Atomium. This daring 300 ft. aluminum structure is in the form of an atom of iron, with a nucleus and eight surrounding electrons joined by spars. The lower spheres house an exhibition devoted to the peaceful uses of atomic energy, whilst in the top sphere there is a restaurant.

The sighting of Brussels as the capital of the E.E.C. (Common Market) heralded a considerable architectural boom. This has brought about a transformation and made Brussels into a high-rise city of steel and glass. Though not unpleasant, the effects of this modernistic explosion can hardly be called imaginative. The supreme example here is the four-winged structure of the Berlaymont building on the Rond Point Schuman, which now houses the E.E.C. Council and Commission, an edifice ideally suited to house a vast faceless bureaucracy.

During the 20th century Belgian artists have also played a significant role on the European scene. Paul Delvaux (b. 1897) took a leading part in the early development of the Surrealist movement. Examples of his work can be seen in the Fine Arts Museums (Museums voor Schone Kunsten) at Ghent and Antwerp. A more individual and perhaps more typically Belgian contribution to the same movement was made by René Magritte (1898–1967), whose ambiguously realistic canvases have achieved world-wide renown. In more recent years, the work of the Belgian-born abstract impressionist Willem de Kooning (b. 1904) is now considered as integral in the development of modern art in America, where he has lived for most of his life.

Literature and Music

As a result of both French and Flemish being spoken in Belgium two distinct literary traditions have evolved. Flemish literature has mostly tended to follow Dutch trends, whilst the French branch has looked more to Paris. However, Belgian literature has remained for the most part of little more than regional interest, with relatively few figures achieving international renown.

The French-speaking writer Charles de Coster (1827–79) is best remembered for his *Legend and Adventures of Til Ulenspiegel*—a story concerning the exploits of the subversive Flemish anti-hero who was later to inspire the German composer Richard Strauss. A memorial to de Coster stands by the lake in the Brussels suburb of Ixelles.

Paradoxically Belgium's two leading contributors to French literature at the turn of the century were both Flemish. Maurice Maeterlink (1862–1949) settled in Paris at the age of 34, where his symbolist dramas achieved great fashionable renown. His most enduring masterpiece is *Pélleas and Mélisande*. He was awarded the Nobel Prize for Literature in 1911. The outstanding Belgian poet of the century is undoubtedly Emile Verhaeren (1855–1916), who also lived in Paris and played a leading role in the Symbolist movement. His work was widely influential on many modern poets, including such figures as Rainer Maria Rilke and T.S. Eliot. Another important Belgian poet is the Surrealist Henri Micheaux (b. 1889) who is also an artist of note.

But the best known of all Belgian authors is undoubtedly the prolific detective-story writer Georges Simenon (b. 1903), creator of the famous Inspector Maigret. It is claimed that only the Bible has been translated into more languages than his work. Marguerite Yourcenar is famous as the author of the historical novel *The Memoirs of Hadrian* and recently achieved the distinction of becoming the first woman ever elected to the prestigious French Academy.

The most widely-played Belgian composer is certainly César Franck (1822–1890), a native of Liège. At the age of 22 he settled in Paris where he became organist at St. Clotilde. He is considered founder of the modern French instrumental school and is perhaps best known for his magnificently rousing organ music. Liège has honoured its famous son in the form of a monument in the Conservatoire de Musique, and his works feature prominently in Belgian concerts and music festivals. A lesser known Belgian contributor to the world-wide musical scene is the instrument maker Charles Joseph Sax (1791–1865) who invented no less than three different kinds of musical instrument—the saxhorn, the saxtromba, and the saxophone.

BELGIAN FOOD AND DRINK

Quality and Quantity

There are more restaurants per head in Brussels than in Paris. The Belgians like to eat at length, often, and well. Their cooking is based on French cuisine, though there are significant local variations. The Belgian gourmet associations such as the *Club des 33, Club des Gastronomes,* and *La Ligue des Amis du Vin,* maintain as high a standard as their French counterparts. There are 29 restaurants in Belgium with Guide Michelin stars, and Brussels also gives its own accolade in the form of irises—the flower of the City—five being the highest award.

International *haute cuisine* tends to be the same the world over, but Belgians contrive to add their own distinctive touches by the use of more of the expensive ingredients, with emphasis on the richer ones. At the popular levels they concentrate on quantity *and* quality and, while food is expensive here, you will find excellent value for money.

Most Typical Dishes

As befits a nation which likes its food well presented, the most characteristic of their dishes is colorful. This is the *tomates aux crevettes,* a hollowed tomato stuffed with shrimps and mayonnaise. This is served cold, but has a warmer counterpart the delicious *croquette aux crevettes.* These miniature shrimps are renowned for their delicate sweetness (subtly different from prawns) and their popularity provides a plentiful market for the fishermen of Oostende and Zeebrugge.

A dish found all over the country is *anguilles au vert,* baby eels served hot or cold. It owes its charms to the delicate aroma of the shredded herbs—sorrel, mint, sage, verbena and parsley—used in its preparation.

One of the Belgian's favorite meals is *biftec et frites.* The steak varies in size and quality with the price, but it normally comes to table with a lump of butter coyly melting on the summit. The alternative is pork chop or veal chop; lamb is seldom eaten. The *frites* are of course the familiar English "chips" or American "French fries." They are the national dish *par excellence.* On street corners throughout Belgium you will find counters serving fresh *frites*—usually covered with a dollop of delicious home-made mayonnaise, or other exotic sauces (ranging from tomato to curry). This is the Belgians' favorite national snack.

The pride of the Belgian dinner table is Brussels' own vegetable, which we call chicory, locally known as *witloof* (white leaf), and the French *endive.* The Belgians know the cult, as well as the culture, of this delicious vegetable and serve it *poêlé,* or garnish it to make a number of main dishes in which it has pride of place. It produces crops from October to March, and we can think of no more valid a reason for a winter visit. Chicory heads can be stuffed with chopped meat, tied with string or rolled in breadcrumbs and placed in the oven with a slice of ham or bacon. They are often served like this in restaurants, perhaps with white sauce and a sprinkling of cheese added.

Second only to chicory is Belgian asparagus. Reared with care in the sandy soil of the Malines region, it is at its best in May and June. *Asperges à la flamande* is asparagus with a sauce of hard-boiled eggs crushed in melted butter.

Belgium's choicest fruit is, surprisingly, the grape. Good grapes are produced in hothouses all the year round; but to see them at their best you should come in late September to the grape festival at Hoeilaart, on the fringe of the forest of Soignes.

Sausages and Fish

Another national dish is the *boudin* sausage. All Belgian sausages are generously filled with meat, and their flavours are distinctive. The *boudin de Liège* is made with herbs and is particularly savory. The *boudin noir* appeals most to connoisseurs; the *boudin blanc* is more popular. The latter is a separate sausage and is served hot with varied accompaniments. Apple sauce goes well with it, but in the Ardennes it is served with grapes and is unusually delicious. Another Ardennes specialty is ham, and you can get *jambon d'Ardennes* in almost any restaurant; accompanied by *saucisson d'Ardennes* (salami) it makes a most appetizing hors d'oeuvre.

Unless you are an early-summer visitor, delicacies you will not want to miss are mussels *(moules),* which can be eaten during the months with an R in them. Although they are products of the seaside, you will find them at their best in Brussels: several restaurants in the Soho of Brussels, the Rue des Bouchers quarter, serve them in many guises.

Remember, you don't order mussels as part of a general meal; you either eat mussels or something else, for you will be surprised, not to say shaken, at the size of the bowl set before you. You can, indeed you usually do, eat them with *frites,* but by the time you have mastered the dish you will be far from hungry. Belgium has a number of other fish specialties to offer, notably *bisque de homard* (a very rich lobster soup), *écrevisses à la Liègeoise* (crayfish cooked in white wine sauce with butter and cream), and fillet of sole *Saint Arnould,* dressed with hops and pieces of toast. You will also find fried eel very commendable and, at Namur especially, you can have them served *à l'escavèche.* The essence of this dish is that your eel is first pickled. Later it is fried and served cold in jelly. The practice of serving fish *à l'escavèche* is largely local, though it is found too in the Chimay region. Down by the Ourthe and the well-stocked Semois, they will serve your trout *meunière,* fetching it for you not from a tank but from the river, or even inviting you to do so yourself.

Fish Soup and Other Specialties

A dish you must try on any visit to Belgium is the *waterzooi,* a variety of fresh or seawater fish boiled with herbs, as good as the vaunted *bouillabaisse* of which Thackeray wrote. You will get the best *waterzooi* at Ghent, but both Brussels and Antwerp can cook them very creditably. In Brussels, especially, you should try the *waterzooi* version that contains chicken instead of fish. Chicken is a Brussels specialty, but you can eat broilers off the spit everywhere.

Even for that supreme masterpiece of poultry cooking, *oie à l'instar de Visé,* the goose is boiled before it is carved up and fried. Here, however, the boiling has a special function, for it is from this that the flesh takes on the savor of the vegetables and, most especially, of the garlic which reappears in the cream sauce. *Oie à l'instar de Visé* is certainly a dish to try. Gourmet historians, incidentally, say the recipe probably survives from the days of the Roman conquest of Gaul, though there is a legend which attributes it to a much later Commissaire de Police who ingeniously acquired a boiled goose in settling a dispute among his fellow-townsmen. Pride of place on a good restaurant's menu belongs to *rognons de veau à la Liègeoise,* a serious confection of roast kidney, prepared with crushed juniper and a dash of gin.

During the game season there are some very fine dishes prepared with wine-soaked roebuck *(chevreuil),* hare *(lièvre)* and *marcassin* (young wild boar of the Ardennes). These dishes are called *civet,* and are not unlike English jugged hare.

There are, of course, far more sophisticated ways of serving game, including game birds, especially partridge and quail. Many of them are specialties of individual inns in the Ardennes region. The same applies to trout, which are also native to the region. You may well regret that you can't try every dish.

It is a pity that modern tendencies are destroying much of the character of local cooking. As its name suggests, *carbonades flamandes* (a type of goulash, more sweet than hot) is essentially a Flemish dish—though you'll find it all over the country. In the same way, the practice of serving prunes with hare, a dish known as *civet de lièvre à la fla-mande,* is ceasing to be characteristically Flemish. You will find it everywhere in Belgium. Another Flemish specialty is *choesel au Madère,* small slices of various meats prepared with Madeira wine-sauce and garnished with mushrooms. In general, the characteristic of most Belgian food is its richness. The cooks use a great deal of fat, and fat bacon (or, for the purist, sliced pig's ear and a trotter) is almost always one of the ingredients of the soup. You should not, by the way, neglect the soups. Every restaurant serves a *potage du jour,* which is nearly always very much cheaper than the special soups. Many cafés, too, though they do not cater for meals, serve soup cheaply and you can take it with your own sandwiches. This is one of the ways of getting a meal quickly, apart from in self-service restaurants and snack bars.

Cakes and Sweets

There are, too, a great number of typical biscuits and cookies, some of which have become associated with certain towns. Among these are the *kletskoppen* of Bruges, the Beaumont macaroons, and the *couques de Dinant* (gingerbread). *Tarte al djote,* a specialty of Nivelles, is made with beet leaves and cheese. *Pain à la grecque* is found throughout Belgium, but has nothing to do with Greece. It was named after the bread which the Augustinian monks of Brussels used to distribute to the poor. As their abbey was in the "fosse aux loups" (wolves' ditch), the Flemish called the bread "wolf gracht brood," later simply "gracht brood," which became "pain à la grecque" in French. The Greeks, of course, have never heard of it!

Gaufres (waffles) baked in front of you in cast-iron moulds at street-stalls, are delicious when warm. The teashops contain great quantities of cream cakes, and you will notice that these are made on the same models from one shop to another, though they differ in excellence and in the richness of the buttercream *(crème de beurre).* You will notice, too, that few of the cakes are made with pastry. The *tarte au sucre* (sugar tart) is another Belgian specialty which really should be tried by anyone with a sweet tooth.

Sweets and candies follow traditional lines, though you will see a great deal of nougat, and special stalls full at fairs. Marzipan has a place of its own, for the cakeshops are filled with marzipan animals and fruits in preparation for Saint Nicolas' Day (6 December). "Custom-made" Belgian chocolates are the finest in the world. You'll find them on sale in special shops, where you can make up your own box from the arrays of stupendously rich varieties. These are the last word in luxury.

Wines and Liqueurs

So far as wine is concerned, the last of the Meuse-side vineyards disappeared during World War I. Belgian buying has helped the Mo-selle wines of Luxembourg get onto their feet and, because the wines are imported duty-free under the customs union arrangements, they are very good value as beverage wines. It used to be a tradition that the pick of the Burgundies came overland to Charleroi and the pick of the clarets by sea to Antwerp. Nowadays, you will find the best of either in any city; for though time has broken down the exclusiveness of the main consignment centers, it has not altered the fact that Belgium gets much of the best wine France has to offer. The Belgian palate is discriminating; and you will find really excellent cheap wines even in the self-service stores. Like the British, the Belgians have a distinct taste for Côtes du Rhône wines—for a good wine at a moderate price, this is a safe bet in both cafés and restaurants. The great growths and the prime vintages are, of course, bound to be expensive here as elsewhere. An attempt was made recently to introduce (under the trademark *Isca*) wine and champagne made from the renowned Belgian hot-house grapes.

The grandest restaurants usually don't stock national liqueurs, though three of them are excellent. *Elixir de Spa* successfully captures the scent of the Ardennes pinewoods, while *Walzin* and *Elixir d'Anvers* are of the Benedictine-type.

Belgians are not allowed to drink spirits in cafés. If you want a gin drink, therefore, you must go into a café labeled as a private club *(cercle privé)* and sign a membership form. The usual apéritifs are vermouth (which is curiously expensive) and light port *(porto)* which may be either red or white.

Beer, the Belgian Beverage

The national drink of the Belgians, however, is beer. For an ordinary glass of beer, the Belgian equivalent to "a half of bitter" is *un export* or *un pils,* a light, palatable drink, sweeter than the English bitter. Though standardization and large-scale brewing is winning the market on grounds of cheapness and wide distribution, Belgium has by an ingenious tax structure managed to keep alive quite a number of the small-scale and individual breweries. Their products, by their very nature, are not very widely distributed, but there are a number of old and amusing cafés where you can find many of the lesser known beers.

Beer has, in Belgium, a very respectable history, interwoven with such eminent figures as Van Artevelde and Charles V. The wheat-based beer called *Faro,* which celebrated its 1,000th birthday a few years ago is still brewed. It is now made in a modern brewery, and may have lost some of its character since the days when the Sire of Cantersteen, unable to choose between two beers competing for his favour, left it to a crow to be the judge. The high-density drink that you should certainly try is *Geuze* (so called when it is bottled, but *Lambic* when it is on tap), a strong beer based on half wheat and half barley, and slightly vinous in flavour. A similar drink is *Kriek-Lambic,* which is essentially *Geuze* but with a flavouring of cherries added after the brew. The old-style *Peetermans* has almost disappeared but there are still strong, frothy white beers to be drunk at Louvain and Hoegaarde. The golden beer of Diest is still very individual, but you will not find a great deal of *Uitzet* and *Doppel-Uitzet* even around Oudenaarde, which is its home district. In a country with so many abbeys and monasteries it is surprising that there are so few monastic brews on the market, but two outstanding ones are *Orval* "made by the Trappists" and the even stronger "triple" from the abbey at Westmalle near Antwerp.

Most of the Belgian beers are of the lager-type. Though the Belgians are great brewers, their market is not closed to foreign brews, and you will find abundant supplies of beers from Germany, France, Denmark, the Netherlands and, most of all, Great Britain and Ireland. Guinness, incidentally, is imported from Dublin, and most connoisseurs agree that it is superior to its counterpart in England. Several British brews are bottled in Belgium; and, more recently, investments by the big British brewery companies have resulted in the British beers (which require a special type of fermentation) being actually brewed here. In recent years, British brewers, mainly Watneys, have introduced the Belgians, not only to British beer, but to the British way of drinking it—standing at the bar rather than sitting at the café tables, with all this implies in friendliness and bonhomie.

The general impression emerges that the Belgians eat well and drink well. Moreover, they eat copiously, and it may be well to utter a word of warning against attempting to cope with two full-scale meals in one day. At all levels, the amount of fat used in the cooking is very large by Anglo-Saxon standards; and, though it is good to the taste, it often takes a day or two to get used to it. A bottle of Spa water in your hotel bedroom is a wise, and almost universal palliative.

EXPLORING
BELGIUM

BRUSSELS

Belgium's Capital, Heart of Brabant

Brussels is now the capital of Europe, the boomtown home of the Eurocrats and their legendary expense accounts. This means that at the highest level Brussels is as well-equipped as any other city in Europe. However, side by side with this bureaucratic creation lies the old traditional capital, the ancient heart of the Brabant. As a duchy, it was once the buffer state between the Lotharingian empire and the marauding counts of Flanders—now it is where the two separate Belgiums meet, a true mixture of both Flemish and Walloon cultures.

In Belgium, all roads lead to Brussels. And this goes for the railroads and airlines too. Though Antwerp may still be *La Métropole,* the country's commercial and economic hub, Brussels is very much *La Capitale.* In its buses and cafés you will hear every language in Europe.

In many respects, Brussels is a thoroughly modern city. Shining steel-and-glass office blocks dominate the skyline, while smartly-dressed Eurocrats patronize elegant shops or brightly-lit places of entertainment. The city has an impressive network of expressways and road tunnels, and the metro-system trains are fitted with some of the most comfortable seats you'll find on public transport anywhere in the world. But within the city there are still corners of cobbled streets which even the most experienced motorist will find it difficult to navigate, canals where old barges still discharge their wares, and forgotten spots where the city's eventful and romantic past is plainly visible through its 20th-century veneer.

Cavalcade of History

You will not see much, if anything, of the River Senne, which now takes its unlovely course underground through the city, and which could be the origin of the capital's name—*broeck* (brook), *sele* (dwelling). It was an island on this stream which was the South's bastion against the Flemish a century before William of Normandy invaded England. Here, too, the Senne's course ceased to be navigable to craft coming up from the Schelde and the sea beyond. A merchant community grew round the discharge point of the barges, and for this community the Duke of Brabant, Graaf Jan, or Jean le Victorieux, fought and won the Battle of Woeringen (1288). In this he wrested from Renalt the Bellicose, not only the Duchy of Limburg, but also the safeguarding of the open road from flourishing Bruges to Maastricht and the Rhine at Cologne. This road ran through Brussels, and the battle consolidated the city's position as capital of the duchy.

This was the age when the merchant communes were struggling with feudal princes for their liberties. In 1356 the reigning Duchess Jeanne, and her husband, Wenceslas of Luxembourg, were forced into signing the *Joyeuse Entrée*, a declaration of rights as basic and as confusingly drawn as Magna Carta. A few months later, however, Duchess Jeanne was brought to book by the quarrelsome Count of Flanders who, having married her sister, came with an armed force to claim the dowry. At Anderlecht, now a suburb of Brussels, the Flemish swept the floor with the men of Brabant, and hoisted their standard in the Brussels Grand' Place.

The first of Brussels' many liberations came six months later, when Everard 't Serclaes led 70 patriots on a surprise assault of the occupying garrison. He became the first of Brussels' heroes and was deputy mayor. While defending the city 30 years later he was assassinated by order of the Lord of Gaasbeek, Sweder Abcoude, who coveted the city. This brought the citizens of Brussels to a vengeful storming and destruction of the Castle of Gaasbeek, a few miles away.

During World War II when German troops occupied Brussels people made a practice of visiting Serclaes' statue off the Grand' Place and touching the brass figure's arm or the head of his little dog as a mark of respect and to bring them luck. It is still visited today, and if you make a wish when you touch the shiny arm or the nose of the dog, your wish should come true.

From 1430 onwards, Brussels became more and more the pivot of the Low Countries with their varying fortunes in the next five centuries. Both the dukes of Burgundy and, later on, the Spanish Habsburg kings made Brussels into an elegant center of the arts. This was the golden age of Flemish painting, tapestry, and lace-making.

Under Philip the Good, Brussels was on the crest of a wave. The Coudenberg Palace was enlarged and beautified, and was to be the court center of Brussels life till it was burned down three centuries later. The nobility of the Golden Fleece built their stupendous mansions nearby. The foundations were laid of the collection of manuscripts which the Spaniards were later to centralize as the Bibliothèque Royale—now the great reference library of the Belgian state. Fountains decorated the streets, and Roger van der Weyden brought to Brussels the skill and fervor of an artist.

Brussels passed through another period of splendor, 40 years after Philip's death, with the court of Charles V in the first phase of the Spanish ascendancy. It was Charles who enclosed the Parc de Bruxelles, at either end of which now lie the Royal Palace and the Palace of the Nation (Parliament). Contemporaries tell us the park then contained "valleys with vines and divers manner of fruit." Already, however, the Reformation was sweeping across Europe.

Charles had abdicated in Brussels in 1555. Persecution started in earnest under the Duke of Alba as governor for Philip II. Those who resisted were called the *gueux* or *geuzen* (tramps or beggars) and the leaders of the revolt, the counts of Egmont and Hornes, were brought from Ghent to Brussels for execution in the Grand' Place (1568). The central figure of the resistance was William the Silent, Prince of Orange, who was called to Brussels in 1577 and received by the people on bended knee as a liberating "angel from Heaven." William, however, was assassinated seven years later, and the Italian Prince Alexander Farnese re-liberated Brussels for the king of Spain, despite Olivier van den Tympel's brilliant defense.

The 17th-Century Occupations

Resistance was virtually over, and the Spanish Lowlands had comparative quiet during the first half of the 17th century. Brussels, indeed, became known as a refuge for exiled princes. But Spain was on the decline, and soon the France of Louis XIV was in the ascendant. In 1695 a 46-hour bombardment by the red cannon balls of Marshal Villeroy reminded Brussels of the French defiance of the Augsburg league. Four thousand houses were destroyed, including the entire Grand' Place apart from the Hôtel de Ville.

The Austrians who had been nominal masters of the Spanish Lowlands since 1713, had begun oppressively but, under Maria Theresa, were more accommodating when they recovered the country in 1748. Forty years after the disastrous fire of 1731, when the Coudenberg Palace was wholly destroyed, this part of Brussels and the Parc de Bruxelles was replanned, and put more or less into its present form. Nevertheless, after all the trials Brussels had been through, it is small wonder that there was much poverty and illiteracy. Voltaire wrote, "In Brussels the arts are no more alive than the pleasures. A calm, retired life is the lot of private people, and this is so akin to boredom that it is easy to call it so."

It was against this background that Joseph II, son of Maria Theresa, started constitutional reforms on too ambitious a scale, even going so far as to cancel the *Joyeuse Entrée.* Brabant led the uprising against this at the very time when the French Revolution was altering the main currents of European thought. Under the leadership of Henri van der Noot, the people of Brussels took arms, troops deserted *en masse* from the Austrian service, and the United States of Belgium were proclaimed in January 1790. The Austrians, however, were back by the end of the year. Two years later revolutionary France was at the door. Brussels changed hands three times in as many years, and remained under French control till 1814. It was at Brussels that Napoleon's last thrust was aimed in 1815, only to be halted at Waterloo.

William I made many mistakes, not least of which was the sending of an armed force under his son to suppress growing dissatisfaction; this had reached crisis point one summer night in 1830, when the audience of the opera *La Muette des Portici* burst out of the Theatre de la Monnaie to sing nationalist songs and support anti-Dutch dissidents. The Dutch prince's 14,000 men converged in four lumbering columns, and a 4-day battle was fought in the Brussels streets and in the Parc de Bruxelles. The result was the evacuation of the Dutch, and the setting up of the kingdom of the Belgians, with Brussels as its capital (27th September, 1830).

Modern Brussels

This is the background of the Brussels of the defiant burgomasters Adolphe Max in 1914 and Van der Meulebroeck in 1940. Adolphe Max, after whom the main shopping street in Brussels is named, openly encouraged people to defy the Germans for a whole month before he was arrested and sent to prison. Now capital of the European Community and NATO, Brussels has become a magnet for politicians, diplomats, reporters, bankers, brokers, and businessmen. More and more cars speed along the flyovers and underpasses. Yellow trams remain, but many have gone underground to form the city's subway system whose immaculate stations greet you with soothing piped music.

Despite the creeping commercial takeover, much of old Brussels remains with its *fin de siècle* houses, monuments and unique Grand' Place—all so attractive to the visitor.

If you come to Brussels by air, you will land at Zaventem airport, begun by the Germans in World War II, which has jostled the old Château of Steenokerzeel almost off the map. A highway and railway spur connect Zaventem Airport with Brussels. The railway takes less than 20 mins. to the Air Terminal, adjoining the underground Central Station.

Discovering Brussels

You can buy a map *(guide-plan)* of Brussels at any stationer's or bookstall. The central city is enclosed by a heart-shaped boulevard (the line of the Ramparts), with the Nord station at one end and the Midi Station at the other. Its name changes every few hundred yards, so the practical Brussels people call it *petite ceinture* (small belt) in contrast to the outer boulevards *(grande ceinture)* that enclose several boroughs. The outermost expressway is called the Ring, and it by-passes the city altogether. These roads are models of their kind for fast-moving automobile traffic. A central boulevard (beginning at the north with the boulevard Adolphe Max) connects the two stations.

Taking the southward line, the streets on your left run uphill towards St. Michael Cathedral, the administrative government area and the Parc de Bruxelles. Farther on, the uphill streets lead towards the Palais de Justice, the high dome of which is the landmark you will have seen from many miles away. In doing so, they traverse the once poor but colorful quarter of the Marolles (gradually being replaced by new housing projects), and the place du Jeu de Balle, where there is a flea market every day (largest on Sunday). The streets on your right as you pass down the central boulevard lead to a more popular, and more populous shopping quarter, the high point of which is the street market in the place Sainte Catherine, which you reach by turning right opposite the Bourse.

Typical Features

The first thing to strike you in the Brussels streets is the enormous number of cafés. The Belgians are, indeed, great coffee drinkers, great beer drinkers, and great drinkers of light port *(porto),* which they take as an apéritif. These are the main trade of the small cafés, many of which, however, seem to do very little business. There are of course a large number of popular cafés, that are busy most of the day.

A second thing to notice is the great amount of very fine ornamental ironwork. The Belgians have for centuries been forgers of iron and have learnt to express themselves in iron in ways that deserve special admiration. You will find, especially in the streets around the Grand' Place, a number of shop signs, some of which are of considerable age, and many that have histories of their own. You will also find wrought-iron park railings, balcony railings, and banisters of private stairways, of intricate and generally highly-pleasing design. Though much of this work is old, wrought-iron work in general is far from being extinct. There are, for example, butchers' shops where the joints hang on hooks and from battens of exquisite design which are of recent execution.

There is nothing self-conscious or pretentious in the way this iron work is used and it is seldom pointed out to the visitor. For this reason, as you walk through Brussels, it is wise to be observant of little things. This will also ensure your seeing the many streetcorner shrines, with their effigies of the Madonna and the saints let into the walls of houses, though often too high for detailed scrutiny.

Walk out of the southwestern corner of the Grand' Place, along the rue de l'Etuve, and here you will come upon a rather self-conscious corner surrounded with lace-and-souvenir shops. On this corner you will find Brussels' "Oldest Inhabitant," the charmingly outrageous little statue known as *Manneken Pis.* No apology is needed for bringing him in at the start of your visit. He is the most-loved piece of the Brussels of the Bruxellois, whose origin is wrapped in mystery, though it is certain that a similar effigy, moulded in sugar and similarly occupied—with rose water, however—garnished one of the banquets of Philip the Good. The figure is identified with the fortunes of Brussels. Many amusing legends surround it, the most persistent being his sprinkling of a Spanish sentry, passing under the windows of the little man's parents. The statue in bronze was ordered by the city from the

17th-century sculptor, Duquesnoy, to replace the one in stone, whose origin was unknown. Hidden during the 1695 bombardment, he was carried off by British soldiers before Fontenoy and later kidnapped by the French. On this occasion he was invested with a gold-embroidered suit by no less a dignitary than Louis XV of France. He has many other suits, which he dons on ceremonial occasions. On September 3rd you can see him dressed in the uniform of the Welsh Guards, who liberated Brussels on this day in 1944; and on October 27th he wears an American sailor suit in honor of United States Navy Day.

The Grand' Place

The Grand' Place is the noblest of market places, with ornate gold-scrolled facades making an irregular skyline of guildhouses which have been likened to a stage set. They are, however, as solid and enduring as the flagstones in the square and much more sacrosanct; yet they certainly are theatrical, especially when you emerge from one of the dark, narrow side streets as if from the wings of a stage at night. The magic remains year after year. You will see the Grand' Place to its best advantage if you go on Sunday mornings, when there is a bird market in the center. It is also very beautiful at night when it is floodlit with changing colored lights.

By a municipal ruling passed in 1972, the parking of cars in the Grand' Place has been prohibited, a sensible decision which gives the visitor a proper chance to contemplate this unique square at leisure from one of the many sidewalk cafés.

The highlight of the Grand' Place is the Hôtel de Ville, with its Lion Stairway as entrance to the original building and the main gateway surmounted with the exquisite tower and its copper figure of St. Michael. This was designed by Martin van Rode in 1454, and the statue of St. Michael has been crushing a figure of the devil beneath its feet ever since. Over the gateway are statues of the prophets and female figures representing Peace, Prudence, Justice, Strength, Temperance and Law, attributed to the 14th-century sculptor, Claus Sluter. Within the gateway is the inner court, with its two fountains representing Belgium's two main rivers, the Scheldt and the Meuse (Schelde and Maas), and its lovely flowers.

Inside the Hôtel de Ville, the burgomaster's antechamber contains an extremely interesting set of pictures, painted in the 19th century by Van Moer, of Brussels, before the river Senne was taken underground. In the Council Chamber the brilliant ceiling (Assembly of the Gods, by Victor Janssens, early 18th century) is especially noteworthy, and there are three excellent 18th-century Brussels tapestries depicting historical scenes. There are other fine tapestries in the Maximilian Chamber, but the most interesting are modern (about 1880) Mechelen (Malines) tapestry panels in the Gothic Chamber representing the crafts of Brussels. They were the work of Belgian weavers, said to have inspired the Gobelin factory in France. Their tapestries make use not only of wool and fine silk but also of precious metals and exquisite embroidery.

In the Grand' Place itself, the buildings were erected soon after the French bombardment of 1695, and are a curious mixture of French and

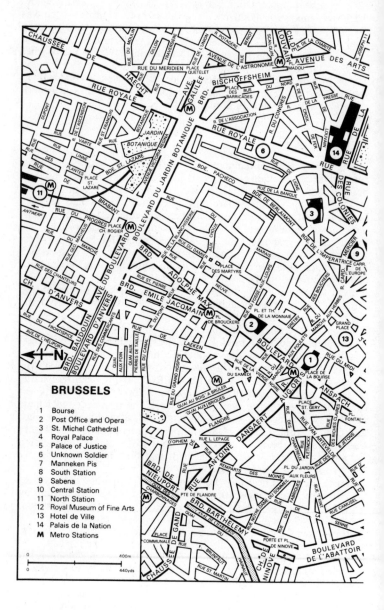

BRUSSELS

1 Bourse
2 Post Office and Opera
3 St. Michel Cathedral
4 Royal Palace
5 Palace of Justice
6 Unknown Soldier
7 Manneken Pis
8 South Station
9 Sabena
10 Central Station
11 North Station
12 Royal Museum of Fine Arts
13 Hotel de Ville
14 Palais de la Nation
M Metro Stations

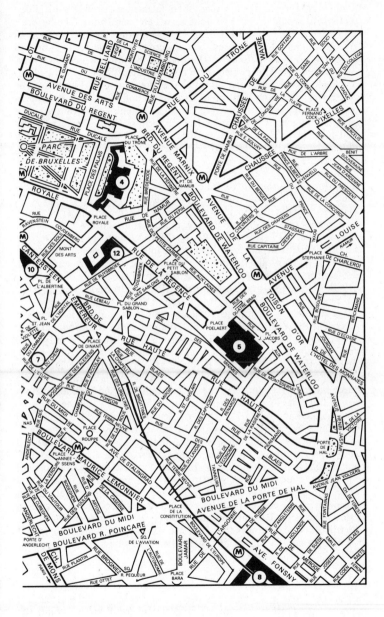

Italian Renaissance architecture, their facades decorated with gilded scrollwork and statues. The houses, which were built for the craft guilds, have been described by a Belgian author as "ostentation in opulence." One of the houses, No. 4, known as "The Sack," still has the ground and first floors of the original building which, however, dates from only 50 years before the bombardment. No. 10, "The Golden Tree," was the meeting house of the Brewers' Guild and today is the Brewery Museum. On top of its ornate roof there is an equestrian statue of Charles of Lorraine. No. 26, "The Pigeon," was for a time the home of the great 19th-century French writer Victor Hugo, when he lived in exile in Brussels. Round the corner from No. 8, under the colonnade, is the memorial to Everard 't Serclas with its "touch-for-luck" statue and its little dog.

Opposite the Hôtel de Ville, a 16th-century Flamboyant Gothic palace known (although no king ever lived there) as Maison du Roi today houses the City Museum. It is said to have been the scene of Charles V's abdication in 1555 in favour of his son, Philip II of Spain. Arch enemy of the kings of France, master of an empire "over which the sun never set" (Austria to Peru), Charles spent the rest of his life as a simple monk at Yuste, in Spain. The museum houses an important collection of 18th- and 19th-century ceramics, with some remarkable 14th-century rood-screens and sculptures from the facade of the Hôtel de Ville. Here, too, are the Manneken Pis wardrobes.

You should not miss the little Church of St. Nicholas, almost invisible because of the tiny houses close up against its walls. It lies between the Grand Place and the Bourse. St. Nicholas is the traditional church of aspiring dancers, and hopeful ballerinas light candles in prayer for a role. There is a small *Virgin and Child* attributed to Rubens and, outside beside the porch, the exquisite *Milkmaid* by Marc Devos.

Keeping the Grand'Place on your right, you now head east along the Marché-aux-Herbes and the rue de la Madeleine, and come out to a view of the best of Brussels' new buildings. You are facing the equestrian statue of King Albert. Over to the left of this statue is the Central station and, beyond it, the Telecommunication building. To the right, flanking the formal gardens is the Albertinum, Belgium's National Library. As you walk up through the gardens, do not neglect to look back at the clock over the lower archway. You should try to hear (and see) it strike the hour (preferably at noon). The building in front of you at the top is the Palais des Congrès. Through the upper archway, in mellow brick, is one of the rare remaining traces of the Burgundian period. This is the Ravenstein Palace, birthplace of Anne of Cleves, the "Flemish mare" who was fourth of the six wives of King Henry VIII of England and subject of one of Holbein's loveliest portraits.

The Place Royale

You now arrive at the place Royale, a classical square of elegant proportions. This is the site of the Coudenberg Palace. Behind the statue of the crusading hero, Godefroy de Bouillon, is the neo-classic facade of St.-Jacques-sur-Coudenberg, the interior of which contains a number of sculptures worth seeing, including a *Moses* by de Marseille and a collection of pieces by Godecharle. As you stand on the steps of the church, the re-decorated Belle Vue Palace, former home of King Leopold III and Queen Astrid before their accession, is at the corner on your right. Beyond this is the rue Royale, alongside the Parc de Bruxelles.

To your left, the rue de la Régence runs up to the Palais de Justice, sometimes called the ugliest building in Europe. The large museum on the right is the Musée Royal d'Art Ancien, with its magnificent collection of Flemish and Dutch paintings, among numerous other works of art. Down the side of this building runs the rue du Musée, which luckily still preserves the fine façade of the former National Library building. Nearby, the strikingly rebuilt Musée d'Art Moderne specializes in the more recent periods of painting, although it includes works by Ingres and Sir Thomas Lawrence.

Returning to the place Royale, you may care to remember that Brussels has much music to offer. You can get to the Palais des Beaux Arts—with its many art galleries, concert and lecture halls (not to forget its cinema), all located below street level—by the rue Ravenstein or down a broad stairway from the rue Royale. Even if you have little taste for music, it is always worthwhile finding out what there is at the Beaux Arts to be heard or seen. The Orchestre National de Belgique has an excellent name. In the rue de la Régence is the Conservatoire Royal.

Back down the rue de la Régence and diagonally opposite the Petit Sablon museum is the Church of Notre Dame du Sablon, originally a small chapel built by crossbowmen in 1304. The church itself, which took a century to build, is a 15th–16th-century masterpiece. It is the church rather than any particular monuments or treasures that deserves a visit, though there is a delightful statue of St. Hubert just beyond the porch, with a stag at his side and between its horns a hanging Christ. There is also some very fine work in the choir, though much of it is too high to see easily. Here is held the Mass of Saint Hubert, patron saint of huntsmen, on 3 November each year.

Behind the church lies the Grand Sablon, one of Brussels' most pleasant squares. It contains many cafes and restaurants as well as antique and bookshops. In the evenings it is a regular rendezvous for the "in" crowd prior to embarking on more raucous nightlife elsewhere.

On the other side of the rue de la Régence is the attractive little garden square, the Petit Sablon. You should notice the variety of railings, but above all the little statues representing Brussels' medieval guilds. There are 48 of these and it is easy to guess each trade for the furniture-maker holds a chair, the wine merchant a goblet and so on. At the far end of the garden is a large statue of the counts of Egmont and Hornes, surrounded by a semi-circle of statues of Belgian scientists of the 16th and 17th centuries.

Immediately beyond the square is the Palais d'Egmont. It now houses the offices of numerous semi-public bodies, but, if security permits, you can enter from this end, walking through what were once the stables and emerging into the Palace gardens. Here you will find a replica of Frampton's Peter Pan (the original is in Kensington Gardens), "given by the children of London to the children of Brussels", and come, rather to your surprise, to the outdoor terrace leading into the coffee shop of the Hilton hotel. (If the Palace is closed for an official function, go round the block to the rue du Grand Cerf and cut through the garden from there.)

The Palace of Justice to the Boulevards

At the end of the rue de la Régence is the Palais de Justice in the big square called after the architect Poelaert. You cannot fail to notice the size and style of the building (the definition "Assyrio-Babylonian" would fit it best). The impression of immensity as you mount the steps is well designed to impress upon you the majesty of justice. If you climb the 500-odd steps to the cupola, you will get a view of the Brabant countryside worth remembering. This site is the former Gallows Hill.

The precipitous descent from the Palais de Justice brings you quickly into the quarter known as Les Marolles, and sometimes also called after Pieter Breughel the Elder, who died here in 1569 and whose tomb is in the Eglise de la Chapelle, in place de la Chapelle at the foot of the hill. Parts of this church date back to the 12th century, and it contains the beautiful statue, *Our Lady of Solitude,* wearing a black lace mantilla and attributed to the Spanish master Becerra. It is said to have been brought here by the Infanta Isabella, "light of the eyes" of her father, the cruel but pious Philip II, who ceded the Low Countries to his daughter a few months before he died of gout in 1598.

The puppet theatre of Toone VII has been moved from this square down the hill, to a little blind alley called Schuddevelde, near the rue des Bouchers. It is no longer in the father-to-son tradition, but its charm and fun have been maintained, and it has an attractive cafe. It is a good place to spend an evening.

To appreciate Les Marolles you should visit it during the fun of the Braderie Bruegel in October. These autumn *braderies,* or shopkeepers' festivals, are held as joint efforts in all the shopping streets in Belgium. They are a time of fairy lights, amplified music at street corners, shopping novelties aimed to catch your attention, and stupendous shop-window decoration. On the Braderie Bruegel you will see how little the faces, and the spiritual gusto, of these people have changed through the centuries since Bruegel painted them—though the damsel elected "Miss Bruegel" for the year habitually conforms to 20th-century standards of beauty. It is not true, as is sometimes alleged, that the title is reserved for the winner of the sausage-eating contest.

Returning along the rue Blaes, which runs parallel with the rue Haute (both are one-way streets) you will pass the place du Jeu de Balle, scene of the Sunday flea market (it also functions on weekday mornings), which is also the traditional center of all the black markets in Belgium. During the Occupation, it was hunting ground for Hitler's scouts seeking forced labour for deportation, and the Church of the Immaculate Conception opposite provided the citizens with emergency exits into adjoining roads with the ready connivance of the Capuchin fathers. At the end of the street you are again on the ring boulevard;

50 yards higher up is the Porte de Hal, last survivor of the city's fortified gates, which houses an arms museum.

The boulevard, which stretches downhill past the Midi station for almost a mile from this point, is the scene of the Brussels Fair (sometimes called the Foire du Midi) from mid-July through August. The Belgians are devoted to fairs, and the peripatetic amusement caterers are to be found running fairs on a small scale in almost all the city squares at various times during the spring and summer. The Foire du Midi is the meeting place for all of them, and you will find everything that is newest and most thrilling in this peculiarly Belgian form of amusement brought together here as at a gathering of old friends.

Taking the uphill route, you quickly reach and pass the Porte Louise. The outer section of the avenue de la Toison d'Or, between the Porte de Namur and the rue des Chevaliers, has been made into a pedestrian zone. The pavement has been brightly colored in red and white stones in diamond shapes, evergreen bushes and shrubs have been laid out, benches and fountains installed. It is a pleasant place for shopping and strolling in winter or summer. From the Porte de Namur you can best take a bus down the long and crowded chaussée d'Ixelles to the place Eugène Flagey (named after the former burgomaster of Ixelles). The square itself is a morning food market which often finds room for a fair and even a circus.

Beside it you will see where the lovely Ixelles lakes rise. To see these at their best you should come in May, when the white and red chestnuts are in full bloom. Do not miss the delightful walk round these lakes (they are the center for a firework display in June), and leave plenty of time for a visit at the far end to the Abbaye de la Cambre, the serene setting of which is somewhat spoilt by the new ITT office tower. The history of the Cistercian sisters, from the early 13th century to their dispersion after the French Revolution, epitomises the troubled story of the Low Countries. Here, too, lie the remains of St. Boniface who died here in 1260.

A bus returning the length of one of the lakes will take you back through the place Eugène Flagey, up rue Malibran and into the rue du Trône. If you alight at the chaussée de Wavre crossing and turning downhill, you can fork up the rue Vauthier to the Musée Wiertz, a collection of the works of a single powerful painter.

From this vantage point you walk round into the Parc Léopold, once a zoo. Here, among a number of institutional buildings, you will find the Natural History Museum with several extremely interesting prehistoric remains, including the Lierre Mammoth and the reconstructed skeletons of some Stone Age miners.

Having left the park and walked up the rue Belliard, you again come to the ring boulevard. Crossing it and taking the short rue Lambermont, you will find yourself in the Parc de Bruxelles. Byron resided for a time on the rue Ducale, a fine, late 18th-century street bordering the park. It was here that he wrote the third canto of *Childe Harold* on the Battle of Waterloo. The street now contains the residences of the United States and British ambassadors.

The City Park and Cathedral of Saint Michael

To your left is the Royal Palace with at the farther end the white block of the Belle Vue Palace. The Royal Palace owes its present appearance to Léopold II, who had it altered several times by architects who drew their inspiration from Versailles and the Tuileries; there are magnificent crystal chandeliers in the Throne Room and remarkable Gobelins tapestries in the Grand White Drawing Room.

Opposite the center of the palace, a wide avenue leads you across the park, past two lake-fountains to the rue de la Loi where, surrounded by a row of government departments, stands the Palais de la Nation, housing the two chambers of the Belgian Parliament. It has an impressive frontage by Barnabé Guimard. The building is accessible to visitors when the chambers are not sitting.

The government offices on either side of the Parliament building have a good deal of historical interest. No. 16, now the Prime Minister's office, was built by Montoyer for a religious community. No. 2, again the work of Guimard, has been a private house and a hotel and it housed the meetings of the revolutionary committee in 1792; it is now the Ministry of National Defense. At the farther end of the park, opposite the Royal Palace, is the Palais des Académies, home of the Academy of Sciences, Arts and Letters and other learned bodies, and an occasional mise-en-scène for top-level international conferences.

Crossing the park to its corner on the rue de la Loi, a hundred yards' walk downhill and a short turn to the right bring you before the Cathedral of St. Michael. The church stands on the site of a Chapel of St. Michael, to which were carried in the year 1047 the remains of Gudule, a saintly lady of Ham, near Alost, who had died 335 years earlier. As a young girl she had carried a lantern which was extinguished by the wind and, in answer to prayer, re-lit by divine power. Although known for years as the church of Ste. Gudule, it is now dedicated to St. Michael, and only recently (on the creation of the See of Malines-Brussels) became a cathedral.

The church itself was begun in 1226, and there is 13th-century work (restored in the 19th century) in parts of the nave and choir. You will find a beautiful statue of the saint as Guardian of the City, but the chief treasure of the church is its stained-glass, designed by Bernard van Orley, early 16th-century painter at the court of Margaret of Austria, regent of the Lowlands during Charles V's infancy. Note in particular the two magnificent lights in the north and south transepts, and the windows in the Chapel of the Holy Sacrament showing the incidents connected with the Profanation of the Host, a Jewish-Christian episode of 1370 often used as a subject by Brussels artists. The chapel was in fact built in the 16th century to house the remains of the Host salvaged from its defilers. In summer, the great west window of the church is illuminated at night so that its color values are strikingly apparent to people coming uphill into the Place Sainte Gudule.

On the north side of the church is the 1940s-built National Bank of Belgium. Again climbing the hill on this side, you emerge into the rue Royale by the Column of the Congress, which commemorates the first

National Assembly of independent Belgium in 1831. In front of it, flanked by two huge bronze lions, are the tombs of Belgium's Unknown Soldiers, one killed in the First World War and the other in the Second. The statue that crowns it is of Léopold I, the country's first king. Behind is the new Civil Service building (Cité Administrative), with a vast public terrace overlooking the lower town. Slightly further on you can stroll into what remains of the botanical gardens, now that the upgraded *ceinture* has been built through one side of them.

The Heart of the City

From here you can easily find your way downhill, and you will be able to reach the rue du Marais and the rue aux Choux, to find the place des Martyrs. This architecturally attractive square is also a cemetery, since the Brussels citizens who lost their lives in expelling the Dutch in 1830 are buried here in a mass-grave. The monument is perhaps less worthy than the neo-classic square itself, which, despite its commercial importance, is curiously quiet and dignified.

From here you emerge into the commercial bustle of the rue Neuve, and on the right is the little church of Notre-Dame de Finistère, a triumph of religion over circumstance: originally planned to be built from the proceeds of a lottery the treasurer of which absconded with the funds. It houses the statue of Our Lady of Good Success (the Aberdeen Madonna), presented by Scottish Roman Catholics to the devout Infanta Isabella in 1625.

If you cross the place de Brouckère diagonally and turn into the narrow busy streets behind Ste. Catherine's market, you will see on place Sainte Catherine the Black Tower, part of the first fortifications of Brussels, which dates from the mid-13th century, long before the fortified circle of the ring boulevard had defined the city's growth. This market quarter has existed since Brussels was founded. Today it houses the city's finest seafood restaurants.

Across the market square is the entrance to the rue de Flandre. The side streets leading from it have a picturesqueness of their own. If you go round to the right through the Marché-aux-Porcs and the rue du Grand Hospice, another right-turn takes you in front of the Eglise du Béguinage. This is all that is left of the Béguinage, the hostel for the order of lay sisters named after the Liège monk, Lambert le Bègue (Lambert the Stammerer), who have been active since the 13th century. The 17th-century church is known as Brabant Baroque, a local version of the Italian form. Its furnishings are rich and there are paintings and carvings, and a lovely ivory crucifix attributed to Duquesnoy.

Three Side Trips

There are three trips outside the center of Brussels which, if you have time, are worth taking. The first is to Laeken, which can be reached by several tram routes. You can walk round the Royal domain (on some days in spring the greenhouses are open to the public) and see the Chinese Pavilion and Japanese Tower imported by King Léopold II from the Paris Exhibition of 1900, also the fine Neptune statue. The original (in Bologna) from which it was cast is by Giambologna. Across the public park you will skirt the Atomium, the symbol of the 1958 World Fair with its nuclear museum, and arrive at the approaches to the Palais du Centenaire, site of the Brussels World Fairs in 1935 as well as in 1958.

Another trip is a walk along the rue de la Loi to a decorative archway (visible all the way), which is approached at the last through a small park and is in fact the Cinquantenaire Memorial. (The less active can go directly by metro.) The buildings on either side house the Museum of Art and History and the Museum of the Army. The former is one of the richest and most complete in Europe and includes lace among its many collections. The latter, perhaps because of the amount of fighting that has taken place on Belgian soil at one time or another, also has a notable series of displays. The 13-story office complex which you can pass in front of at Rond-Point Schuman is the Berlaymont building, headquarters of the E.E.C. Commission. It is in the form of a cross, and contains over a thousand offices. From the Cinquantenaire Arch it is only a ten minute drive (or a ride to the end of the 44 tram route) out along the tree–lined avenue to the royal estates at Tervuren. Here you can wander in the ornamental gardens of the park (watch the Common Market functionaries jogging in the lunch hour) and visit the Central Africa Museum with its fine collection of loot from the former Belgian Congo.

In Anderlecht you will find a colony of interest centered upon the Church of Saint Peter and Saint Guidon. The latter is buried here, and as patron of farm animals, especially horses, and peasants attracts devout throngs on given dates in spring and autumn. The lovely 15th-century church is marred by a hideous 19th-century spire, but its crypt with the tomb of the saint are of real interest. In the rue du Chapelain, behind the church, is an old Béguinage (Begijnhof) dating from 1252. On the other side of the church is the rue du Chapitre, where you will find (No. 31) the house where Erasmus, the great Dutch humanist and leading light of the Reformation, stayed when in Brussels in 1521. It is now a museum, highly evocative of the great man. Its diamond-paned windows overlook a quiet walled garden, and the library contains a fine collection of his works including *In Praise of Folly* in Latin, English and French, and a first edition with the date 1512 under its original title *Moriae Encomium*. Engravings show him on his many travels, and in one he is engaged in animated conversation with his great friend Sir Thomas More. A copy of Holbein's portrait of Erasmus hangs in the study and there are several other portraits of this unusual scholar. Sayings attributed to Erasmus are still used by us today, such as "Call a spade a spade," "One swallow does not make a summer" and "As plain as the nose on your face."

Finally, after these town pilgrimages, it is good to know that it's only a 20-minute tram- or bus-ride to the ancient and magnificent trees of the Forêt de Soignes, via Ave. Louise to the gates of the Bois de la Cambre, a public park and forepart of the forest, with open-air cafés. Beyond this, the Drève de Lorraine plunges through the forest, the road running almost to Waterloo. On the fringe of the forest is the Boitsfort racecourse.

PRACTICAL INFORMATION FOR BRUSSELS

HOTELS. The rôle of Brussels as capital of the European Community has enormously increased the pressure on hotel accommodation, especially during the week. So it is best to book ahead, except for weekends when business and official visitors leave. As an inducement to weekend tourists, several of the big hotels offer a booklet of vouchers for free visits to most of the sights of Brussels, including Boitsfort racecourse, and give reduced weekend prices. To make hotel bookings from abroad, call Belgium Tourist Reservations on 230 5029, or write to BTR, PO Box 41, B-1000 Brussels 23. The Tourist Office at rue Marché-aux-Herbes 61 (tel. 512 3030) will also arrange hotel reservations locally. These services are free, but guests are asked to pay a deposit, which is deducted from the final bill. Open 9–6 (8 in summer, 7 weekends). *Acotra* on rue de la Montagne 38 (tel. 513 4480) is a youth organization which has a free room-finding service for student hostels.

Deluxe

Amigo, rue de l'Amigo 1–3 (tel. 511 5910). 183 impeccable rooms. Classic hotel (though built in '50s) just off the Grand'Place. Superb French restaurant. Still a haunt of European High Society.

Astoria, rue Royale 103 (tel. 217 6290). 120 rooms, all sumptuously furnished in Louis XV or Empire style. In the heart of the ministerial quarter, close to the Parc de Bruxelles. Dine under classic chandeliers; and don't miss the Pullman bar.

Europa, rue de la Loi 107 (tel. 230 1333). 240 air-conditioned rooms. Right by European Commission. Enjoy (taxpayers') expense-account luxury at reasonable prices by making a week-end booking.

Hilton, blvd. de Waterloo 38 (tel. 513 8877). 365 rooms. Overlooks the place Louise shopping area and the tiny Parc d'Egmont. Outclasses most other Hiltons in Europe, with its excellent restaurants and personal service.

Hyatt Regency, rue Royale 250 (tel. 219 4640). 315 superb rooms. Overlooks the Botanical Gardens; close to the rue Neuve shopping complex. Good French restaurant.

Jolly Hotel Atlanta, blvd. Adolphe Max 7 (tel. 217 0120). 240 rooms (some with shower only). Very central; recently refurbished. The view from the rooftop breakfast-room is superb.

Mayfair, ave. Louise 381–383 (tel. 649 9800). 99 well-equipped luxury rooms. Slightly south of the city center, within easy jogging distance of the beautiful Etangs d'Ixelles (ponds). Excellent French restaurant. Undoubtedly the top-ranking business hotel.

Métropole, place de Brouckère 31 (tel. 217 2300). 400 rooms. They still sing songs about this downtown square, where the 19th-century boulevards slice through the medieval heart of the city. The hotel is an Art Nouveau classic, now wonderfully restored to its former glory. Some Bruxellois maintain the restaurant is still the best in the city; it is certainly one of the most elegant.

Président World Trade Center, blvd. Emile Jacqmain (tel. 217 2020). 300 luxurious rooms and stupendous suites. Despite its very recent construction, this hotel, close to the Gare du Nord, has become an instant classic. Two restaurants, both excellent.

Royal Windsor, rue Duquesnoy 5–7 (tel. 511 4215). 300 rooms. Between the Grand'Place and the Mont des Arts. Excellent restaurant and a good nightclub, the Crocodile.

Expensive

Arenberg, rue d'Assaut 15 (tel. 511 0770). 158 rooms, all with bath. Close to St. Michael's Cathedral.

Bedford, rue du Midi 135 (tel. 512 7840). 280 rooms, all with bath. Just south of Grand'Place. Reliable restaurant.

Chambord, rue de Namur 82 (tel. 513 4119). 70 rooms, all with bath. Tucked in between the Porte de Namur and the Royal Palace. Beautiful rooms; no restaurant.

County House, square des Héros 2–4 (tel. 375 4420). 96 rooms, all with bath. South of city center along avenue Brugmann. Excellent restaurant.

Delta, chausée de Charleroi 17 (tel. 539 0160). 250 rooms, all with bath. Modern hotel, close to pl. Stéphanie.

Fimotel Expo, ave. de l'Impératrice Charlotte (tel. 479 1910). 80 rooms, all with bath. Between the Atomium and the Exhibition Center; convenient for the Ring expressway and the airport.

Forum, ave. du Haut Pont 2 (tel. 343 0100). 78 rooms, all with bath. Modern hotel in quiet area, south of the city center.

New Siru, pl. Rogier 1 (tel. 217 7580). 100 rooms, all with bath or shower. Overlooking Brussels' busiest square. Two good restaurants.

Président Center, rue Royale 160 (tel. 219 0065). 73 rooms, all with bath. Comfortable, distinguished and very central. No restaurant.

Trois Tilleuls, Berensheide 8 (tel. 672 3014). Just 8 rooms (all with bath or shower); but individually decorated. Close to the lakes in Watermael-Boitsfort. Truly excellent restaurant—with service to match.

Moderate

Ambassade, pl. des Barricades 1A (tel. 218 2061). 17 rooms, all with bath. Just north of the ministerial quarter. Family run, with excellent-value restaurant.

Arcade Sainte-Catherine, rue Joseph Plateau 2 (tel. 513 7620). 234 rooms, all with shower. Right by St. Catherine's church, a few blocks from the Grand'-Place. You'll only pay for a tv or telephone in your room if you want one. No restaurant.

Argus, rue Capitaine Crespel 6 (tel. 514 0770). Newly-built hotel, with 40 well-equipped rooms. Close to pl. Louise. No restaurant.

Armorial, blvd. Brand Whitlock 101 (tel. 734 5636). 15 rooms, 11 with bath or shower. East of city center, near pl. Montgomery. Impressive converted mansion; no restaurant.

Ascot, pl. Loix 1 (tel. 538 8835). 58 rooms, all with bath. Overlooking quiet square between pl. Stéphanie and Porte de Hal. No restaurant.

Charlemagne, blvd. Charlemagne 25–27 (tel. 230 2135). 60 spacious rooms, all with bath. Right next to European Commission. No restaurant.

Elysée, rue de la Montagne 4 (tel. 511 9682). 18 recently refurbished rooms, 12 with bath. Between the Central Station and the Grand'Place. No restaurant.

Lloyd George, ave. Lloyd George 12 (tel. 648 3072). 15 rooms, 8 with bath or shower. Recently refurbished mansion overlooking the Bois de la Cambre. Have a treat by booking one of the beautifully furnished suites. No restaurant.

Marie-José, rue du Commerce 73 (tel. 512 0842). 17 rooms, most with bath or shower. Close to Parc de Bruxelles. Excellent restaurant.

Van Belle, chaussée de Mons 39 (tel. 521 3516). 137 rooms, 110 with bath or shower. Just west of city center on the way into Anderlecht. Underground parking; moderate restaurant.

Inexpensive

Aux Arcades, rue des Bouchers 36 (tel. 511 2876). 17 rooms, 4 with bath. Close to Grand'Place; more noted for its position than its creature comforts. No restaurant.

Barry, pl. Anneesens 25 (tel. 511 2361). 30 rooms, all with bath. Between Gare du Midi and Grand'Place. Good value restaurant too; nearly always full, so book.

Concorde-Louise, rue de la Concorde 59 (tel. 513 9372). 18 rooms, all with bath or shower. In quiet street near pl. Stéphanie. No restaurant.

Congrès, rue du Congrès 42 (tel. 217 1890). 38 rooms, most with bath or shower. In the ministerial quarter.

De Boeck's, rue Veydt 40 (tel. 537 4033). 30 rooms, 17 with bath. On quiet street, parallel to ave. Louise.

Derby, ave. de Tervuren 24 (tel. 733 0819). 28 rooms, all with bath or shower. Close to Cinquantenaire park. No restaurant.

France, blvd. Jamar 21 (tel. 522 7935). 27 rooms, 12 with bath. Close to Garde du Midi. Good value. No restaurant.

International, rue Royale 344 (tel. 217 3344). 25 rooms, almost all with bath. Convenient for Gare du Nord. No restaurant.

La Légende, rue de l'Etuve 33–35 (tel. 512 8290). 31 rooms, 8 with bath. Very central location, right by Manneken Pis. Good family restaurant offers real Belgian cooking.

Léopold III, square Joséphine Charlotte 11 (tel. 762 8288). 15 rooms, most with shower or bath. Overlooks tree-lined square on eastern side of city center. Friendly service. No restaurant.

Mirabeau, pl. Fontainas 18–20 (tel. 511 1972). 28 rooms, all with shower or bath. A short stroll from the Grand'Place. No restaurant.

Paris, blvd. Poincaré 80–82 (tel. 523 8153). 27 rooms, most with shower or bath. Close to Gare du Midi. No restaurant.

Plasky, ave. Eugène Plasky 212 (tel. 733 7530). 30 rooms, most with shower or bath. A quick taxi-ride from the airport on the eastern edge of the city center. No restaurant.

Vielle Lanterne, rue des Grands Carmes 29 (tel. 512 7494). Only has 6 rooms (all with bath). No restaurant—but there's a view of Manneken Pis on every floor!

Airport hotels. Most of Brussels' airport hotels are in Diegem. The best is the **Holiday Inn** (L), Holidaystraat 7 (tel. 720 5865). 288 rooms; two restaurants; swimming pool and sauna. Closer to Zaventem is the **Sofitel** (L), Bessenveldstraat 15 (tel. 720 6050). 125 rooms; good restaurant; swimming pool (with poolside bar); sauna, etc. **Fimotel Brussels Airport** (E), Berkenlaan (tel. 721 4801). 79 well-equipped rooms and restaurant. Good value in its class. **Novotel** (E), Olmenstraat (tel. 720 5830). 159 rooms, all with bath or shower. Recently refurbished; airport shuttle; good restaurant and swimming pool. **Campanile** (M), Excelsiorlaan 2 (tel. 720 9862). 46 rooms, all with bath. Good eat-all-you-like restaurant.

Student accomodations. There are several youth hostels and student residences around the city. The latter are always full during the university terms. The camp sites are a long way out.

Breughel, blvd. de L'Empereur (tel. 511 0436). Brand new hostel with 136 beds and good cafeteria.

C.H.A.B. (Centre d'Hebergement de l'Aglomeration de Bruxelles), rue Traversière 7 (tel. 219 4750). Near Botanical Gardens.

Centreurope, rue Verte 124. Youth hostel with 216 beds. North of city center.

Huizingen, at Beersel, Provinciaal Domein 6 (tel. 380 1493). Campsite, A long way out of the center—7 miles to the southwest—but the best there is. For other campsites see the *Environs of Brussels* section.

Maison Internationale des Etudiants, chaussée de Wavre 205 (tel. 648 8529). Former monastery with 25 rooms (all single).

Sleepwell—Auberge de la Marais, rue de la Blanchisserie 27 (tel. 218 5050). 86 beds. Right by Gare du Nord. Shower and breakfast included in price. Lockers available. No youth or student card required.

GETTING AROUND. There is a regular train service from the airport to the Central Station calling at the Gare du Nord. This leaves every 20 minutes, takes 16 minutes and costs BF 120 (or BF 90 if you take the trouble to buy a ticket before boarding the train). A taxi will cost you around BF 750 for the same journey (luggage included) and will take approximately 35 minutes.

Getting about the city is easier as an easily-comprehensible **Metro** system takes over more routes from the less predictable **Trams.** Line 1 links the EEC Commission with the Central Station, the central shopping area, St. Catherine, and the western suburbs. Other lines are basically "trams in a tunnel" but two lines link Nord and Midi stations, via either blvd. Adolphe Max or Ave. Louise.

The trams and **buses** run as part of the same service. A single ticket anywhere in the city by public transport costs BF 40. A BF 150 Tourist Pass entitles you to unlimited travel on all public transport for one day. A 10-trip ticket costs BF 250 (less if purchased at a newsstand). You can get up-to-the-minute information or leaflets from the Tourist Office, rue Marché-aux-Herbes 61 (tel. 513 8940).

Tram and bus services are numbered, but the numbers have changed and rechanged during the metro construction, and are almost certain to be changed again. Any attempt to suggest useful route numbers would therefore be misleading. The Tourist Office will provide up-to-date information.

Best get to know the names of destinations you are likely to want, such as Nord, Midi, Bourse, Bois, place Royale, Cinquantenaire, place Flagey, which are marked on the destination boards. If you are uncertain where to get out, ask a fellow passenger, not the driver.

Taxis. These are expensive, but the tip is included in the fare. To call a taxi phone *Taxis Verts* (Green Cabs) on 347 4747 or pick one up at one of the many stands. If in doubt, ask your hotel to phone for one.

Car Rental. Again, this is expensive. The better firms run better cars but cost more. Back-street hiring may appear to be cheaper, but can lead to greatly increased expenses with unreliable cars. Among the better firms are—Avis, rue Americaine 145 (tel. 537 1280) and Sabena Air Terminal near Central Station; Hertz, blvd. Maurice Lemonnier 8 (tel. 513 2970) and Brussels Airport; ABC Service Rent-a-Car, rue d'Anderlecht 133 (tel. 513 1954).

SOURCES OF INFORMATION. For current events see the English-language weekly, the *Bulletin*. For further information, contact TIB (Tourist Information Brussels), rue Marché-aux-Herbes 61, tel. 513 8940, where you can pick up their *Visit Friendly Belgium: Weekends and Excursions* booklet. Open 9–6 (7 weekends, 8 summer).

SIGHTSEEING. Guided tours of the city are organized by *Sightseeing Tours*, rue de Colline 8, Grand'Place (tel. 513 7744); and *Panorama Tours*, rue Marché-aux-Herbes 105 (tel. 513 6154).

Brussels at a Glance organize guided tours of the city center on foot—and in a VW microbus around the suburbs. All tours in English and French. Tel. 217 4985.

Alternative Tourism. Bus tours are also organized by ARAU, an urban workshop group concerned with conservation and environmental issues. These are excellent value, but you won't see many of the conventional sights this way. *Brussels seen by her inhabitants* is a 2½ hour bus trip around the city starting from St. Michael's Cathedral every Sat. at 10 and 2, July–Sept.

Guides. To hire a qualified guide (any of 12 languages) phone Mme. Le Bon at the Tourist Information Center (tel. 513 8940).

Cassettes. Tape equipment can be hired from the TIB office (rue Marché-aux-Herbes 61), for a walking commentary in 8 languages to cover a visit to the Grand'Place.

SPORTS. Football (soccer) is the most popular sport. Important international games are held at Heysel Stadium and S.C. Anderlecht sports grounds (see newspaper announcements). **Athletic meets** are held at the Racing Club Stadium. Covered **swimming pools:** rue de Chevreuil 28; rue St. François 25; rue de la Perche 38; open-air pools, rue de Genève 121; Solarium Beausoleil; Solarium du Centenaire, ave. de Meisse. **Water-skiing** at Genval and Hofstade lakes.

Tennis, Lawn Tennis Federation, ave. Louise 164 (tel. 648 0934). Several large hotels have courts available for residents. **Horseback riding:** L'Etrier Belge, Champ du Vert Chasseur 19; Country Riding Club, Welriekendedreef, Jezus Eik. Poffé, Chaussée de Waterloo 872a. Duwez, Allée du Vivier d'Oie 55.

Flying at Grimbergen Airfield. **Horseracing** at Boitsfort, Groenendaal, and Zellik racetracks (see newspaper announcements). **Bowling.** There are plenty of bowling alleys. A few: Brunswick, quai au Foin 43, downtown; Crossly, blvd. de l'Empereur; uptown, the Molière, ave. Molière 115.

CHURCH SERVICES. Catholic: All parish churches. Especially convenient for visitors are St. Nicholas (Bourse); Notre-Dame au Sablon (rue de la Régence); Ste. Marie (rue Royale); Carmes, ave. de la Toison d'Or. Weekday Mass at 6 P.M. at the first two and 6.15 P.M. at the others.

Anglican and American Episcopal, Holy Trinity, rue Capitaine Crespel 29. Sun., Holy Communion 8.30, 9.20, 10.30. Wed. and Fri. 12.30. Morning Prayer 10.30; Sung Eucharist 11.30, Sunday school and crèche for infants; Evening Prayer 6.45.

American Protestant Church, Kattenberg, Boitsfort (in grounds of the International School). Sun. service and school, 10.30 A.M.

MUSEUMS AND PLACES OF INTEREST. Brussels has over twenty major museums and innumerable minor ones, specializing in exhibits that range from torture to tapestry. Admission fees also vary a lot, ranging from BF 5 to 75, with some galleries charging more for special exhibitions. Churches tend to be free. The Tourist Office, rue Marché-aux-Herbes 61, has an excellent brochure *Brussels—Guide and Street Plan*, price BF 35, which will give you all the up-to-date details of both museums and events.

Abbé de la Cambre, blvd. Général Jacques, Ixelles. Ancient abbey containing remains of St. Boniface, situated south of the lakes of Ixelles. Opening hours vary, but usually around 2 to 5.30.

L'Arbre d'Or (The Brewers' House), Grand'Place 10. One of the beautiful guild houses that surround the square. This one is still connected with the same medieval trade, and houses, too, a small Brewing Museum; open weekdays 10 to 12, 2 to 5; Sat. and hol. 10 to 12; closed Sun.

Archief en Museum van het Vlaams Leven te Brussel (Museum of Flemish Life in Brussels), Vieux Marché-aux-Grains 5. Open 10 to 5; closed Sun., Mon. and holidays.

Atomium, at Laeken in the northern suburbs. Built for the 1958 World Fair, and now very much a symbol of the city. It houses an exhibition on the peaceful uses of atomic energy (open daily 9.30 to 5.30) and a restaurant. Admission BF 90.

Bibliothèque Royale Albert I (Albert I Royal Library), blvd. de l'Empereur 4, Mont des Arts; collections of manuscripts, engravings, medals and coins, books, and printing. Opening hours vary according to department, but generally 9 to 12 and 2 to 5. Closed Sun., public holidays, and last week in August.

Le Cathédrale de Saint Michel (popularly known as Sainte Gudule), close to the Parc de Bruxelles. Started in 13th century, since 1962 Brussels' cathedral. Open 7.30 to 6 (8 in summer), 1.30 to 5 Sun.

Eglise Notre Dame de la Chapelle, place de la Chapelle. Parts of this fine church date from 12th century; burial place of Brueghel the Elder. Open 10 to 12, 2 to 4; 9 to 12 Sun.

Eglise Notre Dame du Sablon, rue de la Régence. 15th- to 16th-century masterpiece; contains the celebrated statue of St. Hubert.

Eglise St. Nicholas, rue au Beurre. At back of the Bourse beside a number of fine old houses. The "Dancers' Church," it contains Rubens' *Virgin and Child*.

Erasmus House, 31 rue de Chapitre, Anderlecht. Home of the great Renaissance humanist; now a museum with many personal and historic exhibits. Open 10 to 12, 2 to 5; closed Tues. and Fri. Admission BF 50.

Hôtel de Ville (Town Hall), Grand'Place. The jewel in Brussels' architectural crown. Famous for its relics of the Duchy of Brabant and the tapestries in the Maximilian Chamber. Open weekdays 9 to 5 in summer, 9 to 4 in winter; Sat. and Sun. 10 to 12.

Musée d'Art Ancien (Museum of Classic Art), rue de la Régence 3. Admission BF 5; sometimes free. Contains some well known Belgian masterpieces from the 14th to the 17th centuries. There are three sections: Flemish Primitives —Van der Weyden, Bouts, Memling etc.), Renaissance—Bosch, Breughel; Baroque—Rubens, Van Dyck; as well as good examples of foreign work. Qualified guides are available. Reconstruction of the galleries may still be in progress and cause considerable disruption. Check on status before launching out. Open, by and large, 10 to 12, 2 to 5. Closed Mon.

Musée d'Art Moderne (Museum of Modern Art), off Place Royale. Good collection of 20th century Belgian and international art. Open 10 to 1, 2 to 5. Closed Mon. Admission varies according to exhibition.

Musée du Centre Public d'Aide Sociale de Bruxelles (Museum of the Brussels Welfare Center), Saint-Pierre Hospital, rue Haute 298A; paintings, sculpture, tapestries, and furniture from the 15th to 18th centuries. Open Wed. 2 to 5.

Musée Charlier, ave. des Arts 16. Collection of the sculptor Guillaume Charlier—his own work and also pieces by other turn-of-the-century artists. Sun. 9 to 12.30 only.

Musée des Chemins-de-Fer Belges (Railway Museum), Gare du Nord, rue du Progrès. Open weekdays 9 to 5.

Musée du Cinéma (Film Museum), rue Baron Horta 9. Both museum and screenings. Fascinating revivals. Evenings, usually 5.30 to 10.30.

Musée Communal (City Museum) in the Maison du Roi, Grand'Place (rue du Poivre 1). Traces the city's story. Much fascinating material—on the guilds, artists and crafts of Brussels. Also has the Manneken Pis costumes. Open Mon. to Fri., 10 to 12, 1 to 4 (5 in summer), Sat. and Sun. 10 to 12.

Musée des Enfants (Children's Museum), rue Tenbosch 32, Ixelles. Largely a practical display, with lots for kids to do as well as see. Mon., Tues., Thurs., Fri. 9.30 to 11.45, 1.30 to 3.30; Wed., Sat., Sun. 2.30 to 5. Closed in Aug.

Musée Horta, rue Americaine 25, St. Gilles. Private house of the *art nouveau* architect, built 1896. Open 2.30 to 5.30, closed Mon. and holidays. Admission BF 50.

Musée de l'Hôtel de Belle-Vue, place des Palais 7. Former royal residence, with memorabilia and restored 18th- and 19th-century rooms. Open 10 to 4.45, closed Fri. and holidays.

Musée Instrumental (Musical Instrument Museum), Petit Sablon 17. Over 5,000 musical instruments from all over the world and from all ages. Open Tues., Thurs., Sat. 2.30 to 4.30; Wed. 5 to 7; Sun. 10.30 to 12.30.

Musée Royale de l'Armée et d'Histoire Militaire (Royal Museum of Army and Military History), Parc du Cinquantenaire 3, Etterbeek. Traces Belgian history from 1789; displays of arms, uniforms, battle pictures; Waterloo section. Open 9 to 12, 1 to 4. Closed Mon. Admission free.

Musée Royale d'Art et d'Histoire (Royal Art and History Museum), Parc du Cinquantenaire 10, Etterbeek; built to commemorate the 75th anniversary of the founding of the kingdom. Antiquities from Egypt, Greece and Rome, China and South America. Open 9.30 to 12.30, 1.30 to 5; closed Mon. The same building contains a **Museum for the Blind.**

Musée Schott, rue du Chêne 27. Medieval sculpture, furniture and objets d'art. Open Tues., Thurs., 2 to 5, but double-check with the Tourist Office.

Musée Wiertz (Wiertz Studio), rue Vautier 62. Workplace of an unusual 19th-century painter; a kind of Edgar Allan Poe of paint. By appointment only. Check with the Tourist Office or call 648 1718.

Palais d'Egmont, pl. du Petit Sablon. Showplace site for international receptions. Varying, though limited, opening hours.

Palais de Justice (Law Courts), pl. Poelaert. The huge "Assyrio-Babylonian" structure which dominates the city skyline. Climb 500 steps to a dome larger than St. Peter's in Rome. Open 8.30 to 4. Closed Sat. and Sun.

Palais du Roi (Royal Palace), overlooking the Parc de Bruxelles, the King's state residence. Many of the rooms are open to the public, especially the throne room. Open from end-July to early-Sept., dates depend on the King's absence. Open 9 to 4 Aug. to Sept.

Pavillon Chinois (Chinese Pagoda) at Laeken in the outskirts of the city in the Palace Park. A collection of Chinese porcelain. Open weekdays (except Mon) 9.30 to 12.30, 1.30 to 5; Sat. and Sun., 1.30 to 3.30.

ENTERTAINMENT. Opera and ballet may be seen at the **T.R.M.** (Théâtre Royal de la Monnaie), pl. de la Monnaie (tel. 218 1202). Founded by Bombarda in 1659 and rebuilt in 1855 by Poelaert, it today maintains a full international repertory for most of the year. June is traditionally devoted to operetta, and the famous Ballet Béjart also dances there from time to time.

All theaters, except the **Flemish** (rue de Laeken 146, tel. 219 4944) play in French. The charming **Parc** has a good company presenting modern comedies and serious plays. The same applies to the **Théâtre Royal des Galeries,** Galerie du Roi 32 (tel. 512 0407) where top Paris companies quite frequently try out their plays before presenting them in the French capital. For other French classics, try **Molière,** sq. du Bastion 5 (tel. 513 5800).The **Théâtre National** is a troupe with a mission and has its home in the place Rogier skyscraper (tel. 217 0303). For more avant-garde theater, try the **Théâtre 140,** ave. Eugène Plasky 140 (tel. 734 4631). Tipping (about BF 20) is essential in all theaters.

Classical concerts are held in the two concert halls of the **Palais des Beaux Arts** by the Place Royale, home of the Belgian National Orchestra (tel. 512 5045). Other concerts can be attended at the **Conservatoire Royale de Musique,** rue de la Régence 30a (tel. 512 2369).

There is a famous marionette theater **de Toone** at rue Bouchers 21 (tel. 513 5486), where popular plays are performed with puppets. Most of the dialogue is in Brussels dialect, which is often incomprehensible to outsiders. Even so, this is a sight not to be missed.

Details of all theaters and cinemas can be found in the daily newspapers.

SHOPPING. The main shopping areas are blvd. Adolphe Max and rue Neuve, running from pl. Rogier as far as the Bourse, and, turning left uphill, the rue Marché-aux-Herbes; the rue Royale, sedate and rather select, continuing through pl. Royale, and uphill through the archway, along the rue de Namur; both sides of the boulevard between porte de Namur and porte Louise, and the first part of the wider section of ave. Louise. The latter are the best spots for fashionable shopping.

Rue Neuve, now a pedestrian precinct, has most of the large shops such as *Innovation, Marks and Spencer* and *C. & A.* The surrounding area is most attractive.

Among the shopping arcades are: the little *Passage du Nord* in the Metropole block and the more ambitious *Galeries Saint Hubert* which, besides its smart shops, shelters two theaters, a cinema and several cafés. Using the street levels of tall new buildings, there is the *Agora Gallery* near Grand'Place; the *Ravenstein Gallery* near the Central Station, adroitly using the differences of level; the ultra-smart *Galeries Louise,* almost opposite the Hilton; with a few hundred yards along the boulevard the *Galeries de la Toison d'Or.*

Up the ave. Louise, too, is the *Garden Stores,* an imaginative architectural venture, and the honeycomb of galleries in the Post Office Building (place de la Monnaie). The *Manhattan Center* is also another gallery in pl. Rogier. At the corner of place Rogier and rue Neuve is the new underground shopping center *City 2,* an attractive, plant-filled complex built on a number of different levels. These are linked by escalators, the deepest of which leads to the Metro. In addition to a variety of shops, City 2 contains banks, and some attractive restaurants.

Markets. These are a traditional part of Brussels life, and in addition to the fruit and vegetable markets found in most of the Communes there are many of interest to the tourist.

Grand'Place: daily flower market, bird market on Sunday mornings. Both the surroundings and the colorful stalls make this a must for anyone wanting to take home enviable snaps.

Place du Grand Sablon: antiques and books, Saturday 10–6, Sunday 10–1.

Place du Jeu de Balle: daily flea market, 8–4 in winter, 8–6 in summer.

Midi market, around the Gare du Midi: food, clothing, and people from all over the world. Bicycles are sold nearby in the Blvd. du Midi. Sunday morning.

Rue Ropsy—Chaudron, 1080 Brussels: pet market, Sunday morning, 10–1.

Place de la Duchesse, 1080 Brussels: horse market, Friday morning, 9–12.

 TEA SHOPS AND CAFES. Brussels' streets are lined with places of refreshment. "Tea Rooms" offer coffee, patisserie and ice-creams to a largely day-time clientele. Similar fare can be obtained in cafés, which offer the added inducement of beer, and a wider range of food. They also tend to stay open later. With their marble-topped tables and relaxed art-nouveau atmosphere they are fine places to while away a wet hour with a newspaper and a coffee, to snatch a quick sandwich lunch or to spin out an evening chatting with the locals.

In the *Tea-Room* category, try **le Candy,** rue de l'Enseignement 27 (tel. 218 5426); **Tony,** rue Malibran 22, near pl. Flagey in Ixelles (tel. 647 6424); or the **New Diplomat,** ave. Georges Henri 279 (tel. 762 8998). Alternatively try one of the major department stores cafes.

In the *café* category, you are quite simply spoilt for choice. In the city center, the best known are—**The Golden Boot** and the **Roy d'Espagne** on the Grand'-Place (the latter picturesquely decorated with inflated pigs' bladders and a lifesize stuffed horse). **Falstaff** on the rue Maus opposite the Bourse and next door to Mr. Stone's Fish and Chip Shop. **Café de l'Opera,** on the place Monnaie, just opposite the National Opera House; does a good line in smoked-salmon sandwiches and champagne after the theater when many restaurants are already closed. For more serious evening eating see the *Bistro* listings on p. 86.

 RESTAURANTS. Brussels has more than 400 restaurants offering all classes of real Belgian cuisine (with French undertones). Foreign restaurants are most popular; the city boasts 200 Italian and 175 oriental restaurants. US-style hamburger joints are popular too. (Brussels now has its own *McDonalds,* which also serves beer). You can eat in so many places and in so many styles in Brussels that our listing can only be representative; and remember that the fashionable restaurant of one month may be *démodé* in the next. Hotel restaurants are not included; for these, see our *Hotel* listings.

Brussels has an unusual system of grading its best restaurants. Instead of giving stars, for example, it awards irises—the iris being the flower of Brussels. Few hotel restaurants achieve such awards but two that have received 3 irises are those in the **Europa** and **Hilton.** The former for its *Beefeater,* and the latter for both the *Maison du Boeuf* and the rooftop *En Plein Ciel.*

A word of warning is necessary: do not expect quick service. Ingredients are plentiful and rich, the food is prepared to your order, and it can't come till it's cooked. Allow two hours for dinner and put all other thoughts aside.

Except for a very few deluxe establishments, even the best restaurants offer a fixed menu at a price substantially less than your bill is likely to come to if you order *à la carte*. This menu, however, does not cover wine or extras, although VAT and 16% service is included; so if you add wine, coffee, and so forth the price will be considerably augmented. At lunchtime you need not order a complete meal, but in the evening a full-course dinner is almost an obligation, but a pleasant one—the cooking is excellent, even at the bottom of the price-scale. Most high-class restaurants close on Sundays, so best telephone to check, and in any case, best reserve ahead.

A word about prices: you can eat modestly but well for about BF 350 a head at one of the impeccable department store restaurants, in pleasant surroundings. You will dine better for BF 1,500 in one of Brussels' gastronomic temples, and you may pay almost as much elsewhere for the pleasure (or discomfort) of sitting on a barrel or some other atmospheric gimmick. To find the place that suits you, consult the bill of fare that is usually exhibited at the restaurant's entrance or in one of its windows.

For an evening in quest of culinary adventure, go to the rue des Bouchers, a street of restaurants—mostly small—which climbs the hill between the Galerie du Roi and the Galerie de la Reine, just behind the Grand'Place. Every restaurant here has its own style and its own specialties.

Finally, a **warning:** as Brussels is now the capital of Europe, the city is full of expense-account people who don't mind paying huge bills. Accordingly, some restaurants have been inclined to raise their prices more than inflation would warrant, and it is also hard to get reservations in many instances. So book well ahead and be prepared to pay, pay and pay.

Expensive

Astrid, Chez Pierrot, rue de la Presse 21 (tel. 217 3831). Classic French cuisine. Exceptional fish dishes. In the heart of the ministerial quarter—the politicians' favorite spot.

Bernard, rue de Namur 93 (tel. 512 8821). Specializes in caviar, oysters, foie gras and other delicacies. Near the Porte de Namur.

Bruneau, ave. Broustin 73–75 (tel. 427 6978). This unusual restaurant is located near the wedding-cake Basilica in Koekelberg. The cuisine changes according to the food which is in season and the chef's ideas for the day.

Chez Christopher, pl. de la Chapelle 5 (tel. 512 6891). One of the Marolles' newer gastronomic temples, specializing in French cuisine with the accent on sea-food.

Comme Chez Soi, pl. Rouppe 23 (tel. 512 2921). Considered by many to serve the best seafood in town. If it's not Sunday or Monday visit Pierre Wynants and try his sole done in Riesling. Quite small so book in advance. Closed Sundays, Mondays and the whole of July.

Ecailler du Palais Royal, rue Bodenbroek 18 (Grand Sablon) (tel. 512 8751). A top specialist in shellfish. Try the crab consommé and the crêpes Normande—delicious pancakes with apple rings and caramelized sugar. Oysters and other seasonal tidbits are excellent. Small, so book ahead. Run by the same management as the *Villa Lorraine* out in Bois de la Cambre. Closed Sundays.

Filet de Boeuf, rue des Harengs 8 (tel. 511 9559). An intimate restaurant, just off the Grand'Place. As its name suggests, this is the place to come if you're tired of fish. Closed weekends.

Huîtière, quai aux Briques 20 (tel. 512 0866). Superb seafood restaurant, renowned for its lobster.

La Maison du Cygne, Grand'Place 9, entrance under archway (tel. 511 8244). This is one of Brussels' best, if not *the* best. Attractive decor in an old house; really splendid food. Try the *Waterzooi de Homard.* Piano in the evening. Closed Sun., Sat. midday and two weeks in Aug.

L'Oasis, pl. Marie-José 9 (tel. 648 4545). Worth the trip to the south side of the University campus—especially if the weather is good enough for the terrace. Don't miss the vine-leaves stuffed with wild salmon and *foie de canard.* Sadly, closed in Aug.

Parc Savoy, rue Emile Claus 3 (tel. 640 1522). Just off ave. Louise near the Bois de la Cambre. Excellent veal dishes.

Ravenstein, rue Ravenstein 1 (tel. 512 7768). A 16th-century nobleman's house—a rare survival in the city's business center. Delicious seafood specialties such as *Sole Albertine;* also saddle of rabbit with raspberries and onions.

La Tête d'Or, rue de la Tête d'Or 9 (tel. 511 0201). Traditional restaurant located in beautiful 17th-century building near the Grand'Place.

Trente rue de la Paille, rue de la Paille 30 (tel. 512 0715). This is *the* place to dine in the Sablon area. Classic French cuisine.

Moderate

L'Amadeus, rue Veydt 13, just off the ave. Louise (tel. 538 3427). Lively, good value wine-bar with excellent food.

Anmougar, rue de Rollebeek 21 (tel. 511 2437). One of the best North African restaurants in town, and the best in the Sablon area. Try the *tajine de poissons.*

L'Armagnac, chaussée de Waterloo 591 (tel. 345 9279). As its name suggests, this restaurant specializes in the cuisine of France's southwest. Don't miss the cassoulet.

Aux Armes de Bruxelles, rue des Bouchers 13 (tel. 511 5598). Traditional Brussels restaurant on street famous for its eating spots.

Le Canard Sauvage, chaussée de la Hulpe 194 (tel. 673 0975). Dinner and dancing in romantic candle-lit atmosphere. Apart from excellent duck, their scampi is highly recommended.

Cheval Blanc, rue Haute 204 (tel. 512 4016). The attractive interior of this Marolles favorite suggests France's *belle époque*—and the food is of a similar flamboyance. Booking is essential.

China Town, rue Jules van Praet 1, near the Bourse (tel. 511 3722). Highly recommended Chinese fare, frequented by cognoscenti and Chinese.

Les Deux Singes, rue Blaes 150 (tel. 511 5963). This is the "in" dining-place in the Marolles, with more than a hint of '50s "retro" elegance. The cuisine is post-nouvelle French.

L'Eléphant Bleu, chaussée de Waterloo 1120 (tel. 374 4962). Brussels' most exotic Thai restaurant. Well worth the trip to the south side of the city center.

Éperon d'Or, rue Éperonniers 8 (tel. 512 5239). French specialties, mostly sea-food.

Henri I, ave. de Messidor 181 (tel. 345 2629). Popular for its charcoal grills and varied cuisine. South of the ave. Molière in Uccle. Book well ahead.

Marie-Joseph, quai au Bois-à-Brûler 47 (tel. 218 0596). Another fine seafood restaurant, with a pronounced nautical ambience.

Ming's Garden, rue du Grand Cerf 11 (tel. 511 8412). Chinese cooking, two steps from the Hilton.

L'Ogenblik, rue des Dominicains 15 (tel. 511 6151). Contrives to give the impression of an everyday French brasserie; but the food is superb. On the corner of the Gallérie des Princes, slap in the historic center.

L'Orangeraie, ave. Winston Churchill 81 (tel. 345 7147). Set in an elegant mansion on Brussels' south side, this restaurant offers superb French cooking at moderate prices. Try their asparagus with mange-tout.

Samambaïa, rue Philippe Dewolfs 7 (tel. 672 8720). Fabulous Brazilian restaurant in Watermael-Boitsfort. Try the classic bean dish, feijoada.

Samourai, rue Fosse-aux-Loups 28 (tel. 217 5639). Most typically Japanese of Brussels' restaurants.

Sugito, blvd. Brand Whitlock 107 (tel. 733 5045). Indonesian fare. Excellent *rijsttafel.*

Taverne du Passage, Galeries de la Reine 30 (tel. 512 3731). Moderately priced Belgian cuisine in fashionable area. Try their *croquettes aux crevettes.*

Au Vieux Bruxelles, rue Saint-Boniface 35 (tel. 513 0181). Tucked away in a street running between the ch. de Warre and the ch. d'Ixelles, this is *the* place to come for that Belgian stalwart, mussels, and their ubiquitous companions, *les frites.* But remember that mussels are out of season in June and July.

Inexpensive

The fact that most of Brussels' cheaper restaurants tend to be ethnic doesn't imply that they are second-rate. Freed from the Belgian conventions of vast quantities of red meat or expensive fresh shell-fish, they offer exquisite food at affordable prices—probably better for your health too.

Le Corfou, rue Marché au Charbon 69 (tel. 512 4678). Open late at weekends; guaranteed to get you dancing. Excellent *meze.*

Le Docteur, rue Linné 32 (tel. 217 9549). Good, honest Italian food.

La Houblonniere, pl. de Loudres 4 (tel. 513 1483). Small, but typically Belgian. Watch out for the beer!

The King, blvd. General Jacques 149 (tel. 649 2537). This is a real low-budget address. Open through to midnight.

Kochavata, ave. du Parc 4 (tel. 537 4296). If you haven't tried Bulgarian food, start here.

La Maison d'Attila, ave. du Prince de Ligne 36–44 (tel. 375 3805). For a crazy evening's dining, you can't beat Brussels' one and only Mongolian barbecue. Children pay according to their age.

La Marée, rue de Flandre 99 (tel. 511 0040). This restaurant offers Belgian sea-food specialties at half the price of the others.

Mezza Luna II, chaussée de Charleroi 157 (tel. 537 6262). Italian food at reasonable prices.

Montana Feed & Fuel Co., chaussée de Waterloo 508 (tel. 344 9446). Open late for ribs, Tex-Mex dishes and other Americana.

Le Paradoxe, chaussée d'Ixelles 329 (tel. 649 8981). Good vegetarian food; unlike most of the others, open until 10 P.M.

La Quincaillerie, rue du Page 45 (tel. 538 2553). A turn-of-the-century hardware store turned over to purveying American favorites.

Rosticceria Fiorentina, rue Archimède 43 (tel. 734 9236). One of many keenly priced restaurants close to the Berlagmont Building.

Les Routiers Sympas, rue Picard 18 (tel. 428 6391). Like the truckers (after whom this restaurant is named) you'll have to head for the canal-side wharves; but it's worth it if your budget is tight. Closed weekends—but open from 5 A.M. weekdays.

Sahbaz, chaussée de Haecht 102 (tel. 217 0277). Turkish cooking at its best; low prices.

La Table d'Asie, rue Haute 187 (tel. 511 4435). Vietnamese cuisine in the heart of the Marolles.

Un Violon sur le Toit, place du Nouveau Marché aux Grains 35 (tel. 513 0900). Specializes in the Russian/Jewish food of *Fiddler on the Roof* fame; hence the name.

Outskirts of Brussels

Some of Brussels' finest—and most expensive—restaurants are to be found some way from the center of the city. Indeed, the two contestants for the ultimate accolade—the **Barbizon** and the **Villa Lorraine**—are both on the outskirts. You can sell your car and judge for yourself which is the best, or alternatively settle for some more modest treats in delightful surroundings.

BOENDAEL. Not far from Brussels University. *l'Auberge de Boendael* (E), square de Vieux-Tilleul 12 (tel. 672 7055). Converted farmhouse serving expensive *haute cuisine*. Smart without achieving elegance. *Doux Wazoo* (M), rue du Relais 21 (tel. 649 5852). Small, busy brasserie offering excellent value food.

BOIS DE LA CAMBRE. Large park just southeast of city. *Villa Lorraine* (E), chaussée de la Hulpe 28 (tel. 374 3163). Held by many to be the best in the country; patrician atmosphere, impeccable service, superb food—with prices to match.

FÔRET DE SOIGNES. Southeast. *Barbizon* (E), Welriekendedreef 95 (tel. 657 0462). Vies with the Villa Lorraine as the best in Brussels. On the cover of its menu it quotes *La Cuisine Francaise est une Princesse qui se fait attendre mais . . . qui ne peut attendre.* The Barbizon's seafood is especially good. Quite small—so be sure to book.

On the edge of the forest is another famous restaurant, the *Romeyer Maison de Bouche* (E), Groenendaelse-steenweg 109 (tel. 657 0581). Many claim that the most celebrated chef in Belgium works here. A lovely spot with the atmosphere of a luxurious hunting lodge, and a fine garden. Closed Sunday evening, all day Monday and all of February.

WEMMEL. Just off the main road to Antwerp. *De Kam* (E), Steenweg op Brussel 7 (tel. 460 0365). An authentic 17th-century inn, with dining in the garden in summer.

WOLUWE ST.-LAMBERT. 4 miles east of center. *Moulin de Lindekemale* (E), ave. J.F. Debecker 6 (tel. 770 9057). An ancient converted water mill.

 NIGHTLIFE. Brussels nightlife is growing in sophistication, and its level has risen markedly in recent years. In the floorshow clubs you must expect to be asked over BF 1,500 for a bottle of champagne, and find it compulsory at floor-side tables, while lesser wines, at about half the price, are served at the others; in most cases, too, you can dally at the bar and see the show for far less cost in drinks. In many cases the establishments are indeed clubs, but membership can be arranged at the door and costs little.

For a floor show one of the best known night clubs is **Show Point,** place Stephanie, 14, (tel. 511 5364). **Moulin Rouge,** blvd. du Jardin Botanique 9, (tel. 219 5261), has a show with an oriental atmosphere **Au Gaity,** rue Fossé-aux-Loups 19, has a good nude cabaret; and **Le Jonathan,** rue Wilmotte 10, has a show catering to unaccompanied men.

Male gays should try **La Cage,** rue des Bouchers 71; and for female gays there's **Madam,** Galerie du Roi 25. These are both bars.

For dancing/disco the choice is wide, including **Crocodile Club,** Royal Windsor Hotel, rue Duquesnoy, 6; **Golden Gate,** Galerie Louise, 98; **L'Equipe,** rue de Livourne, 40; **Mirano,** chaussée de Louvain, 38; **Take Off,** rue Vilain XIIII, 55 (weekends only). There's also a wide variety of nightspots on the avenue Louise and just south of the Gare du Nord.

For great jazz, try the **Brussels Jazz Club,** Grand'Place 13. **Café Henry,** blvd. de Waterloo 8, and **Chez Lagaffe,** rue de l'Epée, are also good.

A word of warning. Brussels is now full of lonely, highly-paid executives, so expensive hostess bars abound, especially around the avenue Louise and south of the Gare du Nord. These are usually just costly clip joints. The latter region especially can be dangerous.

BOTTLE CLUBS AND PICTURESQUE BISTROS. Since hard liquor cannot be sold in cafés, there is a thriving branch of the catering industry that calls itself the *club privé.* As soon as you comply with the statutes by becoming a member for a nominal fee, you are entitled to your well-earned drink.

Ballon Nord, rue de Brabant 24, is the place for bar billiards enthusiasts. **Bierodrome,** place Ferdinand Cocq, 21, is also a jazz club. Those who like a gypsy atmosphere should try **Le Hischier,** pl. du Grand Sablon 42, and **Le Fleur en Papier Doré,** rue des Alexiens 53, is a 'temple of surrealism.'

Au Bon Vieux Temps, impasse St. Nicolas 4, just off the rue Marché-aux-Herbes, will give you a good idea of Brussels in a bygone era. Another typical 19th-century Brussels bistro is **A la Mort Subite,** rue Montaigne-aux-Herbes-Potageres, not far from the Grand'Place. Don't miss the excellent beers: Kriek, Geuze and Favo. Also try **Vieux Spijtigen Duivel,** chaussée d'Alsemberg 621, at Uccle, and **Moeder Lambic,** chaussée de Waterloo 786, now enlarged as a restaurant (in the Orangery). All their beers, Geuze, Faro, Orval, Lambic should be drunk with caution—they're strong. If you want to discover the latest secrets of the European Commission, go to **The Corkscrew,** ave. d'Auderghem 17, the best English wine-bar in Brussels.

British-style pubs are growing popular, serving English beer and also Irish Guinness, the latter direct from Dublin, and of excellent quality.

MAIL AND TELEGRAPH. The General Post Office, pl. de la Monnaie (facing Opera House), is open weekdays 9 to 5; for express and airmail, 9 to 8. An office is open at ave. Fonsny 48 (Midi Station) 24 hours a day. Stamps and postcards may be purchased, and correspondence mailed, at the Banque de Bruxelles, rue de la Régence 2; you may also send cables from their private telegraph office. There is a general telegraph and telephone service in the building next to the Sabena Air Terminal at Putterie 20, near Central Station.

USEFUL ADDRESSES. Embassies and Consulates. American, blvd. du Régent 27; Australian, ave. des Arts 52; British, rue Joseph II 28; Canadian, rue de Loxum 6; Irish, rue du Luxembourg 19.

Tourist Office. Brussels Tourist Information (TIB) is at rue Marché-aux-Herbes/Grasmarkt 61 (near the Grand'Place), tel. (02) 513 89 40. The office is open every day from 9 to 6 (to 8 in summer, weekends 7). Alternate phone number—(02) 512 30 30.

Tour Offices. American Express, place Louise 2 (tel. (02) 512 17 40); Wagons-Lits Tours, blvd. Adolphe Max 52 (tel. (02) 217 62 40).

Emergencies. Police tel. 900; Ambulance, Red Cross (Croix Rouge) tel. 447 010.

ENVIRONS OF BRUSSELS

History and Rural Calm

Brussels is ideally situated in the midst of the attractive Brabant countryside. Sites of historic interest, large woods, and peaceful rural retreats are all within easy reach. It is also an easy city to get out of—many places of interest are signposted from the *petite ceinture* (inner ring of boulevards), and Belgian railways operate buses and fast electric trains which leave the principal stations at regular intervals.

A spot not to be missed is the Hoeilaart-Overijse. You can reach Hoeilaart by train from the Gare Quartier Leopold, or you can catch a bus to Boitsfort (site of the racecourse) and take a three-mile walk through the Forêt de Soignes. This will bring you into the fantastic capital of the glasshouse industry, which has 30,000 hothouses, and boasts that it can produce you a bunch of grapes fit for the table on each day of the year. There is a "Grape Fair" every year in August at Overijse, end-September at Hoeilaart. And it's all just 13 km. (8 miles) south of Brussels.

On the Charleroi Road

A delightful drive 8 km. (5 miles) or so to the southeast will take you into the Bois de la Cambre, on the edge of the Forêt de Soignes. This is the Bois de Boulogne of Brussels, studded with super-smart restaurants and modest inns. Or buy some charcuterie and a bottle of wine and picnic beneath the centuries-old trees.

19 km. (12 miles) to the south lies the Battlefield of Waterloo, reached by the local "W" bus. Most tourists content themselves with climbing the lion memorial, which almost obliterates the battlefield. Nearby, a panorama gives you an overall picture of the battle, but you may grasp more of the tactics from the cinema reconstruction (opposite). To get a real knowledge of the battle, study the excellent phase-maps in Wellington's Headquarters in Waterloo, now a museum. Hougoumont farm is still privately owned, but you can visit the tiny mutilated chapel which housed the British wounded. Inside its simple, whitewashed interior, you can still see the wooden statue of Christ against which the flames miraculously died when the French tried to set it on fire. Another farm, Le Caillou, has been transformed into an interesting museum. It is said that Napoleon spent a restless night here before the battle.

In 1973 preservationists won a new battle at Waterloo. A motorway was to have passed a mere 5 m. (15 feet) from Mont St. Jean farm which was also used as a field hospital for British wounded during the battle. It is now some 15 m. (45 feet) distant.

21 km. (13 miles) to the southeast, between Waterloo and Wavre, you come to Genval. Here there is a charming lake, with a dozen lakeside restaurants, though it can be crowded on Sundays.

Villers-la-Ville is 40 km. (25 miles) southeast of Brussels, and is best reached by road through Waterloo and Genappe. By train it is 20 minutes from Ottignies. The interest here lies in the quite astonishing remains of a 12th-century Cistercian abbey. Worth seeing, too, are a restored 10th-century church and a castle. 8 km. (5 miles) away, at Gentinnes, is the memorial shrine to the missionary martyrs of the Congo, erected in 1967. It draws 50,000 pilgrims and visitors each year.

On the Ghent Road

At Groot Bijgaarden, 8 km. (5 miles) out of town on the Ghent motorway, is Grand-Bigard Castle, which dates back to the Frankish period, although its recorded history begins with Almeric de Bigard in 1100 and ends with its sack in the French Revolution. Its remains span several centuries. The manor house itself, with its long rows of windows and dormers is a good example of Brabantian 17th-century architecture, reminiscent of the French Louis XIII style. The gateway with its twin towers and the moat covered with water lilies have a romantic air, and the interior decoration of the château in general is remarkably well preserved.

You will pass through Asse as the first major town on the old road from Brussels to Ghent, which runs parallel to the Brussels-Oostende highway. The town lies on an ancient Roman site and as recently as 1829 was the starting point for as many as 35 stage coaches per day. The church, which has a tower dating from the 13th century, contains one or two fairly important paintings, including those by Otto Venius and the younger Brueghel.

A little farther on is Hekelgem, where several of the cafés proclaim *Zandtapijten* (sand carpets). These are well worth stopping to see. You pass into the back parlor of one of the cafes, where you may find an artist busy preparing a picture with saucers of colored sand. This is a local folk art, and some time ago its foremost practitioner, Roger de Boeck, was invited to Florida to teach the technique. Unfortunately the motorway has resulted in so much traffic, with visitors bypassing Hekelgem, that it has lost some of its character as the center of this art.

Along the Mons Road

Only 9 km. (6 miles) south of the capital is Beersel. This beautiful 13th-century castle is surrounded by water-filled moats and is worth a visit in itself. During the summer, Shakespeare plays and outdoor folk-dramas are staged there. Nearby is the attractive domain of Huizingen, where you can indulge in various sports. There is also a restaurant.

Gaasbeek lies off the road to Mons, 13 km. (8 miles) out. Turn right while in the suburb of Anderlecht, or farther on where signposted. A castle of real historic and artistic interest, dating back many centuries, it has all the trappings of medieval gracious living: superb carved furniture, tapestries, and paintings. The rooms are so well arranged that you have the feeling people still live there. A copper-gilt icon, a gift from the Grand Duchess Marie of Russia, hangs in Count Jean Arrivabene's bedroom. In the richly-paneled large gallery a 15th-century silver reliquary head of Isabella of Castille and some repoussé and engraved silver-gilt salvers and ewers are among the numerous *objets d'art.* Before each guided tour there is an eight minute introductory talk in 4 different languages with projection of color slides. If some of the landscapes look familiar, it's because Brueghel painted many scenes from here.

Halle (Hal) lies 16 km. (10 miles) to the southwest and on the Mons road. This curious town is devoted to the cult of the Virgin Mary, and there are processions of great devotion at Whitsun and early in September. The church, though nominally dedicated to St. Martin, is known as the Church of our Lady because of the miracle-working Black Virgin Statue, which, according to the legend, played an active part in the defense of the town against the siege by Philip of Cleves. The church itself is especially interesting. Not only is it a comparatively unspoilt example of 14th-century architecture, it contains a number of important 13th- to 15th-century sculptures. The best examples are those from the school of Claus Sluter, the leading sculptor in Northern Europe at the end of the 14th century and whose work in many ways anticipated later Italian Renaissance developments. He was to gain considerable fame as court sculptor to Philip the Bold, Duke of Burgundy. The font is a specially good example of Tournai (as opposed to Meuse-side) brassware, dated 1446, by Lefebvre; and the high altar is the only signed and recorded work of Jan Mone (1533), one of the few major works in Belgium to have caught the spirit of the Renaissance.

Halle was the birthplace of Adrien Servais, the master violin-cellist, and at his house here the guests included Liszt, Berlioz, Anton Rubinstein, and even La Malibran, one of the greatest operatic prima donnas of the last century.

Taking a southeastward byroad from Halle, you come to the little township of Braine-le-Château nestling in a hollow of the rolling country. This is the domain of the counts of Hornes, whose moated manor is here. The chief object of interest is the rather original pillory, set up by the ruling count in 1521. It is of unconventional design, consisting of a small caged platform mounted on a pillar, the cage being beautifully ornamented for a pillar of penance. Here, too, in a water mill seven centuries old, is an interesting Mill Museum (Musée de la Meunerie).

From Nivelles to Tienen

The same byroad brings you down to Nivelles, on the main road from Brussels to Thuin. The damage done to this town during World War II was a major tragedy. It included a fire that melted down all but a small part of the famous reliquary of St. Gertrude. Still more, it destroyed hundreds of ancient dwellings, the Hôtel de Ville and, with it, the four town giants: Argayon, Argayone, Lola, and their horse Godet. These eminent citizens were, in their lifetime, privileged to follow the wholly devout procession of "Madame Sainte Gertrude," whose remains were annually taken from the reliquary and led on a 13-km. (8-mile) pilgrimage across fields and meadows. St. Gertrude was a daughter of Pepin de Landen, great-grandfather of Charlemagne. She was born in Nivelles, and here she founded her abbey, so richly endowing it that it became one of the greatest and most powerful in Christendom. The canonesses were carefully chosen as being "of good lineage and nation," a family tree of four quarterings on both the spear and distaff side being draconically demanded. These "white-surpliced young ladies" seem to have led a life of some luxury. The convent routine permitted them to make regular visits to their homes, even when these were in foreign countries. On the tombstone of one of these ladies, who died in 1558, in her 28th year as provost of the college, it was inscribed that "she lived decently and died virtuously; in paradise God owes her room and a seat." (The stone itself was destroyed in 1940.)

The glory which had lasted a full thousand years had already departed from Nivelles before the destruction of 1940. Bombs destroyed much that was interesting and exciting in the town, but they left the lovely Romanesque cloister and much of the fabric and furnishings of the church. You can still admire the pulpits by Laurent Delvaux, a Nivelles man who together with his pupil, Philippe Lelievre, achieved great renown in the local woodworking revival of the 18th century.

The town has contributed much to the history of the arts. Jehan le Nivellois was the 12th-century troubadour and composer of the *Vengeance of Alexander;* Gerard de Nivelles painted at Dijon for Philip the Brave, first of the Dukes of Burgundy; Jan Tinctoris, one of the first systematic explorers of counterpoint, and master-musician to the king of Naples in 1480, was a Nivelles man; and in the late 13th century, it was a Nivelles silversmith who worked with others from Douai and

Anchin to break away from the Meuse-side tradition in the design of St. Gertrude's reliquary.

Work is under way to restore the remains of Merovingian and Carolingian churches discovered after the town's bombing.

You reach Wavre from Nivelles through Genappe and Court-St.-Etienne with its 17th-century treasures. The main cultural sight here is the *Madonna of Peace and Concord* in the church at Basse-Wavre. However, there is also one of the best and most popular amusement parks in the country here. It's called Walibi, and is open from April to September. Besides all kinds of spectacular rides there are performing dolphins.

The road to Jodoigne leaves to the north Hamme-Mille, site of the ancient Valduc Castle, where only a farm and a mill now remain. At Jodoigne you are in a hamlet of special interest to Welshmen because of the sojourn there of the Welsh Guards during World War II, an event which is commemorated by a tablet on the outer wall of the Hôtel de Ville under the shadow of the mighty lime that commemorates Belgium's independence. The main point of interest in Jodoigne is the reliquary in the 12th-century Church of the Knights Templar, said to contain the jawbone of St. Médard. This saint occupies a position in Belgium similar to that of Saint Swithin in England—if it rains on his day (June 8) it will rain on the next 40 days as well. This belief leads to devout agricultural-religious observances on the eve of the Saint's day.

Tienen (Tirlemont) which you reach from Jodoigne through Hoegaarden, with its rival churches and its white beer, is another once-famous spot. It was a tourist town when it was a stage on the Roman road that through the Middle Ages linked Cologne and Maastricht with the sea at the fabulously prosperous city of Bruges. It is known as the "White City," to commemorate the limewashing which was one of the precautions taken during a cholera plague that once swept the area. The old glory of Tienen has given place to another, for it is now the capital of the sugar industry, as sugar beet has been grown on a large scale in Belgium since the continental blockade of the Napoleonic Wars. The Church of Our Lady of the Lake is more interesting outside than in, especially for the sculptured portal by Jean d'Oisy (1360).

Hakendover is 5 km. (3 miles) from Tienen on the road to Sint Truiden. It has a curious legend of three Frankish virgins who hired 12 workmen to build the church and duly meted out 12 pay-packets, only to find there were 13 workers on the job. The site of the church had been miraculously revealed to them on the 13th night after Epiphany; and on this night there is nowadays the procession that honors the 13th worker, a procession that gets under way with prayers in the winter midnight and does not end till the hour appointed for the first Mass. The legend is fully illustrated in a remarkable carved reredos dating from 1430. The town has another procession, of a less religious kind, on Easter Monday. The participants come on horseback, and the cortège proceeds over the fields around the town. According to local legend, the field that is most trampled is the one which will yield most abundantly at the coming harvest.

The Art City of Zoutleeuw

From Hakendover it is worth going a little further on the Sint Truiden road before turning north to Zoutleeuw (or Léau), which lies near the farthest eastern boundary of Brabant province. This is another town that is no longer what it was, for in the 13th century it had a direct water route to Antwerp, which it supplied with cloth as a part of the early competition against the Flemish cloth carried overseas from Bruges.

Zoutleeuw has a Stadhuis carrying the arms of the empire. It is the work of no less an architect than Rombaut Keldermans. The town's greatest treasures, however, are in the Church of St. Leonard which dates from the 13th century and is altogether out of proportion to the township's present population. All the more fashionable artists seem to have been commissioned, when the town was at its prime, to contribute to the decoration. Cornelis Floris made the 50-foot stone tabernacle in which the Gothic seems to be fading into the Italian style; Cornelis' brother Frans painted the *Coronation of Christ* triptych; and Matthew de Layens created one of the more intricately ornamental altarpieces. The great treasure, however, is the tall Pascal candlestick, by Renier de Tirlemont (1483), surmounted with its Crucifix, around which are statues of the Madonna, Mary Magdalene and St. John, and below which sprout the six branches of the candlestick supported by a wrought column on which there is an effigy of St. Leonard. This is one of the finest pieces of brassware in Belgium. It came from Brussels, where Renier was installed at the time, as did the gilded-wood reredos of St. Leonard. This was executed some five years earlier by Arnould to enshrine the painted and jeweled statue of the saint, which dates from about 1300.

Zoutleeuw shows little sign of eminent foreign residents or visitors, but it was one of the seven free towns of the Duchy of Brabant, and it has a 16th-century Renaissance Town Hall and a 14th-century Cloth Hall, now occupied by the local police.

On the Leuven Road

One of two roads from Brussels to Leuven (Louvain) continues through Tervuren. Follow route N3 to Tervuren, or take a No. 44 tram. The Central Africa Museum, favorite brain-child of King Léopold II in the days of colonialism, and today an active research center on African problems, is well worth visiting. There is a good swimming pool (Beausoleil). You should also visit the Bois des Capucins, a vast and beautifully-kept park, and admire the collection of tree species known as the Arboretum, covering 250 acres. The Ravenstein Golf Club is in the vicinity—not more than a 30-minute ride from Brussels —exclusive and expensive.

PRACTICAL INFORMATION FOR
ENVIRONS OF BRUSSELS

HOTELS AND RESTAURANTS. Most probably you will set up headquarters in Brussels and make an excursion or two into the Brabant countryside. If you want to put up at an hotel in the quiet green belt surrounding the capital, here are some addresses in attractive spots. There are too many restaurants and inns in the immediate vicinity of Brussels to be included in this list; we shall quote only a few selected ones. You can't go far wrong by having a meal at the others—the standards are very high.

BEERSEL. About 8 miles south of city center; famous feudal castle. *Centrum* (M), Steenweg op Ukkel 11 (tel. 376 2615). 20 rooms, 6 with bath or shower. Good restaurant offering Belgian dishes.
    Restaurant. *Saint Lô* (M), Schoolstraat 1 (tel. 376 9933). Pleasant, recently opened, small restaurant in the heart of town. Closed Tues. evening and Wed.

ESSENE. 11 miles northwest of city on route for Ghent and Oostende. *Bellemolen* (E), Statiestraat 9–11 (tel. 053–666 238). A converted 12th-century mill. Has 6 rooms with bath and an excellent restaurant.
    Restaurant. *Hostellerie Heembos* (M), Brusselbaan 420 (tel. 452 5419). Excellent French cuisine in elegant surroundings.

GENVAL. 15 miles outside city by charming lake. *Château du Lac* (L), ave. du Lac 87 (tel. 654 1122). If you're looking for a luxurious spot outside the Brussels conurbation, this is it. 38 top-class rooms and suites; marble everywhere. Gourmet restaurant.
    Restaurant. *Jardin du Lac,* (E) Zilverbeekdreef 2 (tel. 653 4404). Excellent sea-food; on northern side of lake.

GROOT BIJGAARDEN. Restaurant. *De Bijgaarden* (E), Van Beverenstraat 20 (tel. 466 4485). Sophisticated hostelry serving traditional cuisine of the highest order. Famous for its seafood.

HALLE. Restaurant. *Les Eleveurs* (M), Basiliekstraat 136 (tel. 356 5309). Classic cuisine. Also has 13 rooms. Across canal from station.

HOEILAART. In the Soignes Forest southeast of city. **Restaurant.** *Fol Atre* (M), Gemeenteplein 24 (tel. 657 1363). Deservedly popular, for its fine value; be sure to book.

HUIZINGEN. Just outside Beersel. **Restaurant.** *Terborght* (E), Oud Dorp 16 (tel. 380 1010). Candlelit dinner in rustic 17th-century surroundings. Off the Brussels–Paris highway.

NIVELLES. Historic city, full of good eating spots.
    Restaurants. *De La Collégiale* (M), ave. Leon Jeuniaux 2, (tel. 222 843). Noted for first class cuisine, pleasantly individual; by the park. *l'Haubergeon*

(M), rue des Brasseurs 14 (tel. 067–22 2914). Turn of the century furnishings; good bistro food. *Pascal* (M), Grand'Place 3, prepares excellent grouse in wine sauce (in season).

TIENEN (TIRLEMONT). 30 miles from Brussels. In the station square is *Nouveau Monde* (M), Vierde Lancierslaan 75, (tel. 016 81 4321). 11 rooms, all with bath; its restaurant is far and away the best in town. Try their woodcock in season. *Alpha* (I), Leuvenstraat 95 (tel. 816 640). 17 rooms with bath.

Restaurant. *Al Parma 2000* (I), Grote Markt 41 (tel. 061–81 8655). Jovial Italian restaurant, open late.

WATERLOO. Site of the famous battle, 10 miles south of Brussels. Best hotel is about 4 miles north of the battlefield: *Auberge de Waterloo,* (E) chaussée de Waterloo 212 (tel. 358 5963). 76 rooms, almost all with bath. Good Italian restaurant. **Restaurants.** Two miles northeast of the village on the N17, *Maison du Seigneur* (E), chaussée Tervuren 389 (tel. 354 0750). Serves *haute cuisine* in the rural atmosphere of a 17th century farmhouse. *Clos Joli* (I), chaussée Tervuren 155 (tel. 354 7781). In the village, with a good set menu. Close by the lion monument, try *le Bivouac de l'Empereur* (M), route du Lion 315 (tel. 384 6740). Attractive 1720s farmhouse, serving authentic Belgian food.

WAVRE. *Macas* (M), pl. A. Bosch 33 (tel. 010–22 8383). 20 rooms, all with bath or shower. No restaurant.

Restaurant. *Le Grand Duc* (M), rue Fontaines 60 (tel. 010–227517). Classic cuisine.

ZOUTLEEUW. Restaurant. *Pannenhuis* (I), Grote Markt 25 (tel. (011) 789 485). Pleasant unpretentious spot, handy for St. Leonard's Church.

CAMPING. Rising land prices have made camp sites more expensive, and rarer. Closest to Brussels is **Huizingen** (Beersel) in the Provinciaal Domein, 6 miles southwest of the city. Open mid-Mar. to end-Sept. (tel. 02–380 1493). 6 miles north is the camp-site at **Grimbergen,** open Apr. to end-Oct.; tel. 02–269 7628. **Neerijse** (12 miles east) has two or three good sites.

MUSEUMS AND PLACES OF INTEREST. Naturally, the attention of most Anglo-Saxon visitors will be drawn to the battlefield of Waterloo. It is very easily reached from Brussels, being only 23 km. (14 miles) away, and public transport, route W, or the many coach tour firms will take you there.

BEERSEL. Early 14th-century **Château** (16 km., 10 miles) to the south of Brussels. Open daily 10 to 12, 2 to 6, Mar. to mid-Nov. Rest of the year Sat., Sun., and holidays only. The route through the castle is clearly marked.

GAASBEEK. The **Château,** former home of the Counts of Egmont, is magnificently furnished, with some especially notable tapestries. 12 km. (7½ miles) southwest of Brussels. Open April to Oct., 10 to 5, closed Mon. and Fri.

GROOT BIJGAARDEN. Grand Bigard Castle (5 miles west). Site of ancient castle with 17th-century Brabantian manor house, fully restored in the 19th century. Open 10 to 5, summer only.

HALLE. Basiliek. Superb 14th-century church with many fine relics. Avoid morning visit, when there are religious services. Also, **Musée de la Meunerie** (Mill Museum) at nearby Braine-le-Château; open 10 to 12, 2 to 5.

NIVELLES. 34 km. (21 miles) from Brussels. **Collégiale Ste. Gertrude** (Church of St. Gertrude). The heart of the city, notable for its architecture, excavations and treasures. Open 10 to 12 (except festal days) and 2 to 5; closed Tues.

Musée d'Archéologie, a great grab bag of fascinating material—from prehistoric, Merovingian, 18th century times, and most between. Open daily 9.30 to 12.30, 2.30 to 5; closed Tues.

TERVUREN. Koninklijk Museum voor Midden-Afrika (Royal Museum of Central Africa). One of the major memorials to Belgian colonialism. A must for anyone interested in the art and topography of the Congo, etc. Set in lovely park. 13 km. (8 miles) southeast of Brussels. Open 9 to 5.30; winter, 10 to 4.30.

VILLERS-LA-VILLE. Cistercian Abbey. 12th-century ruins of abbey founded by St. Bernard, with 13th-century well opposite. Floodlighting Sat. and Sun. in summer. Open 9 to 6 (winter, Sun. only, 9 to 4).

WATERLOO (see note at head of this section). The **Wellington Museum,** open 10 to 12 and 2 to 7, except Mon.; in winter, 4 to 6 only; **Battle Panorama,** near Lion Monument, open all year, 9.30 to 12, 1.30 to 4.30; **Musée du Caillou** (Napoleon's headquarters), on the Charleroi road, houses relics of historic interest; open 9 to 7 in summer, closes at 5 in winter and Tuesdays.

ZOUTLEEUW (Léau). **Sint-Leonarduskerk.** Fine 13th-century church with many marvelous relics, including one of the best examples of brassware in Belgium. Open 9.30 to 12, 1.30 to 6 (to 5 Sun., 4 in winter).

CATHOLIC BASTIONS

Mechelen and Leuven

Two Flemish towns, though neither of them is in Flanders proper, are the center of Belgium's Catholic faith today. Mechelen (Malines to the French, Malinas to the Spaniards and Mecklin to our ancestors) lies in the province of Antwerp; while Leuven (Louvain) is in Brabant. The people of both towns speak Dutch, although French still has a place in the metropolitan archepiscopal see at Mechelen.

On maps both Mechelen and Leuven have the look of fortresses, with their encircling boulevards that mark the line of ancient fortifications. Leuven, indeed, has a military record of which to be proud. In 1925 it was decorated with the French *Croix de Guerre* at the hands of no less a hero than Marshal Foch and in the presence of Cardinal Mercier, the Cardinal-Archbishop of Mechelen, whose courageous attitude during World War I put to shame many self-conscious patriots.

Leuven was the domain of the dukes of Brabant. It grew around the fortress built by Arnold of Carinthia against the Normans, and it was in the 12th century that the Count of Louvain, Henry II, incorporated Brussels into his realm and took the title of Duke of Brabant. The town had the worst of the bargain after Duke Wenceslas' reprisals against the communal uprising led by Pieter Coutereel in the 14th century, when the nobles hid in the Stadhuis and the populace threw them out upon the pikes of the mob below. Weavers (the town had a good

96

business in the cloth trade) emigrated to England. Leuven sank in importance till the 15th century, when it was revived by the founding of the Catholic University, which is its chief glory today. This union of the Flemish element and the Catholic element is politically of the highest importance, and Leuven is now the nursery of much of the political and economic thought which governs the destiny of a country deeply Catholic at every level and predominantly Flemish.

Mechelen has two great names in its history. Besides Cardinal Mercier, there was Margaret of Austria, and her court, four centuries earlier. It was at Mechelen that this remarkable princess, as regent for her nephew (later to rule as Charles V), held her devout and cultured court. At 26 she was already twice a widow; having decided not to make a third attempt—after all, both she and her brother had been deprived of the throne of the newly united Spain, he by his own premature death and she by the death of her spouse—she was able to devote the whole of her thought and energies to the affairs of the Low Countries. It was she who persuaded her father, Emperor Maximilian, into alliance with the Holy League against Louis XII, and, having done so, saw that his forces and those of Henry VIII of England kept the Low Countries in a safe neutrality, and even added to them the city of Tournai. Erasmus and Sir Thomas More visited her court, Michiel Coxie and the prolific Van Orley were among the painters who counted her as a patron; and her architect was Rombout Keldermans, whose partnership with the younger De Waghemaker was to be so fruitful for Antwerp, Ghent and Tongerlo.

Discovering Mechelen

Mechelen was known to Margaret as the seat of the Grand Council, or Supreme Court of Justice, under the system created by her grandfather, Charles the Bold. The town itself, lying on the banks of the River Dijle, had been an appanage of the prince-bishops of Liège and a bargaining-counter between the prince-bishops and the Berthout, the *sept* (7) in control of the free town lying on the left bank of the river. For a time Mechelen came under the See of Cambrai, and it was not until 1559 that it became an archbishopric.

You can look down from the heights of St. Rombout's tower over the white palace of the cardinal-archbishops and the dignified line of its trees in the refreshing green of its garden. Chiefly, however, you will have climbed the tower to see the bells and the manual of the *carillonneurs,* who carry on here the great tradition of Jef Denijn. It was in the last two decades of the 19th century that Denijn became conscious of the decline in the bellringer's craft in the towers of Belgium, and set to work to create a musical idiom for this great art, to revive the craft and mystery of the *carillonneur*—in short, to put belfries, and Belgian belfries most of all, firmly on the map. Denijn's life as a refugee during World War I gave him the chance to reawaken interest in bells and in bell-founding in other countries (notably at Loughborough and Croydon in England) and now there are carillons as far afield as Florida (Edward Bok's Singing Tower), New York (Riverside Church), Philadelphia, and Wellington (N.Z.) that owe much to his inspiration. Staf

Nees worthily carried on the school (the only one in the world) founded by Denijn at the corner of Sint Janstraat and Mérodestraat; you will often find in the tower that the player is one of the school's younger pupils, who has been through the arduous apprenticeship of the dummy keyboard.

The ancient art of tapestry-making has pride of place among the surviving home-crafts in Mechelen. With improved methods and designs adapted to contemporary tastes, some firms not only weathered modern times, but made this art, allied to interior decoration, a paying proposition. The magnificent tapestry offered by Belgium to the United Nations Building in New York was designed and executed in Mechelen.

Saint Rombout's Cathedral

Half a millennium has passed since the raising of St. Rombout's tower, the work of Wauthier Coolmans in the 15th century. The original plans from which this structure was built are still in existence, so we know today, in spite of the lapse of five hundred years, how magnificent the tower would have been if it had risen to its full height. Even as it stands, it is a fine example of late Gothic design. Parts of the cathedral church itself are in fact much older, dating back to the early 13th century. The building contains the armorial bearings of members of a Chapter of the Golden Fleece who met here in 1491, and also a Van Dyck *Crucifixion*.

The high altar is the work of Luc Fayd' Herbe in the 17th century, who was responsible for a good deal of work in his native town. He was a disciple of Rubens, and even if the Church of Onze Lieve Vrouw van Hanswijk is not an architectural masterpiece, there are highly original elements in its construction. The big high-reliefs inside the dome are also by Fayd' Herbe and with his work in the Church of the Groot Begijnhof (Beguinage) are unique in Belgian decorative art. Onze Lieve Vrouw van Hanswijk also contains a fine pulpit by another Mechelen craftsman, Theodore Verhaegen. The confessionals by Boeckstuyns date from half a century earlier.

The Begijnhof itself, with its curious array of gables and turrets, is an interesting piece of 17th-century building. From here, passing the Church of St. Katelijne, you come to the museum of the archbishopric, which is worth visiting if only for the sake of the souvenirs of Cardinal Mercier. The building itself is the former refuge of Tongerlo Abbey. It is not the only one of these abbatial refuge houses; that of the Abbey of Sint Truiden, lying as it does beside the Dijle, is one of the most charming sights in the town.

The Church of St. John (St. Janskerk—closed between Easter and mid-September, call for doorman, from 2 to 4, at Mérodestraat 57) contains on the high altar a triptych, an important work by Rubens, the *Adoration of the Magi*, and also some carving by Theodore Verhaegen. Mechelen has two other Rubens paintings, the more important of which is the *Miraculous Draft of Fishes*, in Onze Lieve Vrouw van Overdijl. The other is a *Crucifixion*, which you will find in the Busleyden Mansion (1503), now given over to the Communal Museum. This is a very absorbing small museum, and well worth an hour or two.

The first courthouse of Charles the Bold's Grand Council was in the House of the Aldermen (Schepenhuis), separating the Grote Markt from the Square of the Iron Railings (IJzerenleen), beyond which, and past the houses reconstructed following the 1914–18 bombardments, you come to the 16th-century Fish Market building; thence to the Haverwerf across the Dijle, where three colorful houses of the same period are worth special attention. They are, in the usual way, named after the main features of their decoration. The corner building, known as Paradise because of the bas-reliefs of Adam and Eve, is specially characterized by the fine moldings in curve-patterns of a geometrical complexity *(anses de panier)*, which was used in Mechelen in the late Gothic period but is not much found elsewhere in Flanders.

Go along the Haverwerf, and to the left you will find the house of Beethoven's grandparents in the small street bearing this famous name.

Following the Dijle back over the Guldenstraat, you come to the Zoutwerf, with an interesting guild-house, De Zalm. Inside is a small museum. Further on, cross a bridge to the Botanical Garden, with its modern statue of the 16th-century botanist Dodoens, who was from Mechelen. On the farther side of the gardens you come, suitably enough, to the great present-day vegetable market. It is a forcible reminder that Mechelen is in the heart of the hardworking market-gardening country, which, founded as it largely is upon family enterprise, keeps Belgium so magnificently supplied with vegetables that she can afford to be choosy about the condition in which they come to market. Returning through the Botanical Gardens and turning right at the bridge, the street called Bruul takes you back to the Grote Markt past the Church of Onze Lieve Vrouw van Leliendaal, a Baroque construction built for the Norbertines, another of the works of Luc Fayd' Herbe.

The old Stadhuis shows many signs of its patchwork history. It was begun in the early 14th century as a Cloth Hall, on the same lines as the belfry-topped market building at Bruges. The work was never finished, and two centuries later Charles V began its conversion into a palace, which was to be the seat of the Grand Council. The façade on the Befferstraat dates from this period, but once more the work hung fire, so that the building seems to taper into the Renaissance and shows little real unity, though the colonnaded street level is pleasing. Passing down Befferstraat, you come to another Baroque church, that of Saints Peter and Paul. Continuing to your right (Keizerstraat), you pass the theater, housed in the old building of the Imperial Court, opposite which is the Law Courts building.

The latter is perhaps the most interesting of the secular buildings in Mechelen, because it includes the most important contribution rendered by Rombout Keldermans (though he also had a hand in the Stadhuis). The building was originally planned as a palace for Margaret of Austria, and she entrusted the work to Keldermans, who was responsible for the interior courtyard with its attractive galleries and porches. In 1517, however, Margaret imported the Savoyard architect, Guyot de Beauregard, who erected the facade on the Keizerstraat.

This, with its dormers, its pediments, its balconies and gateways, is a Franco-Italian Renaissance achievement as different from Kelder-mans' late Gothic as chalk is from cheese.

12 km. (7 miles) off, at Muizen, is the 90-acre Zoo, the estate of Planckendael, an outstanding collection where lions and bison live in semi-liberty. Open all the year round.

Discovering Leuven

Leuven was more fortunate than Mechelen in its fine Stadhuis, the work of its own architectural master, Mathieu de Laeyens, who made a quick job of it by finishing it in 1459 after only 11 years' work. If you know this astonishing building from photographs, you will be surprised to find that it is really life-size, for its crow's-nested pinnacles, its wealth of Gothic ornament, and its roof recall the art of the jeweller rather than the architect. The interior is less interesting than the exterior, though it contains some good 15th-century ceilings. The building itself, however, stands in the Grote Markt as a perpetual reminder to a religious people that miracles are not impossible. The miracle is not only in the building itself, but in the fact that it is still there after the vicissitudes of two world wars. The same cannot be said of the Round Table building at the entrance of the same square, another de Laeyens masterpiece. The present building is a reconstruction.

The great Church of St. Pieter (Sint-Pieterskerk) has the place of honor on the Grote Markt. Despite much effort, this fine edifice was for long little more than a memory. Mathieu de Laeyens had a hand in it and so, before him, had Sulpice van der Vorst from Diest, and Jan Keldermans, of the great Mechelen family of architects. A shifting foundation led to the drastic shortening of the tower in the 17th century and the replacement of the spire by a cupola in the 18th. In 1914, cupola and roof were almost completely destroyed, as were other build-ings, due to the wanton burning of the city by the Germans in reprisal for the alleged firing of shots at their occupying troops from the win-dows of houses in the town. The damage, in fact, proved repairable, but the bombardment of 1944 was more serious, and World War II left a large part of the church in ruins. It has now been repaired. In St. Peter's you will find a remarkable polyptych, painted in 1464 by Dirk Bouts and representing the Last Supper.

A Great University

The important feature in Leuven, however, is the Catholic Universi-ty, whose fame reached its apogee in the 16th century. It had among its alumni such men as Bishop Jansen of Ypres; Dodoens, the botanist of Mechelen; Mercator, the geographer; Erasmus; Justus Lipsius (who occupied a Chair here); and it housed the presses that first printed the *Utopia* of Sir Thomas More. There were some 50 colleges attached to the university at its most flourishing period, but the French suppressed the university altogether in 1797. Under the Dutch domination that followed the fall of Napoleon, William I founded here a Philosophical

College, which was one of the grounds for protest by the clerical interests that led to the Belgian revolution of 1830. The university, dependent on the Catholic Church, was established at Mechelen in 1833, and transferred to Leuven two years later. It remained a bilingual institution until the late 1960s, when intercultural tensions forced the transfer of the French language faculties (UCL) to Louvain-la-Neuve, leaving the Dutch (KUL) still in Leuven. Today, however, KUL remains one of the controlling influences in Belgian thought, especially in the politico-economic sciences, and its Board of Faculties is called upon to produce the men who fill the highest places in public life. The surviving college buildings of the original university date mostly from the 18th century. They include the College of the Pope, the College of the King, that of the Premonstrants, of Viglius, Van Dalle (this dates from 1569), Arras, and the Haute Colline.

The fact that the Stadhuis escaped the 1914 fire was due to its occupation by the German staff, but the library of the university was less fortunate. Priceless manuscripts were lost with it, and the building opened in 1928 in the square named after Monsignor Ladeuze was the gift of American universities and was designed by the American architect, Whitney Warren. In 1940 it was again burned out, and the Catholic University lost nearly a million volumes. Reconstruction proved possible, but libraries are more difficult to stock than to build, and the filling of the shelves is still going on.

Near the university is the Sint-Michielskerk, a masterpiece of the Antwerp Jesuit, William Hessius, built about 1666. This also suffered very badly in the 1944 bombardment, though a large part of the excellent 17th-century wood carving in the confessionals and the Communion rail were saved. The magnificent choirstalls in the Sint-Gertrudiskerk, carved by Matthew de Wayer around 1543, and accounted the finest work of its type in Belgium, were very badly shattered during an air raid in 1944 but subsequently restored. Don't miss the misericorde seats, with their evocative carvings of biblical scenes. The church has a lovely spire of lace-like stonework.

Two churches that were less badly damaged are those of St. Quentin and St. James. The former contains early 13th-century work round the base of the tower, but the bulk of the church is the work of Mathieu de Laeyens in the Burgundy period. Nearby is the picturesque precinct of the Begijnhof, with a church very much in the Brabançon style dating from 1305. This contains some glass dating from about the same time. St. James' Church, which lies across the Dijle by the main road, dates from a number of periods.

Outside Leuven, at Heverlee, a number of the University institutes are in less congested surroundings in the splendid park of the Renaissance-style Château d'Arenberg. At Heverlee, too, is the renowned Abbaye du Parc, founded in 1128.

Aarschot and Keerbergen

On the border of the Kempen moorland country to the northeast lies Aarschot, sacked many times in its long history. The Church of Onze Lieve Vrouw has resisted the ravages of war, and its haughty, massive tower is visible from afar. It possesses a good Verhaegen painting, the *Disciples at Emmaus*. Asparagus-growing is the major industry of Aarschot's inhabitants—it is in Belgium that you should sample this delicacy—which they export all over Europe.

Keerbergen, with its dunes, pine woods and heather is a favorite weekend haunt of tired business executives. From there the road back to Brussels leads you through Haacht and along the side of Brussels airport. Just before reaching the latter, you cross the road from Waterloo to Mechelen. Along this road, to the right, is Elewijt Castle, which belonged to Rubens, and is now used for temporary exhibitions. Further on is the big pleasure-garden of Hofstade with its 28-hectare (70-acre) lake, a favorite with the people of Brussels.

PRACTICAL INFORMATION FOR MECHELEN AND LEUVEN REGIONS

GETTING THERE. These two art cities are both within 15 miles of the outskirts of Brussels and, in fact, constitute one big excursion from the capital, from which they are easily reached by modern motorways and direct train services. Leuven may also be reached by direct trains from Ghent, Bruges, and Oostende; Mechelen from Ghent and Antwerp. There is also a local train service between Mechelen and Leuven.

HOTELS AND RESTAURANTS. Due perhaps to the proximity of Brussels and Antwerp and the pastoral nature of the countryside, the region has relatively few hotels. However, there are several excellent restaurants which will repay a visit.

BLANDEN. About 5 miles south of Leuven on N251 toward Hamme-Mille. *Chateau de Namur* (M), Naamsesteduweg 68 (tel. 016–201545). 11 comfortable rooms and excellent restaurant.

KEERBERGEN. A good weekend spot 20 miles from Brussels, 8 from Mechelen and 12 from Leuven. Horseback riding in the pine woods. *Hostellerie Berkenhof* (E), Valkeniersdreef 5 (tel. 015–234 803). 7 rooms with bath; also has excellent restaurant—try their salmon in season.

Restaurant. *Paddock* (M), Haachtsesbaan 107, (tel. 015–511 934). An excellent restaurant on the road to Haecht in a converted villa.

KORTENBERG. Halfway between Leuven and Brussels. *Les Trois Sapins* (I), Leuvensesteenwag 175 (tel. 02–759 6507). 14 rooms, 7 with bath. Modest restaurant.

Restaurant. *Hof te Linderghem* (E), Leuvensesteenweg 346 (tel. 02–759 7264). Celebrated spot serving classic cuisine. Closed Mon. evening and Tues.

LEUVEN. *Binnenhof* (M), Maria-Theresiastraat 65 (tel. 016–236 926). 57 rooms with bath. *A.C. Relais Leuven* (M), St.-Jansbergsteenweg 405 (tel. 016–

200 816). *Modern motel* at Heverlee, 4 miles south of Leuven on the E40 autoroute. 41 rooms and a moderate restaurant. *Professor* (M), Naamsestraat 20 (tel. 016–220 442). 8 rooms all with bath; good restaurant. *Al Giardino* (I), Brusselsestraat 114 (tel. 016–233 058). 14 rooms, all with bath. *Royale* (I), Martelarenplein 6 (tel. 016–221 252). 22 rooms, 7 with bath. No restaurant.

Restaurants. There are a number of good restaurants in the city center. *Belle Epoque* (E), Bondgenotenlaan 94 (tel. 016–223 389). Between historic center and the train station. Excellent classic cuisine. *Trilingue* (E), Vismarkt 6 (tel. 016–231 050). Close to St. Peter's Church; good steaks. Less expensive is *Il Fornello* (M), Oude Markt 37 (tel. 016–238 371). Good value Italian dishes. Other good restaurants are close to the line of the fortifications, now the city's inner ring-road. *De Oude Kautien* (M), Kautieneplein 3 (tel. 016–222 084). Close to the modern university buildings; serves Belgian favorites.

Blauwputois (I), Tiensevest 10 (tel. 223 152). For excellent budget value near the station. *La Chasse* (I), Naamsesteenweg 500 (tel. 016–223 647). Four miles south of town at Heverlee for excellent grilled steak.

MECHELEN. *Alfa-Alba* (E), Korenmarkt 24 (tel. 015–420 303). 43 rooms. Modern hotel; no restaurant. *Egmont* (M), Oude Brusselstraat 50 (tel. 015–413 498). 19 rooms, all with bath; no restaurant. *Claes* (I), Onze-Lieve-Vrouwstraat 51 (tel. 015–412 866). 15 rooms, 9 with shower; no restaurant.

Restaurants. *Golden Anker* (M), Brusselsesteenweg 2 (tel. 015–422 535). Just outside the Brussels Gate. Excellent sea-food. *Groene Lantaarn* (I), Steenweg 2 (tel. 015–202 027). Just by the cathedral for a good inexpensive meal. There are several little cafes in the Grote Markt that are good for snacks, and around the station there are a number of reasonably-priced restaurants.

Five miles northeast at **Rumst** is the excellent *Potaerde* (E), Antwerpsesteen-weg 96 (tel. 311 374). Well worth the trip.

TOURS. Leuven's Tourist Office can arrange individual guided tours or make bookings for organized trips. Call at the Stadhuis on the Grote Markt (tel. 061–234 941). The Catholic University also runs some tours. Call at the information office, Naamsestraat 22 (tel. 016–220 321). Guided tours of **Mechelen** are organized by the Tourist Office—Town Hall, Grote Markt (tel. (015) 20 85 11). They take place as follows: Easter—Sept., Sat., and Sun. at 2 P.M.; June—15 Sept., Mon. at 7 P.M.; July and Aug., every day at 2 P.M.

 MUSEUMS AND PLACES OF INTEREST. LEUVEN. As a great university town from the Middle Ages, Leuven is bursting with interesting survivals, historic and artistic. One of the latest additions is the **University Library,** Monsignor Ladeuzeplein, donated by American universities after the original burned down in the First World War. The walls of the library bear the names of the many U.S. contributors.

Groot Begijnhof (The Great Beguinage), half-mile south of Grote Markt, really a town within a town. More than a hundred houses and convents and Brabantine Gothic church of St. John the Baptist. All carefully restored and well worth wandering around.

St. Gertrudiskerk (Church of St. Gertrude), Naamsestraat. Contains magnificently restored choirstall. Contact Tourist Office for varying opening hours.

St. Michielskerk (Church of St. Michael), off Mechelsestraat. Fine 17th-century church designed by William Hessius.

St. Pieterskerk (Collegiate Church of St. Peter), Grote Markt. Many beautiful artifacts in the church itself, and more in the museum in the west transept, including a *Last Supper* triptych by Dirk Bouts. Museum open from 10 to 12. On Sat., Sun. and holidays from 2 to 5. Admission free.

Stadhuis (Town Hall). Rather like an enormous version of a medieval reliquary, this has to be one of the most striking Town Halls in Europe. Guided tours at 11 and 3 except weekends. Apply Tourist Office. Under the Town Hall is a **Municipal Brewery Museum,** open every day 2 to 6, closed Tues.

Stedelijk Museum (Municipal Museum), Savoyestraat 6. In an old nobleman's house, with a fine collection of Brabantine artwork. Open 10 to 12, 2 to 5; Sat. and Sun., 10 to 1.

Stella Artois Brewery. Groups can arrange a free guided tour (with tasting) inside Belgium's most famous brewery. Call 247 299.

MECHELEN. The main point of interest here is the magnificent **Cathedral of St. Rombout,** with its wonderful carvings, marvelous stained glass, and its paintings by Van Dyck. Open 9.30 to 4 (7 in summer), Sun. and hols. 1 to 5. Other churches worthy of a visit include the **Sint Janskerk** (church of St. John), which has guided tours (apply Tourist Office) and the **Kerk van Onze Lieve Vrouwe van Overdijl** (Church of Our Lady over the Dyle), open 9 to 6 (1 to 4 in winter), both of which contain important works by Rubens. **Onze Lieve Vrouw van Hanswijk,** Hanswijkstraat, has a high Baroque interior. Other places of note are:

Begijnhof (The Hospital of Our Lady), attractive collection of enclosed gardens. The church is a Baroque gem, but is not normally open to the public—visits could be arranged in advance by application at the convent, or ask at the Tourist Office.

Carillon Concerts take place at St. Rombout's Cathedral and in the towers of Our Lady-over-the-Dijle and Busleyden House every Mon. and Sat. 12 to 2, every Sun. at 11.30 from June to mid-Sept., and Mon. evenings at 8.30.

Folklore Museum, XII Apostelenstraat 17. Collection of objects and costumes describing local customs. Open from Easter to end-September, weekends only 10–12, 2–5. Admission BF 33.

Stadsmuseum (The City Museum), housed in the Gothic-style Busleyden House, Frederik Merodestr. The museum follows the course of local history and has a special part devoted to the famous Carillon. Open Easter to end Sept., 10 to 12, 2 to 5. Winter until 4. Admission BF 50.

Toy Museum, Nekkerspaelstraat 21. Relates toys to social history. Open daily (except Mon.), 2–5. Admission BF 55.

De Zalm (the Salmon House), Zoutwerf. Craft museum, open 10 to 12 and 2 to 5 (4 in winter). Admission BF 30.

USEFUL ADDRESSES. City Tourist Offices. Leuven, Stadhuis (Town Hall), Naamsestraat 1A (tel. 23 49 41); Mechelen, Stadhuis, Grote Markt. (tel. 20 85 11).

ANTWERP

Rubens and Diamonds

Wherever you go in Belgium, you cannot avoid being conscious of Antwerp. The mighty port, the fifth-largest in the world, has assumed so much of the commercial power of the country that it has become a great economic, and thus to a large extent a political, force. It claims to have the fastest turn-round time of any port in the world. It is a large and wealthy city, with a long history, but it did not establish its ascendancy until the silting up of the Zwin in the 15th century closed the seaport of Bruges. The prosperity of Antwerp has not been continuous, but the Scheldestad or Métropole as the city is known has had periods of such wealth and such cultural ascendancy that the traces of them are abundant. The city also has a 500 year-old tradition of diamond cutting and its own diamond bourse. 40% of the world's cutting and polishing and 60% of its diamond dealing is carried out in Antwerp. Most of the larger diamond cutting firms can arrange for visitors to tour their cutting and polishing rooms and—if you can afford that kind of tourist memento—to buy a sample or two of their stock. Details are available from the City Tourist Office.

Legend links Antwerp with a giant who would fling into the Schelde (Scheldt) the severed hands *(handwerpen)* of mariners who refused to pay his tolls. Two statues, indeed, commemorate his having suffered a like fate at the hands of the Roman soldier Salvius Brabo; but the older one dates back less than four centuries, and scholars insist that the city's name can be less colorfully explained. In olden times the merchant brigantines could sail up into the central town which, therefore, was located "on the wharf" *(aan het werp)*.

Antwerp's Checkered History

Authenticated history begins in the 7th century, when St. Eloi (best remembered in the early history of Bruges) and St. Amand (who founded the two abbeys which were the beginning of Ghent) were joined by the Irish St. Dymphne (whom we shall meet again at Geel) in their missionary work.

The Norsemen, of course, played havoc with the early civilization, but in the 11th century Antwerp was a marquisate enfeoffed to the De Bouillon family from the south of Belgium, and during the 12th century St. Norbert re-established doctrinal orthodoxy after Godfrey the Bearded had banished the heretic Tanchelin. After the marquisate passed to the dukes of Brabant, Antwerp was caught in the meshes of the anti-French policy of Edward III of England, and though this promised well for a time, Bruges got the best end of the bargain. This was confirmed when the astute Louis de Male, last of the counts of Flanders before the great dynasty of Burgundy, received the marquisate of Antwerp in fee (1357).

In the late 1480s, the strife between Bruges and Antwerp reached its crisis. It was then that the men of Bruges struggled to re-establish their fortunes by holding Maximilian, Regent (or Mambour) of Flanders since the death of Mary of Burgundy, as a prisoner and hostage. He bought his escape by promises he had no intention of keeping, and proceeded to revenge himself on Bruges by giving more and more privileges to Antwerp, including the monopoly in alum and spices.

Thus began a period in which the power and commerce of Antwerp expanded rapidly. The Italians and Germans set up their trade from the port, leaving Bruges little beside the Spanish wool monopoly. A commercial exchange had been founded in 1460, and Sir Thomas Gresham was so impressed that he took the idea back to London, which led to the founding of the Royal Exchange. The banking princes of Germany and Italy—the Fuggers, the Osteters, the Gualterottis, and others—set up their counting houses in Antwerp.

Following Amsterdam's example, Antwerp joined the powerful Hanseatic League that controlled the North Sea and the Baltic. With the arts also flourishing (this was the period of Quinten Matsijs, Cornelius Floris and the younger De Waghemaker), Antwerp was already a city of world renown before the religious troubles began and vessels lay in the Schelde filled with the church statues and decorations saved from the iconoclasts. In the "Spanish Fury" (1576), more than 7,000 citizens were butchered by the Spaniards in a single night. Antwerp was the last citadel and indeed the symbol of resistance in the southern Low Countries to the Inquisition; and when the defenses of Burgomaster Philippe de Marnix collapsed before the besieging armies of Italian general Alessandro Farnese, fighting in the service of Philip II, resistance ended (1585).

This established a line of demarcation between the remaining Spanish provinces (now Belgium) and the independent United Provinces (which were to become today's Netherlands); this left Antwerp on the Spanish side of the line, which is logical enough in view of the territory through which the Schelde flows, though it left the Dutch in control of the estuary. This was to have serious consequences later. Meanwhile the ground was prepared for Antwerp's greatest period, the beginning of the 17th century. This was the reign of Albert and Isabella, the period of Rubens and his· coterie, of Artus Quellin, Jacob Jordaens, Adriaen Brouwer, and Van Dyck. This was the time when Antwerp had the chance of building and decorating, possessed the money to do it, and had at hand the great artistic talents by which it could be carried out. It is for this reason that much of Antwerp's architecture is colored by the rather heavy Baroque style of the time.

Meantime, however, disaster was in store. The United Provinces, freed from the dead hand of Spanish colonial rule, began to exercise political and military power commensurate with their rapidly mounting mercantile wealth. Backed by a strong war fleet, the countrymen of William of Orange had their say in the framing of the Treaty of Westphalia (1648). They insisted on nothing less than the closure of the Schelde. Trading from Antwerp became impossible at the behest of the rich merchants of Amsterdam, and it was small consolation to the men of Antwerp that the Dutch had strengthened their position also against Bruges by closing the now much smaller Zwin.

There followed nearly two hundred years of oblivion. There was indeed a period of hope when the French Revolutionary Convention reopened the Schelde in 1795, and later when Napoleon enlarged the port and built a naval arsenal as part of his campaign against England. The chance of a peaceful enjoyment of these benefits, however, came to very little, owing to Belgium's incorporation in the Netherlands after 1815. After the Belgian revolution, so keen were the Dutch on maintaining their hold over Antwerp that they had to be turned out by force from the citadel (from where they had bombarded the town) by the French in 1832. It was only in the 1860s that the Dutch finally gave up their rights to levy a toll on ships passing through the estuary—the monument at the junction of Tolstraat and Scheldestraat, near the Fine Arts Museum, commemorates this re-establishment of free navigation.

Since then Antwerp has been the chief port and the second city of the Belgian kingdom. For a time in 1914 it was the seat of the government, then fell to the Germans after a short but intensive siege. In World War II it suffered most heavily after its liberation, when it was a constant target for V-1 and V-2 rocket-attacks; some 20,000 buildings were destroyed or badly damaged and almost 3,000 civilians killed. Now, it is one of the water gateways to Europe, with its immense port installations, its pride in the quick turn-round of ships, and its diversified modern industries.

Modern Antwerp

In the past few years Antwerp has grown considerably. The port has been pushed eight miles downstream to the new lock—the world's biggest—at Zandvliet. Big ships (though not supertankers) can now enter. Enormous tracts of land have been developed for industrial use and eagerly snapped up. As a motor assembly center, Antwerp's standing has greatly increased through the big second plant opened by General Motors and by the Ford tractor operation; and, based on the refineries, there is now a thriving petrochemical industry in which nearly all the great international chemical companies have important holdings. Nearer the city center, the Bell Telephone Manufacturing Company's tower building dominates its district, while many other industrial enterprises have set up along the Antwerp–Boom highway. The influx of foreign investment has led to the opening of American, British, French, Dutch and German banks in the city, while the financial services sector—particularly marine insurance—is also strong. Behind and amid the romance of the port and the dignity of ancient buildings, Antwerp has become a boom town.

So great has been the expansion that Antwerp has spilled over from the right bank of the Schelde to the left, where many companies have set up production units and the huge reactors of the Doel nuclear plant loom large over the river bank. The development is mainly industrial and suburban, and will soon lead to further port expansion. The communications problem was brilliantly solved by the Kennedy Tunnel, opened in 1969 and constructed by Swedish and Belgian engineers for both rail and road traffic. The five great concrete sections were prefabricated in a special dry dock on the left bank, towed to their sites, sunk into the river bed and joined up in a series of techniques never before applied and incidentally completing the motor highway between Antwerp and Ghent. A more romantic means of crossing the river, however, is to take a small ferry boat from Lillo to Doel. From midstream you can appreciate just how much the city owes to the waterway for its development.

Discovering Antwerp

For the visitor to Belgium with a taste for atmosphere and history, it may well be that Antwerp will fill the bill better than Brussels. For all that the city has grown and modernized at a rapid pace, it still preserves a great deal to stimulate the romantic juices and feed the imagination.

Directly in front of the imposing Central Rail Station—which dates from the early 1900s and is now a national monument—is Koningin Astridplein, a large square surrounded by cafés and cinemas. Just east of the station is the 25-acre Dierentuin, one of Europe's most modern zoological gardens. In one aviary the fronts of the cages are open, but ingenious use of bright lights dissuades the birds from flying away. In the reptile-house, curtains of cold air prevent the pythons from roaming. Elsewhere, larger animals of the less dangerous sort wander about almost at will.

On the other side of the Central Station there stretches the broad, busy De Keyserlei, with Pelikaanstraat running down the side of the station on your left. The De Keyserlei goes on to the main boulevard between the Frankrijklei and the Italiëlei, beyond which you are in the

ANTWERP

| 0 meters | 500 | 1000 |
| 0 yards | 500 | 1000 |

☆ Information ✪ Public Building ✝ Church 🚢 Boats
✳ Museum \ Theater \ Place of Interest ■ Other Item

main shopping thoroughfare called the Meir, which culminates in Europe's earliest skyscraper, the 24-floor Torengebouw (from the top there's a fine panoramic view). Continuing with this building on your right, you pass down the Schoenmarkt till you find yourself in the wide Groenplaats, containing a statue of Rubens, with the Cathedral of Our Lady occupying the opposite end of the square. Turn right beyond the square into the Oude Koornmarkt, which you follow to the Suikerrui. This leads down to the Schelde where, a hundred yards to your right, stands the fortress-like Steen, housing the Maritime Museum.

The Steen is one of the few traces left of medieval Antwerp. It dates back to the 10th century, though of course it has been much altered through the centuries and much of it is no older than 1520. In the 13th century it was a prison, and one of the things you will see inside is the chapel where condemned men heard their last Mass. A tour through the museum takes you through 13 rooms, each with a specific theme, such as the development of the port, seamen's customs, cartography, navigation and Belgian maritime history. There is a comprehensive library of more than 25,000 items where anyone who is interested in maritime matters is welcome.

Without doubt the most fascinating exhibits are models of East-India clippers and other ships of long ago. Here at the Steen you are upstream from the main port installations, but from these raised terraces you can watch the shipping on the busy Schelde.

The walk you have taken has led you along the boundary between the port and old Antwerp, which lie on your right, and modern Antwerp which, though it contains some survivals, is mainly the product of the city's 19th-century expansion and the growth of the residential area. Facing the river on the Steen, you are about midway between the under-river tunnels, for foot passengers on your left and for vehicles on your right. A five-minute walk through the pedestrian tunnel brings you on to the *Linkeroever* (left bank), from whose riverside park you can obtain the best (photographic) views of the great city's spires and wharves; not unlike the artist's impression at the head of this chapter.

An Incomparable Cathedral

The chief architects in the initial work on the cathedral, begun in 1352, were the Appelmans, father and son. At the end of the 15th century Hermann de Waghemaker made various additions, and about 1520 his son Dominique, in partnership with the Malinois Keldermans —a partnership responsible for the restoration of the Steen about the same time, as also for the original wing of the City Hall at Ghent—was at work on the tower. This single tower, on a structure evidently meant to carry two, gives the building an asymmetrical look, but the tower itself is a masterpiece.

The interior of the cathedral needs some study before you realize how very large it is. There was indeed a scheme, in the days of Charles V, to make it about double its present size, but the work was abandoned. Philip II, maintaining the traditions of the House of Burgundy, revived the Order of the Golden Fleece by convocating a chapter here in 1555. Ten years later the iconoclasts were smashing the statues, and in 1794 the best of the glass was removed, the church deconsecrated and the Rubens masterpieces carried off to Paris, whence they were not recovered till 1816, after the fall of Napoleon.

The great treasure of the church consists of the three works of Peter Paul Rubens, the two main ones, the *Elevation of the Cross* and the *Deposition,* being at the back of the two transepts. The former, painted just after the master's return from Italy, shows evidence of Italian influence, but the latter, ordered very soon after, though not finished for three years (1614), defines Rubens' mature style and is generally considered the greater masterpiece. The painter's later manner is brought out by the treatment of light in his *Assumption,* which you will find in the choir (1626). Other works of outstanding interest in the cathedral include a *Last Supper* by Nicholas Rombouts (about 1503).

Three Remarkable Houses

The Rubens pictures will probably have filled you with enthusiasm to see the house occupied by the artist from 1610 for the last quarter-century of his life. It is in a square off the south side of the Meir, and is partly a reconstruction, but a very conscientious one, and contains a wing with strong Italian influence, added by the painter himself. You will see here the studio in which the master worked, and the big studio for his pupils.

Van Dyck worked here for some time as well as Jordaens, Snyder, and many others. The house contains, besides souvenirs of the master, furniture and *objets d'art* of the 17th century. They help to recall the atmosphere of an Antwerp patrician's home. There is a surprisingly beautiful courtyard, a large Flamboyant Baroque-style portico and a formal garden with tiny box hedges. Continual efforts are being made to enrich the collection in Rubens' House. Important acquisitions have been *Adam and Eve,* painted by Rubens when he was a young man, the two portraits of his grandparents, *The Art Gallery of Cornelius van der Geest,* painted by William van Haecht and a self-portrait of Rubens himself at the height of his fame.

Another outstanding museum which calls for a visit is the Mayer van den Bergh collection, housed in the testator's house and wonderfully presented. This collection is largely composed of primitive paintings from a number of sources, but the furnishings and decorations are worth a visit too, even if you are not a keen student of painting. You will find it on Lange Gasthuisstraat, not far from Rubens' House.

Another period reconstruction is the Plantin–Moretus Museum, the house of the printer, himself a Frenchman by origin, whose name is remembered by a type-face and who was commissioned by Philip II and later made Archtypographer Royal. His famous printing business was continued by his son-in-law Moretus, and existed till the latter part of the 19th century, though it never regained its first eminence. The Renaissance courtyard and the gardens give the house a charm of its own, and the type-foundry and the typographical collection are of unique interest.

Plantin's was, in fact, Europe's most important printing shop in the 16th century. His 22 presses brought out no less than 50 to 60 volumes a year. His sumptuous patrician house was for many decades the meeting place of Humanist thinkers of all nationalities. Behind the latticed windows were produced books that were the admiration of all the universities. Through those doorways Rubens and Van Dyck often passed. Dignitaries of all walks of life have been here, including even the ferocious Duke of Alba himself.

In front of the Plantin–Moretus Museum there is a local antique market on Fridays from 8–1. Interestingly, the market has its origins in the public sale by bailiffs of debtors' impounded goods—so the tradition is that prices are reasonable. Simply ask for the Vrijdagmarkt.

Antwerp's Churches

Among the churches of Antwerp, the most interesting in itself is that of St. Charles Borromeo, built in the early 17th century for the Jesuits —and still known to the local residents as Jesuïtenkerk—and in the planning and decoration of which Rubens and his coterie had the lion's share. This is one of the few Flemish churches with a gallery construction. Unfortunately it has suffered very heavily through the centuries. The Rubens ceiling paintings were destroyed by fire in 1718, and the other chief paintings were taken to Vienna after the suppression of the Jesuits in 1772. Twenty years later the French—in a period when they were at their most unreasonable—turned the church into a Temple of Reason, after which it became a military hospital and then a Protestant church. It was at last restored to the Catholic church, and contains an altar by Rubens and statues by Artus Quellin, besides a number of paintings by Scut, Seghers and others, and an ivory Christ by Duquesnoy.

In front of the church you will see the old part of the city library and a fountain with a small statue of Hendrik Conscience, father of the modern Flemish school of prose writing. In this area, and in the nearby Wolstraat, you will find many small bookshops, as well as a number dealing in antiques and fine art.

If you walk down Lange Nieuwstraat you will pass the restored Chapel of St. Nicholas (now used as a puppet theatre) and the enticing little courtyard where a pillared statue of the saint himself is another link with a remoter past. Farther down the street is the Church of St. James (Sint Jacob), begun by the elder De Waghemaker in 1491, and reopened in 1969 after the previous year's fire. Its treasures include more works of art than most others, notably a marble Communion table by Verbruggen and Kerricx, dating from the end of the 17th century, and an *Apotheosis of Saint James* by the latter. Artus Quellin was responsible for the fine carving in the choir stalls, one of the armorial bearings (of benefactors) being that of Rubens. In the fourth side-chapel is the tomb of Rubens himself with, on the altar, a *Holy Family*, one of the master's last works. You may be interested to compare the Rombout's *Mystic Marriage of Saint Catherine* with that by Memling at Bruges; and there is an intriguing *Temptation of Saint Anthony* by Martin de Vos, in which the painter's wife was model for the temptress.

There is, incidentally, a Rubens version of the *Mystic Marriage of Saint Catherine* in St. Augustine's Church, in the southern part of the city, together with Van Dyck's *Saint Augustine in Ecstasy.* Not far away is the Church of St. Andrew (St. Andrieskerk), largely of interest for the monument put up by the refugees Barbara Maubray and Elizabeth Curle for Mary Queen of Scots. The queen's portrait on copper above the monument is said to be a Pourbus.

St. Paul's Church, close to the Butcher's Guildhall (Vleeshuis), also suffered from one of Antwerp's disastrous church fires in the '60s, in which the local hookers distinguished themselves in saving the fine paintings—Rubens, Van Dyck, Quellin and others—which are among its possessions. It is a striking church to visit, with beautifully carved choirstalls and other furniture. The pictures, whether real Rubens or copied Caravaggio, are worth seeing.

Magnificent Architecture

Among the secular buildings of Antwerp you will find a fragment of the old Beurs, or Commercial Exchange, in the Hofstraat, near the Stadhuis (City Hall). The date of the building is 1564. It was not long before this building was replaced by another, on similar lines, which is still in use, in Twaalf Maandenstraat. The Stadhuis is the work, in the first instance, of Cornelis Floris (or de Vriendt), and it was still barely a dozen years old when the Spaniards burned it out in 1576. The galleried hall, with its 19th-century murals, is impressive rather than beautiful, but there are two rooms full of frescoes by the 19th-century painter Leys, which are worth seeing. In the room of the Burgomaster there is an interesting fireplace by Pieter Coecke of Aalst (1548). The Stadhuis is, in the usual manner, surrounded by the Guild houses of the corporations. These, for the most part, are opulent examples of early 16th-century architecture. They are of a more sober style than those for instance in the Brussels Grand' Place. You will find a great number of old houses, of about the same period, in the surrounding streets. In the middle of the Grote Markt stands the Brabo fountain, which has no basin, the water running off through the rocks.

Those interested in folklore will find a great pleasure in visiting the five restored corporation houses in the Gildenkamerstraat which runs behind the City Hall. The museum is a complete survey of Flemish popular activities, customs and art.

Passing down towards the Schelde by the Oude Beursstraat, you come to the Vleeshuis, the Butchers' Guildhall, built above the level of the street at the beginning of the 16th century. It is the biggest and best-preserved building in late-Gothic style in Antwerp. The most remarkable of the beautifully-furnished first-floor rooms is the stately council chamber of the ancient Butchers' Guild. It now houses one of the city's museums.

Proceeding along Vleeshouwerstraat you come to St. Paul's; on its farther side is the old Potagiepoort, a little closed-off square, which is an attractive survival. Reaching the Schelde and passing beyond the Loodshuis, the river pilots' building, you can turn down Adriaan Brouwerstraat to find the Brouwershuis at No. 20. The work of the engineer

Gilbert van Schoonbeke, this interesting relic is the remains of the system by which water was brought down from the Kempen for the city, and more especially for the 20 or more breweries in this street. The system, started in 1552, was in service till well into the present century. Quite apart from the house itself, the study of the water system here is of interest.

From the river end of Brouwersvliet, you can head back towards the city center, either along St. Pietersvliet and St. Paulusstraat, or through the parallel but altogether more atmospheric sidestreets slightly further east. This second route is definitely *not* recommended for those with young children or prudish dispositions: the dingy whorehouses of the Schippersstraat, the seamen's shops, the old one-eyed seadogs and the romantic faraway names of the bars add a touch of 19th-century color —of windjammers and epic voyages—to what is an increasingly sanitized city.

Further south, much restoration work is being undertaken on the 16th- and 17th-century merchants' houses lying to the east of the line of medieval fortifications (St. Paulusstraat-Minderbroedersrui). In Keizerstraat you can now visit the imposing Rockox mansion—Nicolas Rockox was an avid art collector friend of Rubens—while in the same area some of the facades of the patrician houses in the Venusstraat are worth a look. Near here, too, are the charming Stadswaag Square (literally "town scales") and the 19th-century Academy of Fine Arts.

Paintings and the Port

Strongly recommended is a visit to the Koninklijk Museum voor Schone Kunsten (Royal Museum of Fine Arts), which lies in its own grounds down the Nationalestraat at Leopold de Wael Plaats (take a tram from the above-ground stop in the Groenplaats). Even the uninitiated in matters of painting can hardly fail to realize how much Antwerp owes to Peter Paul Rubens and the painters of his circle, and there is no gallery in the world where the work of a painter can so easily be studied in its historical perspective. The collection of Dutch and Flemish masters is indeed formidable, and spans nearly four centuries. A representative collection of all that is best in modern Belgian painting can also be seen here.

South of the city center, beyond the Stadspark, you should seek out the Museum Ridder Smidt van Gelder. The eponymous benefactor bequeathed his 18th-century patrician dwelling to the city of Antwerp in 1949. It contains unique collections of antique furniture and china, and some very fine paintings. What strikes the visitor is an atmosphere totally different from other museums: it is the richly furnished home of a cultured art collector.

The countryside around Antwerp lacks the picturesque quality of the environs of Brussels. Thoughtful city fathers have been successful in creating a green belt, and Antwerp can today boast a large number of beautiful parks on its outskirts. One of the finest is the Rivierenhof, east of the city, where there is an 18th-century manor of fine proportions. Another is the Middelheim Park, which has gradually accumulated one of Europe's best open-air displays of modern sculpture.

Your visit to Antwerp will not be complete without a visit to the port, the world's fifth-largest. The quays extend some 95 km. (60 miles), and the harbor and docks cover an area of 40 sq. miles. You'll enjoy one of the boat excursions that start from the landing stage by the Steen. Within the modern port complex you will find the tiny walled village of Lillo, which is a suitable refreshment halt on your journey up to the Dutch frontier at Zandvliet. You can also visit the port by bus. Seats must be booked in advance from the City Tourist Office, Gildekamersstratt 9, 2000 Antwerp. If you plan to drive in the dock area, try to follow the signposted "Havenroute" and watch out for opening bridges and railroad switchers!

A cruise to the mouth of the river Schelde and the Dutch "island" of Walcheren by fast pleasureboat is a unique experience. You'll have a wonderful time at little cost visiting one of the picturesque towns on the island: Vlissingen (Flushing) or Middelburg. On your outward journey you will notice that the *polders* are well below water level. On your return trip you will be impressed by the ancient city's skyline, dominated by the elegant tower of its cathedral.

PRACTICAL INFORMATION FOR ANTWERP

HOTELS. Antwerp's hotels are less numerous than those in Brussels, though they tend to be less expensive, too. With very few exceptions they all have restaurants. Pay no attention to adverts for "Tourist Rooms" in the cafes around Central Station. These are inhabited by local ladies who ply a far more ancient trade than that of hotelier.

Deluxe

Crest Hotel Antwerpen, Gerard Legrellelaan 10 (tel. 237 2900). 250 top class rooms. Best of the bunch on the city's ring expressway.

De Keyser, De Keyserlei 66 (tel. 234 0135). Luxury establishment with 117 rooms near the Central Station.

Plaza, Charlottalei 43 (tel. 218 9240). 81 rooms, near Stadspark; no restaurant.

Switel, Copernicuslaan 2 (tel. 231 6780). 350 rooms, indoor pool, sauna and gymnasium. Close to the zoo and the diamond quarter.

Expensive

Empire, Appelmansstraat 31 (tel. 231 4755). 70 well-equipped rooms, but no restaurant. In the heart of the diamond quarter.

Novotel, Luithagen-Haven 6 (tel. 542 0320). 119 rooms, heated swimming pool, tennis courts; north of the city in the docks area.

Theater, Arenbergstraat 30 (tel. 231 1720). 83 rooms in the older part of town, near Rubens' house and various theaters.

Moderate

Alfa Congress, Plantin en Moretuslei 136 (tel. 235 3000). 66 rooms, between ring expressway and center of town.

Arcade, Meistraat 39 (tel. 231 8830). Modern hotel with 150 well-equipped rooms. No restaurant. Right in front of the weekend Vogelmarkt.

Columbus, Frankrijklei 4 (tel. 233 0390). 27 rooms, most with bath or shower. No restaurant. Very convenient for sightseeing.

Drugstore Inn, Koningin Astridplein 43 (tel. 231 2121). 27 rooms, all with bath; close to Central Station. Definitely the best of the Astridplein hotels, although it lacks a restaurant on the premises.

Firean, Karel Oomsstraat 6 (tel. 237 0260). 12 well-equipped rooms. No restaurant. Close to Ring expressway.

Terminus, Franklin Rooseveltplaats 9 (tel. 231 4795). 45 rooms, 35 with bath; no restaurant.

Inexpensive

Antwerp Docks, Noorderlaan 100 (tel. 541 1850). 80 rooms, all with bath. A favorite with ships' officers. (And really much better than its name suggests!)

Florida, De Keyserlei 59 (tel. 232 1443). 40 rooms, 21 with bath; no restaurant; handy for Central Station.

Rubenshof, Amerikalei 115 (tel. 237 0789). 20 rooms, 6 with bath; no restaurant. Close to Royal Fine Arts Museum.

Tourist, Pelikaanstraat 22 (tel. 232 5870). 148 rooms, most with bath; right beside the Central Station. Always a reliable low-budget stalwart; no restaurant.

For students

Antwerp has several traditional youth hostels (communal dormitories, bring your own sleeping bag, closing time 11 P.M., etc.) and two reasonable, well-sited municipal camping grounds. In addition there are a few rooms in the following establishments that offer low prices without giving the feeling of "roughing it" unduly.

Square Sleep-Inn, Bolivarplaats 1 (tel. 237 3748). 30 rooms, available for up to four people.

New International Youth Pension, Provinciestraat 256 (tel. 230 0522). 27 rooms (with annex of 9 rooms on Isabellalei), available for 1–4 occupants.

International Seamen's House, Falconrui 21 (tel. 232 1609). Despite its name, some of its 100 rooms are available to non-seafarers.

Hotels and Restaurants in Antwerp's Environs

The environs of Antwerp vary considerably. The south and southwest, for instance, are largely industrialized. This outer suburban landscape is hardly recommended for sightseeing—Hoboken, which gave its name to the township across the Hudson from New York, is no more inviting than its American counterpart. To the east of Antwerp, however, there are pleasant woodlands—especially around 's-Gravenwezel (just outside Schoten) where there are three fine châteaux. Across the Schelde to the west you enter East Flanders—a land of poppies and grazing sheep. (For further details see chapter on *Flanders and its Art Towns.*)

AARTSELAAR. 11 km. (7 miles) south of city just off A12/N277 to Brussels. *Kasteelhoeve Groeninghe* (L), Kontichsesteenweg 78 (tel. 457 9586). 7 luxury rooms in old Flemish farmhouse; superb restaurant. **Restaurant.** *Lindenbos* (E), Boomsesteenweg 139 (tel. 888 0965). Château set in its own park grounds; excellent cuisine.

BRASSCHAAT. Pleasant outer suburb, 8 km. (5 miles) north of city center, on old road to Breda. *Kasteel van Brassschaat* (M), Miksebaan 40 (tel. 651 8537). 16 rooms, 8 with bath; and restaurant. Castle set in its own park grounds. *Pendennis Castle* (M), Augustijnslei 52 (tel. 651 8318). 24 rooms, 9 with bath;

restaurant. *Dennenhof* (I), Bredabaan 940 (tel. 663 0509). 19 motel-style rooms, all with shower; restaurant.

BRECHT. Pleasant spot 24 km. (15 miles) northeast of Antwerp on the main highway to Holland. *Privacy* (I), Pierrelaan 33 (tel. 663 2403). 11 rooms, 7 with shower; no restaurant. **Restaurant.** *E 10 Hoeve* (M), Kapelstraat 8a (tel. 313 8285). Excellent grills served in converted farmhouse.

KALMTHOUT. About 24 km. (15 miles) due north, favorite outing for weekends. *'t Keienhof,* (I), Putsesteenweg 105 (tel. 666 8528). 6 rooms, 4 with bath. Top-class restaurant. **Restaurant.** *'t Ven* (M), Putse Steenweg 43 (tel. 666 6838). Surrounded by pleasant countryside.

KAPELLEN. Small town, 15 km. (9 miles) north of city, on road to Bergenop-Zoom. *De Draak* (I), Hoevensebaan 2 (tel. 664 5393). 15 rooms, 4 with bath; restaurant. **Restaurant.** *De Bellefleur* (E), Antwerpsesteenweg 253 (tel. 664 6719). Renowned for its venison; bookings essential.

KONTICH. 11 km. (7 miles) south just off main route E19 to Brussels. **Restaurant.** *Alexander's* (M), Mechelsesteenweg 318 (tel. 457 2631). A relaxed out-of-town road house.

MORTSEL. 5 km. (3 miles) south of city center. *Bristol International* (I), Edegemsestraat 1 (tel. 440 0002). 26 rooms, all with shower; no restaurant. Right by train terminus; terrific value.

SCHOTEN. 5 km. (3 miles) northeast of city center. *Koningshof* (I), Kapellei 26 (tel. 6587 901). 8 rooms, 4 with bath; good restaurant. **Restaurant.** *Ten Weyngaert* (M), Winkelstapstraat 151 (tel. 6455 516). Converted 17th-century farmhouse. Good steaks.

WIJNEGEM. 11 km. (7 miles) east of Antwerp. **Restaurant.** *Ter Vennen,* (E), Merksemsebaan 278 (tel. 353 8140). Converted farmhouse; classic cuisine.

GETTING AROUND. By tram. In town, the traditional mode of transport is the tram. These are smaller, but no less rapid than those in Brussels; and a slightly shorter network means that the flat fare is a few francs cheaper. Some lines have been rebuilt in tunnels (look for signs marked *Metro*); the most useful for visitors being that between the Central Station (metro stop *Diamant*) and the Groenplaats (for the Cathedral). If you intend to make more than a few journeys you should invest in a *toeristenkaart*. This is a go-as-you-please ticket, valid on all the municipal trams and buses in the Antwerp area. It is available at MIVA offices at Diamant, Opera/Frankenlei and Groenplaats metro stations. It costs 100 francs for one day, 150 for two.

By bus. The long-distance buses of the NMBS and NMBV start from the Franklin Rooseveltplaats. These travel to such excursion spots as the picturebook town of Lier (Lierre), Schoten, 's-Gravenwezel, Brasschaat and Lillo, as well as deep into the Kempen (to Geel and Mol). Municipal bus lines mostly begin outside the Central Station in the Koningin Astridplein, while the special Sabena bus to Brussels National Airport starts from the airline office 75 yards down De Keyserlei.

Trips on the river Schelde or visits to the port can be made by the *Flandria,* at the Steen landing. Regular departures in summer, 10 to 4. Call Flandria (the name of the company as well as the flagship) on 233 7422.

By car. Several major highways converge on Antwerp's inner-city Ring expressway. It's a 10-lane racetrack, so be sure you maneuver in time to take the exit you want. On the Ghent route, the A14-E17 passes through the J. F. Kennedy Tunnel under the Schelde. The more northerly Waasland tunnel links with an expressway N49 direct to Knokke, Bruges and Zeebrugge (avoiding Ghent).

There are two (almost equally fast) motorways to Brussels. The more recent A1-E19 goes via Mechelen and gives a better link with Brussels airport than the older A12-N277 (via Boom), which, however, has a more direct route into the capital via Laeken.

 MUSEUMS AND PLACES OF INTEREST. Most museums are open 10 to 5 daily, except Monday; all close Christmas and New Year, also May 1, Ascension Day, and November 1/2. Exceptions are indicated below. Admission, unless otherwise indicated, is BF 50 for adults, BF 20 for children. A combination ticket, giving entry to any three museums during a 7-day period, costs BF 100; an annual ticket BF 200.

Churches are more autonomous and opening times vary considerably. A small entry charge is common; some may be visited by prior request only from the City Tourist Office.

A useful museums and general sightseeing folder may be obtained.

Archief en Museum voor het Vlaamse Cultuurleven (Archive and Museum of Flemish Culture), Minderbroedersstraat 22. Documents depicting the Flemish cultural reawakening since the 18th century.

Béguinage (Begijnhof), Rodestraat. Typical enclosed religious community. The church, restored in the 19th century, contains works by Jordaens and Van Noort, and may be visited daily 9 to 5. No admission charge.

Brouwershuis, Adriaan Brouwerstraat 20. This building combined the functions of a quasi-ceremonial brewers' guildhall with the entirely practical role as a water-distribution center for the breweries nearby.

Burgundian Chapel, Lange Nieuwstraat 31. Dates from 1496. Open Mon., Wed., Fri., 9.30 to 11.30 in mornings. No admission charge.

Diamond Museum. Housed in same building as the Provincial Health & Safety Institute (Provinciaal Veiligheidsinstituut) at Jezusstraat 28. Closed Tues. and Mon. Diamond-cutting demonstrations sometimes given Sat. afternoons. No admission charge.

Handelsbeurs (Commercial Exchange), Twaalfmaandenstraat (but accessible from many surrounding streets). Galleried building, heavily restored in the 19th century. Can be used as a handy shortcut on weekdays from 7.30 A.M. to 7.30 P.M.

International Cultural Center, Meir 50. Former royal palace. Usually houses art exhibitions. Pleasant café. No admission charge.

Koninklijk Museum voor Schone Kunsten (Royal Fine Arts Museum), Léopold de Waelplaats 1–9. The first floor contains one of the best collections of the Flemish school anywhere in the world. The ground floor is given over to more modern, but no less interesting, paintings. The neo-Classical building also houses a pleasant snackbar. No admission charge.

Maagdenhuis, Lange Gasthuisstraat 33. A 16th-century girls' orphanage now housing a collection of (largely household) items from that period. Open

Mon. to Fri. (except hols.) 8.30 to 4.30. Group visits at weekends may be arranged by calling 232 9835. No admission charge.

Mayer van den Bergh Museum, Lange Gasthuisstraat 19. Works by Flemish masters, sculpture, furniture, china, lace.

Nationale Scheepvaartmuseum (Steen), Steenplein 1. Last remnant of the city's early fortifications, the bastion now houses a small maritime museum. Open daily.

Onze Lieve Vrouwekathedraal (Cathedral), Groenplaats 21, but tourist entrance is via shopfront on the Blomstraat. One of the finest Gothic churches in the world. Open Apr. to mid-Oct., 12 to 5 weekdays, 12 to 4 Sat., 1 to 4 Sun. and hols. Rest of year, to 4 weekdays, 3 Sat., otherwise same. Admission charge BF 20.

Openluchtmuseum voor Beeldhouwkunst (Openair Sculpture Museum), Middelheim Park. Contains over 200 sculptures including works by Rodin and Meunier. Open daily, 10 to around sunset. No admission charge except during Jun. to Sept. Biennial Exhibitions (odd-numbered years).

Oude Beurs (Old Exchange), Hofstraat 15. The forerunner of all the world's mercantile exchanges can be seen from its inner courtyard on weekday mornings, free of charge.

Polder Museum. In the walled village of Lillo (in the port area), at Tolhuisstraat 14–16. Exhibition of the lifestyle of the traditional polder-dwellers from along the banks of the Schelde. Open Apr. to Sept., Sun. and hols. only, 2 to 6. Admission charge BF 20.

Plantin-Moretus Museum, Vrijdagmarkt 22. Home and workshop of the great family of printers from the city's Golden Age; priceless first editions. Open daily. (Visits to adjoining Prentencabinet, housing major collection of engravings, may be made on request.)

Provinciaal Museum Sterckshof, Hoofdvunderlei 160, in Deurne, about 5 km. (3 miles) east of city center (take tram 10). Flemish Renaissance castle (reconstructed 1938), located in beautiful Rivierenhof park. Contains collection of regional craftwork and items on local history. Open Easter to end-October, 10 to 5, closed Mon. and Fri.

Rockoxhuis, Keizerstraat 10–12. Patrician mansion, once belonging to Burgomaster Nicolas Rockox, a close friend of Rubens. Several fine interiors and some pictures. No admission charge.

Rubenshuis, Wapper 9, just off the Meir. Home of the greatest of Antwerp's 17th-century artists, Peter Paul Rubens. The building, constructed in 1610, contains the artist's studio, as well as several noteworthy pictures by the master himself and by his pupils. The garden is also worth a look. Open daily.

Sint-Andrieskerk (St. Andrew's Church), Sint-Andriesstraat 5. Gothic interior dating from 15th and 16th centuries; Mary, Queen of Scots monument. Group visits only—call 2320 384 between 10 and 11.30 A.M.

Sint-Augustinuskerk (St. Augustine's Church), Kammenstraat 73. Early Baroque interior. Currently undergoing restoration.

Sint-Carolus Borromeuskerk (St. Charles Borromeus Church), known to all locals as the Jesuïtenkerk, Hendrik Conscienceplein 12. Despite much subsequent damage, the richness of this high Baroque masterpiece is still evident. Notable galleried interior, Rubens chapel, and collection of lace. Open weekdays except Tues., 7.30 to 1, Sat. 7.30 to 12 and 3 to 6.15. Tourists are recommended to join the guided tours Wed. afternoons at 2 and 3. Admission charge BF 5, tour BF 20.

Sint-Jacobuskerk (St. James's Church), Lange Nieuwstraat 73. Gothic style, dating from the 15th and 16th centuries. Rubens' tomb. Open daily except Sun. from Easter to end-Oct., 2 to 5; rest of year 2 to 4. Admission charge BF 20.

Sint-Niklaaskapel (St. Nicolas' Church), Lange Nieuwstraat 3. Small 15th-century building, normally visible only from pleasant walled courtyard unless you attend one of the performances of the Vancampens puppet theater!

Sint-Pauluskerk (St. Paul's Church), Sint-Paulusstraat 20. A 16th-century Gothic exterior hides a gilded Baroque interior; several famous pictures. Open Tues. to Sat., May to Sept. from 9 to 12 and 2 to 5, rest of year 9 to 12. No admission charge.

Smidt van Gelder Museum, Belgiëlei 91. A beautifully-furnished 18th-century mansion, containing an excellent ceramics collection.

Stadhuis, Grote Markt. Majestic City Hall built at the height of Antwerp's mercantile greatness; 19th-century murals adorn much of the interior. Open Mon. 9 to 12, Tues. 9 to 12, Tues. to Thurs. 9 to 12, Fri. and Sat. 12 to 3, Sun. 10.45 to 12, 12.45 to 2, 2.45 to 4. Admission charge BF 20.

Vlaeykensgang, Oude Koornmarkt 16. Not actually a museum, but this tiny ancient alleyway is typical of the old city—and takes some finding.

Vleeshuis, Vleeshouwersstraat 38–40. The old butchers' guildhall; various exhibits, including collection of old musical instruments.

Volkskundemuseum, Gildekamersstraat 2–6. Old guildhouse; collection of artefacts and costumes depicting Flemish culture and folklore.

Zoo (Dierentuin), Koningin Astridplein 26. Several interesting sections including a dolphinarium. Open daily, 8.30 to 6.30 in summer, to 5 in winter. Admission charge BF 240.

 ENTERTAINMENT. Theaters. Antwerp has ten theaters, but for those who don't understand Dutch (or the local Flemish dialect) there are always symphony concerts held at *Queen Elisabeth Concert Hall* (near Zoo Gardens). A visit to *Vancampens Puppet Theater* (on Lange Nieuwstraat, at junction with Sint-Katelijnevest) is also worthwhile. Shows Fri. to Sun. afternoons. Call 6519 911 for details. Antwerp also likes to think of itself as Belgium's **cinema** capital; there are at least six large "commercial" cinemas near the Central Station, often showing English language films. In addition, there are a couple of art-film movie houses that show modern classics and also present a film festival in Sept. Details from *Het Filmhuis,* on Lange Brilstraat.

 SHOPPING. Head for the main thoroughfare, De Keyserlei, which starts at the Central Station, and you are in the big shopping district. This continues into the Meir, where you will find the major department stores. The surrounding side streets are sometimes specialized—Léopoldstraat goes in for *haute couture,* lace shops are in the streets around the cathedral. The *Antwerpse Lloyd* book shop on the Eiermarkt has one of the finest collections of nautical books in the world, while a good street for second-hand books is the Hoogstraat. Hi-fi buffs should make for the Minderbroedersrui, which is also good for antiques. Sat. and Sun. mornings there's a major openair market, the Vogelmarkt, stretching from the Oude Vaartplaats up to the Graanmarkt.

 RESTAURANTS. If the choice of hotels—for Antwerp's size and importance—is somewhat restricted, we can't complain about restaurants. In addition to those in the hotels, there are over 150 native, or classic, and nearly half as many exotic, or ethnic, eating places. You'll find everything from gastronomic temples to humble *fritures* in this city of good living.

If you reserve at least 1 week ahead, you can take the one-day gourmet cruise from Antwerp to Rotterdam aboard the *Flandria,* and return by bus; apply: Flandria, Steenplein (tel. 233 7422).

Expensive

Epicurus, Verbondstraat 44 (tel. 237 3699). Lives up to its name, with fine seafood and original specialties. Near Royal Museum of Fine Arts. Closed Sat. lunch, Sun. and Mon.

Het Fournuis, Reyndersstraat 24 (tel. 233 6270). Classic dining amid country-style decor.

Den Gulden Greffoen, Hoogstraat 37 (tel. 231 5046). A 15th-century survival, offering excellent local cooking.

La Pérouse, on the Steenplein on a ship's pontoon (tel. 232 3528). Exquisite seafood and other classic cuisine, in a great small restaurant. Must book. Closed Sun. and Mon., plus May through mid-Sept.

Sir Anthony van Dijck, Oude Koornmarkt 16 (tel. 231 6170). Down an ancient alleyway close to the cathedral; upstairs, with rural decor. Superb seafood, also try their goose-liver dishes.

'T Vermoeid Model, Lijnwaadmarkt 2 (tel. 233 5261). Literally built into the walls of the cathedral, with rustic Flemish atmosphere. Smoked trout a specialty.

Vateli, Kidporpvest 50 (tel. 233 1781). Classic cooking, with duck a specialty.

Moderate

Cambodge, Bourlastraat 19 (tel. 234 0979). Best Cambodian cooking outside Asia—a must.

Cigogne d'Alsace, Wiegstraat 9 (tel. 233 9716). Excellent cuisine at comparatively reasonable prices.

De Twee Atheners, Keiserstraat 2 (tel. 232 0851). A wide range of Mediterranean cooking in the best Greek restaurant in town.

Dragon Vert, Van Schoonhovenstraat 26 (tel. 233 0728). Excellent Chinese food.

Pottenbrug, Minderbroedersrui 38 (tel. 231 5147). Good food, delightful decor, relaxed atmosphere.

Rooden-Hoed, Oude Koornmarkt 25 (tel. 233 2844). Near the cathedral. Antwerp's most ancient restaurant, specializing in various preparations of eel and mussels.

Terminal, Leopolddok 214 (tel. 541 2680). An atmospheric spot in the north of town in the heart of the port. Dining with a fine view over the docks.

V.I.P. Diners, Lange Nieuwstraat 95 (tel. 233 1317). In the Old Quarter on a corner near St. Jacobskerk.

Inexpensive

Carmel Snack-bar, Hovenieresstraat 36–38 (tel. 231 8180). A cultural and gastronomic experience; kosher food in the heart of the diamond quarter.

In de Schaduw van de Kathedraal, Handschoenmarkt 17 (tel. 232 4014). As its name implies, it is in the center of the Old Quarter in the shadow of the cathedral.

Lido, Hanegraefstraat 8 (tel. 219 3590). Across on the Left Bank of the Schelde. One of the best Chinese restaurants.

Mini-Lunch, Sint'Katelijnevest 42 (tel. 231 6116). Good snack bar, excellent value for soup and sandwich lunches.

Rimini, Vestingstraat 5 (tel. 231 4290). Reliable Italian restaurant in diamond quarter.

NIGHTLIFE. Like every self-respecting port, Antwerp is teeming with nightclubs and especially discos. Prices, with one or two exceptions, are not high. Closer to the docks, there's a dubious red-light district; everything listed here is above-board.

In the neighborhood of Central Station, concentrated in Annessenstraat and vicinity: **Cactus, Popking** and **Retro** are currently popular laser-equipped disco-bars. In the nearby Statiestraat, try old favorite **Luna** or **Tropic.** If you want something a bit up-market from teeny-boppers, try some of the clubs (a U.S. or British passport usually gains you temporary membership): **le Richelieu,** Britselei 70; **Siam Club,** Frankrijklei 123; **Papillon,** Amerikalei 67; or **Jimmy's,** van Ertbornstraat 12—home of Antwerp's *jeunesse dorée.*

More like music-hall is **De Lachende Koe,** Statiestr. In the vicinity of the Flemish Theater are numerous bars and cabarets, others may be found in and around De Coninckplein.

USEFUL ADDRESSES. Consulates: American, Nationale Straat 5 (tel. 225 0071); British, Lange Klarenstraat 24 (tel. 232 6940).

Travel Agents: American Express, Frankrijklei 21 (tel. 232 5920); Wagon-Lits/Cook, Meir 11 (tel. 231 0830).

City Tourist Offices: Gildekamersstraat 9 (tel. 232 2284 and 232 0103); and the tourist pavilion opposite the central station, Koningin Astridplein, (tel. 233 0570). Both are open weekdays 8.30 to 6, weekends and holidays 9 to 5.

Provincial Tourist Office: Karel Oomsstraat 11 (tel. 216 2810). Other useful touring information can be obtained at the Touring Club of Belgium, Quellinstraat 9 (tel. 231 8718) and from the Flemish Tourist Association (VTB), Sihr-Jakobsmarkt 45 (tel. 234 3434).

Emergency Calls: Police 906; Ambulance 900.

LIMBURG AND THE KEMPEN

Land of Strange Contrasts

The Kempen (Campine) is Belgium's most deserted area, a lonely moorland alternating with sandy plains. It stretches from the Schelde to the Maas (Meuse) in the country north of Liège and Visé, where it becomes the Dutch frontier. The Kempen includes the bulk of the provinces of Antwerp and Limburg, and it is a country of sandhills and scrub, where indeed most of the fertility—and there is much—is the product of human endeavor. Men and women in wooden *klompen* toil long hours on the land; it is here that one may still encounter such homely scenes as were painted by Brueghel, Teniers, and latterday painters such as van Gogh in his earlier years.

It is a Dutch-speaking country, full of strange contrasts between old and new, and above all between a traditional simplicity of outlook and all the trimmings of modern mass-architecture. It was in the heart of this country that not long ago a woman was accused by her neighbors of witchcraft. Among her alleged accomplishments was the practice of turning herself after nightfall into a particularly ill-omened cat. This she was supposed to achieve in her ultra-modern kitchen, in a row of new redbrick residences which, apart from the pig-and-poultry back-yards, were indistinguishable from any London suburb.

There are two great economic features in this country, the coalfield and the Albert Canal. The discovery of coal in the Kempen basin dates from just after World War 1, and the collieries have outlasted their 19th-century counterparts near Mons, Charleroi, and Liège. The coal-field stretches east and west, roughly from Maasmechelen to the big army establishments of Beverlo. The Albert Canal leaves the Maas just north of Liège, following much the same course as the river until, near Lanaken, it curves round to flow past Hasselt and carry the heavy Liège traffic to Antwerp.

Sint-Truiden: Religious Art Center

For the Brussels-based visitor, the best approach is the Liège road through Leuven, which brings you into Limburg province at Sint-Truiden (St. Trond), in the very heart of the cherry country. In blossom-time a drive round the neighborhood is an experience never to be forgotten, and every day while the crop is being marketed the streets are full of the brightly colored fruit. At Sint-Truiden you are still in the Hesbaye (Haspengouw) country, but the elegant little spire of the town hall belfry demonstrates very graphically that the Kempenaars are proud of their public buildings and have seldom disfigured them with bulbous growths such as those which mar the tower at Mons.

In Sint-Truiden, however, most architectural activity has has been concentrated in numerous religious buildings. The town owes its name to an abbey established in the 7th century by the Bishop of Metz on land granted to him, in 655, by Saint Trudo. Most of the town's churches and monasteries date from the 12th to the 15th centuries, however. Sint-Truiden was, none the less, the center of an interesting outburst of civic consciousness in the mid-18th century, when the people took exception to the carillon cast for them in the first years of the century and were not satisfied until they got the bells, 41 in number, that you hear today. The Grote Markt (Market Square), severe but elegant, is a jewel of medieval architecture; and the second largest in Belgium (after Sint-Niklaas).

This is the place to come to if you are interested in fresco work. In the Begijnhof there are 38 large frescos, varying in age, for some date from as early as the 13th century, while others are a full four centuries later. There is no indication of any outstanding artist having had a hand in this work, but the frescos are interesting in themselves for their simplicity and sincerity. A hundred yards from the church is an astronomical compensation clock, nearly 20 feet high and comprising 20,000 mechanical parts. The frescos in St. Genevieve's Church at Zepperen, which lies 5 km. (3 miles) eastward, date back to the early 16th century; and in Sint-Truiden the fresco in the Onze Lieve Vrouw-kerk (Church of Our Lady) on the Grote Markt is dated 1625.

Just to the north of the Grote Markt stands the Benedictine Abbey (now a seminary), whose oldest tower dates back to the 11th century. Enlarged in the 17th, 18th and 19th centuries, the seminary was badly damaged by fire in 1975 and is still not restored to its former glory. Further down the Diesterstraat from the abbey is the Sint-Gangulfskerk, containing an 11th-century nave. Overlooking the Minderbroedersplein is the Minderbroedersklooster, a large 18th-century baroque edifice containing a display of numerous religious works of art—including an illustrated hymnal from 1515.

Following the main road eastward, you soon come to Borgloon, an attractive little town, ancient capital of the former county of Loon, which covered practically the whole of the present province of Limburg. Its principal curiosity is the Romanesque Sint-Odolfuskerk with its early 15th-century Gothic spire. The former residence of the counts of Loon, 's-Grevenhuis, the present town hall, was built in 1680. From Borgloon, you can head northeast for 2 km. (1 mile) toward Kerniel, until you reach the abbey at Kolen, known as the Mariënlof. In the shrine of Saint Odile you can see painted paneling dating from 1292—the oldest in Belgium. Also you can marvel at the 12th-century chair that belonged to Saint Lutgart—the oldest piece of furniture in Belgium. Alternatively, if you're tired of religious art, head northwest for 3 km. (2 miles) to the impressive 17th-century Kasteel van Rullingen.

Tongeren, Cradle of Resistance Movements

The road east from Borgloon leads you on to Tongeren, which lies at the intersection of seven roads, serving to remind you that the town owes much of its importance to its location on the great Roman highway from Cologne to Bavay. This ancient town is the cattle market for the rich Hesbaye country, the country of Charlemagne, and heifers are bargained for under the statue of Ambiorix, who was the father of all Belgium's resistance movements. He rallied the tribes against the Roman invader in 54 B.C., and massacred the legions of Sabinus and Cotta, only to be frustrated by the treachery of the enemy's collaborators. He was finally driven underground by a top-speed counter-offensive led by Caesar himself. Tongeren then became the Atuatuca Tungrorum of Roman Gaul. It reached its greatest size and eminence in the days of Tiberius Caesar, so that, most surprisingly in view of normal trends in town life, the remains of the medieval 13th-century fortifications are often well inside the towered Roman wall.

The Salian tribes destroyed Tongeren in the 4th century; and five hundred years later Norsemen pillaged, sacked, and burned it. Duke Henry I of Brabant sacked it again in the early 13th century, and in 1677 it was burned by the French.

The outstanding Romanesque relic is the 12th-century cloister in the Onze Lieve Vrouwebasiliek (Our Lady's Basilica), a church of some architectural interest with a very rich treasury containing, in particular, the 7th-century reliquary of St. Remacle and also that of the martyrs of Trier (West Germany), early 13th century. The lectern and chandelier, both made by Jehan Josès in the latter half of the 14th century, are excellent examples of Dinant brassware. Near the south door of the church is an underground Roman tower, the sole remaining relic of the 4th-century fortification which replaced the 2nd-century Roman wall, 4½ km. (3 miles) in length, extensive remains of which can be seen to the west of the center (Julius Caesarlaan, Legioenlaan, Cottalaan and Sabinuslaan). The medieval fortifications lie almost entirely within the line of the 2nd-century wall. They are best followed by heading north up the Vermeulenstraat as far as the Maternuswal.

Turn right (east) along the Elfde Novemberwal, then you can follow the ramparts south—along the 2nd-century alignment—to the Moerenpoort, one of the six medieval city gates, built in 1379. Slightly farther round the fortified perimeter, you reach the Begijnhof, one of the loveliest in Belgium, with its late 13th-century church and 17th-century cottages.

While you are at Tongeren, you should walk out to the Beukenberg, a man-made hill built apparently as part of the Roman city's water-supply system, at the order of Emperor Diocletian, which now marks a conventional boundary between the valleys of the Maas and the Schelde. From here you can see the *tumuli* that cover the remains of the legionaries slaughtered by the ambush laid by Ambiorix; and you can pass on to the Pliniusbron (Fountain of Pliny), a spring that has not had the commercial success of Spa, but with which it disputes the claim of being the spring mentioned for its invigorating qualities by Pliny the Elder.

There are a number of châteaux in this neighborhood, including the leafy 17th-century Kasteel Betho and the very lovely 18th-century Kasteel van Heks, which now stands in a large and stately park. It has a richly-appointed and well-preserved interior and may be visited on request. One you will not want to miss is some miles farther north, the castle of Alden Biesen (Vieux Joncs) at Rijkhoven, which can be seen on Sunday afternoons except in winter. The commanders of the Vieux-Joncs, an order of knights, were still here until the last years of the 18th century. The château, which is quite intact, portraits, tombs and all, had Louis XIV and Louis XV among its guests, as well as the young Duke of Cumberland, son of George II of England. The Tourist Office in Tongeren produces a useful little folder describing these (and about a dozen other) châteaux, which can sometimes be off the beaten track.

From Tongeren you can go on to Liège or Visé, or you can make for Eben-Emael, site of Belgium's "impregnable" frontier fortress, which was captured by a daring German attack, using parachute troops, in the early summer of 1940.

Hasselt, Capital of Belgian Limburg . . . and Distilling

If however you are systematically touring the whole of Limburg and the Kempen, you will strike northwestward to Hasselt, capital of the Belgian Limburg, a fragment of the old Duchy left on this side of the frontier by the events of 1830. Its Grote Markt is dominated by the 18th-century tower of the 12th–13th-century Saint Quintin's Cathedral. Also overlooking the market square are a number of fine patrician houses "The Pelican" and "The Sword" (in't Sweert) from 1633 and 1659. The Onze Lieve Vrouwekerk (Church of Our Lady), which was badly damaged in 1944, none the less contains a fine altar by the Liège sculptor, Jean Delcour, brought to the church from the abbey at Herkenrode. It also houses a celebrated 14th-century image of the Virgin, the Virga Jesse. Every seven years, in August, the image forms the centerpiece of a major religious procession (next celebrated in 1989). If you long for more secular pleasures, Hasselt will not disappoint you, since it is the center of the Belgian jenever-distilling industry (and we call it *Dutch* gin!). The Municipal Museum contains an interesting distillery exhibit—and *borreltjes* are available in local cafés.

Hasselt is also the gateway to the arid Kempen heathland and to its colliery district. You can come to the latter conveniently through Genk, a picturesque holiday resort with its lakes and woods and open-air theater. It has grown rapidly, due to the Ford plant and other industrial ventures, and has an ultra-modern shopping center (park on the roof); many Italians and Turks work in the mines and factories.

Bokrijk, halfway between Hasselt and Genk, should be visited. The administration of Limburg province has set aside a nature reserve which shows in all its unspoilt originality the Kempen country of heather and pine, sand and broom, and marshes and ponds frequented by waterfowl. In this beautiful setting, many old farmhouses from all over Flanders have been carefully reerected and restored, and their interiors show old peasant furniture, ancient utensils and beaten copper-work, all familiar from paintings of the Flemish masters. Since the late 1970s, more urban buildings have been brought to the site, and the archetypal Flemish village is gradually taking shape. Even a few mock-peasants walk around in traditional garb. It is the largest open-air museum in Europe.

Through As and Dilsen you can reach the Maas at lime-fringed Maaseik. A trip which is purely a pilgrimage to the birthplace of the van Eycks will reveal little of the great painters' lives, save a statue in the main square. None the less, the elegant 17th- and 18th-century facades of the houses on the Grote Markt and the Bosstraat are worth a second look. In the mansions known as "Orange Tree" and the "Blue Lion" on the Grote Markt you will find the local museum—largely uninspiring save for the old apothecary's shop interior and suitably gruesome equipment. More impressive, perhaps, is a visit to St. Catherine's church treasury to see the *Gospels of Aldeneik,* an illuminated version prepared by two Valenciennes nuns who came to Limburg in A.D. 730. This is one of the few examples of Carolingian art and craftsmanship to be found in Belgium.

The valley of the Maas (Limburgse Maasstreek) is a pleasant region stretching from Lanaken in the south to Ophoven in the north. Many anglers practise their favorite sport here. From Maaseik itself you can take a leisurely cruise up the Maas into the Netherlands. Or you can settle down in your tent, camper or chalet at one of the region's well-equipped tourist centers: swimming, boating, horseback riding and extensive nature trails are all on offer.

For those unable to linger, the route returns westward along the Leopoldsburg road (N73). You will pass through a country where the villages were once important towns. Having never recaptured their cloth-based prosperity of the 14th and 15th centuries, they have fortunately for us never had money enough to replace their Gothic churches by more pretentious edifices conforming to the tastes of later periods. At Neeroeteren (just west of Maaseik) the late Gothic church contains some fine statues. Further on, at Opitter and Bree, there are fine churches of the early 15th century. At Opoeteren (farther south) the church is older (partly 9th century) and here too you will see the château that served as a hunting lodge to the prince-bishops of Liège.

Geel, Pilgrimage Center

Striking westward across the open moorland, passing the spoil tips of the coalfield and the nuclear research center of Mol, you will reach Geel.

For many centuries Geel was a center of pilgrimage for the mentally ill and, if they were not at once cured, they would often stay on in the homes of the townsfolk. Their pilgrimage was to the shrine of Saint Dymphne who, about the year A.D. 600, fled here from the attentions of her Irish father, who eventually caught her and split her skull open right in this very town. Her relics are in a wooden reliquary in the church which bears her name and which contains some beautiful stone and woodwork. In the northern part of the town, on the south side of the 16th-century tower, is the sickroom where pilgrims in search of cure were required to lodge during the nine days of their pilgrimage. The hospital has retained all the architectural features of its epoch (17th century) while the town hall has lost much of its original appearance because of clumsy renovation.

Today, Geel is a byword among the Belgians for its main occupation, which is the care in private houses of the mentally handicapped. You will have to wander about Geel and the neighboring country to get an idea of the patients and the work this seeming freedom is doing for them. It is basically charitable work, though nowadays it is paid for by the families of the patients, or, more often, by the state. If you come by train you cannot avoid the scrutiny at the station of the male nurse who, in these modern times, will lead the patient to the infirmary where the non-dangerous cases are vetted before they are placed with families.

The countryside here is charming, dotted with ancient castles and mansions. Heading north from Geel, through Kasterlee (a useful overnight halt), you reach Turnhout, the local administrative center and market town. Turnhout, however, offers little architectural interest. Its only outstanding building is the Gerechtshof (Law Court), formerly a hunting castle of the dukes of Brabant. St. Peter's Church contains some fine Baroque furniture, and paintings by Teniers. Since 1826 Turnhout has printed playing cards and has an unusual museum centered around them.

Baarle-Hertog, a Medieval Enclave

Your journey to Turnhout has not been in vain, however. From the Paterstraat you should head north, following the signs for Baarle. In about five miles you will reach the Dutch frontier. Here you cross the border and pass along an unmistakably Dutch stretch of road for a couple of miles until you find yourself back inside what is legally, and administratively, Belgian territory: in one of Europe's last remaining territorial enclaves.

Baarle-Hertog is not only surrounded by Dutch territory, it is a town within a town. The surrounding land is not empty fields—but the twin town of Baarle-Nassau. You will not discern any visible "frontier" running between the houses; but look at the two telephone cabins a few yards apart in the main square. One is Belgian, hooked up to one network; the other is Dutch, requiring an "international" call to ring just down the street. Likewise, there are two town halls, two post offices, two churches, two fire brigades, two schools, and two police stations—in what appears to be a single town of just over 7,000 people.

There is no Berlin-style median line. Apart from the main Belgian nucleus south of the main square (which is itself Dutch—except for one cafe), there is a hopelessly confused jumble of plots of both nationalities. Thanks to a 12th-century land settlement, there are parcels of Belgian territory all over Baarle; some too small to accommodate a modern house, some over a mile from the town center, and some which even contain Dutch enclaves within them.

The rule of thumb is that the "nationality" of a house is determined by the position of its front door. As part of each house number you will notice a small tricolour plaque: red-black-yellow for Belgian houses, red-white-blue for Dutch. Simple, unless of course the doorway straddles the frontier, in which case the house has dual nationality and two sets of numbers. After walking round the charming streets, trying to spot which country you're in, visit some of the town's inns (and try to pay in the "home" currency to get a slightly better price), which serve excellent local food. The (Belgian) church of St. Remigius is also worth a visit, while the 19th-century Belgian Stadhuis has much of the appeal of a provincial French *Mairie*.

From Baarle you can return to Turnhout, then head southwestwards toward Herentals, the Ypres of the north which, in the early days of the 14th-century cloth trade, was a serious rival to the Flemish industry. Its best buildings, the Stadhuis and the Church of St. Waudru (Sint-Waldetrudiskerk), are early 15th century, and the latter contains a carved reredos by Pasquier Borremans, considered one of the masterpieces of Brabant wood carving.

Moving southward across the Albert Canal you will come to Olen. It has pre-Roman remains and a radium factory. It is also the home of a unique drinking vessel—the Pot van Olen—which is a three-handled beer mug, said to have been first made for Charles V to facilitate his taking a drink from his servants while still on horseback. You can emulate the 16th-century emperor in one of the local inns. Further on are the two Norbertine abbeys of Tongerlo and Averbode. Tongerlo has a strikingly decorated church and owns a particularly valuable copy of Leonardo da Vinci's *Last Supper* which, in view of the restorations of the original in Milan, is thought to show more clearly the painter's original intentions. It is usually accepted as the work of Leonardo's pupil Andrea del Solario and is attractively displayed. Moated Tongerlo is one of the most active religious houses in Belgium. Its rich library has among its treasures a complete *Acta Sanctorum*, one volume of which was actually published from Tongerlo.

The buildings at Averbode, one of Europe's most important monasteries, are for the most part later than those of Tongerlo. Well restored, they contain some magnificent Louis XV interiors and some old masters. In the Abbot's House there is an embossed plaque by Rubens, some four feet in diameter, depicting a man on a galloping horse, so lifelike that one recalls Reynolds, saying, "His horses are perfect in their kind." The Baroque church, with the choir longer than its nave, contains a particularly fine sacristy decorated by Feuillen Houssart of Namur (18th century).

Between Averbode and Tongerlo is Westerlo, with its two châteaux of the house of Mérode and the fine *Annunciation Triptych* by Robert Campin of Tournai, presumably the Maître de Flémalle who, because of this picture, has sometimes been referred to as the Maître de Mérode.

Diest and Lier, Prettiest Towns of Belgium

Continuing south toward Zichem, you can turn eastward through Molenstede to Diest, famous not only for its beer but also for its ramparts, an excellent example of a totally fortified town remaining largely intact. For its size, it is Belgium's richest town in monuments of the past, and in the absence of new buildings, one of the most unspoiled. Its principal attraction is the Grote Markt, where 17th-century houses present a fitting background to the 18th-century Town Hall and the largely 15th-century Church of Saint Sulpice. There is an unusual museum beneath the Town Hall, laid out in three cellars at different levels, but linked together: no cameras allowed, but there are excellent postcards on sale.

A pleasant walk in the old town will take you to the Schaffen Gates, showing distinctly Diest's triple line of fortifications. Despite the town's having been successively occupied and fortified by Spanish, Austrian, French and Dutch troops, most of the remaining vestiges date from the early years of the Belgian state. During that period, the Dutch were thought to harbor revanchist ideas and so, right up to 1855, Diest was progressively ringed with ramparts and interlinked forts— just in time for military tactics and strategic realities to make the whole system obsolete.

In a less martial guise, Diest has a delightful begijnhof, where the church is dedicated to St. Catherine, and a Cloth Hall dating from the 14th century. In the Henri Verstappenplein you can see the former mansion of the princes of Orange-Nassau, dating from the early 16th century. Opposite is the Warande Stadspark, the princes' former hunting ground—now a pleasant green space with a small open-air theater. To the east of Leopoldvest, some of the old moats and ravelins have been turned into an open-air recreation center, de Halve Maan (the Half Moon), an attractive place devoted to sport and spare-time activities. You can swim, row, fish or sunbathe, and children will enjoy the well-equipped playground. At nearby Schaffen, there is a well-known parachuting center, where you can watch the participants or try your luck.

West of Diest lies Scherpenheuvel (Montaigu), a small town created at the behest of the Archduke Albert and Archduchess Isabella, to which a large-scale religious pilgrimage, known as the Procession of the Candles, comes on the Sunday after All Saints' Day each year.

Beyond this you can head roughly northwestward, through Aarschot (see page 101) and Heist-op-den-Berg (which, as its name suggests, is on what passes for a hill in these parts), toward the town of Lier (Lierre), which you should on no account miss. Already described in the 13th century as a little paradise, it is still today (despite the damage done during the German invasion of August/October 1914), an attractive little town. You will enter it over a bridge, and so perplexing is the course of the Nete that the town is almost all at the riverside, with willows leaning over the water. Everything in such a town is bound to be charming, and the 18th-century town hall accords miraculously well with the belfry, which stands at its side, and is prominently dated 1369. This is one of the more elegant towers of its kind in Belgium.

Lier is rich in history, political and cultural, a miniature walled town of cobbled streets and houses ranging in period from the Renaissance to the last century. If you want to know the time of day, the season of the year, the phase of the moon, or even the date of the next eclipse, you have only to climb the old (but rebuilt) tower to the much more modern studio of the astronomer Louis Zimmer, whose "Centenary Clock" was one of Belgium's exhibits at the New York World Exhibition in 1933.

The Church of Sint Gummarus, 15th-century Gothic at its best, planned by Hendrik Mijs of Mechelen and worked on by the de Waghemaker-Keldermans partnership, is rich in works of art. Particularly outstanding are its 15th- and 16th-century stained-glass windows. On the first Sunday after Trinity and after October 10, the relics of the saint, in their massive silver *châsse*, are the focus of a long procession through the streets. See the Wuyts Museum's fine paintings, and the Begijnhof, one of Belgium's most beautiful, with an outstanding monument of the Calvary in one of the courtyards.

PRACTICAL INFORMATION FOR
LIMBURG AND KEMPEN

HOTELS AND RESTAURANTS. The Kempen country is well provided with moderate and inexpensive hotels. They are on the whole cheaper than elsewhere in Belgium, probably because this region is touristically as yet "undiscovered". Farmhouse holidays are also available. Contact *Transeurope*, Petrus en Paulusplein 10,8400 Oostende, or see the appropriate section of the *Groene Gids* (Green Guide) published by the Limburg Province tourist bureau. Good restaurants abound.

AS. 8 km. (5 miles) northwest of Genk. *Mardaga* (M), Stationstraat 89 (tel. 011–657 034). 18 rooms; excellent and reasonably priced, as is their restaurant. Try one of their preparations of eel.

BAARLE-HERTOG. Picturesque enclave of Belgian territory 2 miles across the border in Holland. *Den Bonten Os* (I), Pastoor De Katerstraat 23 (tel. 014–699 016, Belgian). 30 rooms, 14 with bath; no restaurant. **Restaurants.** *Den Engel* (M), Singel 3 (tel. 0031–4257—9330, Dutch). *Lotus* (I), Sint-Annaplein 9 (tel. 9988, Dutch). Good Chinese food.

132 EXPLORING BELGIUM

BOKRIJK. Model village of bygone era. Halfway between Hasselt and Genk, take a signposted private road to the left. **Restaurant.** *Kasteel Bokrijk* (M), Bokrijklaan 8 (tel. 225 564). On private estate; serves great provincial cuisine.

DIEST. Charming old art town, home of good beer. *Modern* (I), Leuvensesteenweg 93 (tel. 013–311 066). 13 rooms, all with bath or shower; and recommended restaurant. *Falstaff* (I), Eduard Robeynslaan 2 (tel. 013–311 634). 7 rooms, 4 with shower; just outside ramparts.
Restaurants. *De Keizer/L'Empereur* (M), Grote Markt 24 (tel. 013–335 482); their tourist menu offers excellent local cooking at a bargain price.

EISDEN (MAASMECHELEN). Well-located overnight halt, with interesting modern church. *Lika* (M), Pauwengraaf 2 (tel. 011–760 126). 17 rooms in this comfortable hotel; and pleasant restaurant on third floor.

GEEL. Restaurant. *De Waag* (M), Molseweg 2 (tel. 014–586 220). 1/2 mile east on the N71.

GENK. *Atlantis* (I), Fletersdel 1, Sledderloweg (tel. 011–356 551). 19 well-equipped rooms and good restaurant. *Europa* (I), Sledderloweg 85 (tel. 011–354 274). 17 rooms, on southeast outskirts. *De Schacht* (I), Noordlaan 36 (tel. 011–356 180). 15 rooms, 10 with shower; modest restaurant.
Restaurant. *Ludo's Bistro* (M), Europalaan 81 (tel. 011–357 467). Cheerful and centrally located.

HASSELT. Chief city of province and art town. *Crown Royal* (M), Sint-Truidersteenweg 381 (tel. 011–273 628). Comfortable hotel with 9 rooms, just south of town center. *Parkhotel* (M), Genkersteenweg 350 (tel. 011–211 652). 27 rooms and restaurant 2 miles northeast of center. *Century* (I), Leopoldplein 1 (tel. 011 211 652). 27 rooms and restaurant 2 miles northeast of center. *Century* (I), Leopoldplein 1 (tel. 011–224 799). 18 rooms, 14 with shower; good restaurant.
Southwest of Hasselt at **Stevoort** (follow Runkstersteenweg about 3 miles) there is a converted 18th-century farm which is one of Belgium's most exclusive hotels, *Scholteshof* (E), Kermtstraat 18 (tel. 011–250 202). 18 comfortable rooms—and a world-class restaurant.
Restaurants. *'t Claeverblat* (M), Lombaardstraat 34 (tel. 011–222 404). Centrally located with excellent cuisine. *Roma* (I), Koningin Astridlaan 9 (tel. 011–222 770). Good Italian food; between the station and the town center.
Between Hasselt and Diest at **Lummen** (5 miles northwest) there is a small castle, *Kasteel St Paul* (M), Lagendalstraat 1, (tel. 551 809), which is now a gourmet restaurant.

HERENTALS. Interesting town hall and church. *Golf* (M), Lierseweg 321 (tel. 014–211 836). 12 rooms, 8 with bath, and good restaurant; west on the N13.
Restaurants. *De Zalm* (I), Grote Markt 21 (tel. 014–221 417). Flemish cuisine right on the main square. *Snepkenshoeve* (E), Lichtaartseweg 220 (tel. 014–213 672). Gourmet restaurant with authentic Flemish decor. 2 miles northeast on the N123.

KASTERLEE. Typical small Kempen town—a better overnight halt than Turnhout. *Bosrand* (M), Geelsebaan 69 (tel. 014–556 215). 34 rooms, 24 with bath; good restaurant. *Sparrenhof* (M), Lichtaartsebaan 77 (tel. 014–556 161). On edge of built-up area. 15 rooms, about half with bath; restaurant.

Restaurant. *Kastelhof* (E), Lichtaartsebaan 33 (tel. 014–556 360). Open-air dining in summer.

LIER. The gateway to the Kempen. *Handelshof* (I), Leopoldplein 39–41 (tel. 03–480 0310). 10 very basic rooms, and modest restaurant; handy for station.
Restaurant. *Marnixhoeve* (M), Kesselsesteenweg 79 (tel. 03–480 3310). In a rustic setting, 2 miles east on the N13.

MAASEIK. Birthplace of the van Eyck brothers, *Aldeneikershof* (M), Hamontweg 103 (tel. 011–566 777). 8 comfortable rooms, good restaurant. *Van Eyck* (I), Markt 48 (tel. 011–564 051). 8 rooms, 4 with shower; pleasant restaurant. At **Neeroeteren**, 2 1/2 miles west on N73, *Jagershof* (M), Diestersteenweg 221 (tel. 011–865 632). 6 rooms in rural setting; no restaurant. At **Opoeteren** (about a mile beyond Neeroeteren), *Oeterdal* (M), Neeroeterenstraat 43 (tel. 011–863 717). 25 well-equipped rooms; with pleasant restaurant.

MOL. Road junction, nuclear center, strictly an overnight halt. *Molinas* (M), Turnhoutsebaan 46 (tel. 014–313 588). 18 rooms all with bath, and restaurant.
Restaurant. *Resto Gerard* (M), Statiestraat 24 (tel. 014–310 950). Classic cuisine, convenient for the station.

SINT-TRUIDEN. *Cicindria* (M), Abdijstraat 6 (tel. 011–681 344). Modern hotel, centrally located in well-designed new development. 19 comfortable rooms, but no restaurant.
Restaurants. *New Astoria* (E), Grote Markt 18 (tel. 011–689 962). Gourmet dining in modern decor in the town center. *Amico* (I), Namenstraat 3 (tel. 011–676 150). Just south of Grote Markt, open late, with fish a specialty. *Jacques* (M), Luikersteenweg 268 (tel. 011–683 965). 2 miles southeast at Brustem.

TONGEREN. The oldest (Belgo-Roman) city in the country and fine art center. *Chemin de Fer* (I), Stationslaan 44 (tel. 012–233 105). 14 rooms, 2 with bath. *Lido* (I), Grote Markt 19 (tel. 012–231 948). 7 rooms, 3 with bath; in the historic central market place.
Restaurants. *Biessenhuys* (M), Hasselsestraat 23 (tel. 012–234 709). Historic building offering top-class Flemish cooking. *Sir Charles* (M), Maastrichtersteenweg 447 (tel. 012–230 209). 2 miles east of town at Elderen; recommended for their game dishes. *Speedy* (M), Grote Markt 36 (tel. 012–230 723). Mussels are a specialty; terrace in summer. *Mokkakopje* (I), Kloosterstraat 2 (tel. 012–230 187). Friendly cafe.

TONGERLO. Famous abbey and Leonardo da Vinci Museum. **Restaurant,** *Torenhof* (M), Geneinde 1 (tel. 544 391). Pleasant inn opposite the abbey. Good for lunch en route.

TURNHOUT. Short on hotels (try **Kasterlee,** 6 miles south). *Ter Driezen* (M), Herentalsstraat 18 (tel. 418 757). 7 comfortable rooms and good restaurant. Located just south of the Grote Markt.
Restaurant. *Alta Ripa II* (M), Engelstraat 6 (tel. 677 461). Excellent rustic inn, 4 miles east on road to Arendonk.

WESTERLO. Fine châteaux and 15th-century church. *Geerts* (M), Grote Markt 50 (tel. 014–544 017). 18 rooms, some with bath; garden restaurant.

Restaurant. *Het Loo* (M), Bergveld 107 (tel. 014–545 405). Provides good provincial cuisine in a rural atmosphere. Two miles west of town on the N152.

MUSEUMS AND PLACES OF INTEREST. Some of the country's oldest and finest art towns are in this region. In fact, Tongeren is the oldest Romano-Belgian settlement in Belgium. There are also a sprinkling of wonderful abbeys and châteaux to carry the story on through the Middle Ages.

BOKRIJK. Vlaams Openluchtmuseum (Flemish Open-Air Museum). Europe's largest folk-museum contains typical rural and urban buildings from throughout Flanders. Open daily from April to mid-October, 10 to 6. Admission BF 100.

BORGLOON. Klooster Marienlof. Kolenstraat 1, Kerniel. Richly endowed Cistercian convent. Open weekdays 10 to 11.30 and 2 to 5; Sun. 3 to 6. Admission BF 20.

DIEST. Begijnhof. One of Belgium's biggest—a large peaceful area of lanes and small houses and a church, St. Catherine, which can all be entered via a fine archway topped by a statue of the Virgin and Child on Begijnenstraat.

St.-Sulpitiuskerk (Church of St. Sulpice). Open daily 10 to 12, July and August, except Sun.; rest of the year apply to the church authorities (tel. 332 007).

Stedelijk Museum, the Municipal Museum in the 14th-century crypt of the Town Hall; rich medieval atmosphere with carvings, armor and ornate guild relics. Open April 1 to Oct. 31, 9 to 12 and 2 to 5 (to 4 on Sun.).

HASSELT. Stadsmuseum and **Nationale Jenevermuseum** (Municipal Museum and National Gin Museum). Oude Gasthuis, Thonissenlaan 73. The main attraction of the museum is the reconstruction of a 19th-century distillery. Open daily (except Mon.) 2 to 6. Admission BF 40.

LIER. Sint-Gummarus Church. Silver shrine of the saint, white sandstone rood screen and lovely stained glass. Arrange visits with information center in the Stadhuis.

Wuyts Museum, excellent art collection. Open 10 to 12, 1.30 to 5.30; closed Wed. and Thurs.

Zimmertoren, clock and observatory tower. Open 9 to 12, 2 to 7 in summer; 9 to 12, 2 to 4 in winter. Admission BF 25.

MAASEIK. Apotheek- en Stedelijk Museum (Pharmacy and Municipal Museum), Markt 46. Open weekends only from April to September, 2 to 5. Admission BF 15.

Kerkschat Sint-Catharinakerk (St. Catherine's Church Treasury). Fine collection of religious ornaments, with the 8th-century *Codex Eyckenensis* its centerpiece. Open on request—apply to tourist office (address below). Admission BF 10.

Maaseik Historical Display, Markt 17. Models and maps explain the development of Maaseik from earliest times to the present day. Opening times are the same as for the Municipal Museum. Admission BF 40.

SINT-TRUIDEN. Begijnhof Church, now a museum of religious art. Open 9 to 12 and 2 to 4. Closed Sat. and Sun. Visits are also possible to adjoining astronomical clock (studio Festraets). Jul. and Aug., daily exc. Sat., 10.45 and 3.45 (visits begin 15 mins. before the clock "performs"). Rest of year, Sun. and hols. only, 9.45 to 11.45 and 1.45 to 4.45.

Sint-Franciscusmuseum, Minderbroedersstraat 5. Franciscan monastery now displays important collection of devotional art and religious objects. Open daily, 9 to 12 and 2 to 6. Admission BF 20.

TONGEREN. Onze Lieve Vrouwebasiliek (Our Lady's Basilica). Delightful interior, fine cloister. Most memorable are the priceless reliquaries in the treasury. Open May to Sept. 9 to 12, 1.30 to 4. Call 232 654 in winter.

Moerepoortmuseum, Leopoldwal. Collection of weapons and display of Tongeren's military history, housed in old gateway. Open Sat., 2 to 5. Admission BF 20.

Provinciaal Gallo-Romeins Museum (Gallo-Roman Museum), Kielenstraat. Reflects Tongeren's early history; some Roman sculptures. Recommended. Open 9 to midday daily, exc. Mon.

Stedelijk Museum (Municipal Museum), Grote Markt. Paintings and prints depicting the history of the town. Open daily (exc. winter weekends), 10 to 12 and 2 to 4.30.

TURNHOUT. National Museum van de Speelkaart (Playing-card Museum), Begijnenstraat. Open Wed. and Fri. (daily Jul. and Aug.), 2 to 5, Sun. 10 to 12.

USEFUL ADDRESSES. Provincial Tourist Office. Domein Bokrijk, 3600 Genk (tel. 222 958). **City Tourist Offices.** Baarle-Hertog, St. Annaplein 10 (tel. 99 21); Bree, Cobbestraat 3 (tel. 462 514); Diest, Stadhuis (Town Hall), Grote Markt 1 (tel. 332 121); Genk, Gemeentehuis, Dieplaan 2 (tel. 353 911); Hasselt, Lombaardstraat 3 (tel. 225 961); Lier, Stadhuis, Grote Markt 57 (tel. 480 22 33, ext. 212); Maaseik, Markt 45 (tel. 566 372); Neeroeteren, Recreatiepark 't Eiland, Komweg 11 (tel. 863 036); Sint-Truiden, Stadhuis, Grote Markt (tel. 686 872, ext. 190); Tongeren, Stadhuisplein 9 (tel. 232 961).

FLANDERS AND ITS ART TOWNS

Historic Ypres, Ghent and Bruges

Of all the age-long stories of strife, bloodshed and conflicting interests, that of Flanders is among the most eventful. Remotest Gaul to the Romans, it was the buffer between the Capets and the Lotharingian emperors, and its sandy shore offered no obstacle to the marauding Vikings. It struggled to independent existence under Baldwin Iron-Arm, and its weaving industry became the great market for English wool. Its independence from French or imperial domination became central to English policy. The alliance of the last count of Flanders with the first of the dukes of Burgundy was the cornerstone upon which Philip the Good built the Grand Dukedom of the West, by which time the strife between its patricians and the men of the loom had given place to the strife of the cities for their civil liberties. Ruined as it was by arrivals of cloth that refugee Flemish weavers had taught the English to weave, it lived to become a center in the fight for religious toleration and, in consequence, a victim of the Duke of Alba's persecutions. Fought over time and again, it was the scene of Marlborough's victory of Oudenaarde; and its northwestern corner, centered on Ypres (Ieper), was the final bastion on Belgian soil to stem the German advance on the channel ports in World War I.

The Flemish language is basically Dutch, but the spoken language can still vary from place to place. "God made us Flemish; only politics made us Belgian" is still a much-quoted slogan from their poet, Guido Gezelle. Its people have resisted, with all the stubbornness they showed in the Middle Ages, the real or supposed French domination in Belgian affairs. There is scarcely a Fleming who hasn't a story to tell of victimization of his people during the last century and a half of Belgian history; to be fair, it should be added that such stories are told also on the other side now that the Flemings (grown to 60% of the population) are taking the upper hand. But the effect in Flanders has been a certain self-consciousness in the language, which suppresses the occasional Gallicisms allowed by classical Dutch, yet admits much Gallic phraseology.

The Flemish have a great sense of spiritual unity, and even though they were once supporters both of Jansenism and of Calvinism, their unity today centers more than ever upon the Catholic Church. Luckily for the visitor, the Flemish are good linguists. Moreover, the connection with England dates back over many centuries, not only in commercial matters, but also in tourist visits and more especially in the migrations of political and wartime refugees. You won't go far without finding someone who speaks excellent English, and in times of difficulty simple French will usually help you out.

Ypres, Victim of History

While Ghent is queen of the rivers and islands, and Bruges for some centuries was queen of the sea, Ypres (Ieper), with the spire of Saint Martin's Cathedral and the sturdier but less aspiring tower of the Lakenhalle (Cloth Hall), is queen of the Flemish plain. Senior partner of the three great towns of Flanders, Ypres was probably well-established in the textile industry when Menapian cloth was the prized possession of the matrons of ancient Rome. Centuries before Edward III of England gave Bruges the handling of the English wool trade, Ypres was the active center of a mighty industry that, in the 14th century, gave her the right to annex the countryside round Poperinge and break up the competing looms of the *buiten-poorters* or country citizens.

When you see the Cloth Hall you will realize that only an industry on a large scale—an immense scale by medieval standards—could have justified such lavish architecture. The Cloth Hall dates from the year 1214, and the cathedral is from the same period. Unfortunately, however, little of the original structure is left in either. What you see today has been reconstructed from the ruins of World War I, when the name of "Wipers" stood for the near-destruction, suffering and dogged resistance of that last salient of Belgian soil, which never fell. Fittingly the reconstructed Cloth Hall now houses the informative Salient War Museum, as well as a Museum of Modern Art.

It is right and fitting that the Cloth Hall should have been restored, and so gigantic an enterprise was not an easy accomplishment. The building has, or had, scarcely its like in the world. Its rebuilding was an act of piety hardly influenced by the spirit of social usefulness which was never wanting from the original.

In the cathedral you can still see the tomb of Bishop Jansen, the Bishop of Ypres whose studies of Saint Augustine produced the heresy of Jansenism that divided the Christian world through the second half of the 17th century and caused such suffering. But nowadays the fortunes of Ypres have dwindled. The citizens who originally built the Cathedral and the Cloth Hall would be most surprised to learn that today Ypres is smaller than London. (In the 13th century Ypres was a city of 100,000, today it has around 34,000 inhabitants.)

In a number of the streets of Ypres you will find rows of reconstructed 17th-century house frontages. Ypres, risen out of the rubble of 1914–18, is essentially a modern town. She is lucky in having a great past around which to build; and it is from this magnificent heritage that modern architects involved in the reconstruction have drawn much of their inspiration for the town's modern revival. One of the most impressive 20th-century constructions—designed to blend into the Vauban fortifications—is the Menin Gate (Meensepoort), a masterpiece of classic simplicity, built as a lasting memorial to the 250,000 officers and men of the British Commonwealth who lost their lives on the Western Front in World War I. Of these, some 55,000 have no known graves, and their names are engraved on panels on the gate itself. Designed by the British architect Sir Reginald Blomfield, the Gate was inaugurated in 1927. Since then, every evening traffic has been stopped for a few minutes while buglers, recruited from the local fire brigade, blow the "Last Post" on silver bugles, the gift of the British Legion. Only during World War II was this nightly rite interrupted and, on the night of Ypres' liberation, the "Last Post" was blown before the last enemy had marched out of the town.

The ancient moated fortifications of Ypres were strengthened by Vauban in the 17th century, and even the bombardments of the 20th century did not destroy them. If you walk up the stairway in the Menin Gate, you will find yourself on the ramparts. You can follow them round as far as the Lille Gate (Rijselpoort) where, nestling below a large cypress and with turf greener than is elsewhere to be found in Belgium, is one of the most picturesque of the many British war cemeteries. These cemeteries are maintained by the Commonwealth War Graves Commission on soil given in perpetuity by the Belgian government.

Among all the reconstruction and modern building, it seems unlikely Ypres will forget that of all her eventful history, the years 1914–18 are the most memorable. If you return to the Grote Markt, pass through the archway of the Cloth Hall and follow round past the cathedral, you will come to the little British Church of St. George, with its abundance of war memories and, behind it, the Pilgrims' Hall, built for those who visit Ypres in quest of family graves.

The tremendous events of the 20th century have all but eclipsed the memories of earlier centuries. There is, however, a link with the past: on the second Sunday in May, *Kattenwoensdag* cats (nowadays only stuffed woolen cats) are flung by the town jester from the belfrytop to the crowd below. Cats were required in great numbers during the

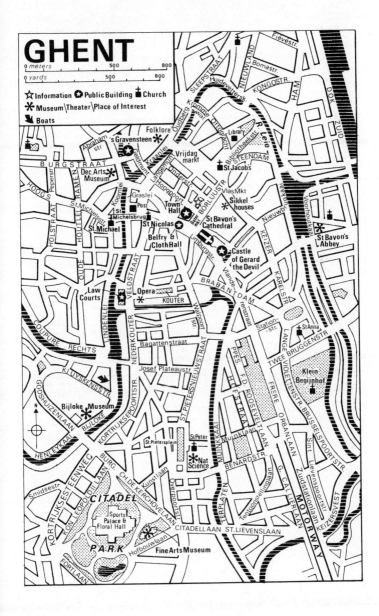

GHENT

| 0 meters | 500 | 800 |
| 0 yards | 500 | 800 |

☆ Information ⊕ Public Building ⬛ Church
✳ Museum\Theater\Place of Interest
⬐ Boats

middle ages to deal with the mice rampant in the Cloth Hall. When the
great yearly sales were over and the storage space empty, the mice
vanished and the cats themselves then became the problem. It is said
that in order to get rid of them the inhabitants conceived the idea of
hurling them from the belfry to the ground. Cat-worship has always
been linked with witches so toy witches are also thrown by the carnival
jester. This is all part of the magnificent procession which has floats
devoted to the history of the town and of course the cats.

The names around Ypres sound like a repertoire of battlefields—
Poperinge, Paschendaele, Kemmel Hill, Ploegsteert. British and Commonwealth cemeteries are almost everywhere. One of the most moving,
the Tyne Cot British Military Cemetery containing 11,908 graves (and
a memorial to 34,888 missing), is built around a German bunker on the
Paschendaele (now Passendale) ridge. A short drive away Hill 60 and
the Caterpillar mine crater at Zwarteleen are more or less as they were
in 1918, and there is a small private Museum of the Trenches in a café
at Sanctuary Wood, just below Hill 62. A section of trenches and
tunnels has also been preserved, remaining authentically horrific. Away
from these memories of the carnage the country is attractive for walking. Westouter, near Loker, is a typical Flanders village, worth a short
halt. Dikkebus, 5 km. southwest of Ypres, has a pleasant man-made
lake with a small hotel overlooking it.

Ghent, "Florence of the North"

If Ypres has lost touch with her remoter past, Ghent (Gent or Gand)
has absorbed hers. No city, except perhaps Florence, has had a history
so full of dark incident and valiant strife, and in none do the buildings
of many centuries jostle one another in so lively an aspect of present
social usefulness. Ghent does not live in the past; her past lives in her.
She has more to show you, if you care to look for it, than any city in
Belgium or than any city of comparable size in the world. Yet she does
not worry unduly about bringing her treasures to your attention.

But the city—one of Belgium's largest—is not an inanimate museum, as is often said of Bruges. Like Florence, it is full of flowers, for
it is the center of a thriving horticultural industry. Due to the flowers
there is always color in the streets of this gray city, where there is much
that dates from the Middle Ages and earlier, but where nothing is
self-consciously medieval and where every stone is part of 20th-century
life. Incidentally, at Lochristi, 9 km. (6 miles) out, a Begonia Festival
is held on the last weekend of August (the begonia is the national flower
of Belgium).

It is true that you can no longer see the palace where Charles V was
born, with its "six gateways flanked with towers, its gardens where
there wandered bears and lions, its 300 halls each with its lock and key,
and above them all its tower of glass." All that is left of this splendor
is the name of Prinsenhof for a dingy industrial street; and indeed,
Charles V, though perhaps the most illustrious of the city's sons, has
been the one she has seemed most to forget. Not until 1966 was a statue
of him erected to replace the one which was removed in favor of the
tribune Jacob (or Jacques) van Artevelde. Ghent has always been

proud of her civic liberties, whose defense against the counts of Flanders, the dukes of Burgundy, and the kings of Spain cost her much blood. She does not seem to have forgotten that it was against Charles that her citizens revolted in 1535, or that it was he who dissolved the Abbey of St. Bavon, even then nine centuries old, for the sake of erecting a military citadel. It is here that Edward III of England stayed during his negotiations with van Artevelde in 1341, and here that his queen gave birth to John of Gaunt, Duke of Lancaster (Gaunt being yet another variant of the city's old name).

If you are to understand Ghent, you must not regard it as an antique. It is no more old than a man is old for having a long line of ancestors. True enough, its pedigree traces unbroken through the history of the two abbeys, those of Saint Bavon and Saint Peter, founded by Saint Amand in the 7th century. Ever since the center of gravity of the wool trade shifted eastward from Ypres, it has been Ghent which has taken the natural leadership in all the troubled days through which Flanders has passed. It was from here that Jan Borluut led his troop of citizens to victory on the field of the Golden Spurs (1302) against the flower of French nobility. From here Philip van Artevelde led his levies against the last of the counts of Flanders to the victory of Beverhout. It was here that the commune executed the councillors of Charles the Bold, and the revolt against princely privilege rebuffed the besieging armies of the Emperor Frederick III. In the religious troubles of the 16th and early 17th century, the Pacification of Ghent (1576) freeing the city from its Spanish garrison, was one of the high points. But the intransigence of the Ghent Calvinists lost them the support of the rest of Flanders and left them an easy target for Alessandro Farnese, Duke of Parma, in the service of Philip II. Returned to the Catholic faith, Ghent had to face a time of economic difficulty; but it was her Bishop, Maurice de Broglie, who in 1814 launched the religious assault that was the basis of Belgium's separation from the predominantly Protestant Netherlands 16 years later and of her establishment as an independent state.

Ghent is as proud of the Vooruit (Socialist) building as it is of its ancient buildings, and as proud to count among its sons such men as Edward Anseele, the pioneer of socialism, and the writer Maurice Maeterlinck, as it is of the 14th-century statesman van Artevelde or the prolific painter De Crayer. It is a town of great civic pride. This is certainly true of all the major manifestations of the city's consciousness, such as the stupendous flower show, Floralies, held every 5 years (next one in 1990), the international trade fair held in a park setting every September, and the European Music Festival, held during the last two weeks of August and the first week in September.

Hub of Trade

You must know the city well to realize that it is built on a hundred islands. It stands at the confluence of two rivers: the Leie, which brings its waters from the flax country around Kortrijk, and the Schelde. These waterways have played a big part in Ghent's prosperity. They were one of the causes for the shifting of pre-eminence in the wool trade from Ypres, and Ghent's nearness to the flourishing port of Bruges was a valuable asset. When the wool weavers of Flanders were ruined by English competition, and Antwerp was handling the hated English cloth that Bruges had refused to touch, Ghent turned her attention to the grain shipments coming downriver from France. Her shipping trade grew important, and you can still see the storehouses around the Graslei and Koornlei where the commune stored the tolls, taken in kind. These were put by against times of scarcity. On top of this trade, Ghent began to develop a trade in linen, but it was not till the early 19th century that her textile industries again became prosperous.

In 1800 Lieven Bauwens, a leading citizen and later burgomaster, whose statue you will find before the castle of Gerard the Devil, returned from England with the secrets of mechanical spinning and weaving of cotton. (The "Spinning Jenny," a power loom smuggled out of Britain piece by piece, is exhibited in the Castle of the Counts.) Within a decade, the Ghent cotton industry had sprung from nothing to employ 10,000 workers, housed in emergency camps.

Since then Ghent has not looked back. The textile industry has had its ups and downs, but the closing of the Liverpool cotton market has given Ghent the opportunity to establish her own, though still on a smaller scale. The seabound traffic, of course, suffered by the closing of the Schelde during the troubles with the Dutch, but this difficulty is now in the far past. A canal has been built through Dutch territory to Terneuzen in the Schelde estuary, making the Ghent maritime traffic independent of Antwerp. In point of fact, the canal needed deepening, and the lock at Terneuzen broadening, to accommodate the demands of present-day traffic. These matters have been settled between Belgium and Holland within the Benelux framework, along with the Antwerp-Rhine canal and the Lanaye bottleneck. Behind the canal, at the northern end of the city, Ghent possesses a first-class seaport, which did outstanding service to the Allied cause in 1944, and has been streamlined and enlarged to give access to freighters of up to 60,000 tons.

Ghent thus combines with its activity as a flower center the roles of seaport, cotton market and textile center. There is much other industry around the canal, and more to come through the modernizing of this most crucial waterway. Oddly enough, it is in the Stadhuis (Town Hall) that the city has its most forceful reminder of its troubled history. The facade on the Hoog Poort, begun in 1518, differs completely from that on the Botermarkt, which was finished almost a century later. The original plans, by Keldermans and De Waghemaker, would have made it a rival to the town halls in Brussels and Louvain but, in the meantime, with civic revolt and the religious troubles, Ghent virtually lost her status as an independent commune. By the time work could be resumed, taste had changed and the old plans were regrettably abandoned. This is one of the city's grievances against Charles V; and, in revenge, she exhibits in the Hall of Civil Marriages a monster canvas showing Charles' grandmother, Mary of Burgundy, vainly interceding with the town authorities against the execution of her two ministers, Hugonet and d'Humbercourt.

Peerless Art Treasures

On a summer evening, viewed from St.-Michielsbrug (St. Michael's Bridge), Ghent's noble medieval buildings assume a fairytale quality under the floodlights; in the background to the left, the truculent lines of the castle; in front, the gabled guild-houses of the Graslei; and farther on, the menacing silhouette of the Belfry, surrounded by the spires of St. Nicholas' Church and St. Bavon's Cathedral. Here is a truly magnificent sight.

The city's greatest treasure is undoubtedly the *Adoration of the Lamb*, the big polyptych by Hubert and Jan van Eyck in a side chapel of St. Bavon's Cathedral. This astonishing 15th-century masterpiece is one of the earliest-known oil paintings (by mixing pigments with such oils as linseed it was discovered that the resulting glaze permitted much greater detail). It has had many adventures. The nude bodies of Adam and Eve were objected to by Joseph II, and even replaced for a time by clothed figures. The central panel was taken to the Louvre in 1799 and only recovered after the fall of Napoleon. It has since been twice stolen by German invaders, and its last recovery was from an Austrian salt mine. In 1934 the panel of the Just Judges was the object of one of the most daring thefts ever known, and the alleged thief died without disclosing its hiding place. (It is a replacement you see today.) Apart from these adventures, the polyptych alone is worth a visit to Ghent.

The Adoration of the Lamb represents Christ on the judgment seat between the Virgin Mary and St. John the Baptist listening to the songs of angels. The Lamb of God is seen surrounded by angels, apostles, prophets, martyrs, knights and hermits on a great grassy plain studded with flowers. So minute is the detail that if you examine each tiny blossom through a magnifying glass, you will find it quite perfect in color and detail. Botanists have identified over 40 plants. The cathedral, in which the rather flashy marble of the choir screen and the richness of the Baroque monuments are more striking than pleasing, also contains another precious 15th-century painting, *Christ On the Cross* by Justus of Ghent (who later went to Urbino to teach the Italians to paint in oils), and an interesting Rubens, painted in 1623, of the conversion of St. Bavon.

Most authorities now deny the legend that the gilded dragon adorning the pinnacle of the Belfort (Belfry) was a crusaders' trophy from Istanbul. The Belfry, indeed, is another building that never achieved its original design, which would have taken it a full 100 feet higher. It houses a carillon of 52 bells, but the famous tocsin bell Roeland—another of Charles V's offences was that he confiscated it—was smashed in the 17th century. On the ground floor of the Belfry is a built-in recess, which housed the iron coffer in which the charters of privilege granted to the city were kept. The ancient prison gate, close to the Belfry, has a fine portal depicting a strange tale: an old prisoner condemned to die from hunger fed from his daughter's breast.

Adjoining the Belfry is the 15th-century Cloth Hall, whose construction, interrupted when the city's Protestant weavers left for England, was only completed in the last century.

Guardians of a Stormy Past

To understand the power of old Ghent, head northeast along Hoogport, through Groetenmarkt, to 's-Gravensteen (Castle of the Counts). Here, overlooking the water of the Leie, and superbly buttressed and elegant even in its massive solidity, the castle of the Counts of Flanders dominates the town. One look at it is enough to make you appreciate the courage which must have underlain the struggle for civic freedom. The count's apartment contains an interesting collection of instruments of torture. There is a fine panoramic view of the city from the top of the imposing tower.

The castle, founded in the 9th century, was built up in the 12th on the model of the crusaders' fortified mansions in Syria. Before it lies St. Veerleplein, where the pillar surmounted by the Flemish lion marks the site of the scaffold used for the religious executions of the 16th century.

It is natural to proceed from here, across the Leie, to the Vrijdagmarkt, passing on the way Mad Meg (Dulle Griet), which was manufactured around 1430. This 16-ton gun, made entirely of wrought iron, fired heavy stone-balls with a noise that earned it a fitting nickname. She stands today opposite the Kraanlei and its charming Renaissance gabled houses. The Vrijdagmarkt was the traditional forum of the city, once used as a place of execution, and also for settling the disputes among the trade guilds. Here the riots broke out on the Bad Monday of 1345 between the weavers and the fullers, resulting in 500 deaths. Here, too, the Counts of Flanders were installed on their entry into their capital, and here they held their armed tourneys, took the oath to maintain the privileges of the city, making their declarations to the people from the Tooghuis, the door of which still exists. Among a number of interesting buildings of several periods, is the guildhouse of the tanners dating from the 15th century.

In the Middle Ages the city was dotted with fortified manors. Behind the cathedral is the best known of these private fortresses, Gerard Duivelsteen (the Castle of Gerard the Devil). Its Romanesque crypt is of exceptional grandeur. The Rabot is a reminder of the 1488 siege by the Austrian Emperor Frederick III, and of his defeat at the hands of Ghent's burghers under Philip van Cleef. When Charles V destroyed the entire defense system of the city in 1540, this fine specimen of medieval military architecture escaped his wrath.

Array of Religious Relics

The Church of St. James (Sint Jacob), near the Vrijdagmarkt, has a central tower dating from about 1200, but the interior is uninteresting. Adjoining the church is a 17th-century Cistercian abbey now used as the town and university library, and housing also a secondary school. On the other side is the Church of St. John. This crowding together of churches is not untypical of Ghent, which has 50 or more churches and was famous during the 18th century for its great number of monasteries. Of the latter, the chief trace is the Byloke, lying beside the Leie a short distance south of the 's Gravensteen. This was founded by the Cistercian sisterhood in 1228 to administer the big civil hospital endowed by Ermentrude van Uttenhove. The abbey buildings are given over to an archeological museum, which contains some extremely interesting pre-Van Eyck mural paintings. The refectory and the Chamber of the Poor are well worth seeing. In addition, the museum contains a miscellaneous collection of articles connected with the history of Ghent, including reproductions of 17th- and 18th-century Ghent homes, and a most entertaining assembly of 18th- and 19th-century means of transport, from the sedan chair to the early motorcar.

Ghent has two relics of medieval religious life typical of the Belgian Lowlands, the Begijnhoven (Béguinages). The *béguines* lived in communities less secluded than those of the convents. The Ancient Begijnhof, founded in 1234, was abandoned during the 19th century, but is still worth a visit. West along Burgstraat, its houses have been preserved and still retain their medieval atmosphere. The Klein Begijnhof (Small Béguinage) is on Violettenstraat (southwest of center). This is a picturesque town within the city, where a few *béguines* still wearing the ancient Flemish headdress occupy quaint cottages.

Of the two abbeys founded by St. Amand, that dedicated to St. Peter survives only in some unclassified remains and in a church built 1,000 years after St. Amand's day. It is the work of the monk Pieter Huyssens of Bruges, though not finished till long after his death. As the work of a leading master in the Baroque, it is worth study though it contains little that is remarkable. You will find it on St. Pietersplein, south of the center.

On the other hand, the beautiful abbey buildings of St. Bavon survive, if not in the original 7th-century form or even in that of the 10th-century reconstruction, at least as 12th- and 13th-century work befitting a religious house of this importance. The abbey was in fact the biggest landowner in Flanders during the 14th century, and it was here that Edward III made his sojourn and John of Gaunt was born. The abbey rose to its apogee near the end of the 15th century, when the abbot was Raphael de Mercatel, one of the bastards of Philip the Good. Most of the buildings survived Charles V's resolve to build a fortress to keep an eye on the ebullient burghers of Ghent; and quite a lot survived the property greed that characterized the early 19th century. The museum of stonework is interesting to students, but to the ordinary visitor the charm of the place is in the buildings themselves, the cloistered gardens, and the magnificent 12th-century *lavatorium* with its canopied vault, one of the earliest examples of crossed-ogive construction. These are east of the center, across the Leie.

Other churches deserving a special mention are St. Nicolas' and the Church of the Augustinians. The former has the third of the great towers of Ghent (the others being the Belfry and St. Bavon's Cathedral). The tower itself dates from about 1230. In the Augustinian Church, the main point of interest is the series of carved confessionals. On the other side of St.-Michielsbrug is the last church to be built in the center of the city, named after the same saint (Sint Michielskerk). Started in 1440 and completed two centuries later—the period of Gothic decadence—it shows many architectural corruptions. Besides some fine stained-glass windows, its main treasure is a splendid *Christ On the Cross* by Van Dyck.

To feel the real spirit of Ghent you must wander in the old town, most of all along the Graslei and the Koornlei, noting the gable-fronted houses with their rich ornamentation, which somehow avoids—as the Grand' Place in Brussels does not—over-ornamentation. See the Butchers' Guildhall from the Kraanlei, and above all see the lordly dwellings of the 13th and 15th century called the Groote Sikkel, Kleine Sikkel, and Achter Sikkel, after the Van der Sikkel family.

Though most of what you can see comes from the 13th to 16th centuries, the patrician heritage of Ghent was never forgotten, and the nobility built mansions as magnificent as any in the world. Most of these are now shadows of their former selves, but in Nederpolderstaat, you will find the old home of the Van der Meersch-Maes (now the Opthalmic Institute), where the magnificent staircase is eloquent of a great period.

You can get a closer view of the same period in the Hôtel Hane-Steenhuyse in Veldstraat, though this is no longer a museum. This was the refuge of Louis XVIII during Napoleon's memorable comeback, the "Hundred Days." You will notice here the characteristically unostentatious front on the street and the superb grandeur of the garden frontage (1768). The house, with its splendid ballroom and its furnishings, which still remain, has had a number of illustrious guests, including Alexander I of Russia and William I of Orange. Châteaubriand, who later met Talleyrand here, was in the house during the period immediately before Waterloo while the Duke of Wellington was a guest in the Hôtel Clemmen on the opposite side of the same street. On the corner of this street and Volderstraat is Hôtel Schamp; in 1814 this was the lodging of John Quincy Adams and the other United States delegates, who, during one of the first of Ghent's giant flower shows, signed the Treaty of Ghent ending the Anglo-American war.

Other buildings from the period of elegance which deserve a mention include the Hôtel d'Oombergen, occupied by the Royal Flemish Academy, in the Koningstraat. A later building with a very exquisite interior is the Royal Opera in Schouwbergstraat, just off Kouter, built in 1848 by the architect Roeland. Also in Kouter is the Hôtel Faligan, built in 1755, the home of the Cercle Noble.

The Waas Country

If you are driving to Ghent from Antwerp, you might consider a detour via Sint Niklaas, Dendermonde, and Aalst (Alost). Onetime capital of the Waas country, Sint Niklaas can look back on 500 years of independence, granted by the Counts of Flanders in 1241. Its vast square is the largest in Belgium. There, among the ancient houses, rises Sint Niklaas' Church, which has undergone many alterations since its construction in the 15th century. The city museum has two rooms devoted to Mercator, the geographer and inventor of the map projection system, born in nearby Rupelmonde in 1512. His famous navigational planisphere is visible there, and so are some of his rare maps.

Instead of following the direct route from Sint Niklaas to Dendermonde via Hamme, a more interesting way goes via the bridge at Temse, (note the shipyards upstream), and St.-Amands-aan-de-Schelde. Alternatively, you can go via Bornem, with its crop of art nouveau villas, known as het Buitenland. St. Amands itself is romantically situated on a wide bend of the Schelde river. This was the birthplace of the poet and bibliophile Emile Verhaeren (who wrote: *"J'aime violemment le coin de sol où je suis né"*); and following his accidental death in 1916 his wish to return here was fulfilled. An imposing black marble tomb marks the spot. Memorabilia are housed in the Verhaeren museum, and the village also has a cultural center and art gallery. The riverside restaurants offer excellent cuisine—with mussels a specialty. Local cafés are lively in the evenings.

Dendermonde, where the Schelde and the Dender rivers meet, was often a victim of its strategic position. Normans, burghers of Ghent, Spaniards, Marlborough and, in 1914, the Germans, sacked this city. On one occasion the city suffered devastation at the hands of its own citizens. Rather than see their town fall to Louis XIV, they inundated the whole region. It is little wonder that only a few monuments survive. One, the church of Onze Lieve Vrouw, right behind the Butchers' Hall, has the air of a fortress. It houses two Van Dycks, an altar by the great sculptors, Fayd' Herbe and Duquesnoy, as well as an early Romanesque baptismal font. The facade of the Stadhuis is decorated with statues of local potentates and of the city's patron saints. The well-proportioned Belfry contains one of the country's finest carillons.

Driving southward, you enter fertile hop country, hence Aalst's centuries-old reputation for beer. St. Martin's Church is yet another Flamboyant Gothic masterpiece of that father-and-son team, the Waghemakers. The highlight of this church is the tabernacle by Duquesnoy. The old Town Hall dates back to the 13th century. Beneath the slogan *Nec spe, nec metu* (Neither by hope nor by fear), two statuettes in the Belfry's recess explain what was meant by these proud watchwords: they represent a down-to-earth merchant and a warrior. Stroll along the few remaining old streets and visit the town museum in the Old Hospital close to the church where there is a good display of medieval furniture and local decorative art.

Bruges (Brugge), Venice of the North

If it were not for people in modern clothes, and the fact that Bruges is also an industrial city, it would be difficult in Bruges to realize that you are living in the 20th century. Scarcely a facade on any street or canal fails to conjure up visions of the past.

During the 15th century, Bruges was a very important trading place on the Continent. Its position at the base of the Zwin inlet giving access to the sea made it strategically powerful. Added to this two deep canals linked it with Oostende and Sluis in Holland. As wealth poured into Bruges, attractive buildings began to appear. Guildhalls and merchants' houses with gabled frontages faced each other across tiny squares and narrow streets, and elegant church spires soared above them. The town was enclosed by shallow ramparts.

Bruges' medieval atmosphere remains. The Zwin has long since silted up, and today the city is 13 km. (8 miles) inland. Small canals lace it together and, as in Venice and Amsterdam, they quarter the town and are crossed by some fifty bridges; indeed the very name Bruges means "Bridges"!

Not so many years ago, rounding a bend in these waterways, again as in Venice, the boatman's nostrils would curl up with distate at the offensive smells. Fortunately this is no longer true, for in recent years the canals have been dredged and cleaned. When this was first done, it is said, the local people were so pleased that they would offer to drink canal water to prove how pure and sweet it was. Certainly there is no smell today, and it is pleasant to view the sights from a leisurely chugging tourist boat, trailing your fingers in the smooth water. Be careful as you do though as this entices inquisitive swans to come alongside your boat, hoping for a tidbit.

While the canals have led to Bruges being called the Venice of the North, there is much in the character of the town to deserve her alternative name—Bruges-la-Morte. She has, in fact, been the victim of circumstances, in that her early splendor was eclipsed through events far outside her control. To understand this, you should begin, not with Bruges itself, but with the nearby townlet, the ancient foreport of Damme, birthplace (in 1235) of the father of Flemish literature, Jacob van Maerlant, and of Thyl Uylenspiegel, a legendary peasant who, through the sanguinary tricks he played adroitly on the occupying Spanish soldiers, succeeded in helping local resistance during Alba's reign of terror in the 16th century.

Here the waters of the Reie, which flows through Bruges, broadened into the Zwin, which, flowing down past Sluis, gave access to the North Sea. The Maritime Law of Damme was the Bible of the Hansa merchants. Today, Damme is a quiet commune with a small population. Both the Church of Our Lady, begun about 1230, and the Stadhuis, dating from about two centuries later, bear witness to a more prosperous past. Indeed, were it not that the nave was destroyed in the religious troubles, the church would look oddly large for a town of this size; and it is still difficult for many to realize that it was important enough to have been the scene of the wedding of two dukes of Burgundy—of Philip the Good to the Portuguese Isabella and, in 1468, of Charles the Bold to Margaret of York, sister of Edward IV of England, who had sailed up-river with her noble escort.

Even at this time, the seeds of Bruges' decline were being sown. The Zwin was silting up with the sands of the Schelde. Eighty years later Lancelot Blondeel, painter, architect, and engineer, was drawing plans for replacing the Zwin by a canal to link Bruges with the sea at Heist. This, however, was never built, for in the meantime English cloth was ruining the Flemish weavers, and Bruges, having haughtily refused to handle it, saw its trade and its privileges transferred to Antwerp.

It was not until the very end of the 19th century that the idea revived of giving Bruges new access to the sea. The canal to Zeebrugge (which means merely Bruges-on-Sea) was completed in 1907, and the Mole, which stretches out for over a mile to protect the outer harbor from the west and north, are both essentially 20th-century achievements. Its port is being steadily improved.

The story of Bruges is so tied to the sea and ships that it is hard to imagine its existence without them. Even a sea town had to fight for its liberties in the early days, though Bruges had by that time possessed a charter, granted by the Count of Flanders, Philippe d'Alsace, for a century and a half. It was the same count who built the sea wall between Bruges and Damme; and the standing of Bruges in Europe is indicated by the fact that there is reference to this in the *Inferno* of Dante.

A highpoint occurred when the Golden Fleece, one of the great medieval Orders of Chivalry, was founded by Philip the Good in 1429 during his wedding celebrations; the number of knights was limited to twenty-four. The King was Grand Master, using the knights as a consultative body in times of war or revolt, their own disputes being settled by the Order, even in the case of the King. Should a knight violate the code of honor, punishment by the others followed. It was a great honor to belong to the Order, whose insignia was a collar from which hung the fleece of a golden ram with curved horns. The symbol comes from the Greek myth of Jason and the Argonauts' voyage to seek the legendary Golden Fleece in Colchis, and signified the basis of Flemish wealth, wool. Many of the treasures of the Order are now in the Treasury of the Hofburg in Vienna.

Bruges retained its glory for about three centuries, and was at its peak under the dukes of Burgundy. It was, in fact, a favored resort of the dukes, and two of the Treasurers of the Golden Fleece lived in the city. Here came merchandise from the seven seas, and around its point of discharge were congregated the merchants and the rest of the trading community, including the agents of the princely banking houses. If Hugo van der Goes' *Nativity* found its way to the Uffizi in Florence, it was because the Portinari were established in Bruges as agents of the Medici.

Bruges possesses two major treasures, one religious, the other artistic. The first is the Relic of the Holy Blood, which is kept in the Heilig Bloedbaziliek (Chapel of the Holy Blood). The facade, dating from 1530, is a fine piece of early work under Italian Renaissance influence. The crypt chapel, dedicated to St. Basil, goes back to the end of the 11th century and contains a bas-relief of this period. The relic itself is in the upper chapel, in a fine *châsse* made about 1617 by the Bruges goldsmith Jan Crabe. The Relic was, according to tradition, given to Count Thierry d'Alsace by the Patriarch of Jerusalem as a recognition of valor during the Second Crusade. It is said to contain a portion of the bloodstained water washed from the body of Christ by Joseph of Arimathea. The Count presented it to the city of Bruges and the Basilica was built especially for it. The rock-crystal phial is contained in a golden reliquary studded with jewels, one being a black diamond said to have belonged to Mary, Queen of Scots. It is on display to the public every Friday. On Ascension Day, it is borne triumphantly in the "Procession of the Holy Blood", a pageant which has become one of the most important annual religious processions. Hundreds of local people take part, dressed in Biblical and medieval costume. One of the

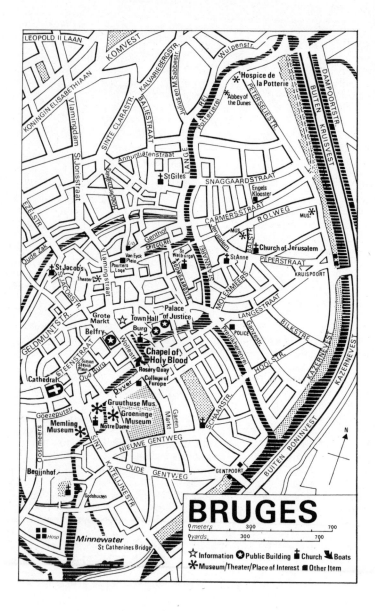

BRUGES

| 0 meters | 300 | 700 |
| 0 yards | 300 | 700 |

☆ Information   ✪ Public Building   ♱ Church   ⬇ Boats
✳ Museum/Theater/Place of Interest   ◼ Other Item

most touching representations is the young David driving his sheep, which are kept in check by a well-trained sheep dog. The phial of Holy Blood is held aloft by bishops and clergy.

The city's second treasure is the collection of the work of Hans Memling housed in the Hospital of St. John (Sint Jans Hospitaal). The hospital itself began its work in 1188, and is one of the best unspoilt examples of the architecture of the period. The Memling collection includes the *Mystic Marriage of Saint Catherine,* a big and rather obscure work, and a delightful portrait presumed to be of Maria Moreel, the daughter of the burgomaster who was one of the painter's patrons. The pearl of the collection, however, is the *Reliquary of St. Ursula,* shaped like a Gothic church and showing the Ursuline legend in small paintings—more akin to miniature work than to the normal work of the master—and in which the characters are robed in the clothes of Memling's own day, thus presenting a fine picture of Burgundian Bruges.

It is said that when the famous painter had been wounded fighting in France, he returned home to Bruges and was nursed at the hospital. He remained there for some time and in gratitude painted several pictures for it. These have been added to through the years, until today it has some of the artist's most interesting works.

Before leaving the hospital grounds, don't miss a visit to the pharmacy, probably the oldest in the world. It continued to dispense drugs and potions until 1971. When you see it you will know why. It has high-polished elbow-high counters, and beneath them are beautifully-fitted small drawers which slide in and out easily and quietly, each with its own tiny label. Silver pestles and mortars are from cup-size upward, and the largest one is like a church bell. Certainly it will chime if tapped. Rows of china jars line the walls, and a small cupboard, again fitted with tiny labelled drawers, has the word "Poisons" outside as a warning.

Almost opposite the hospital is the Church of Our Lady (Onze Lieve Vrouwekerk), the most important of the many Bruges churches, with its nave dating from 1230 and the Paradise Porch (1465). It has a 375-ft. tower, the highest in the city, and contains paintings by Van Dyck, Pourbus and David, but its greatest treasure by far is Michelangelo's *Virgin and Child,* a truly exquisite sculpture. It is set in a black marble niche on the altar of the southern nave. This statue was commissioned by the Mouscron merchants in Bruges, and brought here around 1514. The fondness of the Burgundians for Bruges is emphasized by the tombs of Mary of Burgundy and her father, Charles the Bold. The forest of Wijnendaal, where Mary had the fatal fall from her horse, is a few miles south of Bruges; and it was in the château surrounded by those same woods that King Léopold III made his equally historic decision to surrender with his army in 1940.

Beside the Church of Our Lady is the home of the Gruuthuse family, built in the 15th century. The head of this family was the companion and sage adviser of Charles the Bold. As a museum the house is intensely interesting, especially the 16th-century Flemish kitchen and the collection of old Flemish lace.

A medieval miscarriage of justice is reflected in the Groeninge Museum in the two rather terrifying panels by Gerard David illustrating the Judgment of Cambyses—a story from Herodotus that involves the skinning of the corrupt judge to make a chair-cover on which his son sits as his successor. These works were ordered by the Bench of Magistrates as some atonement for their part in the wrongful death in 1488 of a magistrate, Pieter Lanchals. The painter took some years in their execution, and maybe his heart was not fully in them, for they are not in the same class as his *Baptism of Christ,* in the same museum. This is a later work, dated 1508, and is generally regarded as the finest work of this Dutch pupil of Hugo van der Goes, who was the last important master of the Bruges school. The school can be studied well in the museum. It contains, indeed, none of the rare works of Hubert van Eyck, but it has Jan van Eyck's portrait of his wife, his *Virgin with Saint Donat,* and one of Canon van der Paele, who has obligingly removed his spectacles for the occasion. Memling's *Saint Christopher* is another tribute to the family of Burgomaster Moreel, showing him and his wife with their five sons and eleven daughters. There is also a dramatic *Death of the Virgin* by Hugo van der Goes, and a beautiful *Virgin of the Sorrows* attributed to Roger van der Weyden, the Tournai painter who learned the mysteries of the Bruges school and used them to enrich the life of Brussels.

Public Buildings and Intimate Markets

Bruges, with its historic past and lovely ancient buildings also looks to the future. Its College of Europe was the first university center for European studies to be created after the Second World War. It was opened in 1949. Students must have a thorough knowledge of French and English, be single and less than thirty years of age. Their number is limited to 60 each academic year, and they are chosen by selection boards which sit in 13 European countries. Besides its specific postgraduate program, the college pursues many cultural and scientific activities, and has an 8,000-volume library dealing with problems of contemporary Europe, particularly in the field of European integration.

The Brangwyn Museum in the Arentshuis, which lies between the Gruuthuse Museum and the Groeninge Museum, was given to Bruges by the British artist Sir Frank Brangwyn. It contains etchings, drawings and water colors. His most striking work, however, is outside the city in the strange, very international monastery of St. Andrew, where he designed some of the windows, and his drawings are kept in the chapter house.

Near the fish market there is the Museum Storie, where the enormous 15th-century attic is furnished like a complete dwelling in late medieval style.

If you walk through the fish market and up the narrow street of the Blind Ass (Blinde Ezelstraat) you find yourself in the Burg (Borough Square). Here, besides the Chapel of the Holy Blood, you will find the Stadhuis, the Palace of Justice, and the Old Registry of Civil Liberties (Oude Greffie van het Vrije). The Stadhuis is a lovely building, with octagonal turrets and a facade covered in statues—unfortunately, replacements of those destroyed by the French. The main thing to see inside is the fine Gothic Hall, with its gorgeously painted ceiling and brilliant 19th-century historical canvases around the walls. The Palace of Justice is on the site of the former Palace of the Liberty of Bruges, once a wide-spreading territorial authority, and contains the Brugse Vrije Museum with its famous fireplace, (De Schouw van het Vrije), from designs by Lancelot Blondeel, in which the elders of Bruges are reminded in marble of the story of Susanna and the Elders. The Burg frontage of the Palace of Justice is 18th-century work, but behind, across the canal, you will see the well-preserved facade of the 16th-century Palace with its gables and mullioned windows.

From the Burg, another minute's walk will bring you back to the Grote Markt, under the shadow of the Belfry—"thrice destroyed and thrice rebuilt" (Longfellow)—rising to its famous octagonal tower above the 13th-century market buildings. This is not the mother of all the Belgian carillons—a distinction that belongs to Mechelen—but it is certainly one of the most famous. The climb of the 366 steps to the top is well worth the effort.

Proceeding along Steenstraat, you will pass the colorful fruit and flower market in the Simon Stevin Plein to reach the Cathedral of The Holy Saviour (Sint Salvator). The first chapel on this site was founded by St. Eloi in the 7th century. Though nothing of this remains, the base of the tower dates from about 1120. Its rather uninspired top is unmistakably 19th century. The spatial arrangement of the church is most pleasing, with priceless Gobelins tapestries and a number of interesting canvases. There is a heavy marble screen with some good ironwork, and the stalls beside the choir are fine examples of 15th-century wood carving, with the misericords (tip-up seats) embellished with fascinating scenes of the period. Here, too, are the armorials of the knights present at the 13th Chapter of the Order of the Golden Fleece (1478).

The Cathedral Museum should not be missed. It is full of religious and artistic items—not always the same thing—statuary, embroidery and reliquaries, all of which carry their freight of historical interest.

At the far end of Steenstraat you reach 't Zand, a broad square (formerly the site of the rail station). Happily it has retained a number of hotels and cafés, now patronized by bus travelers and motorists using the extensive underground parking. You might continue your walk along the broad concrete road to the present railway-station, now outside the town. It is a low, functional and unfussy building in a setting of trees, lawns and canal-water, whose garden-display in front makes it one of the more attractive stations in Europe. The building is by Van Kriekinge (1939), and the murals by René de Pauw.

Returning from the station, a right turn from the main road will take you past the modern hospital of St. John to the Minnewater, the most picturesque spot in this picturesque town, once the heart of the harbor, now separated from the canal by an equally picturesque lockhouse. You can sit under the trees by the almshouses (Godshuizen) before crossing the bridge into the Begijnhof. The green, tree-shaded quadrangle with the little old houses and the robed and coiffed beguines is a subject dear to many painters, among them Sir Winston Churchill. There is a small folklore museum to be seen, and the house of the

Grande Dame. The public may attend services in the Church of St. Elizabeth, reconstructed in the 16th century after the burning of the 13th-century chapel.

The gateway to the Begijnhof dates from the foundation of the institution in 1245, by the then Countess of Flanders, Margaret of Constantinople—the same Black Margot (Zwarte Margriet) who was captured by the King of France, imprudently married her tutor at the age of ten, and as impetuously repudiated him and her children at the age of 21 to marry again and raise another family. All Europe was involved in the legitimacy squabble that ensued.

A walk along the ramparts from the Minnewater will bring you to St. Catherine's Bridge, across the encircling canal whence, turning left and following the girdle of the city, you will pass the Gentpoort and re-enter the town by the Kruispoort which leads into Peperstraat and to the astonishing Church of Jerusalem, a pseudo-Oriental edifice. This church, founded in 1427 by the Adornes family, is still privately-owned, but arrangements can be made to visit it. The original building was intended to replicate the Church of the Holy Sepulchre. Unfortunately it was burned down soon after it was built and the present church was raised over the ruins. Stairways lead to the Upper Chapel as they do in Jerusalem and in the crypt there is a model of Jerusalem's Holy Sepulchre. The stained-glass windows bear the coats of arms of the Adornes family. There is a raised choir, and a sculptured altarpiece surmounted by three crosses.

Lace has always been as important to Bruges as wool. Its manufacture gave employment at the turn of the century to at least 6,000 women of the town, and today you can still watch it being made and buy it to take home. In a little street running down one side of the Jerusalem church, there is a lacemaking school where you can watch women at work and children being taught to carry on the tradition.

Striking northward (Balstraat) to Carmerstraat, you will come to the 18th-century Chapel of the English Ladies (Engels Klooster), one of the several aristocratic British religious settlements that took root in Belgium in this period. At the end of the same street is the house of the Guild of the Archers of St. Sebastian, another link with England through the patronage of the exiled Charles II and, less contentiously through the recent honorary membership of Queen Elizabeth II of England, and her husband, the Duke of Edinburgh. Farther north, beside the Reie before it crosses the canal-girdle on its way to Damme, is the Hospice de la Poterie, a 13th-century almshouse for old ladies, with its 14th-century chapel (notice the tapestries) and a museum containing pen-sketches rather doubtfully attributed to the Van Eyck brothers and their sister Margaret.

Also beside the Reie, just south of the hospice, is the old Abbey of the Dunes, which houses a truly remarkable collection of illuminated manuscripts. On your way back into Bruges you pass the Church of St. Walburga, by Pieter Huyssens, whose work in Ghent we have already noticed.

Returning to the Grote Markt, and leaving it by the northwest corner and the Sint Jacobstraat, you will come to Sint-Jacobskerk Church, which is especially worth visiting for the lovely Luca Della

Robbia Madonna in pottery and the tomb—flanked by his two wives—
of Ferry de Gros, a Treasurer of the Golden Fleece. Another treasure
of the church is the *Coronation of the Virgin* by Albert Cornelis, a
16th-century master of whose work little has yet been identified. There
is also some work by Blondeel, and a *Madonna of the Sorrows* by Pieter
Pourbus. In the Naaldenstraat, Number 19 is the house occupied by
another Treasurer of the Golden Fleece, Pierre Bladelin, who eventually relinquished it to the Medici agent, Tomasco Portinari.

Bearing round from here to the right you will come to the town
theater, and the Poorters Loge, a 15th-century building which was the
house of the "inside" burghers—those who lived in Bruges itself, as
opposed to those who were centered on the Liberty of Bruges, the
"outside" burghers. In the facade of this building is the little statue of
a bear, known as Beertje van de Loge. He was installed there in 1477,
and in his way he is as charming as the Mannekin Pis in Brussels. He
stands in a niche about 15 ft. above the ground, looking over the heads
of passers-by. His fur is white, although the arms of the city display
a brown bear. He has been presented with many costumes, but perhaps
looks most impressive when he wears a long red army cloak with gold
lace fastenings. He stands happily on his hind legs and holds the shield
of Bruges in his front paws. Undressed or otherwise, he is a most
delightful beast. At one time the building was a meeting place for the
local burghers and "White Bear Guild."

The Poorters Loge where the bear stands is not far from ter Buerze,
the old Stock Exchange.

Walking down beside the Poorters Loge, you will come into the van
Eyckplein, with a 19th-century statue of the painter. Beyond is the
Spiegelrei (Quay of Mirrors), now the dead end of the canal that once
linked the Reie with the Grote Markt. The truncated canal leads you
in one block to the Reie; follow the river round to the right (upstream)
when you reach it at the end of the cutting. You follow the river round
to your right again—this is the boundary of 12th-century Bruges—past
Dyver to the Steenhouwerskaai and on again to the Quay of the Rosary.
The canal and river quays are Bruges itself. The popular way of enjoy-
ing them is to take a 40-minutes' trip round them in a motor-boat.
Farther round, beyond the Quay of the Rosary, you will find the
Convent of the Black Sisters, and the 19th-century statue of Hans
Memling.

"Bruges by boat" can now mean more than a trip on the network
of canals in the city. An extra is an excursion on a larger vessel along
the Napoleon Canal that links Bruges with Damme 5 km. (3 miles)
away.

Veurne (Furnes) and a Colorful Procession

A 42 km. (26-mile) drive from Bruges southwestwards and almost
parallel with the coast will bring you to Veurne (Furnes). It is a good
plan to see the one while the other is fresh in your mind, for the
Procession of the Penitents, which takes place on the last Sunday in
July at 3.30 P.M. and to which Veurne owes its fame, has the same
Gothic spirit as the Bruges Pageant of the Holy Blood. This observance

always attracts a great crowd. There is some doubt as to whether the procession dates back, as is claimed, to the 12th century, to the time when Count Robert II of Flanders, after his miraculous escape from shipwreck, fulfilled his vow of presenting to the first Flemish church he saw (which happened to be the Church of St. Walburga) the fragment of the True Cross which he had brought from the Holy Land. This precious relic would of course account for the Holy Cross entering very deeply into the consciousness of the townsfolk, and it may well be that it would serve as basis for the alternative theory that the procession started in 1644, as an intercession against the plague and against an outbreak of war between the Spaniards and the French.

The procession differs from that of Bruges in that it does not center upon the Holy Relic itself, but shows the passage of hooded and black-robed penitents carrying their own heavy crosses through the town. It is interspersed, in the same way as the Bruges event, with costumed set-pieces. It is organized by a local devout society, which is also responsible for the spectacular but very sincere procession making Stations of the Cross every Friday in Lent.

Veurne was strategically important during the Spanish occupation, and the visitor can see a Spanish influence in the buildings. The flamboyant Flemish Renaissance is tempered here by Spanish dignity and severity. Both the Stadhuis and the Palace of Justice date from the Spanish period. The Stadhuis (town hall), which dominates the vast square, has a graceful loggia, and its interior is paneled with magnificent stamped leather brought by the Spaniards from Cordoba. The two churches are older, the oldest parts in St. Walburga dating from a century or more after Robert II, who died in the year 1111. St. Nicholas' has a fine brick tower, erected in the 13th century. Its greatest treasure is the *Crucifixion,* a painting attributed to Van Orley.

Diksmuide's World War I Memorial

A 16 km. (10 mile) drive in a southeasterly direction brings you to Diksmuide; chiefly remarkable for the IJzer (Yser) Tower, which stands by the river as a memorial to the heroic sacrifice of King Albert's (mostly Flemish) troops during World War I. This impressive monument has in the course of years become the symbol of Flemish rather than Belgian national aspirations. It is the center of a pilgrimage, the IJzerbedevaart, on the first Sunday in July, when Flemish patriots crowd into an openair Mass, after which there are speeches and Flemish patriotic songs and an impressive laying of flowers on the memorial. A major theme in every IJzerbedevaart, apart from Flemish nationalism, is deeply religious pacifism. Near the base of the tower, you will see the slogan "No more war" in several languages. This is surmounted by the initials *AVV-VVK;* standing for *Alles voor Vlaanderen, Vlaanderen voor Kristus* (All for Flanders, Flanders for Christ). Within the tower is an exhibition focused on other symbols of Flemish nationalism: the free-flying seagull, the dying warrior brothers, and the heroes' broken tombstones.

This charming old town was completely razed in the first World War, and whatever you see in the way of period architecture is a reconstruction. Visiting the network of trenches outside the town gives a good impression of the fighting conditions in World War I. It was near here that poison gas was first used in warfare; though in this part of the front the mud was often as deadly as the enemy's shells.

Kortrijk and Oudenaarde

The tides of war have swept fiercely over Roeselare, a town which you will pass in the 40-km. (25-mile) drive to Menen (Menin). Here you are at the French frontier, and the town was one of those held against the French in the 18th century, largely because the fortifications had been perfected a century earlier by the French expert, Vauban.

From here, taking the Brussels road, you quickly come to Kortrijk (Courtrai), the capital of the flax and linen industry. The main Cloth Hall was almost wholly destroyed in World War II, but Kortrijk's connection with flax will be obvious to you from the fields round about, even though it is no longer in the chalkless Leie itself that the flax is now retted. The church of Our Lady contains the *Elevation of the Cross* by Sir Anthony van Dyck, painted in 1631 during his Antwerp period. The chapel of the Counts of Flanders is also worth seeing, both for its own sake and for that of the delicate statue of St. Catherine, probably by André Beauneveu in the late 1370s. The Stadhuis, a 15th-century Flamboyant Gothic building, contains two fine fireplaces.

Situated between the churches of St. Martin, with its Baroque tower, and Our Lady, the fine Begijnhof takes us back into the Middle Ages. This little township of whitewashed, gabled houses and the silence that surrounds it exude a rarely-equalled old-world charm. Also medieval, but of a different character, are the indomitable Broel Towers that once guarded the bridge over the Leie.

Keeping on the Brussels road you pass through Oudenaarde, which was the mother of the art of tapestry-making before its workers emigrated—not, like the weavers to England, but to France—and you will see some magnificent early tapestries in the Stadhuis. The building itself is almost as exciting as the town halls of Brussels and Leuven in architectural splendor. It was built in the third decade of the 16th century by the Brussels architect, Van Pede. The interior is well worth seeing, both for the tapestries and for the fireplaces. In the second floor museum are the 12 metal pots in which the municipality would send round the wine required by a visiting nobleman for the banquet he would undoubtedly be giving. This early gesture of encouragement for the tourist industry fixed 12 as the number of filled pots to be presented to an emperor, though a king's ration was limited to six and a prince would get only two.

St. Walburga's lofty tower was made top-heavy by the bulb crowning it. The church of Onze Lieve Vrouw van Pamele (13th century) is of a much purer style, and one of the finest examples of Romano-Gothic in northern Europe. The Cloth Hall is of the same period, while Margaret of Parma's House is late Gothic. Charles V used to come and visit the lovely Jeanne van der Geenst in this house, where Margaret, child of this love-affair, who later became regent of the Lowlands, was born.

In front of the Stadhius is the fountain presented by Louis XIV, a reminder that here you are not far from the French frontier, and that the importance of Flanders in Anglo-French, Franco-Spanish, and Franco-Austrian rivalries led to Oudenaarde's being four times occupied by the French—and eventually to the Duc de Vendôme's defeat by Marlborough under its walls (1708). In St. Walburga's Church you will find more tapestries and the tombs of four priests drowned in the Schelde by Protestants in 1572.

Two war memorials connect Oudenaarde with the New World. It was here that the Belgian corps of volunteers was formed in 1864 to help maintain Maximilian's shaky empire in Mexico. One monument commemorates those who fell at the Battle of Tacambaro. The other memorial honors American soldiers who gave their lives helping to defeat Imperial Germany in World War I.

From Oudenaarde the return route to Ghent leads via Deinze, one of the oldest towns in Flanders, though little remains of its past glory. There is a good deal of 13th- and 14th-century work in the church, but the blowing up of the tower in 1918 did a great deal of damage necessitating extensive restorations.

A little farther west lies Tielt, which was a fortified town as long ago as 1172, and a prosperous textile center when Burgundian troops set fire to it in 1579. The 13th-century carillon tower rises above the market building. The carillon itself, which is Tielt's main attraction now, was installed in the 17th century. The old hospital of the Alexian sisters is another foundation of Black Margot, or Margaret of Constantinople, Countess of Flanders and foundress of the Begijnhof of Bruges. Another attraction in Tielt is the church of St. Peter, which dates from the late 17th century. Its centerpiece is a superb Rococo pulpit, one of Flanders' greatest treasures. Tielt also has a Bee Museum in the restored outbuildings of the Château.

A wandering barber and native of Tielt, Oliver Necker was one of the greatest self-made men of the Middle Ages. Better known as Olivier le Daim, he became the friend and confidant of ruthless Louis XI, the Spider King, one of France's greatest and wiliest rulers. After Louis' death in 1484, Parliament's first action was to have Olivier hung.

Leaving Oudenaarde on the Brussels road, however, you are soon at Brakel in green, hilly country with a fine view over the Flemish plain. A right-hand road leads you quickly to Geraardsbergen (Grammont), a curious survival, fast becoming industrialized. This is at the extreme apposition of the French and Dutch languages, and within a mile or two of the formal frontier between Flanders and Hainaut provinces. You will be surprised to see in a niche in the Town Hall a replica of the Brussels Manneken Pis, a memorial presented by the city of Brussels in 1745 in tribute to the courage of the people in recovering the original statue from the Duke of Cumberland's soldiery after the Battle of Fontenoy. Geraardsbergen is built on the sides of two hillocks, on one of which, grandiosely called La Vieille Montagne, stands a little chapel containing the little black miracle-working Vierge de la Vieille Montagne, to which a processional pilgrimage is organized on the first Sunday in Lent. This is the prelude to the Cracknel Festival, which begins with the filling of a cup of wine containing a number of small live fish. The burgomaster, aldermen, and certain other notables pass the cup from hand to hand, each drinking till he has swallowed one or more of the fish. After this the cracknel cakes are flung among the crowd, and the festival has begun.

PRACTICAL INFORMATION FOR FLANDERS

GETTING THERE. By train. The quickest way to see the two principal cities is to take the fast electric train from Brussels in the morning, returning in the evening—quickest but the least satisfactory. Bruges and Ghent merit at least a two-day visit unless you are pressed for time. There are numerous train and bus services to the smaller art towns.

By car. Via the Brussels-Oostende motorway (A10/E40), Ghent is 35 km. (22 miles) and Bruges 98 km. (61 miles) from the capital. From Brussels, St. Niklaas is about 48 km. (30 miles); or, alternatively, 10 miles outside Antwerp on the motorway to Ghent. Oudenaarde is 40 km. (25 miles) from Brussels, and Kortrijk 86 km. (54 miles); Ypres 116 km. (72 miles); Veurne 147 km. (91 miles)—all by good, fast roads.

HOTELS AND RESTAURANTS. The whole region is well supplied with hotels and restaurants. Flanders is too central to the rest of the country to have retained a distinctive cuisine of its own; though you will find the *carbonnades flamandes* better here than elsewhere. It is generally agreed that you get the best *waterzooi* at Ghent, so don't miss the opportunity while you are there. Another local dish is *gentse hutsepot,* a hotpot containing all sorts of meats and most of the vegetables native to the region.

AALST (ALOST). A good overnight stop 16 miles west of Brussels when rooms are scarce in summer. *Graaf van Vlaanderen* (M), Stationsstraat 37 (tel. 053–789 851). 6 rooms with bath; handy for station. *Borse van Amsterdam* (I), Grote Markt 26 (tel. 053–211 581). 6 rooms in 17th-century Flemish building in town center; also has good restaurant dating from 1630.

Restaurant. *La Marmite* (M), Molenstraat 63 (tel. 053–778 599). Close to center of town.

BRUGES (BRUGGE). It is worth noting that comparatively few of Bruges' hotels offer full restaurant facilities on-site (although most provide breakfast). There are many cafes and restaurants to make up this deficiency, however. *Holiday Inn* (L), Boeveriestraat 2 (tel. 050 340 971). Built in a 17th-century monastery on the outskirts of town. 128 comfortable rooms, plus restaurant, indoor swimming pool and sauna. *De Orangerie* (L), Kartuizerinnenstraat 10 (tel. 050–341 649). 19 fully-equipped rooms with classic views; canal-side location.

Duc de Bourgogne (E), Huidenvettersplein 12 (tel. 050–332 038). 19 rooms, all with bath; in old hotel on a canal bend with 17th-century decor. Closed Jan. and July. Good restaurant. *Prinsenhof* (E), Ontvangerstraat 9 (tel. 050–342 690). Lavish hotel in old manor house. 16 comfortable rooms. *Die Swaene* (E), Steenhowersdijk 1 (tel. 050–342 798). 28 comfortable rooms overlooking a beautiful canal.

Adornes (M), Sint-Annarei 26 (tel. 050–341 336). Beamed, canal-side hotel with 20 rooms, all with bath. *Ter Brughe* (M), Oost-Gistelhof 2 (tel. 050–340 324). Delightful canal-side hotel with 20 rooms, all with bath; a wonderful 15th century survival. *Bryghia* (M), Oosterlingenplein 4 (tel. 050–338 059). 18 rooms with bath or shower in friendly, family-run hotel. *Pandhotel* (M), 16 Pandreitje (tel. 050–334 434). Modern hotel with 18 rooms behind old facade.

de Krakele (I), St.-Pieterskaai 63 (tel. 050–315 643). 14 rooms, 65 with bath. Lively restaurant; on outskirts of town. *Notre Dame* (I), Mariastraat 3 (tel. 050–333 193). A small hotel tucked away close to the Memling museum. 11 rooms, all with shower. Good value restaurant. *Van Eyck* (I), Korte Zilverstraat 7 (tel. 050–335 267). Only 8 rooms, 5 with bath or shower. A stone's throw from the Markt. Modest restaurant.

Restaurants. *'t Presidentje* (E), Egelstraat 21 (tel. 050–339 521). Excellent food and charming personal service. *Weinebrugge* (E), Koning Albertlaan 242 (tel. 050–384 440). The best restaurant in Bruges, but 4 km. from town center. *De Witte Porte* (E), Jan van Eyckplein 6 (tel. 050–330 883). Well-run family restaurant with wonderful seafood.

Oud Brugge (M), Kuipersstraat 33 (tel. 050–335 402). In vaults under 16th-century building. *'t Pallieterke* (M), 't Zand 28 (tel. 050–340 177). Family-run restaurant with good food. Book. *d' Eiermarkt* (I), Eiermarkt 18 (tel. 050–300 346). Best of the bunch on this small square of modest restaurants. *Gistelhof* (I), West Gistelhof (tel. 050–336 290). Pleasant old Flemish house with good fish casseroles. *Taverne Curiosa* (I), Vlamingstraat 22 (tel. 050–342 334). Crypt restaurant close to the market. Good for local beers and cheese.

DAMME. Historic small town 4 miles north of Bruges. *De Gulden Kogge* (I), Damse Vaart Zuid 12 (tel. 050–354 217). 6 rooms, 2 with shower; good restaurant. A mile northeast of town at Oostkerke. Close by is best of Damme's restaurants, *Breughel* (E), Damse Vaart Zuid 26 (tel. 050–500 346). Superb cuisine on the canal in rural surroundings. In town, try *Drie Zilveren Kannen* (M), Markt 9 (tel. 050–355 677). Dining amidst Flemish decor.

DENDERMONDE. *West* (I), Hoofdstraat 41A (tel. 052–211 407). 9 rooms, 3 with shower; modest restaurant. Restaurant. *Het Vaderland* (M), Grote Markt 16 (tel. 052–211 136). Real Flemish cuisine, right in town center.

GHENT (GENT, GAND). *'s-Gravensteen* (L), Jan Breydelstraat 35 (tel. 091–251 150). 17 luxurious rooms, all with bath. Between the Castle of the Counts and the Decorative Arts Museum, this beautifully restored 19th-century mansion is a gem. No restaurant. *Sint-Jorishof* (E), Botermarkt 2 (tel. 091–242 424). 66 rooms, 45 with bath. Reputedly the oldest hotel in Europe, housed in 13th-century building, a stone's throw from St. Bavon's cathedral. *De Fonteyne* (I), Goudenleeuwplein 7 (tel. 091–254 871). 16 rooms, 11 with shower. Overlooks the belfry. No restaurant. *De Karper* (I), Kortrijksesteenweg 2 (tel. 091–215 924). 15 rooms, 11 with shower. Slightly south of city center, close to Fine Arts Museum. Good restaurant.

Restaurants. *Apicius* (E), Maurice Maeterlinckstraat 8 (tel. 091–224 600). One of Ghent's great gastronomic locations, south of St. Peter's station. Small, so book. *Buikske Vol* (M), Kraanlei 17 (tel. 091–251 880). Classic French cuisine in 17th-century surroundings. *Raadskelder* (M), Botermarkt 18 (tel. 091–254 334). In 14th-century vaults; good value. *De Warempel* (I), Zandberg 8 (tel. 091–243 062). Good-value selection of fish dishes and vegetarian food.

Resorts for sailing, angling and swimming along the Leie, between Ghent and Deinze include **Deurle** 8 miles southwest, where you can dine superbly at *Rally St-Christophe* (E), Pontstraat 100 (tel. 823 106)—just try their boeuf en route.

Further on is **Astene** where we recommend you try *Wallebeke* (M), Emiel Clauslaan 141 (tel. 825 149), on the banks of the Leie.

IEPER (YPRES). *Continental* (M), Colaertplein 29 (tel. 057–200 065). 17 rooms, 10 with bath. *Regina* (M), Grote Markt 45 (tel. 057–200 165). 18 rooms, all with bath or shower; moderate restaurant. *Sultan* (I), Grote Markt 33 (tel. 057–200 193). 12 rooms, 6 with bath or shower; good restaurant.

Restaurants. Easily best in town is *Yperley* (M), St. Jacobstraat 1 (tel. 205 470), just opposite the Lakenhalle and renowned for its French cuisine. Three miles southwest of Ieper on the shores of the Dikkebus Lake is pleasant *Dikkebus Vijver* (I), Vijverdreef 31 (tel. 200 085).

KORTRIJK (COURTRAI). *Broel* (E), Broelkaai 8 (tel. 056–218 351). 49 rooms and pleasant restaurant, by the river. Near the station is the *Hotel du Nord* (M), Stationsplein 2 (tel. 056–220 303). 44 rooms, all with bath; restaurant. In the center is *Kopke* (I), Grote Markt 53 (tel. 056–221 563). 11 rooms, all with bath or shower; cheerful restaurant. Just off ring expressway to southwest (exit Marke) is *Marquette* (E), Kannaertstraat 45 (tel. 056–201 816). All 8 rooms offer top-class luxury; the food is exquisite.

Restaurants. *Eddy Vandekerckhove* (E), Sint-Anna 5 (tel. 056–224 756). Sophisticated dining south of town. Fairly small, so book. *Bistro Duprez* (M), Kapucijnenstraat 27 (tel. 056–200 110). Pleasant, central.

OUDENAARDE. *Elnik* (I), Deinzestraat 55 (tel. 055–313 788). 14 rooms, 10 with bath. *Pomme d'Or* (I), Markt 62 (tel. 055–311 900). 6 rooms, all with bath or shower; restaurant. *De Zalm* (I), Hoogstraat 4 (tel. 055–311 314). 8 basic rooms; inexpensive restaurant.

POPERINGE. *Palace* (I), Ieperstraat 34 (tel. 057–33 093). 11 rooms, 9 with bath.

Restaurant. *D'Hommelkeete* (E), Hoge Noenweg 3 (tel. 057–334 365). A gastronomic high spot just 2 miles from the center, but in the heart of the countryside.

VEURNE (FURNES). *'t Belfort* (M), Grote Markt 26 (tel. 058–311 115). 8 rooms, 5 with bath.

Restaurant. *'t Groonhof* (M), Noordstraat 9 (tel. 058–313 128). Try their fish dishes.

TOURS. Boat Excursions. The most interesting excursion from Bruges is on the *MS Zeehond* to historic Damme, on the canal that connects Bruges with Sluis, a small Dutch border town. Bus 4 from the city center takes you to the landing stage. For excursions from Ghent on the Leie and Schelde rivers, embark at Bartsoenkaai, near Verlorenkost (May-Sept.). To visit the port, apply to Port Authority, Vliegtuiglaan 1. For information about trips from Ghent to Deurle, contact Benelux Co., Voormuide 77, Ghent, or local tourist office.

 MUSEUMS AND PLACES OF INTEREST. BRUGES (BRUGGE). Bruges, the purest of medieval towns in Northern Europe, has several art collections of the first importance. From Apr.-Sept., when not otherwise stated, Bruges museums and historic buildings are open to the public from 9.30 to 12 and from 2 to 6 (in winter 10 to 12 and 2 to 5). Transferable season tickets entitling one to visit all museums are obtainable at the City Tourist Office and at the museums.

Arentshuis, next to the Groeninge Museum, contains a collection of objets d'art plus a small gallery of the works of the British artist Sir Frank Brangwyn. Open March to Sept., 9.30 to 12, 1.45 to 6. Rest of the year, 10 to 12, 1.45 to 5; closed Tues.

Begijnhof, south of city center. Historic nunnery for gentlefolk founded in 13th century by Marguerite, Countess of Flanders. Fine 17th-century church, gardens and whitewashed cottages. Open 9 to 6 (less in winter). Admission BF 30.

Church of Jerusalem. Originally a replica of the Holy Sepulchre in Jerusalem; founded in 15th century.

Groeninge Museum, on the Dyver Canal. Shows some of the best known masterpieces by Jan van Eyck, Van der Goes, Memling, Pourbus, Gerard David, and Hieronymus Bosch.

Gruuthuse Museum, originally the palace of the lords whose name it bears today, was King Edward IV's refuge in 1471 during his exile from England. It shows lace, pottery, goldsmith's art, etc.

Heilig Bloedbaziliek (Basilica of the Holy Blood), and the **Museum of the Holy Blood,** form part of the Burg complex. See text for description of the contents. The sacred reliquary is the focus of a ceremony of worship every Friday 8.30 to 12 and 3 to 4, and from May to Aug., daily 3 to 4. Procession of the Holy Blood, Ascension Day at 3 P.M.

Memling Museum, a onetime chapter-room in St. John Hospital's precincts, just by the Onze Lieve Vrouw (Church of Our Lady). A unique collection of the master's paintings. Interesting old furniture and household utensils can be seen on the cloister premises next to the medieval pharmacy. Open 9 to 12.30, 2 to 6 (less in winter). Admission BF 40.

Museum voor Volkskunde, Museum of Folklore, converted from seven adjoining almshouses, is found in the little street to the left of the Church of Jerusalem.

Onze Lieve Vrouwekerk (Church of Our Lady). Originated in the 12th century. Has 400-ft. tower; contains Michelangelo's *Virgin and Child.*

Schuttersgild Sint Sebastiaan (the Archers Guild of St. Sebastian), is a unique architectural complex in Carmerstraat and has a remarkable collection of paintings and silverware. Open Apr. to Sept., 9.30 to 12, 2 to 6, daily except Tues.; Oct. to Mar., 10 to 12, 2 to 5, Mon. to Sat, closed Tues.

Storie Museum, Steenhouwersdijk 2. An old Bruges 15th-century house with objets d'art, paintings, furniture and lace.

DAMME. Ouze Lieve Vrouwekerk (Church of Our Lady), Kerkstraat 37. 13th-century exterior containing Baroque furnishings. Don't miss the view from the tower. Admission BF 100.

St. John's Hospital Museum, Kerkstraat 33. Mainly devoted to religious works of art. Open mid-March to end-Oct., 9.30 to 12, 2 to 6.30.

Stadhuis (Town Hall). Overlooks the Markt. Interesting Gothic structure with attractive carved interior. Open May to Sept., 10 to 12, 2 to 6. Admission BF 30.

Til Uilenspiegel Museum, Jacob van Maerlantstraat 3. Contains a collection of books and other works dedicated to Charles de Coster's legendary anti-hero. Open May to Sept., 10 to 12, 2 to 6. Admission BF 20.

GHENT. Abbey of St. Bavon. The ruins of an abbey founded in the 7th century. Though little actually remains of the original abbey, there's still much of interest dating from later centuries. Steeped in history—be sure to buy the brochure. Open 9 to 12, 2 to 5.

Bijloke Museum, Godshuizenlaan 2. Officially archeological, by its contents more of a historical museum. Reproduction of late medieval Ghent homes, ironwork, weapons, costumes, etc. Open 10 to 12 and 1.30 to 5.

's Gravensteen Castle. Superb 12th-century moated castle, former residence of Counts of Flanders. Open 9 to 6 (4 in winter).

Museum voor Schone Kunsten (Fine Arts Museum), in the Citadel Park. Fine collection of paintings by Breughel, Rubens, Jordaens, Tintoretto, Reynolds, etc. Open 9 to 12 and 2 to 5.

Museum voor Sierkunst (Museum of Decorative Arts), Breydelstr. 7, the former De Coninck mansion (1752). Rich collection of furniture arranged so as to recall the atmosphere of domestic life in a patrician family of the period. Exhibitions of modern arts and crafts. Open 9 to 12, 1.30 to 5.15.

Museum voor Volkskunde (Folklore Museum), Kraanlei 41, commemorates customs and traditions in the city of Ghent. Interesting and entertaining. Open 10 to 12 and 1.30 to 5 (closed Tues.). April to Oct., 9 to 12.30, 1.30 to 6.

St. Bavon's Cathedral. A magnificent building, started in the 10th century. Contents include *Adoration of the Lamb* by the Van Eyck brothers.

Schoolmuseum Michiel Thiery (Michel Thiery Natural Science Museum), St. Pietersplein 12. Open 9 to 12 Tues. to Sat., Sun. 2 to 5.

Stadhuis (Town Hall). Superb 3-story structure, begun in the 15th century. The restored interior includes a marvelous Gothic staircase.

IEPER. Battlefields. Sites of many World War I battles, including Ypres, Salient and Paschendaele. Sections of trenches are still visible, and there are several maintained cemeteries, notably at Tyne Got, 15 miles east of town, which has a vast British memorial garden.

Herinneringsmuseum (1914–18 Museum), records the life of the town during World War I. Open Easter to Oct., 9.30 to 12, 1.30 to 5.30.

Lakenhalle (The Cloth Hall). The focal point of Ieper, with its Belfry and a museum of modern art. Open daily April 1 to Oct. 31, 10 to 12.30, 1.30 to 6, closed Mon. Nov. 1 to Mar. 31, 1.30 to 5.30.

Menin Gate (Menenpoort). 130-ft. memorial arch designed by Sir Reginald Blomfield to commemorate 55,000 British lost in World War I.

St. George's Church. English church built in 1929 to commemorate British and Commonwealth dead in World War I. Many moving memorials.

VEURNE. Stadhuis (Town Hall). See description in this chapter (p. 156). Open Easter and June 1 to Sept. 15, check at Tourist Office for times.

CARILLON CONCERTS. The principal concerts given by the carillonneurs take place in the following localities. **Bruges:** year round from 11.45 to 12.30 on Sun., Wed., and Sat.; from mid-June through Sept., 9 to 10 P.M., Mon., Wed., and Sat. **Ghent:** less regularly, enquire at City Tourist Office.

THEATERS. Ghent offers opera at the **Koninklijke Schouwburg,** plays in Flemish, puppet shows, and music hall entertainment. In the **Belfry Cloth Hall,** an audio-visual spectacle, *Ghent in the 14th century.*

USEFUL ADDRESSES. City Tourist Offices: Bruges, Markt 7 (tel. 330 711); Ghent, Stadhuis crypt, for personal callers (tel. 241 555); for advance bookings write to Belfortstraat 9, B-9000 Gent (tel. 253 641). Ieper, Stadhuis, Grote Markt (tel. 202 626); Veurne, Markt 1 (tel. 312 154).

Certified guides: in Bruges, at the City Tourist Office in Ghent, at Guides' League, Lieven de Wimmestraat 58, (tel. 258 302) or at the Stadhuis crypt.

Car hire: Van Renterghen Travel Agency, Grote Markt 13, Bruges; Autolux, Ghent.

THE BELGIAN COAST

Family Resorts—Unlimited

The Belgian coast is an all-but-unbroken belt of sand stretching for 40 miles from the French border to Holland. The country behind is mostly polder country, lying below sea level, relying much for its protection on the line of reeded sand-dunes that hide the sea from large parts of the broad coast road, and on the great seawall (Zeedijk), which adds to the protection of the chief built-up areas. It is a summer paradise for family beach holidays, though in the peak season (July, August and early September) it can be very crowded indeed. This is no place for those who want to get away from it all.

There is good reason for the popularity of the coast and its 20 well-equipped resorts. The sea stretches northward with no landfall for many hundreds of miles, and the freshness of the air strikes many miles inland. The water is shallow and the tides are long. There can be strong currents, however, so watch out for the warning flags, which are flown at the beach stations. There is a huge area of sand kept clean by the forces of nature and firm to the feet and the horse's hoof. Belgian children have but short school holidays except for the two months of high summer, when *de Kust* or *le Littoral* is their summer playland. Landladies expect children with the summer months, and go out of their way to accommodate them. This is a great industry—tourism ranks as the third greatest industry in Belgium—and you will very seldom find any "no dogs or children" notices.

Discovering the Belgian Coast

The coast northeast of Oostende is known as the Oostkust, and everything to the southwest as the Westkust. Oostende, the fishing port, which was enlarged in the 15th century, became the chief port of access to the southern part of the Low Countries; it was fortified, besieged, and fought over in the 17th and 18th centuries, and eventually became one of the smarter watering-places of the early 19th century. Zeebrugge was the final answer to the problems caused by the silting up of the port of Bruges; the old access to the latter, the Zwin, is now a stretch of botanically interesting dry land between the limits of Het Zoute and the frontier of Dutch Zeeland.

Het Zoute, Smartest Resort

Het Zoute (Le Zoute) is generally regarded as the classiest resort on the coast. It has comparatively few hotels and is mainly occupied by expensive villas. It is sometimes known as the Garden of the North Sea, with its 370-acre nature reserve in the Zwin area (part of which even stretches into Holland). The reserve also contains the former residence of Léopold III, where there is a fine restaurant. This silted-up former estuary of the Zwin river, where the salt water washes into the soil at certain seasons, has in consequence some beautiful and rare flowers, and the bird life is unique in Belgium. There is a big tennis club, 50 courts, and an excellent golf club that attracts the best players in the country. There is a shopping street, Kustlaan, which is quite the most fashionable place for luxury-shopping for anything from chocolates to clothes.

Among the staple amusements at Het Zoute is the hiring by the hour of small motorscooters. Though this is a rather costly way of moving around, it adds to the feeling that here there is more space than at most of the other resorts. On the eastward side, towards Holland, you can ride or walk in the woods. It is a short ride over the Dutch frontier to Sluis, full of "sex-shops" forbidden in Belgium.

Knokke, Albert-Strand

Albert-Strand used to be thought more democratic than rich Het Zoute or middle-class Knokke. But now, with a casino and a fabulous hotel, Sofitel-La-Réserve, the balance has been swinging towards Albert-Strand. One of the main attractions here is boating and canoeing on the Zegemeer—an apparently unexceptional pastime which has taken on a new lease of life now that boaters can see into the exclusive *piscine* of the Réserve. (A real bonus for those who enjoy watching celebrities at play and spotting the stars in their swimsuits.) The casino over the way is the center of things in Knokke. It contains two nightclubs and a spacious ballroom, which attracts some of the best singers and entertainers from all over the world. There are also congresses and conferences held almost every week at the casino. The gambling-rooms are most easily reached from the back, facing the Sofitel-La-Réserve.

Duinbergen, Heist and Zeebrugge

Once an unpretentious village, Duinbergen is now the fashionable family resort of the Oostkust, with rows of smart villas. It adjoins Albert-Strand at one end and Heist at the other. There are tennis courts close to the seafront and others in the pleasant little garden city between the dunes and the road.

Heist has a small fishing port, the fishing village lying beyond the railway line away from the sea. As with Blankenberge, it caters to a clientèle of a more popular sort, tradespeople, office and factory-workers, and their families.

Both these resorts make much of the contrast with the costlier fare at Knokke and Het Zoute. In point of fact, there is not a lot to choose between one resort and another when it comes to hotels—though you'll notice the difference in price if you try the smaller places.

Zeebrugge is of little interest to the tourist. As far as most are concerned, it is simply a ferry port, one that hit the headlines in the worst possible way in March 1987 when a car-ferry capsized outside the harbor with great loss of life. However, if you do find yourself stuck here for a few hours, there is a small resort area beyond the foot of the mole. For those who like wandering about ports there is a fishing harbor, all but continuous ferry traffic at the terminals, and a range of commercial shipping. You will also see the occasional North Sea oil rig undergoing a refit, and several of the oddly shaped ultra-modern oil rig support vessels—a source of endless fascination (and questions) for the children.

Zeebrugge is a center of pilgrimage for English people, and indeed for all whose blood stirs at great feats of heroism, because of the exploit of the Royal Navy in blocking the sea channel to the U-boat base on the moonless midnight of St. George's Day in 1918. This achievement, incidentally, was reminiscent of a deed by the Royal Navy's ancestors six centuries earlier, when they sailed into Sluis (the outer port of Bruges at that time (1340)) and tackled the French fleet.

Blankenberge and De Haan

Next, beyond Zeebrugge, is the great conurbation of Blankenberge, giant of the Belgian seaside, with well over 100 hotels and boarding-houses. Because of tidal characteristics it has changed during the last twenty years from a fishing port to an attractive yachting harbour. A large, elegant wrought-iron windbreak (the *Paravang*) overlooking the harbour offers young and old a sheltered view of the activities, and tourists can sometimes buy shrimps from the odd fishing boat. The 1½-mile promenade is limited to pedestrians in summer, and has many cafés. Here there is the only British-style pier on the Belgian coast; it includes a superb modern aquarium, complete with model ships. There are many flats to let, camping sites and full provision for all the usual seaside sports and pastimes.

A detour of 11 km. (7 miles) to the southeast brings you to Lissewege, a sleepy little village, once a powerful medieval city. Its massive church tower, worthy of a cathedral and visible from many miles away, is the only witness of a rich past.

When you get to Wenduine, you become aware of the terror of the sea in this polder country. The seawall here is called the Graaf Jandijk, after Count Jean de Namur who began its construction nearly seven centuries ago. The choir and sacristy of the church are of about the same period, and the church appears on very early maps. The town is now a small one, and its chief industry is tourism.

Five km. (3 miles) farther on is De Haan (Le Coq), the enchanting little place that is becoming the fashionable resort of the coast. It almost rivals Het Zoute in fashion and expensiveness, and though slightly less crowded than the latter it does tend to be packed on public holidays. Here, too, you can play golf. De Haan is largely a villa resort and, as at all the Belgian bathing places, most of the villas are to let during the "fat months" of summer.

Towards Bredene the dune wall against the sea is naturally broad and there is room on it for the Royal Golf Club. At Bredene itself there is no promenade but the beach is large and perfect for families; at the rear is an 800 m (½-mile) stretch of beautiful sand dunes. This is a great center for camping.

Oostende

So we come to that paradox of watering places, Oostende, which has managed to do away with much that has disfigured it in the past. The Europacentrum skyscraper and the twin spires of the Church of Saints Peter and Paul are the first warning to the mariner that he is nearing the port. The town acquired the title "Queen of the Seaside Resorts" because of substantial Royal patronage. And crowned heads have not been alone in enjoying Oostende. It has been the favorite of many great artists and writers. James Ensor, the English-born painter lived here, and caught much that was colorful in turn-of-the-century Oostende. Victor Hugo and Lord Byron visited on occasions, and more recently, the famous Belgian detective story writer Georges Simenon discovered its attractions.

Oostende is the oldest settlement on the Belgian coast, and its history goes back to the 10th century. From here the Crusaders sailed for the reconquest of the Holy Land. For centuries it was a pirate hideout, and later it held out against the Spanish *reconquista* from 1583 until 1604. One of the first railroad lines on the Continent (Oostende-Mechelen) was built there in 1838, and a regular mailboat service to Dover started as early as 1846. In 1918 the Royal Navy's *Vindictive*, loaded with cement, was sunk at the port's entrance, immobilizing the German submarine-base there. As part of Hitler's Atlantic Wall, the city was bombed several times during World War II.

The town has kept what was worth saving, and lost the rest as completely as she has lost the fortifications of the Dutch, and the speculative fever that made the Compagnie d'Ostende the pale but modish equivalent of the English South Sea Company. It is an attractive Oostende that emerged from the postwar bout of reconstruction, and now you can play roulette and baccarat in the modern Kursaal which has replaced the ugly old one. There is also a racetrack, where meetings are transferred from the Brussels courses in the summer. Oostende is full of the usual sporting facilities and many festivities. It is prettily laid out, and the fishing port keeps you picturesquely in touch with as much as you need of the realities of life. There is always a vital flow of traffic through the town because of its position as the railhead for Europe from Dover, and the fact that main international truck routes over the Continent and to the Middle East start from here. Oostende has a small airport, mainly used by light aircraft.

Proceeding westwards from Oostende, you come to the part of the coastline where mounted fishermen ride their horses through the shallows dragging shrimp-nets behind them. At Middelkerke the main sport is land-yacht sailing on the sands, and the tennis courts are good. Middelkerke is becoming fashionable and has a beautiful, pocket-size casino. Westende, two miles farther on, has a number of reasonably priced hotels, and some excellent holiday facilities. Almost next door to it, Lombardsijde is the ideal spot for camping or caravaning. Its church houses a statue of the Virgin washed ashore in the 16th century.

From Nieuwpoort to De Panne

At Nieuwpoort, 5 km. (3 miles) farther on, you are again on historic ground. Here you are at the mouth of the Ijzer (Yser) River with its First World War associations, and it was here that the sluice-gates were opened, flooding the polder country to the discomfiture of the advancing Germans, and playing a decisive role in the defense of the Ypres salient and the Channel ports. Two cemeteries, one Belgian and the other British, will remind you of the part Nieuwpoort played in World War I. Besides the bust of Geeraert, the water-control expert who directed the flooding, you will find British, French and other memorials. Impressively situated, too, despite its Meccano-like pillars, is the memorial to King Baudouin's grandfather, Albert the Soldier-King.

You will soon discover, of course, that Nieuwpoort town is quite separate from Nieuwpoort Bad. The former has sustained the scars of war, and was all but knocked out of existence. The Onze Lieve Vrouw (Church of Our Lady) was destroyed in 1914, restored, burned again in 1940, and again restored. The attraction of Nieuwpoort for the tourist is largely in its nearness to the estuary, which makes it a good yachting-center and the scene of regattas.

Two Modest Resorts

The next resort is Oostduinkerke, where the broad and finely sanded beach provides a healthy playground for children. Koksijde is, together with St. Idesbald and Oostduinkerke, one commune.

St. Idesbald is a small family resort with many pretty villas. Koksijde has preserved its marvellous heritage of dunes. The Hoge Blekker (108 ft.) is the highest dune on the Belgian coast. You can also discover the ruins of the Abbey of the Dunes (13th century). Like St. Idesbald, Koksijde is known as the resort of flowers.

So we come to De Panne (La Panne), three miles from the French border, the last spot on Belgian soil where King Albert stubbornly endured the war in 1914. The place has another connection with the royal family: it was here that Belgium's first king, Léopold I, set foot on the soil of his realm in 1831. De Panne has attained great popularity as a family holiday base.

PRACTICAL INFORMATION FOR
THE BELGIAN COAST

 **HOTELS AND RESTAURANTS.** There are over a thousand hotels and pensions, from the simplest to the most luxurious, along the coast. During the high season (end of July to beginning of September) you may well find booking difficult. To be sure of a room, write at least 4 weeks in advance to the nearest Tourist Office (see *Useful Addresses*) and ask for a Relobel advance booking form. This reservation service guarantees you a place, where possible. Value added tax is included, but 16% service charge is added to the bill and there is no need for extra tipping either in hotels or restaurants.

Though older hotels have restaurants, often excellent ones, and are willing to quote *en pension* terms, many new ones quote only for bed and breakfast and serve no other meals. The latest construction phase incorporates kitchenettes in hotel rooms, or pairs of rooms, even when there is a restaurant on the premises.

To rent furnished villas or flats (apartments) on coast, apply to estate agents *(agence immobilière)*. A full list is available from the Tourist Office, with indications of the cost. The usual letting period is a month or half month. Enquire whether bed linen, table linen and cutlery are available.

For details of a wide range of package holidays—including winter weekends, tours, summer resorts and specialty holidays—contact Belgian Travel Service, Bridge House, Ware, Herts, England (tel. 0920 61171).

For administrative purposes, five closely-connected resorts have been regrouped as Knokke-Heist. They comprise Albert-Strand, Duinbergen, Heist, Knokke and Het Zoute, stretching about 11 km. (7 miles) along the coast.

BLANKENBERGE. Small fishing resort grown into the noisiest of the beach resorts, with overtones of Atlantic City. Caters to all tastes. Has over 100 hotels and even more boarding houses. Best in town is the *Azaert* (E), Molenstraat 31 (tel. 050–411 599). 36 well-equipped rooms. *Albatross* (M), Consciencestraat 45 (tel. 050–416 077). 20 rooms with bath. 200 meters from the beach. *Marie-José* (M), Marie-Josélaan 2 (tel. 050–411 006). 45 rooms. *Rotessa* (I), Consciences-traat 47 (tel. 050–416 077). 45 rooms, 14 with shower; no restaurant.

Restaurants. *Colonies* (M), Kerkstraat 95, (tel. 050–411 275). *Joinville* (M), Jan de Troozlaan 5 (tel. 050–412 269). *La Grande Marée* (I), Bakkersstraat 6 (tel. 050–413 850).

DE HAAN (Le Coq). Has a splendid beach. *Belle Vue* (M), Koningsplein 5 (tel. 059–233 439). 50 rooms. *Dunes* (M), Leopoldplein 5 (tel. 059–233 146). 27 rooms, breakfast only. Closed Oct.–Easter.

Restaurant. *Coeur Volant* (E), Normandielaan 25 (tel. 059–233 567). Outstanding. Specialties include lobster *à l'américaine* and chicken flambé with whiskey.

KNOKKE-HEIST, ALBERT-STRAND. *Sofitel La Réserve* (L), Elizabethlaan 160 (tel. 050–610 606). 112 rooms, 3 suites; health center; hot-water swimming pool; sauna, etc. Best hotel on the coast. *Ascot* (M), Zoutelaan 130 (tel. 050–608 471). 19 rooms. *Atlanta* (M), Nellenslaan 162 (tel. 050–605 500). 32 rooms. *Elysée* (M), Elizabethlaan 39 (tel. 050–611 648). 10 rooms. *The Lido* (M), Zwaluwenlaan 18 (tel. 050–601 925). 40 rooms.

For slightly more modest accommodation *Bel-Air* (M), Patriottenstraat 26 (tel. 050–511 300). 33 rooms. *Pingouins* (I), Duinendreef 52 (tel. 050–513 340). 12 rooms. *Prince's* (I), Lippenslaan 171 (tel. 050–601 111). 28 rooms.

Restaurants. *Esmerelda* (M), Nelleuslaan 161 (tel. 050–603 366). *Casa Borghèse* (I), Bayauxlaan 27 (tel. 050–603 739). For good seafood and Italian dishes. Closed Thur.

KOKSIJDE-BAD. *Hostellerie Le Régent* (E), Blieeklaan 10 (tel. 058–511 210). 10 rooms and excellent restaurant. *Terlinck* (M), Terlinckplaats 17 (tel. 058–511 694). 22 well-equipped rooms. Overlooking the beach.

Restaurants. *Aquilon* (E), Koninklijkebaan 318 (tel. 058–512 267). Best around, with great seafood. A mile out of town. *Atlanta* (M), Zeedijk 75 (tel. 058–513 592). Good food by the beach.

LISSEWEGE. Restaurants. Just south of Zeebrugge, this old-world village has some outstanding restaurants. *De Goedendag* (E), Lisseweeges Vaartje 2 (tel. 050–545 335). A 15th-century inn. Further south, near the ruins of an abbey, *Hof ter Doest* (M), ter Doeststraat 4 (tel. 050–544 082).

NIEUWPOORT. Small fishing port and yacht harbor slightly inland. The main concentration of hotels and restaurants is a tramride away at Nieuwpoort-aan-Zee. *Parkhotel* (M), Albert I Laan 175 (tel. 058–234 491). 21 rooms, all facilities, and some furnished flatlets. *Regina* (M), Albert-I-laan 137 (tel. 058–235 692). 20 rooms, all with bath.

Restaurants. *Jan Turpin* (E), Albert I Laan 68a (tel. 058–233 452). *Windhoek* (I), Albert I Laan 153 (tel. 058–235 506). Both at beach end of town.

OOSTDUINKERKE. Famous for its horseback shrimp-fishers; has wide sands. *Artan* (E), Ijslandplein 5, Zeedijk (tel. 058–515 908). *Westland* (I), Zeedijk (tel. 058–513 917). 28 rooms.

OOSTENDE. *Andromeda* (L), Albert I Promenade 60 (tel. 059–506 811). 65 rooms. *Ter Streep* (E), Leopold II Laan 14 (tel. 059–700 912). 35 rooms. *Europe* (M), Kapucijnenstraat 52 (tel. 059–701 012). 65 rooms. *Prado* (M), Leopold II Laan 22 (tel. 059–705 306). 31 rooms. *Glenmore* (I), Hofstraat 25 (tel. 059–702 022). 40 rooms. Inexpensive rooms available along Visserskaai, opposite ferry.

Restaurants. *Prince Charles* (E), Visserskaai 19 (tel. 059–705 066). Pleasant spot overlooking quayside; superb seafood. *Le Perigord* (M), Kursaal (tel. 059–705 111). At the Casino, specializes in filet steak with duck livers and Perigord sauce, and Pancakes Comédie Française. Less expensive are *Le Basque* (M), Albert I Promenade 62 (tel. 059–705 444), which is right by the beach, *Marina*

(M), Albert-I-Promenade 2, (tel. 059–703 585). Good Italian food, and *Adelientje* (I), Bonenstraat 9 (tel. 059–701 367), which has good seafood.

DE PANNE. Westernmost beach resort of the coast. Has over 50 hotels and pensions. Renowned for its restaurants. *Seahorse* (M), Toeristenlaan 7 (tel. 058–412 747). 19 rooms. *Val Jolie* (M), Baarkenlaan 55 (tel. 058–412 519). 21 rooms. *Terlinck* (M), Zeelaan 175 (tel. 058–412 621). *De la Grande Place* (I), Zeelaan 69 (tel. 058–411 279). 18 rooms, all with shower.

Restaurants. Best are *Fox* (E), Walkierstraat 2 (tel. 058–412 855), and *Bonne Auberge* (M), Zeedijk 3 (tel. 058–411 398), on seafront. Try also *l'Impérial* (I), Leopold-I-esplanade 9 (tel. 058–414 228).

WENDUINE. Has 2½ miles of wide sandy beach, dunes and peaceful woods. *Les Mouettes* (M), Zeedijk 7 (tel. 050–411 514). 30 rooms. *Odette* (I), Kerkstraat 34 (tel. 050–413 690). 6 rooms. Small hotel with excellent restaurant.

Restaurant. *Ensor Inn* (I), Zeedijk 63 (tel. 050–414 159).

WESTENDE-BAD. Family resort known as the "pearl of the coast"; has splendid promenade. *St. Laureins* (E), St. Laureinstrand (tel. 233 958). 10 rooms; weekends only out of season. *Hostellerie de la Noble Rose* (I), H. Jasparlaan 181 (tel. 300 127). 14 rooms. *Splendid* (I), Meeuwenlaan 20 (tel. 300 032). 17 rooms and restaurant.

Restaurants. *Melrose* (E), H. Jasparlaan 127 (tel. 301 867). Classic cuisine, also has 10 (M), rooms. *Bristol* (M), H. Jasparlaan 175 (tel. 300 401).

ZEEBRUGGE. Beach on left of busy harbor, handy for car ferries. *Strandhotel* (M), Zeedijk 14 (tel. 050–544 055). 30 rooms, handy for the ferry.

Restaurants. Almost all specialize in seafood. *Le Chalut* (M), Rederskaai 26 (tel. 050–544 115). *Rivage* (M), Rederskaai 37 (tel. 050–544 061).

South of the town on the road to Bruges, *'t Molentje* (E), Baron de Maerelaan 211 (tel. 546 164). Excellent newish restaurant, with delicious seafood specialties.

GETTING AROUND. By train. From Brussels to the Belgian coast there are excellent train services with an hourly frequency to Oostende, Blankenberge and Knokke. All the trains call en route at Ghent and Bruges. The fast trains to Oostende take around an hour and a quarter.

By tram. One of the best ways to explore the resorts is to use the Vicinal tramway which runs right along the coast from Knokke via Zeebrugge and Oostende to De Panne which is almost on the border with France. The trams are swift and modern and there is a half-hourly service during the summer. The tramway (from Oostende) is probably the easiest way to get to De Panne.

By car. One of Belgium's main roads also links Brussels and Oostende with exits for Ghent and Bruges, and a good link road up to Knokke. From Antwerp a new fast road via Zelzate saves the detour via Ghent. And there is a good road right along the coast. This, however, does get very busy in the summer months and one should allow ample time when motoring between resorts.

PLACES OF INTEREST. Though you came primarily to laze about and enjoy the golden sand and the sea, you will probably want to vary this pleasant monotony by a short outing. Nature lovers can visit the splendid dunes between De Panne and the French border or, at the other end of the coast, the

Zwin marshes covered with sea lavender that blooms in July and August. This 370-acre reserve is open from 9 to 7 (5 in winter) and contains over 100 species of birds. Birds abound at the Zwin Aviary outside Het Zoute for the benefit of amateur ornithologists. Crossing the Zwin, one can climb up the high dunes and be rewarded with a magnificent view of the North Sea, the mouth of the Schelde, the "Isle" of Walcheren, and the hinterland with its Belgian and Dutch steeples. You can visit the small Dutch township of Sluis, near Knokke. A fast car-ferry crosses the Schelde from Breskens to Vlissingen.

This is not an area with many museums or great buildings. The most notable historical relic is the **Duinenabdij** (Abbey of the Dunes) in Koksijde. Founded by the Cistercians in the 12th century, the site today is an impressive archeological park. Open 9 to 12, 2 to 5. Admission BF 45. Among the smaller places of interest—especially to the art buff—is the **James Ensorhuis** (the house of the artist James Ensor), in Oostende. Open 10 to 12, 2 to 5, closed Tues.; from Nov. to May, Sat., Sun., 2 to 5; closed in Oct. You can also see Ensor's work in Oostende's **Museum voor Schone Kunsten** (Fine Arts Museum) which contains mainly Belgian contemporary works. Admission BF 20. Open 10 to 12, 2 to 5; closed Tues. In the **Harbor,** don't miss the three-masted wind-jammer *Mercator.* Open weekends, (daily in summer), 10 to 12, 1 to 5. Admission BF 50.

At Zeebrugge you can board the M.S. *Groot-Brugge* and visit the port. Or you can visit the **Gemeentehuis,** situated on the Markt, which is partly devoted to the famous battle of 1918 and to the events of the last World War in the area.

At Blankenberge there is a great **Aquarama** on the pier: open 10 to 5 in summer, limited hours winter.

For the kids there is the **Meli-Park** at Adinkerke near de Panne, which has all kinds of fun rides, animals, activities, and even a magic show.

SPORTS. Sailing enthusiasts will find ample opportunity to spend their holidays on the water. A permanent breeze along the coast offers splendid facilities for **yachting.** Regattas are frequently held in Oostende. Zeebrugge and Nieuwpoort have good yacht harbors. There are many navigable canals throughout the area for **canoeing.** You can play **golf** on the 9-hole course at Zoute and the 18-hole course at De Haan.

At De Panne and Oostduinkerke there is 3- or 4-wheeled **land-yachting.** Tennis tournaments take place during the season at Oostende and Zoute. There are hundreds of tennis courts along the coast; all resorts and some hotels have their own facilities. Safe **swimming** at the splendid Olympic pool (with restaurant and café) at Knokke. Many resorts have good public pools.

Warning for swimmers (and especially non-swimmers): bathe only at official beaches patrolled by lifeguards. Red flag means bathing prohibited; green, bathing safe, and lifeguards on duty; yellow, bathing risky, but lifeguards on duty. For more information on sports activities, call 050–604 317 (Knokke); 059–500 529 (Oostende); 058–412 971 (De Panne).

SPAS AND CASINOS. The Palais des Thermes at Oostende offers mineral baths for the treatment of rheumatism with water from a well sunk to over 1,000 feet, along with electrotherapy and other cures.

You may invest your savings in chips of 10 to 1,000 francs at the casinos of Oostende, Knokke-Zoute, Blankenberge, and Middelkerke. What happens from there on is anybody's guess. The casino at Oostende features top-name stars of the entertainment world during the season.

NIGHTLIFE. As you can well imagine, the closure-rate among these seasonal establishments is very high, and you had better check to see whether the place of your choice is still operating. What usually happens is that a year later they open under a different name, so while their names may be different from season to season, addresses may remain.

This general rule is not valid for nightclubs run by local casinos; whatever their losses, they keep right on—roulette will always fill financial gaps. And, although these establishments can be costly, you usually get more than your money's worth: two dance bands and headline cabaret entertainers from Paris, London and New York—and no fleecing.

Blankenberge. Dancing and discos: *The Beatles,* Casinoplein 6. *Columbius,* Casinoplein 8. *Djinn,* Hoogstraat 5. *Free,* Zeedijk 95. *The King,* Weststraat 21. *Matson,* Casinostraat 5. *Old Corner,* Casinoplein 10. *Pebbles,* Zeedijk 104. *Piccadilly,* Breydelstraat 62. *Witte Paard,* Langestraat 44.

De Panne. Dancing at *Stardust,* Slopenlaan 17.

Knokke-Heist is a nightclubbers' paradise; several places open year-round. The casino offers dinner-dancing to two orchestras, gala nights with international stars, theater, films, ballet and exhibitions.

In the casino building are *Patrick's Club* and the *27 Club.* The smart set is found in the *Gallery Club; Toy's Club, Number One,* le *Georgy's,* l'*Opium, Dixieland* and *Downstairs* are reasonable.

Middelkerke. Nightclub at the casino; dancing at *V.I.Ps, Beachclub,* Zeedijk 58, *Clef Club,* Torhoutsesteenweg 3, *Ugly,* Leopoldlaan 83; all moderately priced.

Oostende. Best: *Sporting Club* run by casino. Two bands, short cabaret, prices very reasonable. Girlie shows at *Emmanuelle* and *Folies Club* in Van Iseghemlaan. You can find a large choice of entertainment and discos along Van Iseghemlaan and Langestraat. Also movie theaters (occasional English-speaking films).

 USEFUL ADDRESSES. Police Emergency: Call 906. **Tourist information:** For the whole coastland: Westtourism, Vlamingstraat 55, Bruges (tel. 337 344). For individual towns—Blankenberge, Leopold III Plein (tel. 412 227); De Haan, Leopoldlaan 24 (tel. 235 723); Knokke-Heist, Info-Lichttorenplein (tel. 601 516); Middelkerke, J. Casselaan 4 (tel. 300 368); Nieuwpoort, Marktplein 7 (tel. 235 594); Oostende, Wapenplein 3 (tel. 701 199); de Panne, Gemeentehuis, Zeelaan 21 (tel. 411 304); in summer, most resorts operate information desks at train (or tram) stations and on popular beaches.

HAINAUT AND THE
SAMBRE-MEUSE REGION

Cradle of Walloon History

Two main roads lead from Brussels into the Hainaut region. The chaussée de Mons leaves the capital in a southwesterly direction, and forks at Halle (Hal), giving you a choice between the road through Enghien and Ath to Tournai, and the road through Braine-le-Comte and Soignies to Mons itself. The chaussée de Waterloo leaves almost due south, then forks just behind the Waterloo battlefields, where you take either the road through Nivelles and Thuin to Beaumont, or the highway to Charleroi and into the country between the Sambre and Meuse (Maas). All of these roads lead into France, which will serve to remind you that you are in a proud old country that was the nursery of French kings, the rich dowry of dynastic marriages, and for many centuries the buffer between expansionist France and quarrelsome Flanders.

Hainaut is full to bursting with remembrances of strife between France and her neighbors, it is also alive with the marked contrast between industry and intensive agriculture. You will pass many well-run, highly productive farms. Yet Charleroi is the center of the engineering industry and the central coal basin; and at Mons you forget

174

Saint Waudru in the shadow of the great black country of the Borinage.
Here the slagheaps dot the countryside.

Despite 150 years of industrialization, the region still retains many
essentially rural traditions. At Wasmes, on the Tuesday of Whitsun, a
little girl is carried in procession to commemorate the *Pucellette* whom
the villagers were constrained to sacrifice annually to a nearby monster
until delivered from it by Gilles de Chin more than 800 years ago, a
story which will immediately remind you of St. George and the dragon.
But here you are only a couple of miles from Quaregnon, where the old
mine-tips and pithead-gear still remind the villagers that up to the late
1960s their menfolk were working a mile underground.

The people of the Borinage find in pigeon-racing one of their chief
recreations, though around Charleroi the Sunday morning cock-crow-
ing contests are also popular and characteristic of the café life. It all
marks a strong contrast with the Allied Supreme Headquarters
(SHAPE), with its modern buildings, its satellite communications,
military number plates and all the appurtenances of modernity centered at Casteau, only 8 km. (5 miles) from Mons.

Discovering Hainaut

The Brussels-Tournai road enters Hainaut at Enghien (Edingen), on
the linguistic frontier, where there is the remnant of a fine park laid out
in the 17th century by the dukes of Arenberg, who bought the town
from Henri IV, King of France. The Eglise des Capucines contains a
splendid mausoleum by the well-known Renaissance sculptor, Jean
Mone, in honor of Guillaume de Croy, a Belgian priest, later primate
of Spain.

It is worth taking the turning to Lessines (from Ghislenghien) to see
the hospital of Notre-Dame-à-la-Rose, a 13th-century foundation of
one of the dames of honor to Blanche of Castile, though most of the
buildings date from the 16th and 17th centuries and the chapel from
the 18th.

Lessines (Lessen), itself a town of porphyry quarries, is on the Den-
dre, which you will meet again when you have returned to the main
road and gone on to Ath. Lessines is the birthplace of Hennepin (La
Salle's companion), who was the first explorer to sail up the Mississippi
River to 46° North latitude, in 1680. It is also the birthplace of surrealist painter René Magritte.

The Vauban fortifications at Ath, built by order of Louis XIV after
he had personally supervised the siege and capture of the town, have
disappeared; but there remains a vestige, the Tour Burbant, of a much
older fortification, erected in 1166, with a massive wall some ten feet
thick. The main attraction in Ath, however, is the festival of the last
Sunday of August. The town is famous above all for its giants, eight
colorful reed-built constructions which include Goliath (Gouyasse),
Samson and the four sons of Aymon who spend most of the year in
Wenceslas Cobergher's little 17th-century Hôtel de Ville. Traditionally, Goliath and his bride are married on the eve of the festival.

Chièvres (about 4 miles south of Ath) is a very attractive little village
with a charming square and a 16th-century château of the powerful de

Croy family. Nearby, you can visit the 18th-century château of Attre. Heading south again, through Chièvres and Neufmaison, you take a sharp right turn to Beloeil. Here, by courtesy of the Prince de Ligne and on payment of an entrance fee, you can visit the "Versailles of Belgium," with its great garden-park laid out in the manner of Le Nôtre, its ornamental lake, its swans and its fountains. The château itself, rebuilt from the original plans after the fire of 1900, is not quite the place it was, as described by Marshal Charles-Joseph de Ligne, but its treasures lead you on an absorbing journey through the great events of Europe in which the princely family of the château have played their part for nearly a thousand years. Lovers of antiques and old books will want to spend days on end here; paintings abound, from Holbein to Caravaggio, and there are plenty of curiosities like Marlborough's pistols or a lock of Marie Antoinette's hair; all to be found among Flemish and French tapestries. Not so romantic, but still interesting: there are 240 windows to be cleaned and 10 km. (6½ miles) of hedges to be cut.

The memorial of the de Ligne princes is in Beloeil village church, which stands in a shaded square, where a feudal atmosphere can still be felt. Heading northwest once more from Beloeil you join the main road again at Leuze, where it is worth while visiting St. Peter's church to see the 18th-century carved wooden interior.

Tournai, Cathedral and Art Town

After Leuze comes Tournai (the Flemish call it Doornik), within a few miles of the linguistic frontier on the road to Kortrijk (Courtrai) and of the French border on the road to Lille. Strategic pivot whenever France and Flanders were at loggerheads, Tournai has origins which go into a very distant past. Birthplace of Clovis (A.D. 465) and burial place of Childeric (A.D. 481), there is that within it which is more French than France itself. Early French drama can be traced back to Tournai: it was here that the play *Farce du garçon et de l'aveugle* was performed in 1295. It was the Tournaisian mantle of Clovis that Napoleon assumed when he wore on his coronation robe the emblem of the bees. Childeric's tomb with its fabulous treasure was discovered during excavations for building in 1653.

The town has survived many vicissitudes. It resisted the English in 1340, repudiated the Burgundian suzerainty a century later, and was besieged by Henry VIII of England, who erected defences of which part, the Round Tower, still stands. Wolsey was enriched by appointment to the Bishopric of Tournai a few years before he became a Cardinal. Within a few decades the town was again besieged, this time by the Spaniards who encountered the epic defence of Christine de Lalaing, the governor's wife. In her husband's absence she successfully held out for over two months, leading many sorties, until relief came. The town was later seized by Louis XIV, fortified by Vauban, recaptured by the Allies and handed over to the Austrian regime, from which Louis XV recaptured it after the Battle of Fontenoy.

Tournai was war-scarred indeed when it emerged from the carnage of 1940–44. The Grand'Place had simply disappeared and the Halle aux Draps (Cloth Hall) and the Hôtel de Ville were in ruins. Over a thousand of the city's ancient houses were totally destroyed, and several hundred were badly damaged. Today's Grand'Place is a product of postwar town-planning, respectful of the past and moderately successful in recapturing it. One good thing came out of the bombardment, for the damage of the Church of St. Brice revealed fragments of very ancient frescos which have since been restored.

The Cathedral

More important still was that, for all the bombardment, the great Cathedral of Notre Dame stood intact. Indeed, the damage to surrounding buildings revealed the line and majesty of the cathedral, so that these could be better appreciated. For all that, the cathedral is a strange building. As with Antwerp's, the exterior does not prepare you for the large scale of the interior, and unless you are well-acquainted with Germanic architectural forms, you are bound to fancy there is something unfinished or temporary in the hat-like cones that crown the five towers. However, you will see between the west doors the 14th-century statue of Notre-Dame des Malades (Our Lady of the Sick) which will prepare you for great treasures of more conventional kinds. Begun in 1110, the entire cathedral took only 60 years to build.

Inside the cathedral, you will at first be amazed, perhaps even appalled, by the heavy and over-ornate screen. The nave will in its structure, however, have prepared you for the masterly Ile-de-France grace of the 13th-century Gothic choir. The cathedral contains a great number of treasures. The Rubens *Souls in Purgatory,* in an early-14th century small chapel, is so heavily restored as to be unrewarding to the student, but the remains of the 12th-century mural paintings in the transept are more interesting, as also are the well-restored transept windows by the 14th-century master, Arnold of Nijmegen. There is a number of other important paintings by Metsys, Pourbus, De Vos, and Blondeel, and the high altar is by an 18th-century artist, Gaspard Lefèbvre, and was originally in the abbey church of St. Martin. The great treasure of the cathedral, however, consists in the three reliquaries known as the *Châsse de Notre-Dame,* the *Châsse de Saint Eleuthère* and the *Châsse des Damoiseaux.* The first, in vermeil, is the work of the greatest of the Meuse-side silversmiths, Nicholas of Verdun, and dates from 1205. The second is of around 1247, attributed to an illustrious pupil of Nicholas' Hugo d'Oignies, and is a work in silver, as also is the third, a much later work of Bruges origin (1571). There is also a Byzantine cross-reliquary of the 7th century, containing a relic of the True Cross. An ecclesiastical treasure to Belgian and Briton alike is St. Thomas à Becket's chasuble. He spent some time at St. Medard's Abbey in Tournai in 1170 before returning to England to meet his violent death.

The Belfry, which stands near the cathedral in the Grand'Place, dates from the 13th century and its carillon is one of the finest in the country. If you have either the courage or the stamina you can climb the 256 steps to see a really splendid panorama of this ancient cathedral city.

Tournai has at various times in its history been a school of the arts. Tournai sculpture was famous at least 800 years ago, and you can see evidence of this in the Porte Mantile of the cathedral. In the 15th century Robert Campin was a leading Tournai painter, though little is now known of his work, unless it is right to identify him with the Maître de Flémalle. One of his pupils was Roger van der Weyden, who afterwards worked in Bruges and Brussels, and another was Jacques Daret. At about the same period, tapestry became one of the city's fine arts. It was at Tournai that Simon Marmion of Valenciennes started his school of illumination work. At the same time, Tournai brass- and copperwork rivaled that of Dinant, and wrought-iron also flourished. In the 17th century, a new school of painting appeared, in the followers of Michel Bouillon, and in the next century, Tournai porcelain began to be at its best. Around the turn of the 18th century, carpet-making became another fine-art industry.

Unfortunately, the iconoclasts left little of the Tournai statuary, but the Musée des Beaux Arts houses, in a modern but extremely satisfactory building by Victor Horta, an exceedingly fine collection of all that is best in all the Tournaisian arts, including a number of fine sculptures.

In the rue Barre-St.Brice you will come across two dwellinghouses of the 12th-century Romanesque period, numbers 12 and 14. In the same street and elsewhere you will find rows of Gothic houses, some Renaissance buildings, and a number of Louis XIV dwellings.

The terrible bombing of May 1940 revealed traces of a Roman *castrum* visible near place Reine Astrid. You will get the finest view of Tournai from the fortified water-gate, the Pont des Trous, part of the city's medieval defense system.

No Irishman will want to leave Tournai without a visit to the field of Fontenoy, where the Celtic cross in Irish sandstone commemorates the Irish contingent that fought against the English. It brings back memories of the Treaty of Limerick. Fontenoy is best reached by following the road to Peruwelz.

Barges and Wedding Feasts

The road from Brussels to Mons will take you through Braine-le-Comte and Soignies (which will be signposted as 's-Gravenbrakel and Zinnik for a few miles either side of Halle). From the former you can make a short detour to your left, on the Nivelles road, to see the quite astonishing barge-lift at Ronquières, on the Brussels–Charleroi canal. The Belgians are very proud of it, and often forget it was only saved from disaster through a Swedish firm's energetic investigation to correct faulty estimates of the rock formation. It has, however, been successfully operating since late in 1968; and you will be able to buy a bag of *frites* while you watch a 1,350-ton barge sail into a mammoth tank, and the tank, water, and barge hauled uphill for three-quarters of a mile (a vertical rise of some 220 ft.), then passing through a lock and continuing its trip on a viaduct. The whole thing is worked by closed-circuit TV control, and is surmounted by an elegant 300-ft. tower which, apart from the control-room in the lower part, is largely there to give you a first-class view of the countryside. In addition, it is possible from May to August to take a boat trip up and down the incline (every day except Wed. and Sat.) at 12, 2.30, 4 and 5.30.

Returning to the main road and passing through Braine-le-Comte, you may perhaps want to turn again into the valley of the Sennette, where the Castle of Ecaussines-Lalaing grimly bars the old trade route into Brussels from the French country beyond Mons. It was restored in the 15th century, and is the scene of the annual Marriage Feast held every Whit Monday for marriage-minded spinsters and bachelors. Its vast halls, old kitchen and museum are worth a visit. Ecaussines d'Enghien also possesses a château, a pleasant building with a 16th-century chapel.

If you turn off to the right to pass through Le Roeulx and see the château of the Princes de Croy, with its fine 18th-century façade, you will go on to Mons (Bergen) round the edge of the mining district which gave the Borinage its essential character.

Otherwise, if you stick to the main road through Soignies, some 8 km. (5 miles) from Mons between Casteau and Maisières you will see a big complex of buildings and read the sign: "Supreme Headquarters Allied Powers Europe." Since 1966 this has been the nerve center for the Atlantic alliance's land forces in Europe. Three-quarters of the personnel are English-speaking, and the official languages are English and French. The SHAPE worker has plenty of choice of cultural and sporting clubs, from chess to athletics—the marathon race is an annual event—all helping to make up the base's social existence. Apart from SHAPE village itself inside the H.Q. area, with its own shopping center, nearly 2,000 families are housed around the countryside. The influx has brought much trade to shopkeepers, as well as to cafés and restaurants, in this pleasant district.

Mons is the administrative capital of Hainaut, a town traditionally founded by St. Waudru, daughter of a count of Hainaut, in the 7th century. In the 12th century it was very strongly fortified by Baldwin of Mons, and in the rue du Prince you can still see some vestiges of this. Despite its industrial character, Mons does not sprawl; it keeps pretty well within the limits laid down by Jean d'Avesnes in the 13th century, though the fortifications of the Dutch, built in 1818, were gleefully demolished. The town has been somewhat enlarged without losing its character. Its red-bricked, elegant but grimy 17th-century houses remind us of the reign of Louis XIV.

The first thing to strike you will be the absurd belfry, and you may agree with Victor Hugo that only its size saves it. He likened it to "an enormous coffeepot, flanked below the belly-level by four medium-sized teapots." It is, in fact, a 17th-century construction. It dominates the hillside, and you will be surprised to hear it spoken of locally as the *tour du château,* or simply *le château.* This is a reference to the castle of the counts of Hainaut, which once stood nearby but was demolished in 1866. However, you can still see the subterranean passages and the Chapel of Saint Calixte. The belfry houses a carillon of 47 bells, for the Montois were famed as bell forgers. At the top you have a fine view over the country.

Leave the square by the rue des Clercs to reach the church of St. Waudru, a fine specimen of 15th-century Gothic, though parts date from much later. It was begun in 1450 by the ladies of St. Waudru's noble chapter of secular canonesses—founded on the 7th-century chapel of the saint—and Matthew de Layens is said to have made the original plans. Jacques du Broeucq built the screen, which was unfortunately taken down in 1797, though some of the statues and bas reliefs are still preserved in the church. The artistic traditions of Mons itself are represented in the windows of the choir and transept, by the Eve family, and also in the church's exceptionally fine treasure of plate and reliquaries. One of the latter is probably by Hugo d'Oignies. (There is also a good collection of this craftsman's work in the Convent of the Sisters of Notre-Dame at Namur.)

For examples of Hainaut pottery and glass in Mons you must go to the Musée du Centenaire, housed in the building of the old Mont de Piété (municipal pawnshop) just by a pretty little garden which abuts on the Hôtel de Ville and is fronted by a prehistoric standing stone and a 1940s American tank. The museum covers Mons in the First World War, coins, prehistory and, as we have said, has a fine ceramic collection.

There are also two interesting museums of local interest, that in the Maison Jean Lescarts behind the Beaux Arts and the one in rue Notre-Dame where the Canon Puissant collection is found. In the latter street, too, the restored 13th-century Chapel of Saint Margaret houses a collection of religious art.

On Trinity Sunday, the day of Saint George's fight (for the gallant Cappadocian saint, and dragon-slayer, is now identified in local tradition with the Montois hero, Gilles de Chin) with Lumeçon the dragon, this otherwise sleepy town wakes up. A cavalcade of costumed citizens accompanies the monster, who descends from the castle to the Grand' Place. There, the combat takes place.

Mons is far from being alone in its tradition of a yearly cavalcade with military or religious overtones. The whole of Hainaut is dotted with villages that celebrate a saint, a battle, a giant or a medieval marriage with a traditional procession. While all probably have pagan origins, some have been brought curiously "up-to-date." Many are suffused with Napoleonic nostalgia, and it is quite possible to see a complete troop of the Emperor's Old Guard forming up in a Walloon village street, eagles to the fore. Remember that, as the Duke of Wellington said, Waterloo was a "damn close-run thing" and that as far as these people are concerned, the *wrong* side won!

The Binche Carnival

Some 2 miles east of Mons, on the old Charleroi road toward Binche, you come to Saint Symphorien, where there is a feudal castle and an unusual English-German military cemetery of World War I. Some 10 miles further on, you reach the outskirts of Binche, whose central historic core is still intact behind its 27 towers and 1½ miles of ramparts. Once the delight of the daughters of the counts of Hainaut, Binche is the scene every Shrove Tuesday of one of the most remarkable spectacles in Europe, which has even led to the suggestion that the town gave its name to the English word "binge."

The focal point is the procession and dance of the Gilles. The boys and men don gold, white, black and red padded suits which are decorated with lion-motifs and hung around the waist with gilded bells. Their hats are like something from a Moulin Rouge show—white toppers with tall ostrich plumes. From baskets the masqueraders pelt passers-by with oranges, so if you join in the crowds, leave off your spectacles and don't wear your best clothes. Most important of all, be careful where you tread, because orange-peel can be every bit as treacherous as banana skins! Don't under any circumstances return the Gilles' fire: their "gift" brings good luck and should be kept—or eaten!

On this day, the good burghers of Binche keep their doors open and champagne flows with prodigal abandon. The young men who are not among the Gilles arm themselves with short broomsticks *(ramons)*, and woe betide the tourist who has ventured into the town without wearing a fancy hat or a red nose. He is certain to learn that a blow from a *ramon* can sting.

The festival probably has pagan Teutonic origins, but most experts believe it took on its present form in 1549, when Mary of Hungary, sister of Charles V, arranged a sumptuous reception for the Emperor and his son Philip II of Spain in order to introduce the new king to the nobles of the Low Countries. This was just after Peru was conquered by the Spanish, and it is likely that the oranges of Binche symbolize the gold of the Incas, just as the Gilles are supposed to represent the defeated Indians. The Château of Binche, where Mary lived, is now in ruins, but Binche's museum tells the fascinating story of the Carnival through the ages.

Eastward from Binche, you have three choices for your route toward Charleroi. The simplest is the direct road through Anderlues. The more scenic route takes you south through Thuin. Alternatively, you can follow a northerly route via La Louvière, which is rich in the industrial history of Belgium.

Due north of Binche you will come to Houdeng, which is divided into Houdeng-Gougnies to the north and Houdeng-Aimeries to the south. Houdeng lies astride the Canal du Centre, and major works (like those that brought the Ronquières inclined plane into being) are in progress on this stretch of waterway. The newly built vertical hydraulic barge-lifts are perhaps less scenic than the Ronquières incline, but no less effective. At Thieu (further west) there is a well laid-out display of how the various engineering features work and what they're meant to achieve.

At Houdeng-Aimeries you can visit the "model village" (in the full-size sense) built for the workers of the Bois-le-Duc coalmine in the 19th century. In addition there is a display of the history of the Borinage coalfield. In a less industrial vein, the château of Mariemont, 2 miles southeast of the center of La Louvière, restored by Albert and Isabella, burned out and replaced, was left with its park to the nation. It now contains excellent collections, including one of Tournai porcelain.

From here you can head eastward through Courcelles and Jumet (the center of a major *marche militaire* on the third Sunday in July) toward Charleroi—the metropolis of Wallonia's industrial heartland.

Thuin, and Nearby Abbeys

Alternatively, your route from Binche can take you through a completely different landscape, far from the slag-heaps and abandoned winding gear of the industrial zone around La Louvière. Heading southeast from Binche toward Thuin, you reach the 7th-century Abbey of Lobbes, with its remarkable Romanesque church. Like so many of these half-destroyed ecclesiastical buildings, Lobbes was the victim of French vandalism in the early 1790s.

A couple of miles farther on, you reach Thuin, a little town of pretty hanging gardens, in which there still remains the tower of the fortifications erected in the year 972 by Notger, Prince Bishop of Liège. On the third Sunday in May a religious *marche militaire* takes place in Thuin, one of many such which you will find in the country between the Sambre and the Meuse. In this parade the relics of St. Roch are guarded from putative brigands and robbers by a humorous train in many and various uniforms, all colorful and imposing. A short distance east of Thuin, you come to Gozée, notable for its 20-ton prehistoric standing stone, le Zeupire. A very short, worthwhile detour at Gozée brings you to Ham-sur-Heure and its remarkable château, reconstructed by command of Louis XV of France, a job that was finished in the 19th century. No less remarkable is the 15th-century Gothic altar-screen in St. Martin's church.

The Abbey of Aulne, a few miles northwest of Gozée in the Sambre valley, one of the most important ecclesiastic ruins of the country, is well worth a visit. Of vast proportions, it comprises a hostelry, a farm and a fine church, dating from the 16th century. From here it is only a few minutes' drive to the southwest suburbs of the Charleroi conurbation.

Charleroi

The city of Charleroi is now one of the more important in Belgium. Its history goes back into no remoter past than 1665, when the Marquis de Castel-Rodrigo renamed the village of Charnoy in homage to his monarch, Charles II of Spain. He had seen strategic importance in this crossing of the Sambre with the great road due south from Brussels, and here he erected a fortress which hardly seems to have fulfilled its purpose since it was occupied without much difficulty by Louis XIV a few years later. Napoleon, advancing to Waterloo 136 years later still, captured it again. And it was through here the Emperor fled a few days later. The former village of a thousand souls had become a commune of 20,000 inhabitants by the middle of the 19th century, when industry —Charleroi grew wealthy from metal-working and engineering—began to center upon the coalfields. Today Charleroi is an urban agglomeration with over a quarter-million inhabitants.

Like many of its contemporaries in Europe and North America, Charleroi has suffered badly from the decline of the 19th-century heavy industries and the rise of the Far Eastern industrial nations. Don't expect picturesque scenery; though if you're interested in industrial archeology, the old forges and factories will fascinate you. The modern city fathers are hoping to switch to higher technology industries, while retaining the tradition of excellence in mechanical and electrical engineering. Their undaunted civic pride shows through in the Industrial Exhibition Halls and the Palais des Beaux-Arts (Fine Arts Museum).

The Sambre at Charleroi, with its surrounding canals, is an industrial river—a complex of wharves, warehouses, and cranes. The main road eastward from Charleroi to Namur takes you through Presles (the reputed site of the battle between Caesar and the Nervii) with its Roman ruins. They are more numerous, though perhaps less in their extent, than those at Gerpinnes, further south (site of yet another religious-military parade). So you will arrive at Fosses-la-Ville, with the charming houses of the Canons surrounding the church. Here the best-known of the *marches militaires* of the Sambre-et-Meuse country is held once in seven years on the last Sunday in September (next one is in 1991). It is dedicated to St. Feuillen, the 8th-century Scottish missionary, and lasts from 9 A.M. to 4 P.M. Three thousand participants assemble, wearing all the uniforms in which foreign troops have kept order in southern Belgium for many centuries. From Fosses it is only some 10 miles to the banks of the Meuse at the aptly-named Rivière.

If you intend to visit the whole of this fascinating region, you should follow the N5 from Charleroi, since the axis of Entre-Sambre-et-Meuse is the road running due south from Charleroi. It takes you through Somzée, where you will want to turn off to the right to see Walcourt, on the Eau d'Heure. In the interesting 12th- and 13th-century Church of St. Materne you will find more of the exceptional work by the great Hugo d'Oignies, who was born here, and a miracle-working silver Madonna which is the *raison d'être* of the *marche militaire* on Trinity Sunday each year. The basilica has a glorious rood screen (1531), a Gothic gallery of filigree stonework, covered with statues and other ornamentation.

A little to the north is Berzée, where there is a castle-farm, early predecessor of the walled-in farmyards with their defensive connotations. Returning to the main road, you will find a 17th-century version of the same thing at Daussois.

An interesting example of Renaissance town-planning can be seen in this region. Mariembourg, constructed in 1542 and named after Charles V's sister, Queen of Hungary, fell to the French in 1554 and was destroyed, so that little trace of the quadrangular plan remains. In 1555, after the fall of Mariembourg, Charles had another city built farther north, named Philippeville after his son, the king of Spain. Its ramparts have disappeared but the town has retained its original aspect until this day.

Chimay, Home of Froissart and Madame Tallien

Heading south, you soon reach Couvin. Straight ahead lies the French frontier. To the west is the road to Chimay, which will lead you through Gonrieux and past the Pierres-qui-Tournent, two conical dolmens standing on a plateau. From here you come quickly to Chimay, on the westward edge of the Fagne moorlands where the château, were it not for its ugly bulbous spire, would be strangely reminiscent of Cotswold architecture. The statue of Jehan Froissart, historian of the Hundred Years' War and Canon-Treasurer of Chimay, is in the Grand'Place.

Froissart (1337–1404) was one of the most fascinating characters in an age of brilliant men and women. He spent his life at the very center of the great events of his time, going on an expedition with the Black Prince, visiting the court of his son, Richard II, meeting Chaucer and Petrarch, and reveling in the high-life of France and Flanders. From his own wide experiences and the many eyewitness accounts he collected, he created an unparalleled account of the history of his times. The chronicles formed the source-material for several of Shakespeare's plays, and they can still be read with deep enjoyment.

Chimay's other famous figure was Madame Tallien, known to revolutionary France as Notre Dame du Thermidor. Her great beauty and strong personality saved her from the guillotine. She married her protector, Tallien. He, on her instigation, managed to have Robespierre outlawed and "liquidated" in July 1794, thus putting an end to the reign of terror in which so many were killed. She later married the Prince Caraman de Chimay, and so ruled in this château which had known the lordships of the De Croy, the Chatillon and the Henin, and had been taken by assault by Don Juan of Austria and Turenne. The warrant for her arrest, signed by Robespierre, is still preserved here. One of the features of the château is the little rococo theater, the scene of an annual music festival, end June-early July.

Here the road strikes north, parallel with the French border, toward Beaumont. To your right, the Lake of Virelles invites you to halt. Here you can swim, go boating or fishing, and have your catch prepared at one of the many inns along its shores.

Farther north, Rance has been famous for centuries for its quarries. Its red marble decorates St. Peter's in Rome and the palace of Versailles. Another few miles on is the ancient town of Beaumont, dominated by the ruins of its once formidable fortress. From here you can either return to Charleroi and thence to Brussels, or you can head through Lobbes and Anderlues to Nivelles, and so on to the capital.

PRACTICAL INFORMATION FOR

HAINAUT AND SAMBRE-MEUSE

GETTING THERE. By train. Charleroi—capital of the Belgian "Black Country"—is well served by two trains an hour from Brussels, with the expresses taking around 40 minutes to reach Charleroi. Between Brussels and Mons there is a good service of Belgian trains, as well as international expresses on their way to or from Paris. Tournai has a roughly hourly service from Brussels stations and the trains take about an hour and a quarter for the journey.

By car. By road all of these provincial cities are well under an hour's driving time from Brussels, and the Autoroute de la Wallonie links them rapidly to Namur and Liège.

HOTELS AND RESTAURANTS. This region has an abundance of hotels. None is in the luxury class, but given price range you are assured a high standard of service. This is definitely a gastronomic province: trout is a specialty of the Sambre-Meuse region, and while there, we suggest that you try it *aux amandes* (with almonds), *à l'escavèche* (in jelly), *en papillotte* (wrapped in parchment and fried).

BEAUMONT. Vestiges of a fortified city. *Hostellerie Charles Quint* (I), Grand'Place 8 (tel. 071–588 861). 6 rooms, in center of town. At **Solre-St.-Géry** 2½ miles south *Prieuré-St.-Géry* (M), rue Lambot 9 (tel. 588 571). 5 rooms; it also has a restaurant (E) with ancient decor; serves superb cuisine.

Restaurant. For a more modest meal in the center of town try *Commerce* (I), Grand'Place 7 (tel. 071–588 052).

BELOEIL. Louis XIV-style château. Closest accommodation is some 4 miles south at **Stambruges,** *Le Vert Gazon* (M), route de Mons 1 (tel. 069–575 984). 6 rooms and superb restaurant in rural setting.

BINCHE. Inexplicably the town offers no overnight accommodations; but you can eat extremely well at *Bernard* (M), rue de Bruxelles 37 (tel. 333 775), or less expensively at *Saint Laurent* (M), Grand'Place 12 (tel. 335 084). In the center just by the old town.

You can stay 4 miles north at **Haine-St.-Paul,** where there is a comfortable hotel, *Villa d'Este* (I), rue de la Déportation 63 (tel. 064–228 160). 8 rooms, all with bath.

BOUSSU-EN-FAGNE. To get here head north out of Couvin and turn left after a mile. Another mile and you will see *Manoir de la Motte* (M), rue Motte 15 (tel. 060–344 013). A 14th-century manor which retains an authentic medieval setting; 7 rooms and a good restaurant.

CASTEAU-MAISIÈRES. SHAPE headquarters. There are many hotels and road houses within striking distance of SHAPE. *Crest* (M), chaussée de Bruxelles 38 (tel. 065–728 741). 71 rooms and a good moderately-priced restaurant. Four miles west at **Masnuy-St.-Jean** is the *Amigo* (M), chaussée de Brunehault 3 (tel. 723 685). 55 rooms set in rural surroundings; it also has a restaurant.

CHARLEROI. Historic town renowned for its traditional cuisine. *Socatel Diplomat* (E), blvd. Tirou 96 (tel. 071–319 811). Centrally situated, with 40 rooms, but no restaurant. *Pim's* (M), pl. Emile Buisset 13 (tel. 071–319 870). 30 well-equipped rooms, with restaurant; close to south station. *Méditerranée* (M), ave. de l'Europe 20 (tel. 071–317 424). 19 rooms and a good restaurant.

Restaurants. *Solm's* (M), passage de la Bourse 15 (tel. 071–320 349). The best in the town center. Less expensive is *Europe* (I), ave. de l'Europe 18 (tel. 071–317 245).

Close to the Palais des Beaux Arts is *La Térrasse* (M), blvd. Jacques Bertrand 82 (tel. 071–322 284). Another good spot is *A la Grosse Saucisse* (M), ave. de Waterloo 69 (tel. 071–323 070). Specialties are from Alsace, notably *choucroute garnie.*

At **Loverval,** 2 miles south on the road to Philippeville, in pleasant surroundings, is *Chardon* (M), rte. de Philippeville 73 (tel. 369 221).

CHIMAY. Famous château. 2 miles northeast at **Virelles** is *Hostellerie le Virelles* (I), rue du Lac 28 (tel. 060–212 803). 8 rooms and excellent restaurant. 3 miles southeast at **Bourlers** is *L'Auberge du Poteaupré* (I), rue Potaupré 5 (tel. 060–211 433). A genuine country inn, with 11 rooms and rural cuisine.

Restaurants in Chimay itself include *Froissart* (M), pl. Froissart 8 (tel. 060–212 619) and *Napoléon* (I), rue d'Angleterre 17 (tel. 211 868).

COUVIN. On the Brussels-Rheims road, near the French frontier. *Hostellerie au Petit Chef* (E), rue Dessus-la-Ville 6 (tel. 060–344 175). 7 rooms, all well equipped; excellent restaurant. *Château St. Roch* (M), route de Frasnes 12 (tel. 060–344 034). 16 rooms, 10 with bath. Dining in old-world splendor. South of town, a couple of miles toward the frontier is *Hostellerie les Forges de Pernelle* (M), rue de Pernelle 29 (tel. 344 802). 16 rooms, 7 with bath; romantically located in the Bois de Couvin, with excellent game dishes in season. At **Frasnes-les-Couvin,** 5 km. (3 miles) north of town, *Château de Tromcourt* (M), Gérousart 11 (tel. 311 870). 9 rooms; good restaurant.

HAM-SUR-HEURE. Famous château. **Restaurant.** *Le Pré Vert* (M), chemin de la Folie 24 (tel. 071–215 609). Good regional cuisine.

LENS. 13 km. (8 miles) southeast of Ath on the road to Mons. *Auberge de Lens* (I), Grand'Route 23, (tel. 229 041). A good halt, with 7 rooms, rustic decor and excellent cooking.

MONS. Capital of province and art city. 32 minutes from Brussels on the main Brussels–Paris railway. It has surprisingly few worthwhile hotels. *Residence* (I), rue André Masquelier 4 (tel. 065–311 403). 6 rooms. *St. Georges* (I), rue des Clercs 15 (tel. 065–311 629). 9 rooms. For larger establishments see outside town see **Casteau** (6½ km., 4 miles northeast).

Restaurants. *Devos* (E), rue Coupe 7 (tel. 065–331 335). The best in town, near the Grand'Place; prepares a delicious *caneton aux griottes* (duckling with black cherries) for the asking, and is renowned for its seafood. The nearby *Patisserie Saey* (I), Grand'Place 12 (tel. 065–335 448), is more modest and has two buffets (rue des Capucins and Grand'Place) for those in a hurry. Also worth trying are the Chinese and Vietnamese restaurants in the rue d'Havré.

MONTIGNIES-ST.-CHRISTOPHE. 6½ km. (4 miles) from Beaumont on the main road to Mons. Roman bridge.

Restaurant. *La Villa Romaine* (M), rte. de Mons 52 (tel. 071–555 622). In rural surroundings. Also has 6 rooms.

OLLOY-SUR-VIRON. 10 km. (6 miles) northeast of Couvin. *Rolinvaux* (I), rte. de Fourcimont 46 (tel. 060–399 196). 7 rooms, all well equipped, and excellent restaurant.

PHILIPPEVILLE. Charles V's once fortified city. Renowned for its cuisine. *Croisée* (M), rue de France 45 (tel. 071–666 231). 11 rooms and reasonably priced restaurant.

Restaurant. *Grand Bonnet* (I), Place d'Armes 13 (tel. 071–666 044). Pleasant tavern-style establishment.

TOURNAI. One of Belgium's important art towns. *Aux Armes de Tournay* (M), pl. de Lille 23 (tel. 069–226 723). 20 rooms, no restaurant. Alternatively, there is *de l'Europe* (I), Grand'Place 36 (tel. 069–224 067). 9 rooms and modest restaurant.

Restaurants. *Charles Quint* (M), Grand'Place 3 (tel. 069–221 441). Comfortable restaurant overlooking the belfry. *l'Ecaille d'Argent* (M), Pl. de Lille 26 (tel. 069–235 104). In the bishops' winery; offers charcoal grills as well as liquid refreshment. *Le Pressoir* (M), Vieux Marché aux Poteries 2 (tel. 223 513). Delightful old building housing excellent local cooking.

WALCOURT. Picturesque locality just off the Charleroi–Philippeville road. *De l'Aigle* (I), pl. Hôtel-de-Ville 9 (tel. 071–611 139). Unpretentious; 8 rooms and restaurant. *Hostellerie de l'Abbaye* (M), rue du Jardinet 7 (tel. 611 423) Offers somewhat more luxurious accommodation in its 10 rooms and has an excellent restaurant.

CHÂTEAUX. Attre, near Ath, intact 18th-century interiors. Guided tours, mid-March to end Oct., Sat. and Sun., 10 to 12, 2 to 6; July and Aug., every day except Wed., same hours. Admission BF 100.

Beaumont, midway between Chimay and Mons. The Salamander Tower and ramparts are the remains of a major fortified castle built in the 11th century, reconstructed in 1549, and largely destroyed in 1655. Visits from May to end-September, 9 to 12 and 2 to 7. Admission BF 20.

Beloeil, finest in Belgium. Guided tours, April to Sept., 10 to 12, 1.30 to 6. Park open 9 to 8 in the evening; sunset in winter. Admission BF 170 for park and château.

Chimay, also has a lovely Rococo theater. Guided tours all year round, 9 to 12, 2 to 6. Admission BF 70.

Ecaussines Lalaing, early medieval castle. Tours, April to Oct., 10 to 12, 2 to 6, daily except Tues. and Wed. Admission BF 60.

Fagnolles, 8 km. (5 miles) east of Mariembourg. Largely ruined 12th–16th-century castle, with interesting herb garden in its grounds. Open April to December, daily (except Mon.), 10 to 8. Admission BF 60.

Ham-sur-Heure, 8 km. (5 miles) east of Thuin. Dates from 15th to 19th centuries. Interesting interior decoration. May be visited by request: call 213 339 well in advance.

Le Roeulx, 7 km. (4 miles) northwest of La Louvière. Castle of the Princes of Croy, dating back to 15th century. Façade, however, is early 18th century. Visits daily (except Wed.), April to end-September. Admission BF 50.

Mariemont, 8 km. (5 miles) southeast of La Louvière. Ruins of the château of Charles of Lorraine (built 1756) can be seen in a beautiful park of some 50 hectares. The park also contains a major museum, bequeathed to the State by the Warocqué family. Open daily (except Mon.) 10 to 6.

Thy-le-Château, 6 km. (4 miles) north of Walcourt. Solidly built medieval castle, housing an interesting historical display. Open May 1 until September 15, 1 to 6. Admission BF 50.

MUSEUMS AND PLACES OF INTEREST. BINCHE. International Museum of Carnival and Mask, rue St. Paul. Contains fascinating display on the origins and history of the Binche carnival, as well as a collection of outlandish garments. Open daily (except Mon.), May 1 to end-September, weekends only in October. Admission BF 55.

CHARLEROI. Musée des Beaux Arts (Fine Arts Museum), place du Manège. Housed in an annex of the Hôtel de Ville, the collection contains several works by Navez, the local early 19th-century heroic-realist painter, as well as other paintings by lesser-known artists. Open daily (except Mon.), 10 to 6.

Musée du Verre et de L'Archéologie (Glass and Archeological Museum), blvd. Defontaine 10. Housed in the National Glass Institute, the museum traces the history of one of Wallonia's most important industries, as well as explaining something of the glassmaker's "black arts." In addition, there is a small collection of historic objects in the basement. Open Mon. to Fri. 10 to 6, Sat. 10 to 3, Sun. 10 to 1.

Gallerie du Musée de la Photographie (Photographic Museum), rue Huart-Chapel 19. Display of the history and theory of photography, as well as exhibitions of contemporary work. Open Tues. to Fri. 10 to 6 and Sat. 2 to 5.

LESSINES. Hôpital Notre Dame à la Rose. Interesting museum housed in 16th-century cloister. Open Apr. to Sept., Sun. only. Guided visits 3 P.M. Admission BF 30.

MONS. Maison Jean Lescarts. Collection of furniture and Mons folklore. Open 10 to 12.30, 2 to 6, closed Mon.

Musée Chanoine Puissant, entrance by 22 rue Notre-Dame Debonnaire. Collection of Gothic and Renaissance furniture, and drawings and other materials from the 14th to the 17th centuries. Open daily 10 to 12, 2 to 6, closed Mon.

Musée des Beaux Arts (Fine Arts Museum), rue Neuve. Especially interesting for its periodic exhibitions. Open 10 to 6, closed Mon.

Musée du Centenaire, housed in the old Mont-de-Piété—the state pawnshop —in the Mayeur Garden. War trophies, coins, ceramics and prehistoric exhibits. Open daily 10 to 12, 2 to 6, closed Mon.

Trésor de St. Waudru, the Treasury of the Collegiate Church of St. Waudru. Gold plate, a Book of Hours, statues, reliquaries and so on. Daily, except Mon, July 1 to Aug. 31, 3 to 6.

TOURNAI. Musée des Beaux Arts (Fine Arts Museum), Enclos St. Martin. A fine gallery with some Impressionist masterpieces by Manet, Seurat, etc.; the Flemish Schools represented by Breughel, Rubens, Jordaens, Gossart, as well as work by the native son, Roger van der Weyden. Open 10 to 12, 2 to 5.30, daily except Tues.

Musée d'Histoire et d'Archeolgie (Archeology and History Museum), rue des Carmes, in the medieval pawnshop. Big collection of great variety, including pastel-colored silverware and tapestries. Open 10 to 12, 2 to 5.30, closed Tues.

Musée du Folklore (Folklore Museum), in the Maison Tournaisienne—life of the town through the centuries. Open daily, 10 to 12, 2 to 5.30, closed Tues.

Tour Henri VIII (also called Grosse Tour). Keep built by England's Henry VIII, now houses a collection of weapons, with a section devoted to the Resistance. Open daily 10 to 12, 2 to 5.30, closed Tues.

Trésor de la Cathédral Notre Dame. The cathedral itself is a must; check on opening hours. The Treasury has real treasures—reliquaries and shrines, tapestries and statues; it is open 10 to 12, 2 to 6.

NIGHTLIFE. In Charleroi patronize *Parisiana* (floor-show), rue du Commerce 3; *Pacha Club,* quai de Brabant 37; or *Phil's Club,* rue Tumulaire 37; *La Réserve* at the Palais des Beaux Arts, ave., de l'Europe, *Champi,* place Charles II, and *Mistral,* rue Neuve, are also popular. For the younger set there is *Le Carré Blanc,* rue Léopold 18 or *Square Sud,* blvd. Tirou 70.

In Mons, try dancing at *Voum-Voum,* rue de la Coupe 44; or *New Blue Note,* ave. Roi Albert 667, for jazz.

USEFUL ADDRESSES. City Tourist Offices (Syndicats d'Initiative): Almost every locality has its tourist office, usually in the town hall. Here are the more important ones: Beaumont, rue Sous-les-Cloches 1 (tel. 588 684); Binche, rue St. Paul 21 (tel. 334 177); Charleroi, Pavilion d'Accueil, Square Gare du Sud (tel. 318 218); Mons. Grand'Place 20 (tel. 335 580); Philippeville, pl. d'Armes 12 (tel. 666 213); Tournai, Vieux Marché-aux-Poteries, by the Belfry (tel. 222 045).

Car hire: Avis, blvd. Gendebien, in Mons.

Golf: Royal Golf Club of Hainaut, Erlisoeul, near Mons.

Camping sites are located at Beloeil, Binche, Chimay, Ecaussines-d'Enghien, Ham-sus-Heure, Leugnies, Mons, Nimy, Rance, Stambruges, Tournai, Virelles, and Walcourt.

THE MEUSE VALLEY

The March of Centuries

Certain corners of the earth have an air of remaining pure and untouched by man; others are haunted by the centuries of struggle and hardship which man has invested in their making. It is these regions that are curiously attractive to the traveler. You experience this sense of centuries of history in the Meuse valley, where side by side are graves of primitive hunters and tombs of soldiers killed by the gunfire of World War II. The banks of the Meuse have witnessed man's keenest suffering from ancient times until today.

The Meuse has always marked the historic vicissitudes of Western Europe. The Romans understood its importance as one of their principal routes from Cologne to the sea. Later, its valley was the seat of the Liège Diocese, and the birthplace of Charlemagne's empire.

The marvelous school of Mosan metalwork developed in towns along the whole length of the river's banks. It is this art above all that has honored the name of the Meuse in such masterpieces as the baptismal font of Renier de Huy, the silver ornaments of Hugo d'Oignies, and the reliquaries of Nicholas of Verdun.

The Carolingian civilization was essentially Christian and when the empire of Charlemagne disintegrated, leaving the valley vulnerable between two great powers, the Meuse frontiers were reinforced not only with fortified castles, but with the spiritual aids of monasteries and abbeys. The country developed Christian virtues and magnanimous qualities which were felt throughout the world of that time. Saint Lambert of Liège became known as the "fountain of wisdom," attracting students and divines from the whole of Europe.

As enduring as the bronze and silver of their art, the people of the Meuse early acquired the characteristics they possess today—daring, courage, industry, and independence. Julius Caesar called them the bravest of all the Gauls.

For more than a thousand years these people have battled valiantly for liberty, warring against tyrants and invaders. They have fought among themselves, neighbor against neighbor, cousin against cousin, without mercy. The region is filled with graves of soldiers from every age. But its tragic history has not been able to dim the beauty of the valley, nor to quench the lust for life which is characteristic of its people. Their familiarity with death has given these people a vigorous appreciation of life.

The Changing Face of the Meuse

Although the Meuse rises in France and reaches the sea in Holland, and less than one-third of its length is in Belgium, it is nevertheless only in the latter country that the river shows its true character. From the Ardennes, as a young and impetuous stream foaming along narrow ravines and battering down all obstacles in its path, it gathers to itself other, equally impetuous torrents, and thus, noisy and turbulent, rushes into Dinant.

Between Dinant and Namur it flows serene and beautiful, its banks starred with wild roses and marked by castles and chapels. Elegant people live along its banks, and the lawns of millionaires' villas extend to the water's edge near Wépion and Profondeville.

But at Namur it meets the Sambre, whose waters are tainted by the slag-heaps of the Borinage. The Sambre is a beggarly river, coming from a rustic background, but abruptly exposed to the fire and tumult of coal mines and the flames of blast furnaces, and tainted with the acid scum of rolling-mills. After its confluence with the Sambre, the Meuse becomes deeper and more powerful, apt for useful work. At Liège it is very much a part of the city's life, carrying an endless procession of tugboats, freighters, and barges.

As it flows through Liège the Meuse is grey and sluggish, and occasionally punctuated by canals. After Liège, the river loiters through the Limburg countryside, where fishermen idle on either bank. The Meuse, called the Maas in Dutch-speaking Belgium and the Netherlands, is official guardian of the border between Belgium and the neighboring areas, but its office is a sinecure now since there is never a quarrel between one bank and the other. Each side of the border shows the same red-roofed farm buildings, the same big villages shaded by cherry trees. You can go up or down the Meuse by boat, breaking the monotony of the voyage with excursions into such picturesque river-regions as Marlagne, Condroz, Famenne, or Herve. Each tributary valley is full of interest.

With the coming of spring, from the walnut trees of the Ardennes to the orchards of Limburg, the country is one vast splendor of greenery, resounding with church bells and the music of holiday processions. Distances are so short in Belgium that you can go everywhere and see everything easily. It is never more than a mile or two from one village to another, and the Meuse landscape is subtle and ever-changing.

Discovering the Meuse Valley

Embarking at Hastière-par-delà, quite near the French border (known for its 11th-century Romanesque church and nearby Pont d'Arcole caves), you reach Dinant in about two hours, after a trip between rock cliffs, pierced with caves full of shells and fossils. The bare rocks overhanging the river have been worn by time and weather into curious shapes, and they are named accordingly—The Camel, The Dog, and so on. The ancient Abbey of Waulsort, founded by Scottish monks in the 10th century, has been transformed into a château, and rivals its neighbor, the Château of Freyr (designed by Le Nôtre), in landscaping. The orange trees in the French-style garden are over 300 years old. Louis XIV of France and the King of Spain, Charles II, met here in 1675 to put an end to the prolonged strife between the two countries, on which occasion coffee was drunk for the first time in Belgium.

Anseremme is quite a busy, flourishing community, with riverside restaurants, overlooking its 16th-century bridge, which serve excellent fried fish. In a cave in one of the cliffs overlooking the town (the Grotte de Charlemont), there is an attractive aquarium with a full and well-presented collection of aquatic life from the Meuse and Lesse which, in a whirl of water, joins it here. Long before you reach Dinant, the city's sentinel, the rock of Bayard, comes into view. It is a tall, needle-shaped stone, detached from the sharp cliff. According to legend, it was Bayard, the dauntless steed of the four sons of Aymon, who split the mammoth boulder when jumping across the Meuse. These four sons color all the early lore of the Meuse valley with their eternal strife and patriotic valor. They fought a long war against Charlemagne, and almost every château of the region is supposed to have sheltered them.

Dinant

When Louis XIV laid seige to Namur in the 1670s he installed Madame de Maintenon, his morganatic wife, at Dinant, where she was near enough to comfort him in his trials and tribulations. The city lies in an enchanting background, but it has never been able to keep a single one of its historic monuments through an endless history of war, fire, and siege. Dinant was involved in every war that affected the Meuse valley—with the people of Liège, the Burgundians, the French, and, more recently, the Germans. The sack of Dinant by the Duke of Burgundy in 1466 saw the city razed and 800 of its citizens, tied back-to-back, drowned in the Meuse. No less frightful was the struggle of 1914, and the ghastly reprisals that ensued when 674 citizens were executed by the Germans. Incredibly enough, Dinant not only survived and rebuilt its shattered ruins but maintains its traditions and its gaiety.

The ancient art of hammered copper made Dinant an illustrious center of metalwork; even England sent to Dinant for beaten and engraved copper. This art thrived and prospered through the 13th and 14th centuries, but it received a mortal blow after the pillaging of Charles the Bold. The craft lost its originality, becoming, in the end, commonplace in the shops. For some time, conscientious artisans have devoted themselves to resurrecting and applying the secrets of the old masters of metalwork. Another local craft is the manufacture of *couques:* hard gingerbread baked in moulds which are often little masterpieces of woodcarving. The local artists' fancy knows no limits, and you can buy these edible souvenirs in all *pâtisseries* and candy shops in town.

Dinant is a perfect port of call, for it has fine hotels and restaurants, as well as easy access to the neighboring valleys of the Lesse and Molignée. A lift, by the way, carries visitors up the Rocher (high rock) to the citadel, and another, ascending from the town center, brings you to Monfort Tower. On your way down you can visit the prehistoric caverns of Mont-Fat.

Adolphe Sax, inventor of the saxophone, was born here in 1814. His home has been converted into a small museum.

Castles, Castles Everywhere

Take a boat trip through six river locks and, if the time of year is right, you will have plenty of time to enjoy the purple foxgloves and bluebells along the banks, and to consider the history of the old castles and fortresses that line the way.

Bouvignes, squatting below, shows some traces of its important past: the only remaining gate of the city ramparts; the Spanish House or La Maison du Ballage—the town hall—is a perfect example of the Spanish occupation period; and an early Gothic church. It was at Crèvecoeur, now a ruin above Bouvignes, that three lovely noblewomen threw themselves from a high window to escape Henry II, the infamous French king. Nearby, on the right bank of the river, the ruins of Poilvache Castle appear. The countryside around is dotted with ancient fortified farms.

At Anhée you can make a detour to visit Maredsous Abbey, a successful turn-of-the-century imitation of early Gothic on a site of wild beauty. Romantically set in the Molignée valley, the ruins of Montaigle Castle have a sad tale to tell, for it was in the courtyard that the medieval knight De Bioulx accidentally pierced his daughter's heart while duelling with her lover.

From Yvoir, in a picturesque setting on the right bank, you should make a circular trip to Spontin's feudal castle, the oldest still-inhabited castle in Belgium, open to visitors. It gives one a good idea of the evolution of a baronial hall from the 12th to the 17th century. Continuing towards the Meuse, you will pass Crupet, with its interesting church of St. Martin (mainly 15th century, but with a 12th-century spire) and a fortified moated manor of the same time-span, most curiously shaped, and Mont, a typical village of the region. Opposite Godinne, at Annevoie, there is a small Versailles, all parks, fountains, and little pools. A million tulips can be seen here during April and May, and the lovely Château Montpelier is open to the public in season.

The riverbanks rise higher and higher, becoming more crowded with a chaos of boulders. Some of these conceal hidden surprises, such as the formation at Frappecul, behind which is the Chauveau Cave. The Rock of Tailfer guards the entrance to the delightful valley of Fond-de-Lustin. At each lock the riverbanks offer inducements to come ashore for tea and sightseeing. More houses appear among the wild undergrowth, lawns extend to the water's edge, and the river is alive with swimmers, canoeists, and sailboats. The Meuse is busy all summer with this pleasant holiday traffic, but since the war some of its elegance has been spoiled by ever-multiplying cottages and inns.

Namur

Next you come to a huge double bend of the Meuse, as it snakes its way between high cliffs. At their foot is Profondeville (literally "deep town"), a popular tourist and rock-climbing center. You, too, should venture up to the cave of the Nutons, helpful elf-like characters said to have been miraculously aiding poor inhabitants of this part of the Meuse valley since they "migrated" from Liège in 1399. Beyond Wépion, and the ancient Château of Dave, the stern silhouette of Namur (Namen) comes into view. The citadel broods on a promontory above the confluence of the Meuse and the Sambre. Happily, Namur's greatest treasures have remained intact in the Sisters of Our Lady Convent. They are the works of Hugo d'Oignies, the monk-jeweler who dedicated to Christ his art as silversmith. His crosses and reliquaries are ornamented with squirrels and stags, and jewel-studded interlacing leaves. On one Mosan reliquary you will see represented a joust between men on stilts. This once was a popular sport in the Walloon country. Why did the men of Namur cling so to their stilts? No doubt because the Meuse often flooded its banks, leaving a treacherous film of mud and slime, but there is a much more amusing explanation furnished by an ancient chronicler. Following a rebellion of his subjects the noble lord, Jehan, ruler of Namur, laid siege to the city, and reduced it to a state of famine. Emissaries were sent to plead for mercy, but Jehan outraged, replied that he would see no one who came "on foot, horse, carriage, or boat." It was then that the city fathers conceived the idea of sending their ambassadors on stilts. It worked. The duke laughed when he saw the long-legged committee, and that was the end of the strife.

Namur is a city of immaculately-curtained 17th-century pink-brick houses, rich Baroque churches, gardens, an outdoor theater, and a casino. A comfortable cabin lift takes you right up to the citadel. The fortress owes its present shape to the Dutch who, after the Napoleonic Wars, reinforced the strategic château of the counts of Namur.

The early 18th-century cathedral of St. Aubain is one of the finest examples of the Baroque in Belgium and owes its authenticity to an Italian architect, Pizzini. It has an authentic Jordaens, a debatable Van

Dyck, and several Rubens copies executed under the master's watchful eye by one of his pupils.

The heart of the victor of the memorable Lepanto naval battle, which saved Christendom from the Turks' onslaught, rests here. Don Juan of Austria, camping outside Namur in 1578, was sent a pair of poisoned gloves by a jealous lady. This was a treacherous gift and killed the promising prince at the age of 31. Some historians like to think this was a Belgian patriot's act of resistance. But the shocking way in which Don Juan's body was cut up and smuggled in saddlebags across hostile France into Spain throws a somber light on the most powerful monarch of the age. Philip II of Spain, envious of his illegitimate half-brother's military and amorous successes, had given him the most thankless job in the realm, the governorship of the Low Countries. The fact that the Pope wanted to appoint Don Juan to a kingdom within the Spanish dominion was probably too much for the master of half the world.

The Jesuit Baroque St.-Loup Church nearby was described by Baudelaire as a "sinister and courtly marvel" with "the interior of a hearse, terrible and delightful, embroidered in black, pink, and silver."

Some of the finest works of the silversmith Hugo d'Oignies can be seen at the Convent of the Sisters of Notre Dame, and there is a notable 8th-century Carolingian reliquary at the Diocesan Museum.

You should certainly go to visit the Cistercian Abbey at Marche les Dames, 7 km. away. It is a peaceful sight, with silent cloisters and terraces smelling pungently of boxwood. Not far from the abbey, King Albert I of Belgium met his death in February 1934 while climbing a sheer cliff.

Inland, past the fortified farm of Wartet and the medieval Castle of Fernelmont, lies the Château of Franc-Waret, still owned by descendants of the Marquis de Croix, Spain's governor of California. Admirable paintings of the Flemish Schools and Brussels tapestries designed by Van Orley decorate the walls, and among the many exhibits you can see the gold and platinum keys presented by the city of Lima to Théodore de Croix when promoted to Viceroy of Peru and Chile.

Andenne owes its origin to a convent, founded by St. Begge in 692, the nuns of which, under protection from the counts of Namur, had the unusual privilege of governing this township for over a thousand years until 1785, when Joseph II put an end to their hegemony. The saint's mortal remains are housed in a blue Gothic tomb in the Collégiale Sainte-Begge, built in the 18th-century to the designs of Dewez. On the Sunday following July 7 there is the annual St. Begge procession through the town. Andenne was also an early pottery-manufacturing center, and its Ceramic Museum is worth a visit. In the Christmas–New Year period the locals play a complex, unique card game for *cougnous,* specially baked buns.

Romantic Huy

The birthplace of Renier de Huy and Godefroid de Clair, Huy is the epitome of romantic towns. It may or may not have been the birthplace of the naughty Arlette; but it certainly obtained its civic charter, one of the first in Europe, in the same year (1066) in which William, the fruit of her indiscretion, conquered England. Here, too, Peter the Hermit initiated the first crusade, and his tomb is here to this day. Lying at the confluence of the Hoyoux with the Meuse, Huy is a winding tangle of narrow streets dominated by a towering cliff on whose top broods a fortress. Don't miss the copper fountain in the Grand'Place, the town hall carillon ringing out *Brave Liègeois* every hour, the view from the fort, the Collegiate Church, a fine example of 14th-century Flamboyant Gothic, with its rose window, or the tortuous byways around the Convent of the Black Friars. For a reminder that Huy was once a great metal-working center you can visit a thriving tinsmith's shop, Les Potstainiers Hutois, at avenue des Fossés 34. On the riverbank you can see a fine example of medieval Meuse valley architecture: the Hôtel de la Cloche; dating back to 1406, it has a delightful restaurant with plenty of atmosphere. A cable-car connects the hill beyond the citadel with the left bank, a distance of over two miles, and offers a splendid panorama of town and country.

The Meuse lingers a moment longer beside the mall shaded by lime trees, past the University of Peace, founded by the late Father Pire, the Nobel Peace Prize winner, curves about the Château of Neuville, and then forsakes its borders of ivy and honeysuckle for banks lined with railroads and brick factories.

Liège, the Spirited City

Rows of houses ranged along stone quays serve as introduction to Liège (Luik), and there is the city itself, bustling and clattering in the midst of protecting hills. Now dignified and industrious, the river is covered equally by coal barges and pleasure craft. Reflected in its slate-gray waters are the steeples and coal shafts.

Here the river spreads out and loiters among many islands, lagoons, and shop-lined bridges. Until the beginning of the 19th century, Liège remained a perfect Walloon Venice. But the Meuse, which once covered this entire area, has through the centuries become narrower and deeper. The largest lagoon has been filled in and surmounted with great boulevards, while the old quarter of the city retains nothing of its watery past but a few street names: "Island Bridge," "Sovereign Bridge," "Under Water." If you would capture the true, poignant beauty of Liège, approach it from the riverbanks.

Do not look for grandiose monuments, vast perspectives, or triumphal avenues (except for the motorway accesses). Liège is a symbol of rebellion against rule and regimentation. Paradoxically, Liège, a city that works hard day and night in a glare of strip mills, is also a city of quiet home life, where families dine bountifully, and spend hours sitting about the table. Yet, it must be said, the people of Liège also spend hours *not* sitting about the table, for all the pleasures of café life can be found in this, one of the loveliest cities of Belgium.

In the midst of this uproar of factories, a school of notably gifted musicians sprang up. César Franck and Grétry were born in Liège, and the famous violin school exemplified by Bériot, Vieuxtemps, Ysaye, and Thompson developed here.

Ysaye's studio has been reconstructed in the Academy of Music. Here you will find his scores and well-thumbed books and on a small table a casket containing his heart. The Academy concert-hall can seat 700 musicians as well as an audience of 1700. The stage is large, its width the same as that of the Paris Opera. A monument dedicated to the memory of César Franck is in the foyer. It was donated by French musicians to the town in 1922.

Another outstanding building is the Theater Royal, with its beautiful façade of marble pillars with an ornate pediment by the sculptor Oscar Berchmans.

The city has clung steadfastly to old Walloon traditions some of which are demonstrated in the picturesque and touching Museum of Walloon Folklore. But for a more lively study, perhaps the most typical entertainment of Liège is to be found in the Tchantchès Museum, where all the heroes of Mosan legends can be seen: the four sons of Aymon, Geneviève de Brabant and Charlemagne, along with assorted Biblical or contemporary figures. The puppets are large or small, according to their historical significance. The great Emperor Charles weighs about 78 pounds, while his archers are small enough to be manipulated six at a time. A commentary in the local Mosan dialect by the witty Liègeois Punch, Tchantchès, is part of each performance.

Tchantchès' origin is uncertain. He is a grouser, unruly, wildly independent, but with a heart of gold and a passion for noble causes. He represents the prototype of the true Liègeois. His statue in the town is the work of Zomers, and like the Manneken Pis in Brussels, he has received a number of costumes and uniforms.

The history of Liège is one long struggle by its bishop-princes against powerful neighbors, and by citizens against its rulers. Individual liberty —*pauvre homme en sa maison est roi*—was granted by charter as early as the 12th century, and coincided with the discovery of large coal-fields. The city's increasing prosperity was interrupted by 70 years of Burgundian rule and recurrent insurrections, culminating in the destruction of Liège by Charles the Bold in 1468. After his death the de la Marck family played a prominent role in her resurrection.

A fundamentally boisterous population willingly joined the French Revolution and chased out the last ruling prince-bishop. After Napoleon's fall, the proud city was under Dutch rule. Liègeois volunteers, dispatched in haste to Brussels, played an important part in the 1830 Revolution that finally sealed Belgian independence. The heroic defence of that independence in 1914 is one of Belgium's finest stories. Liège celebrated its millenium in 1980.

Discovering Liège

Do not hope to follow any set route in your rambles through the town; Liège streets are laid out like jig-saw puzzles. If you are surprised by the number of churches, remember that Liège is an ancient Episcopal city. The martyr, St. Lambert, was its founder, and until 1789, it was governed by bishops.

So, in spite of bitter anticlerical demonstrations, like that in which old St. Lambert Cathedral was destroyed in 1794, Liège remains a city devoted to its saints. Each has his particular cult of healing: St. Apolline cures toothaches, St. Donat protects against lightning, and St. Ghislain saves children from nervous disturbances. There must be at least 100 steeples surmounting old churches which may be modest but are never uninteresting. St. Jacques is the most beautiful, in Flamboyant Gothic, but with a Romanesque narthex and a Renaissance porch. St. Paul's Cathedral also mingles three architectural styles. Among its ornaments is the gold reliquary offered by Charles the Bold, Duke of Burgundy, to expiate his sins. It seems small enough atonement, considering the fact that he had razed the entire city—except for the churches—and massacred all the able-bodied men. But the Church of St. Barthélemy is the real gem of Liège. Its baptismal font, dating from 1108, and resting on small bronze statues of oxen, is the finest work of Renier de Huy, and is one of Belgium's greatest treasures.

The old bishop's palace, now the Palace of Justice, hides beautiful courts surrounded by porticos. The galleries encircling the first are supported by 60 columns, each differently carved. The second courtyard has an ornamental pool surrounded by Louis XV railings and flower beds. Coats-of-arms and armorial bearings recall the past. The council-chamber has rich Brussels tapestries. This early 16th-century edifice is one of the most impressive secular buildings left in northern Europe. For guided tours apply to the Tourist Office.

One of Liège's finest houses is the Curtius Mansion, built about 1600 by Jean de la Corte, who supplied munitions to the King of Spain. This red brick Renaissance building cost about one million gold francs. It now houses the Curtius Museum whose rooms display local archeological and craft treasures, giving an excellent idea of the riches of Liège's past—especially its medieval past. Fine houses are grouped on Mont St. Martin, in a maze of winding streets, stairways and secret gardens. In early days, a bishop of Liège who became Pope, instituted Corpus Christi Day, and it is still celebrated with great ceremony.

But the most popular Liège procession is that of Outremeuse, that little island locked between the river and the Ourthe. On St. Nicholas' Day, each window is transformed into a street-altar, and the entire parish follows the parade of the Black Virgin. In August, amidst the happy tumult of a traveling fair, they bring out the *bouquet,* a prodigious structure of artificial flowers.

Outremeuse—across the Pont des Arches, on the opposite side of the river, and nicknamed the "Free Republic"—is a little world apart. People used to live there all their lives without crossing the bridge that leads to the city. The community was enough for them, with its narrow, noisy streets and its sidewalks and savory-smelling shops. Strolling along, you see many niches sheltering doll-faced Virgins bedecked with wreaths. Every house has its potted plants and shining copper decoration, its good smell of hot pies and coffee.

Coal and Industry

Liège citizens are small shopkeepers, artisans, miners, or steel workers. They are proud of their fearsome reputation and even of their nickname "coal heads." Since 1198, when a blacksmith named Hullos discovered coal deposits near Publement, Liège has been a prosperous, industrial city. The first Continental locomotive was built here, and Liège men taught the Swedes over a century ago how to make their peerless steel.

There are tree-lined walkways along the river, and Avroy Park covers an area of no less than 45,000 square metres. Avenue Rogier is bordered by esplanade gardens called "The Terraces." Four bronze groups can be seen here; the Boatman's Horse by Jules Halkin, the Tamed Horse by Alphonse de Tombay, the Plough Ox at Rest by Leon Mignon, and the Bull-Tamer by the same artist.

Facing Place St. Lambert a large "Bon Marché" shop backs on to several narrow shopping lanes for pedestrians only. Here there are delightful little cafés and boutiques.

The General Post Office is in Gothic-Renaissance style, looking like a medieval fortress, although it was built in 1901. The architect, Edmond Jamar gave full rein to 16th-century Liègeois fashion and it must be the most romantic-looking post office in Europe. In complete contrast, the Palais des Congrès, 1958, was planned on most modern lines; and boasts three conference halls, with 1,000, 500 and 200 seats respectively; plus television- and radio-studios.

For a really good view of this city, you should go in the evening to the top of one of the three hills which overlook the city. Robermont is where 50 patriots were executed in 1914. In October 1468, 600 heroic Mosans from Franchimont Castle scaled Sainte Walburge, another hill, in an attempted surprise attack on the Burgundians camped there; the effort failed, and all were massacred. Sainte Walburge was also the scene of a great battle in 1830, when Belgium gained its independence from Holland. The citadel resisted the German attack in August 1914 long enough to allow the French command to regroup its forces for the decisive Battle of the Marne. It was again one of the first objectives of the invasion in May 1940.

But the most pleasant place from which to contemplate the city is the wooded hill of Cointe: the Park of Birds is a charming point from which you can see the great curve of the Meuse gleaming in the midst of the city.

Liège does not forget its indebtedness to coal and its by-products. One of the principal squares near the Post Office is called Place Cockerill, after the Englishman who played an important part in the region's industrial progress. The ugly black mine shafts are called locally, "pretty flowers," and the flaming mill chimneys have earned the city the title of the "burning city." The place exudes a warm cordiality, and if you are looking for elegance, you can find that too. There are fashionable shops and fine hotels, usually adjoining excellent restaurants.

You might consider a river trip in one of the little passenger boats. Embarking from Flémalle, at the city limits, you will pass the industrial complexes of Val Saint Lambert, Ougrée, and Jemeppe. Then rounding the green spur of Cointe you will cross the mouth of the Ourthe River and come to the Botanical Gardens. Next comes the rose-and-gray bishop's palace, then the university. You will come to the old quays of La Goffe and La Batte, with their bird markets and apothecaries, their street singers and ironmongers.

Cutting across rich Limburg pasturelands, the Albert Canal goes obliquely towards the North Sea. You realize its importance as an industrial highway when you visit the mine complex at Blégny-Trembleur, just 20 km. (12 miles) northeast of Liège. Here you can learn at first hand just how the miners worked; you'll have to wear a helmet and lamp, too, if you want to complete the underground tour! Back on the surface, you can take an old steam train, "le Trimbleu," from the mine up to Mortroux, where there is another interesting museum. Just west of Mortroux, after passing through the picturesque village of Dalhem, you rejoin the Meuse at Visé, an old town which possesses the oldest Mosan reliquary, that of St. Hadelin. It is attributed to Godefroid de Huy. St. André's church onion-shaped belfry reminds us of Dinant and that we are still in the Meuse valley. At Maaseik, the Meuse finally leaves Belgium, to pursue its course through the Netherlands to the North Sea.

PRACTICAL INFORMATION FOR
THE MEUSE VALLEY

GETTING THERE. By train. The city of Namur is a major center and several international expresses include it in their schedules. There are good local services from Brussels which take under an hour, and there are also good services from Namur to Liège in the east and Charleroi in the west.

By road. Namur may be reached from Brussels in under an hour, Dinant is only about 28 km (17 miles) from Namur. The roads in general are in excellent condition and even in the most remote spots, are asphalted. At weekends, however, you will find driving is easier (and usually more interesting) on the secondary roads.

HOTELS AND RESTAURANTS. The Meuse valley has no very serious shortage of hotel accommodations. Nevertheless, you should book ahead during July and August, especially if you want a room with bath. The smaller hotels are equipped like most of their counterparts everywhere and are extremely clean. Service is good.

Special features of this region—more so than anywhere else in Belgium—are the culinary *auberges* and *hostelleries.* Behind the often modest facade of an inn lurks not so much the cost of accommodations as the astronomic price of the meals which you are expected to take there. First consult the menu exhibited outside the establishment, and you'll know where you are.

ANDENNE. Halfway between Huy and Namur. *Barcelone* (I), rue Brun 14 (tel. 223 268), 6 rooms with restaurant. *Du Condroz* (I), rue Léon Simon 1 (tel. 222 265), 6 rooms and a modest restaurant.

ANHÉE. 8 km. (5 miles) north of Dinant, on the left bank of the Meuse. Some 7 km. (4 miles) up the valley of the Molignée, at Falaën, you will find the *Grand*

Hôtel de la Molignée (M), pl. de la Gare 87 (tel. 699 173). 31 rooms with restaurant; located in delightfully tranquil spot.

Restaurant. *Vachter* (E), chaussée de Namur 140 (tel. 611 314). One of the finest gourmet restaurants in the country, with prices to match; also has 10 rooms and a lovely riverside garden.

ANNEVOIE-ROUILLON. 16 km. (10 miles) south of Namur on left bank of Meuse. *Belle-Vue* (I), rue du Rivage 20 (tel. 611 474). A simple hostelry with 8 rooms and restaurant.

Restaurant. *Le Blute Fin* (M), rte. des Jardins d'Annevoie 32 (tel. 612 833). Well worth a visit for good regional cooking.

ANSEREMME. Two miles south of Dinant on the right bank of the Meuse. *Hostellerie le Freyr* (M), chaussée des Alpinistes 22 (tel. 222 575). 6 rooms and a good restaurant with a panoramic view. *Mosan* (I), rue J.H. Dufrenne 2 (tel. 22 24 50). 8 rooms, with restaurant. A couple of miles up a side valley, you will find the *Castel de Pont-à-Lesse* (M), rte. de Walzin 26 (tel. 222 844). An exclusive hotel with 84 rooms, restaurant, tennis, fishing, etc. Open April–September.

Restaurant. *La Crémaillère* (M), rue du Vélodrome 2 (tel. 222 458). Overlooks the Lesse, offering fish and game specialties

BOUVIGNES. *Auberge de Bouvignes* (E), rue Fétis 1 (tel. 611 600). 6 well-appointed rooms and the area's leading gourmet restaurant.

CRUPET. 8 km. (5 miles) east of Yvoir. *Les Ramiers* (M), rue Basse 1 (tel. 699 070). Pleasant inn with six rooms and an excellent restaurant (which can be expensive). *Hotel du Centre* (I), rue Haute 8 (tel. 699 321). Simple, 6 rooms.

DINANT. The center of Meuse tourism, has many hotels and pensions. Avoid Sundays in the peak summer season. *Couronne* (M), rue Sax 1 (tel. 222 441). 24 rooms and pleasant restaurant; in center near the bridge. *Citadelle* (I), pl. Reine Astrid 5 (tel. 223 543). Central with 20 rooms and terrace restaurant.

Restaurants. The best is *Hôstellerie Thermidor* (E), rue de la Station 3 (tel. 223 135). M. de Wynter himself presides in the kitchen; pâtés and crayfish *à la Dinantaise* are his specialties. *La Grenouillère* (E), rue Rémy Himmer 445 (tel. 224 190), about a mile north of the town center, on the bank of the Meuse, offers regional cuisine. For less expensive dining try *La Strada* (M), rue Grande 24 (tel. 223 913), which specializes in Italian dishes. Alternatively there is *Hôtel de Ville* (I), rue Grande 119 (tel. 222 318), which offers seafood at a very reasonable price.

If you wish for a great gastronomic experience set out for **Celles** 10 km. (6 miles) southeast of Dinant to the *Val Joli* (M), place de l'Eglise 8 (tel. 666 363) which also has 7 rooms. Tucked away by a fine ancient church, this is a spot to relish. Quite small, so be sure to book.

FALMIGNOUL. 8 km. (5 miles) south of Dinant near Waulsort. Home of one of Europe's largest collections of old bicycles. **Restaurant.** *des Cuves* (I), rte de Dinant 38, (tel. 744 878). A pleasant spot which also has 6 rooms.

HUY. *La Réserve* (M), chaussée Napoléon 8–9 (tel. 230 404). 9 well-equipped rooms, and now with good restaurant. *Du Fort* (M), chaussée Napoleon 6 (tel. 212 403), overlooks the river and has 34 rooms and a restaurant; a 350-year-old stagecoach halt.

Restaurants. *Aigle Noir* (M), quai Dautrebande 8 (tel. 212 341). The best in town, specializing in salmon, lobster and duck. At **Villers-le-Temple,** 13 km. (8 miles) east of Huy, there is first-class fare at *La Commanderie* (M), rue Joseph Peirco 28 (tel. 511 701). A 13th-century manor with 12 well-equipped rooms.

LIÈGE, see page 205.

LUSTIN. Vacation center opposite Profondeville. *Chalet des Fresnes* (I), rue Eugène Falmagne 38 (tel. 411 456). 8 rooms, a good restaurant and fine views over the valley.

Restaurant. *Belvédere des Rochers de Frêmes* (M), rue du Belvédere 5 (tel. 412 790). Precariously perched above the Meuse—excellent trout.

NAMUR. *Château de Namur* (M), ave. Ermitage 1, (tel. 222 546). 30 rooms; restaurant, pool and many other amenities. Out of city center, in park close to Citadel. *Queen Victoria* (M), ave. de la Gare 11 (tel. 222 971). Best among the hotels in the city center; 20 rooms, most with bath.

Restaurants. In addition to the hotel restaurants, there are several other good ones. *Au Bon Vivant* (M), rue Borgnet 5, (tel. 222 314). Handy for station. *La Bruxelloise* (I), ave. de la Gare 2 (tel. 220 902). Inexpensive cuisine, almost opposite the station. *La Grappa,* (I), rue Bas de la Place 25 (tel. 222 235). Cheery Italian decor.

For more sophisticated dining head 2 miles west to **Malonne,** *Relais du Roy Louis* (M), chaussée de Charleroi 18 (tel. 444 847). A 300-year-old farmhouse.

The young set from Namur and far afield spend their evenings dancing at *La Ferme Blanche,* allée de la Maison Blanche 18, also at Malonne. Back in town, try dancing at *le Baccarat, Au 421* or *la Reserve.*

PROFONDEVILLE. Vacation center in pleasant surroundings on the left bank of the Meuse, 13 km. (8 miles) south of Namur. *Au Postillon* (I), rue Colonel Bourg 1 (tel. 411 827). 11 simple rooms, with restaurant. *Auberge d'Alsace* (I), ave. Général Gracia 42 (tel. 412 228). 6 rooms and an excellent restaurant.

SPONTIN. Off motorway, 24 km. (15 miles) south of Namur. *Auberge des Nutons* (I), chaussée de Dinant 13 (tel. 699 142). A first-class hostelry with 6 rooms; also has inexpensive restaurant.

Restaurants. *Maison de Bailli* (M), chaussée de Dinant 6 (tel. 699 193). Classic cuisine served in an old farmhouse.

At **Dorinne,** 2 km. (1 mile) southwest of Spontin, *Vivier d'Oies* (E), rue de l'Etat 7 (tel. 699 571). A famed gourmet rendezvous.

WEPION. Vacation center 5 km. (3 miles) south of Namur. *Valmeuse* (E), chaussée de Dinant 1149 (tel. 460 811). 120 rooms with bath; overlooks the river; many amenities, including pool and good restaurant. *Frisia* (I), chaussée de Dinant 1455 (tel. 411 106). 10 rooms, no restaurant.

Restaurant. *Moulin de Provence* (M), rue André de Prémorel 23 (tel. 460 420), offers good regional cuisine.

TOURS. Excursions. A trip worth making is by excursion boat upriver from Namur to Dinant; from there you may continue, by changing boats, to Heer-Agimont near the French border. The return journey for this second lap necessitates an overnight stop at Dinant. You can also take a short excursion by boat from Dinant to Anseremme or vice-versa. For further details contact—Pitance, rue Coster 2 (tel. 223 120) or Bateaux Ansiaux, rue du Vélodrome 15 (tel. 222 325), both in B-5500 Dinant.

SPORTS. All Meuse valley localities have bathing beaches and some have modern **swimming** pools. **Rowing** facilities are available under the auspices of the Clubs Nautiques at Namur and Dinant, while for **canoeing**—particularly by the not-too-skilful—the Meuse is ideal. You may travel downstream on the Lesse by boat or kayak, with a pilot, from Houyet to Anseremme—a tricky proposition if you do it in your own craft. Kayaks may be hired at Dinant. **Yachting** is also a favorite sport, and there are yacht harbors at Namur, Profondeville, Dinant, and Waulsort. For further information contact—Royal Yacht Club of Sambre and Meuse, chemin des Pruniers 11, 5150 Wepion (tel. 461 130).

For **gliding** and amateur **flying,** there is an attractive little airfield at Temploux.

If the Meuse is not an angler's dream, **fishing** can still be a satisfying pastime. A state license is needed where fishing areas are not privately-owned (mostly hotel proprietors). In local post offices, tourists can purchase licenses for a day's or several days' fishing.

Mountaineers, expert or novice, will find plenty of opportunity to test their **climbing** skill. The abrupt, rocky cliffs provide an excellent training ground for up-and-coming alpinists, but are not without danger. The best known are those of Marches-les-Dames, Dave, Anseremme, and Waulsort.

The Namur country is ideal for **horseback riding.** There are 20 livery stables in the province (list from the Tourist Office), where you can hire horses for around BF 300 per hour, whether for lessons, organized outings or for a private ride. Many of the stables organize treks of several days' duration with overnight accommodations. An enjoyable outing is the ride along the Lesse river.

MUSEUMS AND CASTLES. Certain ancient sites, such as Andenne and Huy, have their own museums, but most of the region's treasures are concentrated in Namur. Note that there are admission fees for all the museums below, mostly BF 30.

There are also some natural treasures in the area that are worth visiting. You will find remarkable grottos at Dinant, Hastière-Lavaux, Rochefort, and, farther inland on a much vaster scale, at Han-sur-Lesse.

ANDENNE. Musée Communal de la Ceramique, rue Charles Lapierre. Open weekends and Tues. only, May 1 to end-August, 2.30 to 5.30. Admission BF 40.

DINANT. Abbaye Notre-Dame de Leffe. At the northern edge of town, this is still a spiritual center for the canons of Premontre. Buildings date from the 17th and 18th centuries. Visits daily at 4 P.M. sharp.

Citadelle. Historical and military displays. Reached by road, cable-car, or 400 steps up from the town. Open daily in summer 9 to 6; in winter, daily exc. Fri., 10 to 4.

Spanish House (Maison Espagnole). Two miles north of Dinant center across river in Bouvignes, facing the Grand'-Place. Local history collection in 16th-century former town hall. Open daily Easter to end-Sept., 9 to 12 and 2 to 6.

FALMIGNOUL. Musée du Cycle et de la Moto. Claims to be the largest collection of two-wheeled vehicles in the world. Open all year, every day except Wed. Admission BF 80.

HUY. Citadelle. The most recent fort on this site was built by the Dutch between 1818 and 1823. Contains various exhibits on its use as a prison and concentration camp. Open weekends, Easter to end-September, daily during July and August, 10 to 7.

Collegiale Notre Dame, entrance in rue des Cloîtres. Built between 1311 and 1536. Contains priceless treasury, stained glass and carvings. Open 9 to 12 and 2 to 5.

Musée Communal (Town Museum), rue Van Keerberghen. Locally made metal objects, glassware and coinage (Huy was for many years a mint). Open daily Apr. to Oct. Weekdays 2 to 6; Sun. and holidays 10 to 12 and 2 to 6.

NAMUR. Citadelle, includes a museum of weapons, 6,000 of them. Reached by road or cablecar, with a superb view over the two rivers. Open 1 to 6. The cablecar runs from Pied-du-Château square, 9 to 7, Easter to Oct.

Couvent des Soeurs de Notre-Dame (Convent of the Sisters of Our Lady), houses the treasure of Oignies Priory, with items made by the goldsmith Brother Hugo of Oignies in the early 12th century. Open 10 to 12, 2 to 5, closed Sun. mornings and Tues.

Musée Africain (African Museum). Housed in old barracks, rue du Premier Lauciers. Collection of items from central Africa. Open all year, Sun., Tues. and Thurs., 2 to 5.

Musée d'Archéologie (Archeological Museum), housed in the old Meat Hall, rue du Pont. Fine collection of Roman, Frankish and Merovingian antiquities, with gold plate and glassware. Open 10 to 12, 2 to 5, closed Tues.

Musée des Arts Anciens (Museum of Old Namur Arts and Crafts), rue de Fer 24. A splendid collection of Mosan art in many fields. In the courtyard, too, is a separate museum of the work of the Namur 19th-century painter Félicien Rops. Open 10 to 12, 2 to 5, closed Tues.

Musée Diocésain (Diocesan Museum), next to the cathedral. More gold plate and religious treasures. Open 10 to 6; Nov. to Easter 2 to 5; closed Mon.

Musée Hôtel de Groesbeeck de Croix, rue Saintraint 3. Virtually intact 18th-century residence, with appropriate works of art. Open 10 to 12, 2 to 5, closed Tues.

Musée Provincial de la Forêt, rte. des Panoramas—the road up to the Citadel. Collection of local flora and fauna, especially butterflies. Open 9 to 12, 2 to 5; closed Fri.

St. Aubain's Cathedral, facing pl. St. Aubain. 18th-century Baroque edifice of Italian design. Open 8 to 6 (to 5 in winter).

Castles. Among the outstanding castles and châteaux of the region are the following—

Annevoie, Louis XIV castle in French-style park; guided visit of gardens, about one hour; periodic displays of antiques. Guided tours: Easter to end Sept., Sat. and Sun., 9.30 to 1, 2 to 6.30. Every day during July and Aug.

Crupet, near Spontin, worth a short detour. Dates from 14th century; still inhabited. Fine example of fortified farm. Cannot be visited.

Falaën, close to Maredsous and Montaigle. The Château-Ferme is an interesting fortified farm, with an excellent exhibition on other local historical sites. Open daily, April to October, 10 to 6.

Franc-Waret, fine paintings and tapestries. Guided tours: June to Sept., Sat. and Sun., 2 to 5.30.

Freyr, near Waulsort; one of the most impressive edifices of its kind in Belgium; beautiful interiors, including Louix XV woodwork and furniture. Recently repaired. Guided tours: 2 to 6.30, Sat and Sun., July and Aug.

Jehay-Bodengée, 16 km. (10 miles) from Huy on road to Tongres; one of finest architecturally; still inhabited, contains fine archeological collection. Visits: July and Aug., Sat. and Sun., 2 to 6. High entrance fee.

Lavaux Ste. Anne, 17th-cent. moated castle, contains hunting-museum, and there is a wild animal park (including boar) in the grounds. Open Mar. to Oct., 9 to 12, 1 to 6 (to 5 rest of the year).

Montaigle, a couple of miles up the Molignee valley from Anhee. Visits to the tragic ruined castle are possible only on Sundays at 2 and 4 P.M.

Noisy, 19th-century, English-designed Gothic castle with romantic park-like surroundings. Excellent views toward Vêves. Open April to October, 10.30 to 6.

Spontin, feudal castle, good example of medieval military architecture; still inhabited. The drawbridge can still be operated by its old system of counter-weights. Inside are secret staircases and a watchman's hidden lookout. A 14th-century cupboard conceals a well which was invaluable during times of siege. Guided tours: April to Sept., 9 to 12, 2 to 6, Sun. only in Oct.

Vêves, near Celles; this 15th-cent. castle is perhaps the most romantic of all. Of irregular pentagon-shape, it is flanked by 4 large towers and a gray stone keep connected by a curtain wall. Open Easter to end Oct., 10.30 to 12, 2 to 6.

Walzin, perched like an eagle's nest on a high rock; built originally in the 13th century, it was all but destroyed in 1554, but rebuilt in 1581.

USEFUL ADDRESSES. City Tourist Offices: Dinant, rue Grande 37, near the casino (tel. 222 870); Huy, quai de Namur 4 (tel. 212 915); Namur, square Léopold (tel. 222 859).

PRACTICAL INFORMATION FOR LIÈGE

GETTING THERE. By train. This city benefits from excellent rail connections both from within the country and without. The intercity train *Saphir* provides a good through service to Liège from Oostende via Brussels when eastbound and from Cologne when westbound, while the *Parsifal* provides an excellent service from Paris and Cologne to Liège. Brussels is under an hour away by the fast trains and there is at least one train per hour. There are also good connections from Namur and Luxembourg to Liège. Local trains cross the Dutch border to Maastricht, passing through Vise. Several of the railway routes which radiate from Liège towards Cologne, Spa and Libramont pass through attractive countryside and are well worth traveling.

By road. Liège may be reached from Brussels—98 km. (61 miles)—via the Brussels-Liège motorway (A3/E40). Good rail and bus networks help to explore the surrounding countryside. Self-drive cars are also available.

HOTELS. There are several good hotels, usually with excellent restaurants. The older ones are small and service, therefore, is more personalized than you will find on the average in cities of this size.

Always remember that it is possible to get a slightly less expensive room in one of the Luxury or Expensive graded hotels. The view may not be much, but the service won't suffer and the final check will be much more acceptable.

Expensive

Holiday Inn, Esplanade de l'Europe 2 (tel. 426 020). Across the river, with 224 rooms and many amenities, including a pool, but no restaurant.

Post House, rue Hurbise (tel. 646 400). Just out of town at Herstal as you come off the Liège-Aachen (A3/E40) motorway. 93 rooms and a heated outside swimming pool. Also has the excellent *La Diligence* (M) restaurant.

Ramada Inn, blvd. de la Sauvenière 100 (tel. 224 910). 105 rooms and a good restaurant; centrally situated on the edge of the old town.

Moderate

Couronne, pl. des Guillemins 11 (tel. 522 168). Tourist stalwart, opposite the main station. 79 rooms, no restaurant.

Cygne d'Argent, rue Beeckman 49 (tel. 237 001). 19 rooms.

De l'Univers, rue des Guillemins 116 (tel. 522 650). 51 rooms, no restaurant.

Métropole, rue des Guillemins 141 (tel. 524 293). 27 rooms and modest restaurant.

Le Petit Cygne, rue des Augustins 42 (tel. 224 759). 7 well-equipped rooms, no restaurant.

Inexpensive

Darchis, rue Darchis 18 (tel. 234 218). 18 rooms and restaurant.

Du Midi, pl. des Guillemins 1 (tel. 522 003), right opposite the main station.

Environs

At **Chaudfontaine,** a small thermal spa 11 km. (7 miles) to the southeast, with a casino: *Palace* (M), Esplanade 2 (tel. 650 070). 25 rooms and a good restaurant.

At **Tilff-sur-Ourthe,** 13 km. (8 miles) out of town on the N33: *Casino* (M), pl. Roi-Albert 3 (tel. 881 015). 6 rooms and a highly-recommended restaurant.

TOURS. Excursions. Boat trips on the Meuse are available during the summer months; contact Naviliege, quai de Maestricht 14, 4000 Liège (tel. 235 907/8/9).

MUSEUMS AND PLACES OF INTEREST. Museums are normally open from 10 to 12.30 and 2 to 5 on weekdays and 10 to 4 on Sundays and holidays. Most are closed one weekday (Monday or Tuesday) and certain holidays. Some can be visited in the evening (7 to 10). Admission is generally BF 50.

Galérie Lapidaire du Palais. A collection of carved headstones sounds boring, but this museum provides one of the few means of entry to the bishop's palace (other than requesting permission from the High Court which meets in it). It also gives access to the various subterranean vaults and Belgo-Roman remains under the place St. Lambert. Open on weekdays during office hours.

Musée d'Ansembourg (the Ansembourg Mansion), En Féronstrée 114. Attractive 1735 house with a fine collection of 18th-century decorative art and furniture, mostly of local make. Closed Tues.

Musée d'Armes (Museum of Weapons), quai de Maestricht 8. Collection of more than 8,000 arms, tracing the history of firepower, in which Liège played an important part. Closed Mon.

Musée de l'Architecture et Studio Ysaye (Architecture Museum and Ysaye's Studio), Impasse des Ursulines 14. Housed in a typically 17th-century regional building, the former Béguinage du Saint Esprit. Flowers vie in the gardens with fountains and carvings, while the interior is packed with lovely panelling and fine woodwork. Next door is a reconstruction of the violinist and composer Eugène Ysaye's studio in a reclaimed post office.

Musée d'Art Moderne, across Pont Albert I, in park. Collection of French painting since Ingres; Corot and Impressionists (Boudin, Monet, Pissaro) well represented; works by Vlaminck, Utrillo, Picasso, Léger, and German Expressionists. Section devoted to modern Belgian painting shows Permeke, Ensor, Evenepoel and Laermans. Closed Tues. At the same location is the city's print collection **(Cabinet des Estampes),** containing some 25,000 engravings, lithographs and watercolors.

Musée de l'Art Walloon, Ilot St. Georges, En Féronstrée 86. Works of Walloon painters and sculptors from the 16th to the 20th century.

Musée Curtius, quai de Maestricht 13. Built in pure Mosan Renaissance style, contains an important archeological collection. The section on glass retraces the history of this material since its origins. Closed Tues.

Musée du Fer et du Charbon (Iron and Coal Museum), blvd. Poincaré 17. In a converted factory. Open 2 to 5; closed Sun. and Mon.

Musée Grétry, rue des Récollets 34. Dedicated to André Grétry, one of Liège's three great composers, the house contains many personal items, manuscripts and documents describing his career. Open daily, except Tues. and Sun., 2.30 to 5.

Musée Tchantchès, rue Surlet 56. Collection of puppets and costumes celebrating Liège's most famous citizen. Open Wed. and Thurs., 2 to 5, Sun. 12 to 2. Performances normally mid-September to Easter.

Musée des Transports en Commun, rue Richard Heintz. A final resting-place for various trams, trains and buses from Liège and district. Open weekends, April to October.

Musée de la Vie Wallonne (Museum of Walloon Folklore and Crafts), Cour des Mineurs, just off En Hors Château. In a 17th-century Franciscan abbey, a delightfully arranged museum on the arts, crafts and recreations of the region. Foreign language commentaries. Closed Mon.

Just south of Liège, at **Embourg,** you can visit one of the 19th-century forts, which played a key role in the defense of Liège in both 1914 and 1940. Open Sundays and public holidays, May to September. Admission BF 60.

 RESTAURANTS. Liège cuisine is refined, and noted for specialties of goose, thrushes *(grives),* and a white sausage that is the pride of local butchers *(boudin blanc de Liège).* In addition to all the classic creations of French and Belgian cuisine, Liège offers such local specialties as *écrevisses à la Liègeoise* (crayfish cooked in white wine sauce and butter) or *rognon de veau à la Liègeoise* (veal kidney cooked with juniper berries, and a dash of gin added before serving). Perhaps your tastes are different, and you'll be quite happy with the illustrious Ardennes ham, cured over smouldering oak. Another simple, and inexpensive, course is *salade Liègeoise,* a stew prepared with French beans, potatoes, onions, and lard. If your culinary ambitions go higher, try *oie à l'instar de Visé,* goose cooked in wine, then fried and served with a *sauce mousseline* made of eggs, melted butter and garlic. For dessert there are fruit tarts of all kinds and pancakes *(crêpes flambées).* Your afternoon coffee session should consist of *gaufres Liègeoises*—prepared in front of you in most places, and coffee with whipped cream, still a bone of contention between Liège and Vienna as to which city makes the better.

Expensive

Dauphin, rue du Parc 53 (tel. 434 753). Beautifully paneled interior, opposite Parc de la Boverie. Excellent game dishes in season.

Vieux Liège, quai de la Goffe 41 (tel. 237 748). Recalls bygone days in a 16th-century Mosan Renaissance house. Probably the best in town, with outstanding cuisine and a view over the river.

Moderate

As Ouhès, pl. du Marché 21 (tel. 233 225). Just across from the Hôtel de Ville; open till midnight; excellent slightly old-fashioned food.

Jardin des Bégards, rue Bégards 2 (tel. 235 402). Open-air eating on the edge of the Old Town, at the foot of Mont St. Martin.

Lion Dodu, rue Surlet 37 (tel. 410 505). On the right bank.

Rôtisserie de l'Empereur, pl. du 20-Aout 15 (tel. 235 373). In the center of the old town by the university buildings. In the top gastronomic class, though not quite so pricey as some.

Aux Vieux Ramparts, rue de la Montagne 4 (tel. 231 717). Old building facing steeply inclined street in the Old Town. Excellent sea food. Terrace open in summer.

Inexpensive

Flo, quai sur Meuse 16 (tel. 235 5040). A reasonably priced brasserie, straight out of the *belle époque.*

Le Lotus Bleu, en Neuvice 33 (tel. 233 441). Excellent Vietnamese cooking.

Le Mas, rue d'Outremeuse 55 (tel. 435 701). Relaxed atmosphere.

La Table de Riz, rue sur la Fontaine 65 (tel. 223 911). Vietnamese cuisine at its best, at very reasonable prices.

Environs

At **Angleur,** 3 miles down the main route for Dinant; *Orchidée Blanche* (M), rte. de Condroz 457 (tel. 651 148). Well recommended; open late. Also *Sart Tilman* (M), rue Sart Tilman 343 (tel. 654 224), for very good food.

In the northeastern suburb of **Herstal:** *Rôtisserie Mosane* (M), rue Large-Voie 47 (tel. 646 529). Really excellent fixed-price menu.

At **Neuville-en-Condroz,** 18 km. (11 miles) south of town, is the best of the bunch—*Chêne Madame* (E), ave. de la Chevauchée 70 (tel. 714 127). In the Rognac woods, with out-of-this-world cuisine and sometimes prices to match. Magnificent wine list and incomparable service.

NIGHTLIFE. Liège people enjoy music and dancing, and *la cité ardente* really lives up to its name in the evening. The Tourist Office lists about 30 discos, clubs and bars with music and dancing. Rue Tete-de-boeuf contains several 'smart' clubs and discos such as *La Plantation* (suits and ties are *de rigueur)* as well as the more relaxed *Estoril* disco. *Carlton Club* in rue Souverain Pont. Jazz fans should make for *Le Clavier,* en Roture 22, or *La Pierre Levée,* rue de Serbie. Students congregate in the cafés and bars on the rue d'Amay. For a Paris-style dinner and cabaret, try Chez Sullon, en Bergerue 6, Friday and Saturday at 8.30. The nearby *Tabarin,* en Bergerue 14, starts its somewhat daring floorshow at 10.30 P.M.; quality debatable, prices reasonable.

Theaters and Music. The *Théâtre Royal* has an opera, operetta, and ballet company. If you understand French you will enjoy a visit to *Al Botroûle,* rue Hocheporte 3, (puppet shows); still more of the puppets at the *Musée Tchant-chès,* rue Surlet 56. At the *Trianon* and the *Trocadéro,* plays are frequently in the Walloon dialect.

The *Orchestre Philharmonique de Liège,* rue Forgeur 14, often hosts best international soloists. Lunchtime concerts are held Oct.-Apr. every Thursday at the *Salle de l'Emulation* and the *Palais des Congrès.*

USEFUL ADDRESSES. British Consulate, Rue Beeckman 45 (tel. 235 832). **City Tourist Office,** en Féronstrée 92 (tel. 222 456), and Guillemins Station (tel. 524 419). **Provincial Tourist Office,** blvd. de la Sauvenière 77 (tel. 224 210).

THE ARDENNES

Forests and Valleys

The Ardennes is more a geographical region than a province. Indeed the Haut Plateau Ardennais (to give it its full title) stretches for well over 100 miles from northern France, through the southeast corner of Belgium's Namur province, most of the Belgian province of Luxembourg, the northern half of the Grand Duchy and on, through the Hautes Fagnes, into Germany.

This perfect vacationland lacks nothing, and is loved by poet and picnicker, geologist and hunter alike. Spa, La Roche and many other places offer comfortable hotel accommodations. But for those traveling on a modest budget, every road has hospitable inns. Certain manor houses are now youth hostels, and camp sites are easily found. In the middle of pine woods, on rocky crests, and near wild caverns, you will find young people from all over Europe and North America sharing the warmth of campfires.

For while life in the cities is expensive, camping is paradise, at half the cost. It is always easy to find good Ardennes ham, smoked over oak chippings. There is fresh white bread, cold beer, and coffee with hot milk kept warm on the cast-iron stoves that electricity seems powerless to make obsolete. The most out-of-the-way inn will serve you wonderful fried potatoes in a twinkling and afterwards, a pie or a sugar tart. So take your walking shoes and a heavy sweater, a bathing suit, and a camera and follow the trail of students, scouts, and young couples who are trying, like you, to explore all the paths, climb all the peaks and photograph all the castles.

You will need to be careful to keep to the beaten track when you get into the highland country in the east. These are the High Fenns (Hohe Venn or Hautes Fagnes), around 2,000 ft. above sea level and close to the German Eifel country (and in fact, German is the most widely-spoken language here). A large part of the country, however, is marshy, and if you are walking, particularly after dark, you must be careful to keep to roads and footpaths which are well laid out; and to avoid most of all following unidentified lights, for in such country the will-o'-the-wisp is no fairytale.

Which road will you take? They strike out from Liège like the strands of a spider's web, each running through the most diverse landscapes, from quiet, outdated watering places to the lonely forest of Malmédy and the high valley of the Ourthe. Motorists have their choice of a score or more delightful drives.

You can also explore the Rivers Ourthe, Semois, Lesse, Sure, Amblève and Our and the Lake of Nisramont, by canoe and kayak.

The Ourthe Valley

The banks of the Ourthe are favorite haunts of the Liège population, rich and poor alike. They are lined with a curious assortment of taverns, summer houses, and castles. Tilff, Comblain-la-Tour and Hamoir are all popular weekend excursion spots. The cliffs of Sy, however, act as a natural boundary marker; and not simply of the fact that you are leaving the province of Liège and entering Belgian Luxembourg. This is where you leave the placid farm-country of the Lower Ourthe to enter the Ardennes, a silent, brooding region. The slate-roofed villages are farther apart and hidden among walnut groves. The cliffs are higher, and difficult to climb.

Durbuy (20 miles from Liège) is like a scene from an operetta. The Grain Market and the Ducal Palace in the main street seem much too big for the village. Its nickname, "the biggest little town in Belgium," has a historical background: Durbuy was granted city rights in the 14th century, but after a brilliant period while the dukes of Ursel were rich and powerful, the community reverted to its former somnolent life, in which everybody knew everybody else. The same applies now.

Following the Ourthe southward through Fronville (with its nearby chateau of Deulin), you soon come to Hotton, famous for its caves, discovered as recently as 1958.

La Roche-en-Ardenne (11 miles southwest of Hotton) is right out of a fairytale. Its romantic ruined castle (with wild game park and *Son et Lumière*) belonged to the counts de la Roche, who were famous for dispensing justice and money. Although it suffered much during World War II, La Roche remains a vacation center; its hotels are good and it makes an excellent centerpoint for long walks. Blue earthenware is the outstanding local craft, and visitors are admitted to the workshop in the Rue Rompré. La Roche is teeming with butcher's shops, and no tourist ought to leave without taking home some *saucisson* or *jambon d'Ardennes*.

A walk to the top of Le Hérou and back takes five or six hours. The going is rough, but from the summit there is a breathtaking view. The cliff falls in a straight line to the turbulent river, and the panorama that spreads for miles before your eyes is vast and profoundly silent. The center of this scenic area is the small village of Nadrin. From here you can undertake the descent of the Ourthe by canoe, a 10-mile course of unique beauty. If you prefer calmer waters, the man-made lake of Nisramont offers excellent water-sports facilities.

Houffalize—a corruption of the French for "high cliffs"—lies 10 miles upstream. Its early-Gothic church has some remarkable treasures, like the brass lectern made in 1372, the altar, and the old local squires' sculptured tombstones. Miraculously, the church escaped destruction during the 1944 Ardennes battle, when almost the whole town was wiped out. Five miles southeast of town there is the romantically situated château of Tavigny, part of which now houses a top-class restaurant.

Head southwest from here through Bertogne and Amberloup and you come to St. Hubert. This is in the magic forest of the Ardennes, where St. Hubert, while hunting on Good Friday in 683, saw a stag bearing a lighted cross between its antlers. A Benedictine abbey was erected on the site—both the abbey and the surrounding town are called St. Hubert—and there the saint's bones were kept. But when Belgium was invaded, the monks hid the coffin, and so well that it has never been found. The sanctuary is still visited by pilgrims, and each year there is a special open-air mass, which includes a fanfare of hunting horns. Appropriately, there is a Game Park (Parc à Gibier) just to the northwest of St. Hubert.

North of the town, at Fourneau St. Michel, is a small museum of ancient crafts, where there is a facinating reconstruction of a foundry which operated for a short time in the late 18th century. Its first cannons were sold to the young American republic during the War of Independence, but no more were ordered when the first batch exploded on being used, and the foundry went bankrupt. In the foundry is what may well be the world's largest collection of ancient waffle-irons.

The Battle of the Bulge: Bastogne

Less than 20 miles east of St. Hubert, you come to Bastogne. Here the villagers themselves look after the graves of American soldiers who fell in 1944 in the Battle of the Bulge.

Von Rundstedt's scheme, bold and cunning, was to launch three offensives, a northern push towards Liège, through Sankt Vith, a southern push towards Sedan, and a central push towards Bastogne. Sankt Vith resisted stoutly, and the southern attack miscarried, but the Bastogne offensive was successful. The area was poorly defended: it had been considered too wooded to permit engagements between motorized troops. German tanks drove furiously through the forest in the direction of Bastogne, an important road center. The American 106th Division was deployed throughout the region but it was an unseasoned unit.

Frightful weather added to the chaos; fog and snow paralysed every movement. Soldiers were continually cut off from base, and their supplies and ammunition were running out. It was soon evident that Bastogne was surrounded, but the American 101st Airborne Division, which had been rushed to the area, held firm. When Brigadier General MacAuliffe was asked to surrender, he calmly replied, 'Nuts." The citizens of Bastogne had good cause to name the main square of their town place MacAuliffe.

The resistance continued, made more difficult by a violent snowstorm and more poignant by the approach of Christmas, and it was a grim holiday for GIs buried in icy mud. Burning houses blazed through the thick fog, lighting up every target. The townspeople helped the troops as much as they could, using their linen sheets to camouflage scouts otherwise clearly visible in the snow. The desperate struggle lasted for days. Finally, the miracle happened. The thick moist veil lifted suddenly one dawn, revealing the German tanks, and the Americans were able to use their last stocks of ammunition to effect. Bastogne was encircled, but it held out. Soon after, Allied planes dropped arms and supplies to the stranded division and 2,000 planes bombed the Germans.

Bastogne is the guardian of the impressive Mardasson Memorial outside the town's precincts, dedicated to the American troops who lost their lives in the Battle of the Bulge. Close to the star-shaped memorial is the Bastogne Historical Center with displays that explain the Battle of the Ardennes.

The Vesdre and Amblève Valleys

East of Liège is the Vesdre, a fine scenic river which has been harnessed almost at source, and made to serve industry. Its tributary, the Gileppe, is dammed just above the textile-manufacturing cities of Pepinster and Verviers. This dam, built in 1867, was considered gigantic at the time, and the lion that dominates it has been photographed as often as that of Waterloo. The artificial lake set amongst green hills has an idyllic beauty. A mighty dam, the Barrage de la Vesdre et du Getzbach, was finished in 1951 just outside the textile center of Eupen, home of the largest German-speaking minority in Belgium. The dam has a tower from the top of which you can get a wonderful panoramic view.

The river has stretches of rustic simplicity, when it flows placidly through orchards or busily turns old millwheels. And famous writers have been entranced with the Vesdre: Sir Walter Scott loved the area near the Château de Theux, and Victor Hugo said the Vesdre "is sometimes a ravine, often a garden, always a paradise." Chaudfontaine's thermal springs, on the outskirts of Liège, have been a convenient reason for the setting up of a well-run casino. A few more kilometers in an unlovely, industralized setting, and the Vesdre disappears into the Meuse.

The Amblève river runs down toward the Ourthe at Comblain. The Amblève and its main tributary, the Warche, pass the noble abbeys of Malmédy and Stavelot, which were ruled for eleven centuries by abbot-princes temporally responsible only to the emperor. They were cultivated, generous and well-informed. The houses here are curious, with their exposed beams, and the old abbeys are remarkable. From the Napoleonic Wars until the Versailles Treaty (1919) most of this region was German-speaking, but the Walloon language never died. Malmédy is renowned for its cuisine and its carnival, one of the merriest in Belgium. During the hunting season, the vast silence of the pine forest is broken by the galloping of horses and the flourish of hunting horns. The local nobility takes great pride in its horses and packs.

It was at nearby Stavelot that St. Remacle discovered in 648 that his mule had been devoured by a wolf, and it is said that he founded the town by the simple expedient of saying "To the stable, wolf"—"*Stave, leu*" in local dialect. It is not recorded whether or not the wolf obeyed, but Stavelot certainly does exist, and a beautiful 13th-century reliquary of its founder is in the parish church. Here you may also see a fine 17th-century silver-gilt reliquary bust of a saint with the improbable name of Popon. Stavelot, though hardly a city, is a particularly active cultural center, holding art exhibitions throughout the year and a summer chamber-music festival. It also treasures the memory of the poet Guillaume Apollinaire with a small museum—though he slipped off without settling his hotel bill in 1899.

At Trois-Ponts, the Amblève is joined by the Salm, a picturesque river that rises on the border of the Grand Duchy of Luxembourg. The Salm valley was once a principality owing vague allegiance to the dukes of Luxembourg. The ruined castle of the princes of Salm lies south of Vielsalm at Salmchâteau.

A couple of kilometers north of Trois-Ponts, the Amblève drops from a height of 45 feet with a great splashing of spray. These are the Coo Falls, with an old stone bridge and water mill. You get an excellent view of countryside traversed by a meandering river, by taking the somewhat frightening chairlift to the Belvedère Jean. The Amblève narrows, and is squeezed between slopes so humid and thickly-wooded that the valley is nicknamed "The Congo." Soon it reaches the strange Fonds de Quareaux and at Nonceveux it is joined by the Ninglinspo, which descends in great leaps, carving out pools with names like "Diana's Bath" or "The Naiads."

Throughout the countryside the Amblève feeds a network of subterranean streams; it has hollowed out the mysterious caverns of Remouchamps, between Sougné-Remouchamps and Aywaille, whose great Cathedral Chamber is more than 100 meters long. After you have left the caves' galleries to admire the Calypso Passage and Titan's Bridge, you can take a boat-trip on the underground Rubicon river. The feudal castle, still inhabited, is not accessible to the public, but you can get a good view of it from the banks of the Amblève.

The High Fenn

East of the Salm and of Spa is the High Fenn (Hautes Fagnes or Hohe Venn) country, which links the Ardennes to the Eifel. The highest point is le Signal de Botrange (694 meters, 2,276 ft.). A few miles south you come to Robertville, just below the Ovifat ski slope, and just above the great man-made lakes which are the retention reservoirs for the power-supply. From here you continue west for Malmédy, and 12 miles later you reach Spa. For a scenic detour which takes you close to the German border, head south from Robertville. This route passes through Amel at the headwaters of the Amblève, on to romantic Sankt Vith, and farther south is Burg Reuland, beside the River Our, which flows southward, dividing Luxembourg from Germany.

Spa Stands for Thermal Resort

The town of Spa used to be a haunt of international society. It was for centuries one of the favorite resorts of tsars, queens, statesmen and philosophers. Pliny the Elder, that Roman precursor of travel writers, even mentions the healing powers of Spa's springs—Aquae Sepadonae. A medieval blacksmith from Breda rediscovered its waters and purchased from the Liège prince-bishops some woodland near the earliest "pouhon" or spring. This spring in the center of the town is now called pouhon Peter the Great, since that sovereign visited it many times. Before him had come Montaigne and Queen Margot, Christina of Sweden and the fugitive Charles II of England. But it was Henry VIII's court physician, a Venetian named Augustino, who first used the waters in the treatment of rheumatism. Illustrious visitors are listed in the town's Golden Book and depicted in frescos.

In the 17th century two English doctors, Andrews and Paddy, came to Spa to study the virtue of its waters. They gave the term *spa* to several ferruginous springs in their own country, and it eventually became the generic term for health resorts throughout the English-speaking world. Spa reached its zenith as a watering-place and rendezvous of high society during the 18th and 19th centuries. Many contemporary fine houses, today classified as historic monuments, give a glimpse of that gracious past.

The cure was not painful, and the neighborhood was delightful. But visitors might have been bored without the high-stake gambling at the casino. They played *pharaon* and *biribi* for roubles, ducats, piastres, francs, or what-have-you. In 1751, Bishop-Prince Jean Théodor gave the gambling monopoly to a Scotsman, who made a fortune. Other gaming houses were opened: the Vauxhall, the Redoute and the Levoz.

Spa has changed considerably. It is now the health center of Belgium's national health scheme. The Vauxhall is an orphanage, a casino has replaced the Redoute. Amusements are a little more varied, and include beauty—and other contests. The golf course is one of the loveliest in Europe. There is even a small airfield tucked into a forest clearing, and a little further, on the way to Stavelot, Francorchamps circuit lies in a most attractive mountain setting. European and Belgian racing-car and motorcycle races are held here several times a year.

In 1918, the Kaiser installed his general headquarters at Spa and had a concrete underground shelter built at the Neubois Château. After the armistice was signed, Hoover, Pershing, and Foch lodged in Spa.

With the introduction of new healing methods, the draw of the seaside, and the expansion of foreign travel, Spa has lost its allure as an international social health center, but it has become a pivot of tourism in the Ardennes, holding the motorist for a day or two but no longer.

Spa is full of excellent hotels, some of which are on Balmoral, a wooded ridge overlooking the city and Warfaz Lake. Its admirable situation has caused many well-to-do townspeople and others to build their elegant villas there. An interesting contemporary sight in this city of memories is the ultra-modern bottling plant of Spa-Monopole; guided tours take place daily during the season. From June till the end of September, there is a display of thousands of begonias on Avenue Reine Astrid in the town center.

A 10-minute drive north will take you to Theux, dominated by the ruins of the Castle of Franchimont. These recall the sacrifice of the castle's 600 defenders, who in 1468 dashed to their capital, Liège, and died to the last man against the overwhelming forces of the French king and Charles the Bold, Duke of Burgundy. Sacked by the French, the castle remains a silent witness to this heroic exploit.

The Lesse Valley of Grottos

If you plan to explore the course of the mysterious Lesse River, you must start at Dinant. After following a number of turns through defiles and gorges, the stream completely disappears in a most disconcerting way, only to reappear a few steps farther on. The Meuse is only 52 km. (32 miles) from the source of the Lesse, but that river is so sinuous and curving that its course measures at least 169 km. (105 miles) before it empties into the Meuse.

It begins deep in the Ardennes between two forests, and almost immediately encounters obstacles in the form of rocks and boulders. Coming up against the Belvaux promontory, the Lesse disappears underground. In the subterranean caverns, the river has carved the crystal palace of the Han Grottos. These were discovered in 1814 by four intrepid young men who ventured into the tortuous labyrinth. They carried torches and left a trail of flour in order to retrace their steps. You can imagine their astonishment when they came upon an enchanted scene of sparkling stalactites in vaulted rooms of cathedral-like proportions. A further room, the Cave of Cataclysms, was discovered in 1962, and one or two more caves opened in 1971. A tram will take you from the town, Han-sur-Lesse, to the entry of the caves; allow at least three hours for the full tour.

The nearby Rochefort Grottos, subterranean work of the Lomme, have their marvels too, including a natural throne made of varicolored stone in the Sabbath Room. In just a couple of miles, you can travel from the depths of the earth into space: just to the west of Han-sur-Lesse is Lessive, Begium's satellite telecommunications station, which is open to visitors during the summer.

The Lesse becomes more and more amazing. Going by boat from Houyet to Dinant you will pass through landscapes more varied and surprising than the scenes of any stage show. The region is called the Chaleux Circle. Here you can see plainly the rock strata showing the stages of the formation of the earth's crust. In Furfooz Ridge, the Lesse hides under a rocky shelf. When it finally emerges, the river flows towards and empties into the Meuse, and for some distance colors that river with a cold deep-green.

The Lesse region boasts many other castles. Villers has three of them: Vignée, Jamblinne and that of the Counts of Cunchy. Vêves, near Celles, is a beautifully-preserved example of medieval military architecture. Lavaux-Saint-Anne, now government property, is farther to the south. It houses an exciting Hunters' Museum, with some wild boar in the paddock across the moat. These castles form a circle around the royal estate of Ciergnon, favorite weekend haunt of the royal family.

The Semois Valley

The Semois is an unpredictable and disconcerting river, flowing toward the Meuse through the chalky Gaumais country from its source in the calm Belgian Lorraine, and jostling its way through rocky Ardennes hills. It follows the highway very often, hiding behind rows of trees and tobacco sheds. At its western end, tobacco is the valley's main source of wealth, and in September you can smell the drying tobacco throughout the entire countryside. At Vresse there is a small museum dedicated to the industry.

If you are prepared to walk a few hundred yards away from the road, as you head eastward you will be rewarded by some splendid views. Leave your car and go picnicking to Roche la Dame near Bohan, to Rocher du Corbeau (Raven's Rock) on a side road between Alle and Rochehaut, or to the Chair à prêcher (Pulpit) near Corbion. Before reaching Bouillon, you can see the Tombeau du Géant (Giant's Tomb), hemmed in by the meandering river. Another fine view is offered by walking across the main road to the Rocher de Pendu (Rock of the Hanged Man).

After crossing the crest of the hills at Frahan, the road drops gradually down the shady slope through Poupehan and Corbion past the Giant's Tomb, at Botassart on the other bank, to arrive at Bouillon and its château perched above the Semois. This was the castle of Godefroy de Bouillon, Defender of the Holy Sepulcher, a heroic crusader who died in the Holy Land after having refused the title of King of Jerusalem. This fortified castle has been defended and conquered countless times, for it occupies one of the most strategic spots in the Ardennes. Its ruins are a grandiose sight, and within their walls you may still see the Hall of Justice, various prisons, the gallows, and a 250-foot well, hewn into the rock. During the tourist season the castle is floodlit every night. Perhaps the best view of Château Bouillon's unscalable walls is from the top of the Tour d'Autriche (Austrian Tower). At this point of vantage, the memories of a thousand years of strife are tempered by the sight of the Semois as it flows past houses and fields. The town was the capital of a small free state from 963 until 1794.

After Bouillon, the Semois is again turbulent and twisting, making its way through great oak forests. You can hire canoes in Dohan or Cugnon for short excursions on the river. Herbeumont, a spotless mountain village, is over a thousand years old. The ruins of its castle and the small church dating back to the 12th century are worth visiting.

From here you can head southwest to Muno or follow the Semois through the picture-book village of Chassepierre, towards the more pastoral landscapes of Gaume.

The Gaumais Country, and Orval Abbey

Belgian Lorraine, called La Gaume, begins at Florenville, a neat little town from where you can reach Orval Abbey in a few minutes by car. Near Chiny, the river is covered with flowers. Here you can take a most interesting boat trip to Lacuisine or you can go still farther on to the Forges Roussel, which once employed 200 workers, until one morning it sank under the lake waters. Now only a little turreted castle remains to mark the spot.

Away from the Semois, south of Florenville and deep in the forest, you come upon Orval Abbey, once so powerful that its yearly revenue exceeded £1,200,000, and about 300 towns and villages were temporally responsible to it. Any traveler was welcome to three days' lodging. But when Napoleon's General Loyson pillaged the countryside, he set fire to the abbey, and its ruins were almost forgotten until 1926, when Cistercian monks set about rebuilding it. By means of a special series of stamps, charity balls and donations, a new abbey was built of warm brown stone. Great artists collaborated in the reconstruction, and so Orval is once more a fascinating sight for tourists. If the monks no longer offer free board and room, at least they offer you excellent bread, and their justly-famous beer. They observe the spirituality and discipline of their medieval predecessors, and their monastery once again exerts considerable religious influence.

The legend of Orval's buried treasure is almost as generally accepted as the yarn of Captain Kidd's. Quite a store of gold could conceivably be hidden in the maze of underground passages which connect the old abbey with seven surrounding lakes. One legend relates that long ago a Princess called Matilda was sitting by a pool in the gardens playing with a golden ring, which she accidentally dropped into the water. Naturally distressed, she prayed that she could in some way get it back. On opening her eyes, she is supposed to have seen a fish swim up to the surface with the ring in its mouth. But the real treasure of Orval is the abbey itself, standing once more amidst its church and cloisters.

Virton, farther south, is a typical Lorraine city with its red-tiled roofs and narrow streets. Its regional museum has old utensils, over a hundred *taques* (artistically-worked fireplace plates made of iron) and many other objects of popular art. One of the excursions will take you to Montauban. On this hill some astonishing 2,000-years-old Roman remains were discovered, and a museum has been erected on the spot to house the finds—the Archeological Park.

But it is in ancient Orolaunum, the Arlon of today, that we can measure the extent of Roman civilization in this province. Its museum contains Romano-Belgian archeological remains of the first importance. The carvings on the 2nd-century tombstones provide an interesting picture of daily life in those times: Christianity had not yet come to this region, and the opulence and hedonism of the Roman way-of-life is revealed.

Endless wars have stripped Arlon if its ancient monuments. This lively city, with its broad avenues and neat houses built of heavy stone, will not impress lovers of the past. Yet Arlon is the oldest-known settlement in Belgium.

PRACTICAL INFORMATION FOR THE ARDENNES

HOTELS AND RESTAURANTS. Ardennes hotels are noted for comfort and good food. While the old-fashioned hotels of Spa have become institutions, the accent today is on more countrified sites, and modern standards have gained ground.

The hotels listed below represent only a few of the many establishments available. You will have no difficulty in finding accommodation, provided you avoid the months of July and August.

Rates are reasonable, probably the lowest in Belgium. Most of the hotels offer special weekend (1 night) or extended weekend (2 nights) terms.

There are several regional gastronomic specialties. Sausage products in general, and Ardennes ham in particular, are deliciously cured over smoldering oak for a long time. During the hunting season ask for some of the dishes prepared with marinaded hare *(civet de lièvre),* not unlike English jugged hare; roebuck *(chevreuil);* or a very special dish of young wild boar soaked in beer from Orval Abbey *(estouffat de marcassin à la bière).*

ALLE. 19 km. (12 miles) from Bouillon near the French border. *Fief de Liboichant* (M), rue de Liboichant 99 (tel. 500 333). 30 rooms, many with bath. *Auberge d'Alle* (I), rue de Liboichant 46 (tel. 500 357). 11 rooms and a superb but fairly expensive restaurant.

A modern recreation center, *Recrealle,* on the banks of the Semois, includes many sports and amusement facilities—a closed park for children, a caravan site and fishing facilities.

ARLON. Largest city in the Luxembourg province, and provincial capital. *Ecu de Bourgogne* (M), pl. Léopold 9 (tel. 220 222). 19 rooms. No restaurant, but is close to *New Arly* (M), pl. Léopold 56 (tel. 222 834). *Hostellerie du Peiffeschof* (M), chemin du Peiffeschof 253 (tel. 224 415). 7 rooms and good restaurant. *Hôtel du Nord* (I), rue des Faubourgs 2 (tel. 220 283). 23 rooms, has no restaurant but is right next to the *Relais du Nord* (I) (tel. 226 790), one of the best restaurants in town.

Also worth trying for a meal is *L'Europe* (I), ave. de la Gare 25 (tel. 212 590), a pleasant inn by the station. Closed last 3 weeks Aug.

ASTENET. 10 miles north of Eupen. *Château Thor* (M), Nierstrasse 5 (tel. 659 037). 4 rooms and a good restaurant; a fortified manor dating from the Middle Ages, with good fishing.

AYWAILLE. *Villa des Roses* (M), ave. de la Libération 4 (tel. 844 236). 10 well-equipped rooms and excellent restaurant.

BARVAUX. East of Durbuy along Ourthe. *Cor de Chasse* (M), rte. de Tohogne 29 (tel. 211 498). 14 rooms; modest restaurant.

Restaurant. *Poivrière* (E), Grand'rue 28 (tel. 211 560). A gourmet's delight. Leave room for the excellent desserts.

BASTOGNE. *Lebrun* (M), rue de Marche 8 (tel. 062–211 193), 23 rooms and a restaurant. *Du Sud* (I), rue de Marche 39 (tel. 062–211 114). 13 basic rooms, no restaurant.

Restaurant.*Au Vivier* (M), rue du Sablon 183 (tel. 062–212 257. Excellent fish dishes. *Au Luxembourg* (I), pl. MacAuliffe 25 (tel. 062–211 226). *MacAuliffe* (I), pl. MacAuliffe 33 (tel. 062–214 100). Suitably nostalgic.

BOUILLON. Historic city and castle situated on picturesque bend in the Semois. *Armes de Bouillon* (M), rue de la Station 9 (tel. 061–466 079). 65 rooms, 55 with bath, and restaurant. *De la Poste* (M), pl. St. Arnould 1 (tel. 061–466 506). 73 rooms, 40 with bath or shower. *Panorama* (M), rue Au-dessus-de-la-Ville 25 (tel. 061–466 138). 45 rooms. Excellent restaurant. Superb view across river to castle.

Restaurants. *Auberge d'Alsace* (M), Faubourg de France 3 (tel. 061–466 588). Classic Franco-Belgian cuisine. In the old town there's *La Vieille Ardenne* (I), Grand-Rue 9 (tel. 061–466 277). Noted for its wide choice of locally brewed beers.

BURG REULAND. For the outdoor minded, there is the *Hôtel du Val de l'Our* (M), Bahnhofstrasse 150 (tel. 329 009). 20 rooms and excellent sporting amenities. *Weisse* (I), Dorfstrasse 1 (tel. 329 630). 10 simple rooms and inexpensive restaurant.

CIERGNON. Summer residence of the Belgian Royal Family. *Auberge de la Collyre* (I), rue Principale 64 (tel. 377 146). 10 rooms, garden restaurant.

COMBLAIN-LA-TOUR. *St. Roch* (E), rue du Parc 1, (tel. 691 333). The best in the valley, has a pleasant garden-terrace overlooking the river; 15 rooms, all with bath; also has superb but rather pricey restaurant.

DURBUY. An ideal vacation center, well provided with hotels, 32 km. (20 miles) from Huy. *Cardinal* (E), rue des Recollectines 66 (tel. 086–211 088). 7 luxurious rooms in old mansion. *Sanglier des Ardennes* (M), Grand'rue 99 (tel. 211 088). 20 rooms, 5 with bath; also has a restaurant which is one of the gastronomic highspots of the region; their game dishes in season are superb. *Roches Fleuris* (M), Grand'Place 96 (tel. 212 882). 30 comfortable rooms and restaurant. *Clos des Recollets* (I), rue de la Prévôté 64 (tel. 211 271). 10 rooms, 7 with bath; eat downstairs in the *Prévôté* (I) (tel. 212 300). Good grilled dishes and trout in a peaceful setting.

EUPEN. With the giant dam just outside the city. *Bosten* (M), Vervierserstrasse 2 (tel. 552 209). 11 well-equipped rooms. *Schmitz-Roth* (I), Rathausplatz 13, (tel. 552 078). 27 modest rooms.

Restaurant. *Gourmet* (M), Haasstrasse 81 (tel. 740 800). Gastronomic food, but not at astronomic prices. Also has 12 rooms.

FLORENVILLE. Good overnight halt. *France* (I), rue Généraux Cuvelier 26 (tel. 311 032). 34 rooms, some with bath.

FRANCORCHAMPS. *Roannay* (E), rte. de Spa 155 (tel. 087–275 311). 21 rooms; pool and top-class restaurant. Right at the motor racetrack and named after its most dangerous curve, *L'Eau Rouge* (M), rue de L'Eau Rouge 287 (tel. 087–275 124). 7 well equipped rooms, patronized by some of the star drivers. *Moderne* (I), rte. de Spa 129 (tel. 087–275 026). 14 rooms, all with bath; has restaurant.

HAMOIR. South of Liège on the road to Durbuy. *La Bonne Auberge* (I), pl. Delcourt 10 (tel. 086–388 208). 6 rooms and restaurant.

Restaurant *De la Poste* (M), rue du Pont 32 (tel. 086–388 324). Excellent fish.

HAN-SUR-LESSE. *Voyageurs* (M), rue des Chasseurs 1 (tel. 084–377 237). 39 rooms, most with bath, plus an inexpensive restaurant. *Ardennes* (M), rue des Grottes 2 (tel. 084–377 220). 24 rooms and restaurant.

Restaurant. *Belle Vue* (M), rue Joseph Lamotte 1 (tel. 084–377 227). Good local food, on offer since 1868.

HERBEUMONT. *Hostellerie du Prieuré de Conques* (E), rte. de Florenville 176 (tel. 411 417). Former abbey; 11 superb rooms. Fine cuisine as you would expect from a *Relais et Châteaux* establishment, well worth the price. Superb location deep in the woods on the banks of the Semois. Hunting parties. Best book ahead.

Châtelaine (I), Grand'Place 127 (tel. 411 422). Good budget value, with 36 rooms, 26 with bath. Restaurant and garden.

HOTTON-SUR-OURTHE. Between Durbuy and La Roche-en-Ardenne. *l'Ourthe* (I), rue de la Vallée 20 (tel. 084–466 391). 11 rooms and restaurant.

Restaurant. *Le Seize Cors* (M), rue des Ecoles 15 (tel. 084–466 290). Try their game dishes.

HOUFFALIZE. *Château des Cheras* (M), route de Liege 10 (tel. 062–288 028). 17 atmospheric rooms in an ancient manor. *Vieille Auberge* (M), rue du Pont 4 (tel. 062–289 060). 6 comfortable rooms. Restaurant offers traditional Ardennes cuisine.

HOUYET. Starting point of canoe or boat trip down to the Meuse. On the road to Dinant 4 km. (2½ miles) outside town is *Marquisette* (I), rue Sanzinne 1 (tel. 666 429). 10 rooms and a pleasant restaurant.

MALMÉDY. *Au St. Esprit* (M), rue Jules Steinbach 17 (tel. 080–777 314). 6 rooms and good restaurant. On hilltop at Bévérce, 3 km. (2 miles) north, overlooking town with great views is *Grand Champs* (M), tel. 777 247, a converted farmhouse with 42 rooms. Back in town there is the *Auberge de la Warche* (I), place de Rome 12 (tel. 080–777 364). 6 basic rooms.

Restaurants. Less than 6 km. (4 miles) on the Eupen road is *Trôs Marets* (E), Mont 1 (tel. 337 917). A gourmet's shrine, which also has 7 rooms and 4 suites. Tops in service, with prices to match. Exceptional views. For an unpretentious meal in town, try *Au Petit Louvain* (I), Chemin-rue 47 (tel. 080–777 415).

NADRIN. Near the Hérou gorge. By far the best is *Les Ondes* (M), rte. de la Roche 15 (tel. 444 111). 13 rooms, 5 with bath; fine restaurant.

Restaurant. *Le Cabri* (E), rte. du Hérou 2 (tel. 444 185). Magnificent and imaginative food in a lovely restaurant with attractive views. Great game in season. Also has 4 rooms.

ROBERTVILLE. *Bains* (E), Lac de Robertville 46 (tel. 679 571). 15 rooms and superb restaurant with great game dishes; 1 mile from town center, beside lake with view. Less expensive is the *International* (M), rue du Centre 76 (tel. 446 258). 14 rooms and inexpensive restaurant.

LA ROCHE-EN-ARDENNE. Has almost two dozen hotels and pensions. *Des Ardennes* (M), rue de Beausaint 2 (tel. 084–411 112). 12 rooms, all with bath. Good restaurant. *Beau Rivage* (I), Quai de l'Ourthe 26 (tel. 084–411 235). 11 rooms, restaurant. *Moderne* (I), rue Chamont 26 (tel. 084–411 124). 12 rooms—good value.

Restaurants. *Vieux Château* (E), Pesserue 6 (tel. 084–411 327). Try their venison in season. *Le Chalet* (M), rue du Chalet 61 (tel. 084–411 197). Good river views, with fish and game to match. A little out of town is *Air Pur* (E), route de Houffalize 11 (tel. 084–411 503). Reopened and rejuvenated spot—excellent food, and 11 rooms. Often closed, so check.

ROCHEFORT. Grottos, ancient city, vacation center. *la Malle Poste* (E), rue de Behogne 46 (tel. 084–210 986). 12 comfortable rooms and restaurant with terrace. *Falizes* (M), rue de France 70 (tel. 084–211 282). On the road to Han, with 6 rooms with bath and a very good restaurant (E).

ST. HUBERT. In the legendary St. Hubertus forest. *Borquin* (I), pl. de l'Abbaye 6 (tel. 061–611 456). 9 rooms, inexpensive restaurant. *Luxembourg* (I), pl. du Marché 7 (tel. 061–611 093). Pleasant spot with 8 rooms. *De l'Abbaye* (I), pl. du Marché 18 (tel. 061–611 023). 20 rooms with reasonable restaurant.

Restaurant. *La Petite Fringale* (M), rue St. Gilles 36 (tel. 061–612 559). Small local restaurant, serving Ardennes cuisine.

ST. VITH. *Zur Post* (E), Hauptstrasse 39 (tel. 228 027). 8 comfortable rooms and top-class restaurant. *Pip Margraff* (M), Hauptstrasse 7 (tel. 228 663). 16 rooms and restaurant.

SOUGNÉ-REMOUCHAMPS. Interesting grottos. *Cheval Blanc* (M), rue de Louveigné 1 (tel. 844 417). 13 rooms and an inexpensive restaurant. *Bonhomme Royal Hôtel des Etrangers* (M), rue de la Reffe 26 (tel. 844 006). 12 rooms, with restaurant offering excellent guinea-fowl.

Restaurant. *Le Bienvenu* (I), rue de Louveigné 7 (tel. 844 585). Good local cuisine.

SPA. Many hotels and restaurants in this classic ancient resort. Overlooking the main square is the traditional *Cardinal* (E), pl. Royale 23 (tel. 087–877 208). 29 rooms, almost all with bath, and an excellent restaurant. At **Balmoral,** with excellent views, is *Dorint Hotel Ardennes* (E), rte. de Balmoral 33 (tel. 772 581). A modern hotel with 95 fully equipped rooms, offering a wide range of facilities. At the lower end of the price range, try *l'Avenue* (I), ave. Reine Astrid 48 (tel. 087–772 067). 12 rooms and restaurant.

Restaurants. Best in town is the *Grand Maur* (E), rue Xhrouet 41 (tel. 087–773 616) which serves superb regional specialties in a 200-year-old building.

For a change try *le Rimini* (M), rue du Marché 56 (tel. 087–771 583). Serves delightful Italian dishes—don't miss the homemade pasta.

On the edge of town, along the road to Francorchamps, stop off at *la Ferme de Malchamps* (M), rte. de la Sauvenière 201 (tel. 275 273). Housed in a whitewashed converted farmhouse, it offers excellent local cuisine. At the other side of town, you should head for **Creppe**, 3 km. (2 miles) southwest of town by the ave. Clementine. There you'll find *Manoir de Lébioles* (E) (tel. 771 020). One of the most expensive restaurants in the country, set in delightful rural surroundings. Also has 6 rooms.

At **Tiège**, 5 km. (3 miles) northeast of Spa, off the road to Verviers: *Charmille* (M), route de Tiège 44 (tel. 474 313). 33 rooms; an old hotel of fine repute. Try the great *boeuf stroganoff* in their restaurant.

Near **La Reid**, an attractive village 8 km. (5 miles) before Spa on the road from Remouchamps, you should seek out *À la Retraite de l'Empereur* (M), Basse Desnié 842 (tel. 376 215). You leave La Reid to the south, and follow the signs to Desnié, where you will soon see signs directing you to the restaurant. Inside it has an old-fashioned atmosphere, antique furniture and open fires. The bar is intimate, with saddle stools.

STAVELOT. *Val d'Amblève* (M), rte. de Malmédy 7 (tel. 882 353). A cozy spot with 18 rooms, outstanding food, and many amenities. *Hôtel d'Orange* (I), rue de Spa 8 (tel. 882 005). 24 simple rooms.

Restaurant. *Au Vieux Moulin* (M), Petit Coo 2 (tel. 684 041). Good food in quaint surroundings. Try their raspberry profiterolles.

VERVIERS. Recent is the *Amigo* (L), rue Herla 1 (tel. 087–221 121). A younger brother of the Brussels Amigo. 54 rooms with bath, restaurant, pool and many other amenities. *Grand Hôtel* (M), rue des Palais 145 (tel. 087–223 177). 11 rooms, 3 with bath.

Restaurants. The best in town is the atmospheric *Maison Moulan* (M), Crapaurue 37 (tel. 312 250). A 17th-century house just by the Palais de Justice. Less expensive is *Porte de Heusy* (I), rue Heusy 96 (tel. 221 950). In a 16th-century house. Just south of the town at **Heusy** is *De la Toque d'Or* (E), ave. Fernand Nicolaï 43 (tel. 221 111). Chalet-style building with alpine ambience.

VIELSALM. *Les Fougères* (M), Baraque Fraiture 39 (tel. 080–418 707). 20 rooms and restaurant. *Belle Vue* (I), rue Jean Bertholet 5 (tel. 080–216 261). 14 rooms and modest restaurant.

VILLERS-SUR-LESSE. *Beau Sejour* (M), rue Village 15 (tel. 377 115). 22 rooms, a restaurant and pool; it is also a well-known angling spot.

VIRTON. *Cheval Blanc* (M), rue du Moulin 1 (tel. 578 935). 11 rooms, 6 with bath; good restaurant.

VRESSE-SUR-SEMOIS. Just inside the Belgian border. *Hostellerie de la Semois* (I), rue Grande 37 (tel. 061–500 033). 26 rooms with pleasant restaurant. *Moulin Simonis* (I), rue de Charleville 42 (tel. 061–500 081). 7 comfortable rooms and excellent restaurants in converted mill.

GETTING AROUND. By train. The Ardennes can be explored quite easily by train. There are several secondary lines from Namur and Liège which run into the region. However in common with most branch lines the services are not particularly frequent or fast. There are several railway stations on these lines from which bicycles can be hired, and they can often be returned to stations other than the one they were hired from. For the energetic this is an ideal way to get off the beaten track and explore this beautiful region.

By bus. There is a widespread network of buslines and you can probably reach even the remotest village by public transport.

By car. To get the maximum enjoyment out of your visit to this area, you should tour the region by car. Its complex network of valleys and rivers makes any other method terribly time-consuming and tiring. From Brussels a direct motorway (A3/E40) will take you east to Liège, 94 km. (58 miles), whence it is possible to branch out on a dozen different routes. For the southern Ardennes, the best route from Brussels is the A4/E411, which passes close to Han-sur-Lesse en route for Arlon and Luxembourg. The A26/E25 links Arlon and Bastogne with Liège.

By scooter. For the adventurous, one good way of seeing the many lovely hidden little châteaux and farm houses is to hire a small motor scooter for a few days; no license needed.

MUSEUMS AND PLACES OF INTEREST. ARLON. **Musée Luxembourgeois** (Luxembourg Museum), rue des Martyrs 13. Merovingian relics and a collection of Roman tombstones unique to Belgium. Open 10 to 12, 2 to 5; Sun. 10 to 4. **Eglise St. Donat.** Located atop a strategic hill, known as *la Knipchen,* this church has always doubled as a fortress. Its towers offer an excellent view of the surrounding countryside. The town also has a **Roman Tower** of the 3rd century near the Grand'Place.

BASTOGNE. Bastogne Historical Center. Modern star-shaped gallery, with material from the Battle of the Bulge, an amphitheater with displays and a cinema that shows footage made during the battle itself. Open June to Aug., 8 to 7; 9 to 6, rest of the year. Closed mid-Nov. to mid-Mar. Admission BF 80.

Au Pays d'Ardenne Original Museum, rue de Neufchâteau 20. This curiously named institution explains how the people of the Ardennes worked for their living in times gone by. Open daily, 10 to 5. Admission BF 80.

Musée de la Parole au Pays de Bastogne, maison Mathelin. Dedicated to local customs, folklore and dialect. Open weekdays, except Mon., 2 to 6; weekends 11 to 12.30 and 2 to 6.

BOUILLON. Château. A fine example of medieval military fortifications. A must for all castle lovers to drool over. Open 9 to around 6 (times change with the year). Closed Dec. through Feb.

Musée Ducal (Ducal Museum), rue du Petit 1. An 18th-century house with archeology and folklore collections. Open April to Oct., 9 to 6.30.

EUPEN. Musée de la Vie Regionale, Gospertstrasse 52. Housed in an elegant town house dating from 1697, the museum explains the history of this unique German-speaking corner of Belgium.

FOURNEAU ST. MICHEL. (5 miles north of St. Hubert.) **Iron Museum.** Fascinating relics and ancient foundry which produced cannons for Americans in the War of Independence. Open 9 to 5 (6 weekends); Sat. and Sun. only in mid-winter.

HAN-SUR-LESSE. Musée du Monde Souterrain (Grotto Museum). Small museum of the exciting things found in the vast grottos, from the Bronze Age onwards. Open end-April to mid-Oct., 10 to 12, 1 to 6. There is also an audiovisual display.

ORVAL. The Abbey. Once one of the richest and most powerful abbeys in Europe. Sacked in 1793. Open 9 to 12, 1.30 to 6 summer; shorter hours in winter—enquire at Tourist Office for details. Admission BF 50.

LA ROCHE-EN-ARDENNE. Château. Reached by steps opposite the town hall. A romantic ruined castle with game park. Open 9 to 7 Easter, Jul., Aug. only.
Pottery, rue Rompré, for famous blue-gray local earthenware. Open 10 to 12, 2 to 4.30 (3 to 5 Sat.).

ST. HUBERT. Church of St. Hubert. 16th-century Gothic church attached to 7th-century Benedictine abbey.
Church of St. Gilles. A much simpler Romanesque structure dating back to the 12th century.
Game Park, to the northwest of the town; open 9 to 6 (5 in winter).

SPA. Musée de la Ville d'Eau (Town Museum), avenue Reine Astrid 77. Historic collection of relics and documents evoking the great old days of the "ville d'eau." Open 10.30 to 12, 2.30 to 6 mid-June to mid-September (otherwise, Sat. and Sun. only).
Eglise de Saints Hermès et Alexandre. This is a remarkably preserved 11th-century church, with vestiges of 7th-century foundations. The ceiling is decorated with 127 17th-century frescos.
Franchimont Castle at Theux, 5 miles north of the town, is open 9 to 8 (5 in winter).

STAVELOT. Musée de l'Ancienne Abbaye (Former Abbey Museum). Regional history and a section on local crafts, especially the traditional craft of tanning; housed in an 18th-century wing of the old Abbey. Art exhibitions are held Easter to end Sept. Open every day from Easter to end Sept., 10.30 to 12, 2.30 to 5.30.
Trésor de St.-Sebastien (Treasury of the Church of St. Sebastian), rue de l'Eglise. One of the richest in the country; includes a gold Shrine of St. Remacle and other marvelous pieces. Open 10 to 12, 2 to 5, as long as services are not in progress.
Musée Guillaume Apollinaire, Hôtel de Ville. Documents relating to the poet's stay in Stavelot and early copies of his work. Open July and August 10.30 to 12 and 2.30 to 5.30. Admission BF 20.

VIRTON. Musée Gaumais (Gaumais Museum), rue d'Arlon. Intriguing museum of local archeological finds, housed in an old convent. Open 9.30 to 12, 2 to 6. Closed Tues.

VRESSE. Musée du Tabac, rue Albert Raty. Displays items on role of tobacco in Semois valley's life and history. Open mid-March to mid-November, weekdays 1 to 5, weekends 11 to 1 and 3 to 7. Admission BF 100.

SPORTS. The rivers Ourthe, Vesdre, Amblève, and Semois are ideal for **canoeing** and is the Lesse, although it is not without danger between Houyet and Dinant. For more canoeing information contact: C.C.C.W., rue Hocheporte 123, Liège. The most attractive **boating** excursions will take you from Houyet to Anseremme on the Lesse and from Chiny to Lacuisine on the meandering Semois. You can devote your vacation to **fishing** for eel, trout, pike, and crawfish in all the above-named rivers as well as the Salm and Warche. Most riverside hotels have their own fishing stretches. You should buy a permit from local post offices.

Well-marked and well-chosen footpaths increase the pleasure of **hiking.**

Barely 4 km. (2 miles) from the center of Spa is an airfield for **sport flying** at Spa-la Sauvenière. There are flying clubs at St. Hubert and Temploux.

There are 6 good **downhill** ski runs in the area and several centers for **cross-country** ski-ing around Malmédy and Spa. For information on snow conditions and pistes ring ADEPS in Brussels (tel. 513 94 40). Locally, call (080) 883 021 for information on downhill pistes and 684 254 for cross-country conditions.

SPAS AND CASINOS. Spa, whose name became a generic term for health resorts, has several mineral springs of high iron content. Baths with carbonized water, as well as mud- and turf-baths are natural therapeutic agents for all forms of arthritis, and particularly for gout. Contact l'Etablissement Thermal, pl. Royale 2, B-4880 Spa (tel. 087–772 535).

Spa's casino has played host to the rich and famous for over two centuries. For more information on games of chance, contact Casino de Spa, rue Royale 4 (tel. 772 052).

USEFUL ADDRESSES. City Tourist Offices: Arlon, Pavilon du Tourisme, place Léopold (tel. 216 360); Bouillon, Bureau du Château Fort (tel. 466 257), during the high season at the Porte de France (tel. 466 289); Durbuy, Halle aux Blés (tel. 212 428); Eupen, Bergstrasse 6 (tel. 553 450); Florenville, place Albert-ler (tel. 311 229); La Roche, Hôtel de Ville (tel. 411 342) or Provincial Office, quai de l'Ourthe 9 (tel. 411 012); Malmédy, pl. de Rome (tel. 777 250); St. Hubert, pl. de l'Abbaye (tel. 611 299); Spa, rue Royale 2 (tel. 771 700); Stavelot, Ancienne Abbaye (tel. 882 330); Trois-Ponts, rte. de Coo (tel. 684 539); Vresse-sur-Semois, Centre Touristique, rue Grande (tel. 500 827).

EXPLORING LUXEMBOURG

LUXEMBOURG AND ITS PEOPLE

Industry in Fairyland

by
D. NED BLACKMER

When you try to locate Luxembourg on a map, look for "Lux." at the heart of Western Europe. Even abbreviated, the name runs over: west into Belgium, east into Germany, south into France, as the country's influence has done for centuries.

The shape of the land is roughly that of a wooden shoe resting on its heel with the toe pointed toward Holland. This is appropriate enough, as there are certain tenuous affinities between the Luxembourg and Dutch languages, and the royal houses of both countries have a link with Vianden, a majestic castle in the Luxembourg Ardennes, ancient cradle of the Orange-Nassau dynasty.

This land of 2,586 sq. km (999 sq. miles) offers variety and contrasts out of all proportion to its size. On the northern borders of Luxembourg and down along the Our and Sûre rivers is a rugged, wildly-beautiful highland country studded with castles from four hundred to more than a thousand years old, rich in history, where industrious present-day Luxembourgers have created a lovely lake and one of the most ingenious hydro-electric installations in the world. Castles still abound as you travel south through rich farmlands lying in the broad, central valleys of the Attert, Eisch, Mamer, and Alzette rivers, or follow the eastern frontier down the Wine Route through the lush Moselle Valley. In the southern plains, above green farms, rise turrets, not of the past, but of great industrial installations that make Luxembourg the world's highest *per capita* producer of steel. If you turn back north from the French border, a twenty-minute drive will bring the capital into view, its spires towering above the south-central plain. Seen through early morning mists it revives the magic of Camelot. It is the nerve-center of a thousand-year old seat of government, a functional working element of the European Community, a spot where the past still speaks, the present interprets, and the future listens.

The Historic Background

There is no scientific evidence that people lived in Luxembourg earlier than the Pleistocene period, although it is not impossible. From that time, however, the evidence is definite and may be seen; much of it in the excellently-organized National Museum, more throughout the land itself. At Oetrange were found traces of Magdalenian man, at Reuland a nearly-complete Mesolithic skeleton. Megalithic remains near Diekirch and Manternach show that Neolithic man lived here, as the Celts, perhaps the best known of our prehistoric forebears, did later.

Despite their different tribes, of whom the Treviri (Trier) and Mediomatrici (Metz) were most important in Luxembourg, the Celts were united in Druidic faith. On the Titelberg, at Helperknapp, Widenberg, and through the Mullerthal were refuges where Celtic priests, the Druids, confirmed the people in loyalty among themselves and resistance to all invaders, deep-rooted traits of character which Luxembourgers exhibit today.

In historic times Julius Caesar, having repulsed the Helvetii and subdued the Belgae, turned his legions toward the Treviri. Although their leader, Indutiomar, perished in battle in 53 B.C., the people fought on until defeated at a river, probably the Alzette below Luxembourg. Roman dominion over the area lasted nearly five centuries, and Ardennes smoked ham and Moselle wines found their way to the Lucullan feasts, to be praised by Roman poets like Ausonius and Fortunatus. Yet Augustus, Tiberius, Vespasian and other of the eagle emperors faced attempts by the people to regain independence. Roman paganism did not succeed in stamping out the officially-forbidden Druidism, but Christianity was established early in Luxembourg, probably before the fourth century.

As archeology and written records span the flow of time, tying today to the remotest past, so the history of Luxembourg is marked by actual bridges, or their remains. During the development of the Moselle waterway, which provides a fine navigational link between the French canal-system and the Rhine complex, there were discovered at Stadtbredimus the iron-sheathed piles which supported the old Roman bridge. At Ettelbruck, the very name of the town (Attila's Bridge) recalls the Hun's passage as he hacked his way to Chalons. Nearby is the Hunnebour, a favorite picnic-spot, where the invaders are supposed to have watered their horses. In Luxembourg City and throughout the land are bridges which recall some chapter of history. To find and identify them, and through their tangible evidence to apprehend some bygone episode of our story, is an engaging pastime.

After the various incursions of the Suevi, Alans, Vandals, Huns and Visigoths, the area had become firmly Frankish by the middle of the 5th century. The urban civilization spread by Rome—which left fine mosaic floors, stonework and many artifacts for us to see—receded, and a new rural culture arose.

With the conversion of Clovis to Christianity in 496, missionaries brought their message through the forests and fastnesses of Luxembourg, where local pagan religions and Druidism persisted (traces still linger in spots). Next, the monasteries were founded, which united the people and exercised a vital educational and civilizing influence from then throughout the Middle Ages. Not the least of these is that of Echternach, founded around 700 by St. Willibrord, an Anglo-Saxon from Northumberland.

Under Charlemagne, Luxembourg was a part of the great Frankish realm. The Emperor caused about a thousand Saxon families to be established in the then thinly populated Ardennes region, an ethnic transplant which left signs in the people and on the land. Out of the dismemberment of Charlemagne's domains rose the beginnings of the Luxembourg of today.

On April 12, 963, the Abbey of Saint Maximin in Trier, by a deed which can still be examined in the Municipal Library, granted Sigefroi, youngest Count of Ardennes, certain lands that included the ruins of a Roman fort known as Castellum Lucilinburhuc. This citadel stood on a land-bridge at the crossing of the great consular road, Paris-Reims-Arlon-Trier, with that running from Metz toward Aix-la-Chapelle. The remains of the fortress Sigefroi erected were revealed to public view on the thousandth anniversary of his purchase, after having been hidden for centuries beneath and within the fortifications which grew from his original castle. From this stronghold, Sigefroi's sword reached out and a town and country grew up that were called Lützelburg.

The House of Luxembourg

It is as well to remember that from these times and for several centuries, countries were defined not so much by boundaries as by the families who lived in such castles and the influence they exerted through prowess at arms, interlocking oaths of fealty, and inter-marriage, both upon the country round about their citadels and often upon distant lands.

The influence of the House of Luxembourg waxed and waned through the centuries. William (1096–1128) was the first to be officially designated Count of Luxembourg. From the fortress-town of Luxembourg and from castles among the Ardennes crags, succeeding counts of Luxembourg extended their domains and sway by the sword. From Esch-sur-Sûre, Hollenfels, Bourscheid and their other strongholds, they sallied forth to the Crusades. Luxembourg knights stood with Godfrey of Bouillon in the Holy City and Luxembourg barons in subsequent Crusades fell in Asia Minor and Mesopotamia. The country suffered from the absence of its lords protector—and from their return. Debt-ridden, they sold, gambled, and generally mismanaged their estates into bankruptcy.

A Medieval Modern Woman

Countess Ermesinde (1196–1247) was, upon the death of her father, Henry IV the Blind, in a sorry plight. A minor, her County of Luxembourg attached by the House of Hohenstaufen, the County of Namur which her father had united to Luxembourg seemingly lost to her, she needed protection. Marriage with Théobald of Bar (Bar-le-Duc), a descendant of Wigerik, Sigefroi's father, restored her lost patrimony and added the Counties of Durbuy and Laroche. After Théobald's death, Ermesinde, now 18, married Waleran of Limburg who brought to their union the Marquisate of Arlon. When Waleran died in 1225, Ermesinde took the government into her own hands.

Her administration re-established Luxembourg's prestige, and her reforms presaged future reforms. Power was drawn from the separate and feuding lords to a central sovereign by the creation of officers of the court, a kind of council of state; by appointing competent provosts rather than allowing functional offices to be handed on hereditarily; by establishing a court of feudal justice (which lasted with modifications until 1795); by bringing villages and free towns under her own authority. Charters of freedom were given Echternach, Thionville and Luxembourg, but Ermesinde furthered the cause of freedom on more essential levels in extending the rights of justice to the burghers in all but criminal cases, giving them freedom to move about and dispose of their own goods and chattels, limiting the *droit du seigneur,* establishing a primitive form of social security, and by other acts assuring individual liberties we today take for granted. Aware that freedom depended upon intellectual and moral development, she established schools, convents, monasteries, and other institutions of education and culture. At her death, she who had begun as a weak and defenseless girl in a cut-throat man's world, left a sovereign and unified nation competently administered, with social institutions whose effects remained for centuries.

The Power Game

In the 14th century the House of Luxembourg made its bid to dominate all Europe. In 1308, Henry VII, known as an enlightened prince, a just man, and gifted administrator, was elected to the throne of the Holy Roman Empire through the influence of his brother Baldwin, Archbishop of Trier, and of Pierre d'Aspelt, Archbishop-Prince-Elector of Mainz, one of the most astute politicians of the day and himself a Luxembourger. Henry VII's reign fulfilled its promise. He lies in the Cathedral of Pisa, prematurely dead of malaria during an expedition which he hoped would bring the continent under united rule.

John, Henry's son, was the full embodiment of the knightly ideal. War was the temper of the time, and John battled his way up and down Europe from the Carpathians to Crécy. For the first thirty years of his reign, until he lost his sight and became known as John the Blind, only four springs passed in which he did not set out upon a major military venture, which carried him triumphantly from the Schelde to the Vistula and from the Baltic to the Po. Count of Luxembourg, King of Bohemia, John the Blind is Luxembourg's national hero still. A man of his word, he responded to the appeal of Philip VI when Edward III of England invaded France and, sightless on the battlefield of Crécy, ordered his followers to lead him into the heart of the fight, where he was slain. The victorious Black Prince is reputed to have said, "The battle was not worth the death of this man." He took the three ostrich feathers of John's helmet and adopted his maxim, *Ich dien*, "I serve." The feathers and motto are still displayed on the coat of arms of the Prince of Wales.

Charles IV, son of John the Blind, achieved by marriage and treaty the dominion his father had sought by the sword; and *his* son, the Emperor Wenceslas, brought the rule of the House of Luxembourg its greatest extension. From the North Sea to the borders of Muscovy, and from the Baltic to the Alpine cantons and beyond, the red lion of Luxembourg held his paw over a domain roughly 500 times the size of today's Grand Duchy. The Grand Duchy proper was, at its largest, four times its present size.

With Sigismund (1368–1437), Emperor after Wenceslas, the greatest era of Luxembourg's imperial glory passed. The people themselves cannot have greatly mourned, for imperial power had meant that Luxembourg's rulers resided abroad, increasingly looking to the home country as a source of troops for their armies and revenues for their support. Six years after the death of Sigismund, the country had lost its independence, its autonomy and its dynasty, to become a province under Philip the Good, Duke of Burgundy. It was to remain subject for just over 400 years—variously to Burgundy, Spain, France or Austria. Throughout this foreign rule the procession of conquerors filed through the capital of the little country that accepted them and tried elaborately to pretend they weren't there. Although it was always a special province with specific rights, Luxembourg's rulers never let the people forget that they were now subject—and the Luxembourgers never forgot that they had been free. Their birthright of freedom was a passion that centuries of occupation could not cool.

Division and Independence

Yet, given the politics of the times, the men who controlled the destinies of nations dared not free Luxembourg. The capital, through successive fortifications and because of its strategic position, had become too significant to bypass and too strong for any powerful nation to leave exposed to others. The Congress of Vienna, attempting to solve this problem among others, gave the eastern portion of the Duchy to

Prussia, ceded the remainder to William of Orange-Nassau, raised the title of the dismembered country to Grand Duchy, and guaranteed its independence. Strange independence! It brought to the capital a temporary Prussian occupation army that stayed for 52 years. In 1839 another dismemberment gave more than half of William's territory to Belgium. Independence, neutrality, and autonomy were guaranteed anew to the tiny remnant—but the Prussian garrison stayed. The trouble was that too many nations turned uneasy eyes to this fortress-capital at the fulcrum of Europe. Accordingly, in 1867, the European Powers met in London to certify Luxembourg's freedom and to insist that the fortress be dismantled.

The usually undemonstrative Luxembourgers danced in the streets as the Prussians departed and hastened to underline their regained freedom by affirming anew their constitution. On October 19, 1868, this charter proclaimed to the world: "The Grand Duchy of Luxembourg forms a free state, independent, and indivisible."

Progress and Stress

The history of Luxembourg since 1868 is that of a country progressing in less than 100 years from the position of a feudal province to that of an autonomous modern nation. Progress has been interrupted twice: in 1914–1918 by Wilhelm II's Germany and in 1940–1945 by Hitler's dream of a thousand-year Reich.

Luxembourg emerged from the turmoil that marked the close of the 18th century and the opening of the 19th, exhausted and impoverished; a primarily agricultural country which could hardly feed itself. Thousands of people emigrated, so that there are few Luxembourg families without relatives in some other part of the world. It was discovered that fine steel could be made from the iron ore deposits in the south of the country, using the innovations of the English engineers Thomas and Gilchrist with phosphorus for smelting, and a great industry arose. The development paid off two ways, for it was found that the wastes from the smelting provided exactly the fertilizers needed to make the soil of the northern and central farmlands commercially productive. Prosperity followed upon intelligent exploitation and hard work, and emigration dwindled.

The war of 1914–1918 put an end to this period and the Grand Duchy was again an occupied country. More than 3,000 Luxembourgers died fighting with the Allies, a huge *per capita* sacrifice for so small a nation. Peace brought unsettled conditions until a plebiscite was held to determine whether the Grand Duchy should become a republic and elect a president, or whether Charlotte, sister of the Grand Duchess Marie-Adelaide (who abdicated at the close of World War I) should accede to the throne. The people voted overwhelmingly for Charlotte and, as Grand Duchess, she enjoyed undiminished popularity throughout her reign.

In 1921, a customs and economic treaty was signed with Belgium: public welfare and social security administrations were inaugurated, and women gained the right to vote. The Grandy Duchy became a member of the League of Nations, and Luxembourg's pavilions in expositions like the Paris and New York Fairs demonstrated to the world what a small country could achieve. Emile Mayrisch, Luxembourg steel magnate, was elected head of the International Steel Cartel, and by the eve of World War II the Grand Duchy ranked seventh among the world's producers of steel. Until 1940, despite the depression, productivity and prosperity grew.

On May 10, 1940, a full-scale Nazi invasion overran the country within hours. The royal family and members of the government escaped to found a government-in-exile. But it was within the country that the people stubbornly, systematically, heroically resisted. After all, Luxembourgers had centuries of training for this. Young Luxembourgers escaped *Festung Europa* to enlist with the British, Canadian, Free French, Free Belgian and United States armies. When military service in the Wehrmacht was imposed, Luxembourgers nailed the country's flag to the masts of their factories and went out on strike. Such acts, of course, inevitably led to reprisals and privations, but no suffering could modify the peoples' determination to maintain their identity. The suffering was monstrous. At war's end, largely owing to the Battle of the Bulge, 35 percent of the farmland could not be tilled, the homes of 60,000 people were rubble, 160 bridges and tunnels had been destroyed, miles of railway track had been removed and the rolling stock hauled away, over half the roads were destroyed, and the steel plants practically burnt out from forced overproduction.

Despite all, Luxembourg was soon on its feet after the war, thanks in large part to the peoples' sense of purpose, and solidarity, and to hard work. The farms, increasingly mechanized, returned to prosperous yields; homes were rebuilt. The country's railway system was restored, as was the highway system, and the steel plants, until other countries overtook their rebuilding program, briefly carried Luxembourg to sixth place in world production. A conscious attempt to attract other industries, to reduce dependence on steel, led to the establishment of factories making among other things rubber tires, plastics, machinery and chemicals, a policy of diversification still followed. By the fifties Luxembourg's gross national product *per capita,* was exceeded only by that of the U.S.A., Australia, Sweden, Canada, and Switzerland. Having attained one of the highest living standards, it is unlikely that the people will relinquish it.

European Involvement

Against this background, Luxembourg rediscovered its European importance. A participant since 1948 in building the Benelux Economic Union, since 1950 in the Coal and Steel Community, in the European Defense Community until its demise, since 1957 in the European Economic Community, in the Council of Europe, EURATOM, OECD, GATT, and a host of other acronymic entities, Luxembourg has demonstrated in practical ways both its faith in a common destiny for Europe and its expertise in international negotiation. More than once the suggestions of Luxembourg diplomats have been a factor leading to closer identification of policy or organization, opening the way for wider collaboration and closer ties among nations. It is a role only a small country can fulfil without arousing suspicions, and one in which Luxembourg has earned respect by its clear, honest, and highly-effective statesmanship.

The largest bridge in Luxembourg, named for the Grand Duchess Charlotte, unites the city proper with the plateau of the Kirchberg, from which the tall European Center building dominates the townscape, a symbol and a nucleus of the European vocation of the capital. It is the home of the Secretariat of the European Parliament and for three months of the year the meeting place of the Council of Ministers of the European Communities. The Grand Duchy is the seat of the Court of Justice of the European Communities, and will be the home of any other juridical bodies to be formed by the Communities. The European Investment Bank has been transferred to Luxembourg, further adding to the country's importance as an international financial center, a development dating back to 1929, as many holding companies know to their satisfaction; and the Luxembourg Stock Exchange both quotes and issues international stocks in all foreign currencies.

In this period of transition, when individuals and nations are preoccupied with the search for identity, may it not be that this small country, which has preserved its character over centuries of contention to rise from economic disaster to a respected place in the councils of the world, affords an example worthy of close study? From experience, Luxembourg knows how dangerous it is to live on past glories, but it draws from its heritage the lessons to seek new initiatives, make new efforts and to maintain its progress in collaborative endeavours.

Yet, on the surface, the city and the country seem to go their placid way, with the customary rhythms of life hardly ruffled by international figures, the comings and goings of diplomats, modern pressures, or the jet flights which tie this country in the heart of Europe to the ends of the earth. A Luxembourger remains a Luxembourger, and this attitude of his, refined in the crucible of history, is cast in steel as tempered as the high-quality product of his mills.

The People's Character

"Mir woelle bleiwe wat mir sin"—"We want to remain what we are," is the national motto of Luxembourg, not only carved above the porticoes of town halls or painted in houses, as you will find, but also written as their history demonstrates in the hearts of the people as a whole. But what *is* it they want to remain? What caprice makes them so ardently insist upon an identity apart from their more powerful neighbors? Joseph Bech, a former Foreign Minister of Luxembourg, noted some years ago, "It has often been said . . . that the Grand Duchy is only an artificial creation of European diplomacy. This is not true. From the 15th century onwards Luxembourg was a distinct principality, enjoying its privileges as such whether under the domination of Burgundy, of Spain, or of Austria." An English historian wrote "Surrounded by France, Germany and Belgium, this little country is neither French, Belgian nor German, nor a mixture of the three, but has an entirely distinctive physical, social and ethnic character of its own."

The saying that Luxembourg is less a country than a state of mind is nearly true, for it is in the minds and hearts of its people that the Grand Duchy's character is found. The people's strength lies in their will to "remain what they are," simple farming and industrial folk whose lines have, nevertheless, gone out to all the earth. Luxembourgers are close to their land, and it is natural that their primary concern should be with simpler, more eternal matters like births, deaths, marriages, crops, or whether the price of steel warrants asking for higher wages. The concerns of the young people are the concerns of young people everywhere; their period of rebellion is of their own time but then, with marriage, a job and children, their nonconformist impulses are integrated into the longer line of traditional progress.

Along with their simplicity, Luxembourgers are quite cosmopolitan. The necessarily international character of Luxembourg's business, its place as co-capital with Brussels of the European Community, a growing population that impels young men to seek employment abroad, and a deep love for travel, have led Luxembourgers to every continent. There are more people of Luxembourg origin in the United States than there are in the Grand Duchy, and more in Chicago and its environs than in Luxembourg's capital. Wherever they go, whatever their adopted country, Luxembourgers settle in as good citizens, but they always retain strong ties with the Grand Duchy. Whoever speaks the mother tongue, Letzeburgesch, has a passport into a sort of club with members in Africa, the Orient, Australia, and the Americas.

Letzeburgesch is a spoken tongue as far removed from modern German as, say, Swiss-German. It is learned from the cradle. Schooling begins in German, and French is added in the early years. Secondary schools offer a choice of English, Italian, or Spanish. The official language is Letzeburgesch, with French and German recognized as of equal legality. English is widely spoken, with French the language of cultural exchange. Truly, the country is bilingual, trilingual—or perhaps more.

Homes in Luxembourg differ greatly. There are farm cottages, thick-walled, with beams black with age, and there are residences which can be described as palatial. Housewives pride themselves on the order, cleanliness, and comfort of their homes, and on their cooking. Despite the use of many modern kitchen aids, including frozen foods, market days see women of all classes shopping with gourmet care. Pastries are a national institution, and an afternoon *klatsch* in tea-room or at home is a regular affair. Cafés, even more numerous and active than pastry shops, function as club, office, and home-away-from-home. There's always time for a glass of Moselle wine or *en gudden Humpen* of Luxembourg's famous beers. Similarly, in the cafés, business, political affairs and sports are discussed.

Life here has its pace, both through the days and through the years. If it seems cut-and-dried, it is a framework only, within which Luxembourgers find ample interest and where cultural development is limited more by the individual than by society.

The Royal Family and the Constitution

His Royal Highness, the Grand Duke Jean of Luxembourg, Duke of Nassau, Prince of Bourbon-Parma, is the executive of a constitutional monarchy. Sovereign power resides in the Nation, while the Grand Duke exercises it in conformity with the Constitution and the laws of the country.

In 1890, when union with the crown of Holland ended, the present Luxembourg National Dynasty was founded; since that time, the members of the Royal family have shown a devotion to the interests of the people which has earned them genuine respect and popularity. With the marriage in February 1981 of Prince Henri, eldest son of the Grand Ducal couple, to Princess Marie-Thérèse, the royal line continues; and to deep general approval.

While the Grand Duchess Charlotte was confirmed by the people of the Grand Duchy in her hereditary rights, these rights began to devolve upon the present Grand Duke not just at birth but with his coming of age on 5 January 1939. Then he was invested as heir-apparent to the Crown and the Grand Ducal property trusts, and assumed, with his other hereditary titles, that of Hereditary Grand Duke of Luxembourg. When, on 9 April 1953, he married Princess Josephine-Charlotte of Belgium, the bride became the Hereditary Grand Duchess of Luxembourg. On 12 November 1964 the Grand Duchess Charlotte, after a 45-year reign, abdicated in favor of her son. In the instant of the signature, the full Grand Ducal powers were transmitted to the present royal couple.

For the exercise of these powers Grand Duke Jean was unusually well-prepared, not only by years of study with tutors and in schools and universities, in one of which he read law and political science, but also by ten years' service on the Luxembourg State Council. This ruler, then, is not simply a symbol but a functioning monarch.

The Constitution of the Grand Duchy, which the Grand Duke in assuming his powers swore to observe, guarantees equality before the law, the natural rights of person and family, the right to work, the organization of social security and health protection, freedom of trade unions, the inviolability of the home, freedom of religion, freedom of speech and of assembly, with guarantees in detail of liberty and justice to individuals and communes. Also, "Every foreigner on the territory of the Grand Duchy shall enjoy the protection afforded to persons and property, except as otherwise provided by law."

The members of the Chamber of Deputies are elected by universal free suffrage from candidates presented by the Christian-Social, Workers-Socialist, Democratic, Communist, and other parties. The communes are administered by councils, and by the college of burgomasters and aldermen.

Luxembourg's Social Structure

To understand the social structure of Luxembourg, its politics, or its spirit, it is necessary to understand the role religion plays in the life of its people. About 95 percent of the population is Roman Catholic. Rome may be the home of the church, but Luxembourg is one of its strongholds. Still, the people differentiate between practising and non-practising Catholics, and the *non-pratiquant* is frequently quite explicit in defining his position. Practising or not, all of the family customs are scrupulously kept—baptism, confirmation, first communion. While there is religious instruction in the schools, in the higher grades there is the choice between Catholic doctrine and a lay course in ethics and morality. Traditions count. The Octave celebrations in early May and the Whit Tuesday *Springprozession* at Echternach draw pilgrims from neighboring countries to keep these ancient feasts. In the capital or walking the country lanes, one can still hear the sound of church bells. Wayside shrines are found everywhere, usually decorated with flowers. The greatest shrine is probably the sanctuary of Our Lady of Luxembourg in the cathedral. To many Luxembourgers she is the first citizen of the country, and is believed to have performed numerous miracles (among others, saving the city from siege and from the Plague).

Freedom of worship is also an old tradition, however, and both the chief Rabbi and the official Protestant pastor (Reform and Augsberg churches) are paid by the state, as are the priests. Many other Christian and non-Christian faiths are to be found. Hospitals, old-age homes, and some other official institutions, are often staffed with nuns but state-owned, as is customary in many predominantly Roman Catholic countries.

The Arts

The arts are thriving and actively encouraged in Luxembourg. The names of Joseph Kutter, an expressionist painter whose work has been compared to Vlaminck's and Rouault's, and of the photographer Edward Steichen are well known abroad, but there are other pleasant discoveries to be made in many fields if the visitor can give a little time to the search. Appreciation of the arts is widespread, and clues can easily be picked up from galleries, the announcements of shows, the *Agenda Touristique,* or from official agencies. Little Theater groups, book clubs, lecture series, concerts and opera-circuits, and the cultural activities of the legations provide many points of contact. Despite connoisseurs of every art, no single genre has a sufficient following to permit artists, and particularly young artists, to live exclusively from the sales of their works. This leads some to go abroad to seek success, but many more take a regular job to support themselves. If the number of professionals is small, the amateur level is highly professional and must stem from a real love.

The artistic activity which most Luxembourgers are at home with is unquestionably music. Every village, suburb, and section of town has at least a band, an orchestra or a choral group. Town and village bandstands get much use from mid-May onwards, and there are concerts of one kind or another regularly in the Place d'Armes in Luxembourg City.

Toward the end of summer a music-competition is held, with different categories of prizes offered. If you stay in Luxembourg a week, you are bound to see a parade, and no parade is complete without half a dozen bands.

Perhaps the best souvenir that you will take away from Luxembourg will be vivid recollections of too short a visit, to a country rich in history; of an easy, friendly people who welcome the stranger without envy since they consider themselves particularly blessed, and want to remain what they are—solid, forward-looking citizens of one of the smallest of the United Nations.

LUXEMBOURG CITY

An International Meeting-Place

Luxembourg is organized to be seen at the pace which best suits the traveler. The railroads, highways, navigable streams and cleared footpaths reach all parts of the land, so that whether on foot or by cycle, canoe or automobile one can race or ramble at will through both the centers of interest and the intriguing, unexpected byways. Even a bird's-eye view can be arranged: enquire at the airport. A glimpse of the entire country may be had in three or four days. The leisurely pace pays, for the Grand Duchy opens its heart most freely to those who muse over ruins, who see more in the grape-harvest than labor in the fields, who sense drama in an open-hearth furnace.

The National Tourist Office is a mine of helpful information on what to do and see in Luxembourg if you write them in advance, particularly if you wish to keep within a budget.

Discovering Luxembourg City

Luxembourg City is like no other city on earth. All periods exist together in a kind of helter-skelter harmony, and yet the place seems ageless. One can live in almost any era. Charming anachronisms, which still reflect the vitality of other days, are in every street. One good introduction is to enter the city from the east. The road winding down

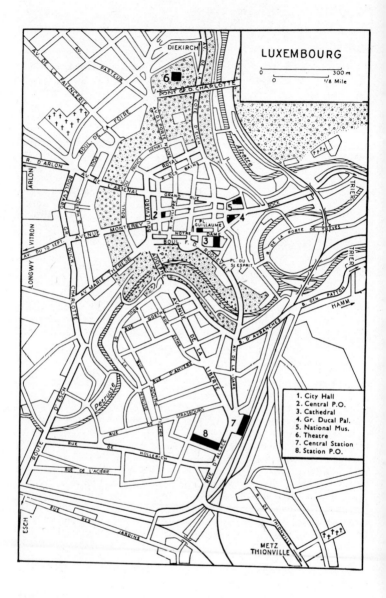

LUXEMBOURG

0   300 m
0   1/8 Mile

1. City Hall
2. Central P.O.
3. Cathedral
4. Gr. Ducal Pal.
5. National Mus.
6. Theatre
7. Central Station
8. Station P.O.

from the plateau into the gorge cut through the centuries by the Alzette and Petrusse rivers goes up into the city across the tongue of cliff known as "the Bock." From pre-Roman times until the later bridges to town were built, this was the principal approach to the settlement on the heights.

The ruined tower, called the "Broken Tooth," is a remnant of the ramparts elaborated from Sigefroi's original fortifications, just beyond it at your left. This once puissant fortress is the cradle of the House of Luxembourg, which gave emperors to Germany, kings to Bohemia and queens to France.

Legendary accounts of Luxembourg's founding differ. Some claim Sigefroi sold his soul to the devil, who built the fortress in a single night. Another story says Sigefroi, riding through the Alzette valley, fell in love with a girl who sat on the rocks, as she combed her hair. He married her, and as a wedding present, the lady Mélusine, in one night built her husband the castle. The bride would say nothing of her origins and made the condition that Saturday was to be hers alone. Sigefroi agreed, and kept his promise for years, but in the end, doubt, jealousy, and friends' solicitude had their way. He followed and watched. Mélusine was bathing and, in her Saturday seclusion, had turned back into a mermaid. Sigefroi gave away his presence. Mélusine turned, saw him and vanished into the rock, where she remains. Every seven years she comes back for a moment, sometimes as a beautiful woman, sometimes as a serpent holding a golden key in her mouth. The brave man who dares kiss the beauty, or take the key from the snake, will release Mélusine and gain all Luxembourg's wealth. Meanwhile, Mélusine knits—only one stitch a year, but should she finish her knitting before she is released, Luxembourg and all its inhabitants will vanish into the rock to share her fate.

Markets and Monuments

From the Bock, walk up rue Sigefroi to the first open square, the Marché-aux-Poissons (Fish Market), site of the oldest buildings. To the right is the National Museum which contains many priceless works of art, as well as archeological, geological and historical exhibits. (A walk outside along the ramparts, and a very little imagination, recreate the past.) Leaving the museum, return to Fish Market Square. To the left, beyond the round bay window, lettered in Gothic script with the national motto: *Mir woelle bleiwe wat mir sin,* the building by the gaslight has been the Masonic Hall since the 19th century. If you stand on the large manhole lid, facing the café with the tawny stone colonnade, you are on the spot where John the Blind received the burghers in the 14th century.

The rue de la Loge, not two yards wide in places, brings one to the back of the palace. The upper windows once marked the apartments of the Royal family. Left and around in front, the double stone stair leads to the Chamber of Deputies. The Spanish section, built in the 16th century, is the oldest part of the Grand Ducal Palace. One of the consoles supporting the balcony shows the cross of Burgundy. The ornamentation bears the stamp of Italian Renaissance influence. Visits to the palace can be arranged: ask at the National Tourist Office or the *Syndicat d'Initiative*.

Down the rue de la Reine, place Guillaume opens out. If it is market-day, it will be filled with stalls, noise, and color and it may be hard to see the City Hall at the left or the statue to the poet Michel Rodange. The arcade at the right connects with the place d'Armes, which has in it a bandstand, where the band of the *Garde Grand-Ducale* and other musical groups perform regularly. In the rue du Curé, just before you come to the *Syndicat d'Initiative* on the corner of the place d'Armes, is a 3-dimensional model of Luxembourg, to orientate you geographically and historically, and a slide show on Luxembourg City.

Down rue de la Poste is the Post Office. A right turn there brings you to the Grand'Rue, now a pedestrian mall. Turn right the length of the shopping center until you see a turreted building on a corner. There, where the main street goes right, turn left through the alley and you come out on a fine terrace with a magnificent view: down below the near-precipice, the old quarter of Pfaffenthal with its medieval buildings; across, the plateau where the Fort of the Three Acorns and the Malakoff Tower are situated; beyond, the tall European Center building on the Kirchberg; down the valley, the Grand Duchesse Charlotte bridge, soaring 280 feet above the Alzette; and immediately below, the Three Towers, which in 1050 marked the outer ramparts of the town. It's an easy descent to the Spanish Tower that hangs over the valley; you can stroll back up rue Wiltheim, passing under the portcullis of the towers, to the Fish Market. A left turn there, and right at the Church of Saint Michael (1320), brings you on to the chemin de la Corniche. Across the valley at the left is Clausen. The villa with the little tower on the right side of its roof, next to the church, is the birthplace of Robert Schuman, the "Father of Europe." Below is the quarter called the Grund, and on the plateau above, the Hospice of Rham and ruins of the second ring of fortifications from the days when Luxembourg was "the Gibraltar of the North." Following the Corniche, mount through the yard of the Vauban barracks, cross the place du Saint Esprit, and follow boulevard Franklin D. Roosevelt right, to the back of the cathedral.

The Cathedral and Casemates

From this side, one enters through the section added in 1935–1938. The sacristan (office to the right) takes pride in showing the treasures of the cathedral to those truly interested: the monumental sarcophagus of John the Blind; the Royal family vault, decorated in blue and gold mosaic to designs created especially by Vatican artists. Leave through the cathedral proper (1613–1623), a splendid example of latter day Gothic in the former Low Countries. This is the shrine of Our Lady of Luxembourg and the object of the chief religious event of the year, the Octave. From the third to the fifth Sunday after Easter, thousands of pilgrims come on foot in procession and pray for the continued protection of the miraculous statue of the Holy Virgin. In the closing ceremony the Madonna is carried in procession from the cathedral to flower-decked altars erected in the streets throughout the city.

Turning left from the porch of the cathedral, and left again in rue Chimay, brings one to the place de la Constitution and an entrance to the casemates. At the height of her power and influence, Luxembourg City was protected by three rings of defenses comprising 53 forts and strongpoints, all tied together by some 25 km. (16 miles) of tunnels and casemates hewn from the solid rock of the citadel. Ten gates controlled admittance through the walls, and the town was, in effect, 440 acres of solid fort. A guided trip through the casemates is a unique experience, a veritable voyage into past ages. (Open only in summer.) From the place de la Constitution there is a good view of the majestic arches of the Pont Adolphe, which span 225 feet and rise to 126 feet. Here, too, is the memorial to all who suffered in World Wars I and II.

The municipal park, which begins just beyond the head of the bridge, is the site of a demolished ring of forts.

Across the bridge rises the lofty tower of the Savings Bank, and two blocks farther down the avenue de la Liberté is the imposing office of ARBED, the steel company that plays so important a role in the economic life of the Grand Duchy.

From the head of the Old Bridge, the Passerelle, the Montée de la Petrusse drops down into the valley. At the foot of the hill is the Chapel of Saint Quirinus, built in the 4th century, one of the oldest shrines in Christendom.

One could walk for days through the medieval suburbs of the Grund and Pfaffenthal or among the ruins on the plateau.

Of special interest to Americans is the United States Military Cemetery 5 km. (3 miles) east from Luxembourg City center. Some 10,000 American soldiers fell in Luxembourg during World War II, most of them in the Rundstedt offensive. A few more than half that number lie buried in a spacious field, surrounded on three sides by pine woods. Among the thousands are the graves of General George S. Patton, Jr., 3rd U.S. Army commander, and Brigadier General Betts, Judge-Advocate General of the U.S. Army of Occupation.

A little under 1½ km. (1 mile) down the road is the German Military Cemetery with some 11,000 graves.

PRACTICAL INFORMATION FOR
LUXEMBOURG CITY

HOTELS. Luxembourg is well provided with hotels, all of which are clean, if simple, with excellent food. Prices are some of the cheapest in Europe. Most hotels have rooms with private bath, but all have bathrooms available, although some charge extra for a bath. Many hotels (list on request from National Tourist Office) offer greatly reduced prices off-season and some of them encourage tourism by granting special terms for a 3-day stay. Many hotels, especially in the capital, welcome the handicapped.

Deluxe

Aerogolf-Sheraton, rte. de Trèves (tel. 3 45 71). 150 rooms. Delightful, wooded surroundings near the airport; all amenities.

Cravat, 29 blvd. Roosevelt (tel. 2 19 75). 60 rooms, TV, parking. Overlooks the valley of the Petrusse and Pont Adolphe.

Holiday Inn, rue du Fort Niedergrunewald (tel. 43 77 61). 260 rooms. Fully airconditioned; TV, indoor pool, sauna. Close to European Court of Justice.

Hostellerie Grünewald, 10 rte. d'Echternach, at Dommeldange (tel. 431 882). 28 rooms, with a superb restaurant.

International Luxembourg, 12 rue Jean Engling, at Dommeldange (tel. 437 81). 348 rooms. All amenities for conducting top-level business in idyllic surroundings; swimming pool, health club, all-weather tennis court.

Novotel Alvisse Parc, 120 rte. d'Echternach, Dommeldange (tel. 43 56 43). 221 rooms. TV, terrace, pool, riding, tennis.

Le Royal, 12 blvd. Royal (tel. 4 16 16). 170 rooms. TV, indoor pool, sauna, solarium, terrace. Quiet elegance in Luxembourg's "Wall Street."

Expensive

l'Agath, 247 rte. de Thionville, at Hesperange (tel. 488 687). 7 comfortable rooms. Excellent restaurant.

Alfa, 16 pl. de la Gare (tel. 49 00 11). 100 rooms. TV, garage. Reliable.

Arcotel, 43 ave. de la Gare (tel. 49 40 01). 30 rooms.

Bristol, 11 rue de Strasbourg (tel. 48 58 29). 30 rooms. No restaurant.

Eldorado, 7 pl. de la Gare (tel. 48 10 71). Centrally-located; good facilities.

International, 20–22 pl. de la Gare (tel. 48 59 11). 60 rooms. TV; a fine restaurant.

Kons, 24 pl. de la Gare (tel. 48 60 21). 136 rooms. Still uses pages.

Nobilis, 47 ave. de la Gare (tel. 49 49 71). 43 rooms. TV, garage.

President, 32 pl. de la Gare (tel. 48 61 61). 40 rooms. Buffet breakfast.

Rix, 20 blvd. Royal (tel. 2 75 45). 21 rooms. TV, parking. No restaurant.

Moderate

Central Molitor, 28 ave. de la Liberté (tel. 48 99 11). 36 rooms. TV, garage. A favorite with visiting businessmen.

Cheminée de Paris, 10 rue d'Anvers (tel. 49 29 31). 24 rooms. Terrace, good restaurant.

City, 1 rue de Strasbourg (tel. 48 46 08). 30 rooms. TV. The restaurant, *City-Cave,* offers French and Luxembourg home cooking.

Dauphin, 42 ave. de la Gare (tel. 48 82 82). 37 rooms. Welcomes youth groups.

Delta, 74–76 rue Adolphe Fischer (tel. 49 30 96). 18 rooms. Garage.

Empire, 34 pl. de la Gare (tel. 48 52 52). 42 rooms. Parking; excellent restaurant.

Italia, 15–17 rue d'Anvers (tel. 48 66 26). 27 rooms. Terrace; Italian and Luxembourg menus.

Schintgen, 6 rue Notre Dame (tel. 2 28 44). 35 rooms. Simple comfort.

Inexpensive

Airfield, 6 route de Trèves (tel. 43 19 34). 10 rooms. Terrace, garage. At Findel airport.

Chemin de Fer, 4 rue Joseph Junck (tel. 49 35 28). 25 rooms. Near the railway station.

San Remo, 10 pl. Guillaume (tel. 472 568). 13 rooms; Italian restaurant.

Touring, 4 rue de Strasbourg (tel. 48 46 29). 15 rooms.

Zürich, 36 rue Jos. Junck (tel. 49 13 50). 13 rooms.

GETTING AROUND. By bus. The blue and yellow buses to your right on leaving the railway station will take you anywhere in Luxembourg City and to some of the immediately adjacent areas: Bereldange, Walferdange, Senningerberg or the EEC complex on the Kirchberg.

From the airport, bus no. 9 takes you to town and this main bus center. Buses no. 9 or 16 go to the Youth Hostel, and nos. 2, 4, 11 or 12 to the town center, across the bridge from the station. Individual tickets cost 25 fr.L. on the bus, but a card for 10 trips is only 175 fr.L. at the ticket windows of the railway station and in those banks or bookstores showing a white and orange seal with *Autobus de la Ville de Luxembourg.* An extra fare may be asked for large suitcases or backpacks and, at rush hours, airport passengers may be refused. A Luxair bus, fare 120 fr.L., leaves from a clearly-marked platform near no. 9's.

Buses to the countryside leave from platforms to the left as you leave the railway station. Ask for information at the Information counter in the arrival hall or the small office under the clock on the south side of the station.

REGIONAL GASTRONOMIC SPECIALTIES. Luxembourg cooking combines German heartiness with Franco-Belgian finesse. Specialties include smoked pork and broad beans or sauerkraut *(Jud mat gardebo'nen),* minced liver balls *(quenelles de foie de veau),* jellied suckling pig *(cochon de lait en gelée).* Pike, crawfish and trout are excellent; the latter poached, in wine or a white sauce mousseline. The smoked Ardennes ham *(jambon d'Ardennes)* is available all year round, and in the hunting season there is wild boar *(marcassin),* and hare—delicious in a thick sauce *(civet de lièvre).* You can also try roast thrush *(grives).*

Pastry shops are numerous and the rich assortment of cakes is excellent. Ask for *tarte au quetsch.* Outstanding desserts are prepared with the aid of local liqueurs, try a delicious *omelette soufflée au kirsch.* During the carnival season a special dry cake is much in favor, bearing the appropriate name *les pensées brouillées* (random thoughts).

Luxembourg's white Moselle wine is quite dry, resembling the wines of the Rhine perhaps more than the fruitier wines of the French Moselle. The main types are *Riesling, Rivaner* and *Auxerrois.* There are sparkling wines *(vins mousseux)* prepared by the champagne method, less than half the price. The *goût américain* has a sweeter tang than *brut.* By another system of fermentation they get the *vin perlé,* less effervescent but very pleasant to the palate.

Brewing beer is a traditional industry. Among the best known are *Diekirch, Mousel, Simon* and *Bofferding.*

Quetsch, Mirabelle, and *Prunelle,* are traditional "firewater" drinks, made from small blue plums. Equally good are *Kirsch* (cherries), and *Cassis* (blackcurrant). All are served ice-cold, often as a chaser to a long drink, and while excellent, they should be treated with caution.

MUSEUMS AND PLACES OF INTEREST. Museums and archeological or historical sites to visit are not lacking in Luxembourg. Trips to the Cathedral in Luxembourg City and the Basilica in Echternach are high on the list. Admissions range from 30 to 100 fr.L. About 30% are free. Check with the ONT. In the capital there are:

Castle of Sigefroi, founder of Luxembourg, Montée de Clausen. Remains of the original fortification built in 963, perpetually open, free.

Historical Model of Luxembourg's Citadel, rue du Curé (tel. 2 28 09). Adults 30 fr.L. Open daily in season, except Tues. and Sun., 10 to 12.30 and 2 to 6. Scale model of the "Gibraltar of the North"; slide show on Luxembourg City.

Luxembourg Casemates. Two entrances: Bock, Montée de Clausen, and Pétrusse, place de la Constitution. Unique, once impregnable, fortifications hand-hewn from solid rock. Intriguing vistas from the embrasures. Open seasonally 10 to 5, adults 30 fr.L.

Pescatore Museum, Villa Vauban, Route d'Arlon. Dutch and French paintings. Open daily, except Tues., from 3 to 7, Sat. and Sun. also 10 to 12. Adults 20 fr.L.

Post and Telephone Museum, 19 Rue de Reims. History of communications. Open Tues., Thurs., and Sat., 10 to 12 and 2 to 5. Free.

State Museums, Marché aux Poissons. Rich collections in painting, sculpture, natural history, history, and archeology. Open daily except Mon., 10 to 12, 1 to 5. Sat. and Sun. 10 to 12, 2 to 6. Free.

 RESTAURANTS. Most hotels have acceptable restaurants, so finding an eating place is no problem. For food that is out of the ordinary, here is a list of restaurants that you might wish to investigate.

Expensive

Au Gourmet, 8 rue Chimay (tel. 2 55 61). Fine regional dishes in a lovely old house. Book in advance to be sure of a table. Closed Sun. even. and Mon.

Bouzonviller, 138 rue Albert Unden (tel. 47 22 59). For *aiguillettes de canard au graines de sesame*. Game in season. 200 wines.

Clairefontaine, 7–9 rue Clairefontaine (tel. 4 22 11). Try *filet de rouget de barbet à la crème de cresson* or *petit nage de sole et de homard à la moderne*.

Cordial, 1 pl. de Paris (tel. 48 85 38). Closed Fri., and noon Sat.

St. Michel, 32 rue de l'Eau (tel. 2 32 15). Try the *blanc de turbot au bourgeuil* or, for dessert, *désir de la reine*. Good wine list. Closed Sat. and Sun.

Patin d'Or, 40 rue de Bettembourge Kockelscheuer (tel. 2 64 99). At skating rink.

Le Vert Galant, 23 rue Aldringem (tel. 47 08 22). Good nouvelle cuisine. Closed Sat. lunchtime and Sun.

Moderate

Bella Napoli, 4 rue de Strasbourg (tel. 49 33 67). Italian and local cuisine.

Caesar, 18 ave. Monterey (tel. 47 09 25). Franco-Italian cuisine.

Le Calao, 47 ave. de la Gare (tel. 49 49 71). Try the *turbot au vinaigre de framboises* or *homard amoricaine*.

Club 5, 5 rue Chimay (tel. 4 67 63). Good salads. Terrace in summer.

Cockpit Inn, 43 blvd. Gen. Patton (tel. 48 86 35). Chili con carne, onion soup, cocktail specialties.

Le Marronnier, 5 rue Marie-Thérèse (tel. 447 43 216). Fine view of the Pont Adolphe and valley of the Petrusse.

Osteria del Téatro, 21–25 allée Scheffer (tel. 2 88 11). Italian cuisine, authentic pasta. Bar, terrace, skittles.

du Passage, 18 rue du Curé–14 pl. Guillaume (tel. 4 06 63). *Raclette Grisons, fondues de fromage* and other Swiss dishes.

Inexpensive

l'Académie, 11 pl. d'Armes (tel. 2 71 31). May be crowded at noon.

Ancre d'Or, 23 rue du Fosée (tel. 47 29 73). Try the *riz du veau.*

Chaves, 21 rue de Bonnevoie (tel. 48 86 08). Portuguese specialties.

City Cave, 1 rue de Strasbourg (tel. 48 44 87). Luxembourg home cooking.

du Commerce, 13 pl. d'Armes (tel. 2 69 30). Reliable everyday fare.

La Lanterne, 2A rue des Capucins (tel. 47 45 12). Home-made pasta *al dente.*

Loch Ness, 13 rue Notre Dame (tel. 2 38 23). Good for a *klatsch* or light snacks.

Maison des Brasseurs, 48 Grand'Rue (tel. 47 13 71). Luxembourgish grills. Try the *jambonneau choucroute.*

La Marée, 37 ave. de la Liberté (tel. 49 08 99). Seafood, Mediterranean décor.

Mister Grill, 15 pl. d'Armes (tel. 275 37). Only best Irish beef used. Salad bar included.

Peffermillen, 61 ave. de la Gare (tel. 48 01 42). Home cooking.

Pole Nord, 2 pl. de Bruxelles (tel. 47 23 23). Luxembourgish and French cuisine.

Star of Asia, 19 rue des Capucins (tel. 47 12 40). Eastern, vegetarian and diet menus.

Taverne Nobilis, 47 ave. de la Gare (tel. 49 49 71). Convenient parking.

Um Dierfgen, 6 côte d'Eich (tel. 2 61 41). Steaks (horse or beef) in a rustic Luxembourg village atmosphere.

Um Plateau, 6 plateau d'Altmunster (tel. 4 23 37). Tasty salads and casseroles.

Waldheim, 28 pl. de la Gare (tel. 48 47 96). The dining section of an ensemble including a hamburger shop and café.

NIGHTLIFE. Pick your leading nightclub (they all close at 3 A.M.) from among the several cabarets available. The floorshows are fair and the prices not excessive. Nightlife rolls along quietly in Luxembourg, except for the discos, which are numerous and vibrant.

USEFUL ADDRESSES. Embassies and Consulates. American, 22 blvd. Emmanuel Servais (tel. 4 01 23); British, 28 blvd. Royal (tel. 2 98 64). **Travel Agencies.** Wagons Lits Tourisme, 80 Place de la Gare (tel. 48 19 19) and 103 Grand'rue (tel. 46 85 11). **National Tourist Office.** Air Terminal, pl. de la Gare (tel. 481 199). **Automobile Club of Luxembourg.** 180 rte. de Longweg (tel. 311 031). Railroad information: Central station (tel. 492 424).

THE GRAND DUCHY

Beauty in Miniature

The northern part of the country, called the Luxembourg Ardennes, is similar in many ways to its Belgian namesake. Romantic winding valleys of fast rivers cut into the plateau of high hills.

The Ardennes Region

To see the Ardennes, take Route 7 from Luxembourg to Diekirch. The church is ancient, some parts dating from the 7th and 9th centuries. Some well-preserved 4th-century Roman mosaics give an idea of the villas the Roman masters of this land built during their occupation. The ancient "Devil's Altar," a Celtic dolmen, has survived. In the people, too, a strong strain of superstition remains. 19th-century Luxembourg folklore has a Druidic flavor, and one may still find an old farm woman who talks just a little too familiarly to her cat. In the Museum of the Battle of the Bulge, scenes from World War II are recreated.

Route 17 leads from Diekirch to Vianden. The castle has been restored to its original plans. Roman stonework can be traced in the ruins, but the castle on the hill dates from the 9th century, even though the important and more beautiful additions were made during the 11th, 12th, and 15th centuries. In 1350 Adelaide of Vianden married Othon of Nassau, and because of this the fortress is the ancestral castle of both Queen Beatrix of the Netherlands and Luxembourg's Grand Duke. A national monument, it was transferred by the Grand Ducal family to the State. For visiting times consult the Syndicat d'Initiative.

Vianden is a picturesque little town, with its old houses and narrow streets stretching from the hill to the two banks of the Our. The Gothic church, quaint in itself, has some interesting old tombs. Nearby is a most rewarding folklore museum. The Victor Hugo Museum, a reconstruction of the house where he lived, commemorates the poet's sojourn here.

You get a fine view from the bridge, but if you take the chair lift, you will see a panorama that includes town, castle, and winding valley. If you walk a short way up-river from the bridge, you will find yourself abruptly in the twentieth century, where a mighty pumping-station takes the river water to the high summit and releases it for sale as a supplier of peak-hour electric power to Germany (across the river).

The remains of the castles of Stoltzembourg, Falkenstein, and Roth are within walking distance. Continuing from Stoltzembourg through the excursion center of Hosingen, one then takes a left turn at Marnach toward Clervaux, in the heart of the Ardennes. Walking along almost any of the wood paths above town, òne can believe oneself to be in Shakespeare's Forest of Arden. Up the hill beyond the new church rises a monument to Luxembourgers' honesty. In 1798 the young men of the country were called to the French army. Ardennes farmers, armed only with ancient weapons, axes, pitchforks, scythes or big clubs *(Kloeppelen)*, led anti-conscription rioting. When experienced French soldiers arrested the leaders of the Kloeppelkrich, the President of the Military Tribunal was moved to clemency. He tried to persuade the farmers to say that their guns had not been loaded and that their aims were misunderstood. *"Mir koenne net lé'ien!"* "We cannot lie!" they replied and the guillotine or the firing squad killed thirty-four men who wouldn't lie to save their lives.

Farther on is the Benedictine Abbey of Sts. Maurice and Maur (1910), built on the lines of the great Abbey of Cluny. The exhibit at the abbey recreating the monastic life is a window on the past which deserves a visit. In the park of Clervaux, near the Chapel of Notre Dame de Lorette (1786), stands the rocky pulpit of St. Hubert, a 7th-century missionary, who became the patron saint of hunters. The unique lines of Clervaux Castle were destroyed in December 1944 but have been completely restored. In 1621, Philip de Lannoi, reputed to be an ancestor of the late President Franklin Delano Roosevelt, left this castle to seek his fortune in America. On display in the castle are scale-models of other medieval citadels, displays of arms and uniforms from World War II, and the "Family of Man" photographic essay by Edward Steichen.

To return, Route 16 through Hoscheid to Diekirch, Route 14 through Medernach and Larochette, Rte. 8 to Mersch, and 7 to Luxembourg lead through beautiful countryside. For the country between Wiltz and Ettelbruck, Route 12 through Bridel and Kopstal leads through Saeul to Redange. There, change to Route 23 through Folschette, Koetschette and Arsdorf. The views of the Upper Sûre at

Hochfels and the countryside around Boulaide are worth seeing. From Bavigne, Route 26 leads to Wiltz.

An industrious little city, Wiltz has a real "uptown" and "downtown," the difference in level being something like 500 feet. The lords of Wiltz, powerful vassals of the counts of Luxembourg, used to dispense justice under the cross, which dates from 1502. The castle was built in the 12th century and remodeled in 1631. In the parish church are the tombs of the counts of Wiltz. But here in these rugged hills more recent history jostles the past. The tank mounted at the bend of the road winding up into Wiltz is a reminder of other and heavier armor than that of the old knights; armor that clanked along these roads to break the back of the Rundstedt offensive. A pleasant drive along the Wiltz River brings you in a few minutes to Kautenbach.

From Wiltz, about 9 km. (6 miles) south on Route 15, a right turn takes you to Esch-sur-Sûre. Sailing and swimming facilities are available above the great dam of the Sûre. Downstream from the dam are fishing and water-skiing areas. Completely circled by hills, this stronghold was well situated for defense. Legend says that an Eschois Crusader brought back a Turk's head and hung it outside the castle gate. The head disappeared, but it is said that the Turk reappears to warn the inhabitants of Esch of impending disaster. Some will tell you that the head was seen just before the country was invaded in 1940. Just over a mile upstream is one of the dams of the Sûre with its artificial lake.

Leaving Esch-sur-Sûre by the same road, follow the Sûre valley to Bourscheid, or turn left from Route 15 at Heiderscheid. Continue through the village to the castle. The seigneurs of Bourscheid must have had an eye for beauty as well as warfare. Commanding three valleys, the situation of the castle, 500 feet above the Sûre, needs no story of the past to evoke a powerful response.

From Michelau, the road will lead you back to Ettelbruck, a tourist crossroad where information and supplies are available. Route 7 leads past the Grand Ducal Castle of Colmar-Berg to Luxembourg.

Echternach to Müllerthal

Route E27 northeast from Luxembourg toward Echternach goes through Junglinster, where certain spires of Radio Luxembourg's transmitter masts tower over 750 feet in the air. Visits to RTL can be arranged by writing in advance to RTL, Villa Louvigny, B.P. 1002, Luxembourg. Route E27 continues into Echternach, where the long-standing bond between Britain and Luxembourg is in evidence.

Echternach still centers upon St. Willibrord, the Northumberland missionary to the Ardennes. In the 7th century, he founded a Benedictine abbey which throughout the Middle Ages exercised an educational and civilizing influence. Today the buildings house primary and secondary schools. In the crypt of the basilica the remains of St. Willibrord are enshrined in a Carrara marble sarcophagus. Frescos dating from the 1100s decorate the crypt, where traces of the original chapel erected by the saint are visible.

Annually on Whit Tuesday some 15,000 pilgrims gather from Western Germany, from Lorraine, from the Grand Duchy—from all the territory in fact that once was Luxembourg for the Springprozession. The origin of this festival is lost in time, but it has become a feast of Saint Willibrord.

About 9 A.M. the solemn tolling of a seven-ton bell gives the signal for the departure of the procession of devout pilgrims, which winds slowly through the streets to the music of bands, of violins, accordions, and singers. To an ancient subtle tune the faithful dance through the streets of the town. Others simply walk along, praying, "Holy Willibrord, founder of churches, light of the blind, destroyer of idols, pray for us." This phrase is chanted over and over again. Miraculous cures are attributed to this act of devotion and to the properties of Willibrord's fountain in the church. About noon, the last wave of dancers has surged into the basilica and been blessed. The streets are still jammed especially in the square in front of the 12th-century Town Hall. Moselle wines speed recuperation shortly, and to godliness is added a gaiety that lasts into the small hours.

This is not the only time when Echternach is crowded. Summer brings floods of visitors, especially Germans, who are very fond of the town. One of the reasons is the possibility for hiking that the area affords. Around Echternach lies a region Luxembourgers like to call their Switzerland. If the hills are not alps, they nevertheless exert a powerful attraction, and you should not shy away from a healthy walk of just under an hour to the Gorge du Loup (Wolf's Throat), a fearful looking crevasse. But Echternach is not all history and hiking. Its recreational facilities include tennis, swimming pools, horseback riding, canoeing and fishing, all in ideal surroundings. The latest addition is a 70-acre lake, set in a large park. As well as fishing, swimming, and sailing, pedalos are available; and the parking areas are discreetly landscaped by trees.

Route 19 up the Lower Sûre through Bollendorf-Pont, Grundhof and Wallendorf leads to Reisdorf, where a left turn winds by Bigelbach to Beaufort's atmospheric 15th-century castle. It still has its torture chamber with an authentic rack. Beaufort kirsch and cassis liqueurs are renowned and available on the terrace.

On the road back to Echternach via Vogelsmuhl is Berdorf, where there is a pagan altar with bas-reliefs of the ancient gods. This is the middle of the Müllerthal (Miller's Dale) which, from the variety of the rock formations, gets its name of "Little Switzerland." Though miniature in scale, it includes enough difficult climbing to provide a good workout. Grottos and caves to explore are numerous in this region and will appeal to enthusiasts. The Hallerbach rock formations challenge rock hounds.

Turning right at the town of Müllerthal, through Waldbillig and Christnach, you reach Larochette, where two castles overlook the Ernz Blanche River. Continuing on Route 14 to Heffingen, you will find that a right turn leads to Fischbach, formerly the residence of the dowager Grand Duchess Charlotte. Farther on there is a splendid view, just before arriving at Rollingen, where a left turn into Route 7 leads you back to Luxembourg.

The Moselle Valley and the Steel Country

The Moselle valley is best reached by taking Route 1 out of Luxembourg City. After passing Roodt-sur-Sûre at the junction with Route 14, the road through Manternach leads to Wasserbillig where the Sûre joins the Moselle at this frontier town. A leisurely way to see the Luxembourg Moselle is to take the *Princess Marie-Astrid* riverboat between Wasserbillig and Schengen, and watch the vineyards roll by.

Route 1 south from Wasserbillig leads to Grevenmacher, whose wine-festival on the Thursday after Easter attracts many connoisseurs. Here you may visit the Cooperative of Vinegrowers' extensive cellars, or the caves of Bernard-Massard. There the method of making champagne will be explained to you and made manifest by several glasses of the sparkling wine that is so popular in Britain and America.

Route 10 continuing south leads through Wormeldange, another wine center, and Ehnen with its wine museum. Continue to Remich, of Roman origin. Remich has a delightful wide and tree-shaded riverside promenade, and facilities for boating and fishing. The wine-cellars of Saint Martin and open and worth visiting. A bit south of Remich at Bech-Kleinacher is a museum in a typical Moselle 18th-century house, with artifacts and explanations which make clear the traditional development of the vintner's art.

The road leaves the Moselle to wind past Ellange to Mondorf-les-Bains. This is Luxembourg's great thermal spa. Many visitors, however, come for the casino which offers roulette, black-jack, slot machines and an international program of variety and dance. There are orchestral concerts during the season and the Luxembourg, French, Belgian, British and American national holidays are celebrated, usually with fireworks. The village church has some interesting frescos.

At Bettembourg, the Parc Merveilleux, with is miniature farm and zoo in a fairy wood setting offers plenty of entertainment.

Route 6 to Dudelange leads to the steel country. Farther on, in Kayl, is the Madonna called Our Lady of the Miners. South from there, at Rumelange, there is what must be the world's most authentic mining museum—in a mine. You can ride the mine cars. Famous for roses as well as great steel production, Esch-sur-Alzette is proud of both; it puts a great rose-garden within a stone's throw of the steel plants. From the nearby Galgenberg, France, Germany, Luxembourg and Belgium may be seen.

Our last stop before reaching the French border is Rodange. For railroading buffs, a steam engine hauls a tourist train from the town to Fonds de Gras on Sunday afternoons. If you are lucky, you'll still find an archeological souvenir at Lamadeleine, at the foot of Mount Titus (Titelberg). Titelberg was an old Celtic settlement, later a Roman camp. There is a monument to the first American soldier killed on Luxembourg soil in World War II, September 9, 1944. Route 4 leads directly back to Luxembourg.

Valley of the Seven Castles

The valley of the Eisch, known as the Valley of the Seven Castles, is one of the most picturesque of the routes near Luxembourg. Route E9 west leads to Steinfort, the entrance to the valley. The road continues through Koerich to Septfontaines, situated below the cliff where there is a ruined castle of the Knights Templar. The old section of the church was built in 1316. The road continues to Ansembourg, where the old castle dominates the height and the valley is graced by the new castle.

Marienthal, once the home monastery of the order of White Fathers, lies in the valley below Hollenfels. At the Castle of Hollenfels is a youth hostel. The castle-tower is 9th-century, and the carving in the Knights' hall merits inspection. Between Hollenfels and Mersch is the Hunnebour (Huns' Spring), an ideal picnic ground. Legend has it that Attila's army camped here. All roads north lead to Mersch, in the geographical center of Luxembourg. The town is a center, too, for excursions. There are wall-paintings, mosaics, a villa, sculpture—all looking much as they did when the Caesars ruled the world. Historically more recent, the castle exemplifies early feudal times. Over the town brood the three towers that identify it at a distance. Route 7 returns to Luxembourg City.

PRACTICAL INFORMATION FOR

THE GRAND DUCHY

HOTELS AND RESTAURANTS

BEAUFORT. Public skating rink, horseback riding, swimming pool. *Meyer* (E), 120 Grand' Rue (tel. 8 62 62), 37 rooms. The top hotel here. There are many others from which to choose. Among them—*Binsfeld* (M), 1 montée du Château (tel. 8 60 13), 20 rooms. Garage. *Saint Jean* (M), 59 Grand'Rue (tel. 8 60 46), 17 rooms. *Thielen* (I), 11 Grand'Rue (tel. 8 60 05), 10 rooms. Terrace.

BERDORF. About a dozen hotels, although most open for the tourist season only. Among the best: *Parc* (L), 39 rte. de Grundhof (tel. 7 91 95), 19 rooms and outdoor pool. *Bisdorff* (E), 2 rue de Heisbich (tel. 7 92 08), 26 rooms and indoor pool. *l'Ermitage* (E), 44 rte. de Grundhof (tel. 7 91 84). 16 rooms. Garage. *le Chat Botté* (M), 36 rte. d'Echternach (tel. 7 91 86). 18 rooms. *Herber* (M), 91 rte. d'Echternach (tel. 7 91 88). 46 rooms. Playground for children. *Kinnen* (M), 34 rte. d'Echternach (tel. 7 91 83). 35 rooms, free garage.

Restaurant. *Auberge de Berdorff* (M), Maison 17 (tel. 7 93 46). Excellent French cuisine.

BIGONVILLE. *Flatzbour* (I), 10 rue de Perlé (tel. 6 45 83). 10 rooms, and good food.

BOLLENDORF PONT. *André* (I), 9 rte. de Diekirch (tel. 7 23 93). 24 rooms, is comfortable and has a good restaurant.

BOULAIDE. 4 km. from the Haut-Sûre lake (where you can fish) is the *Hames* (M), 2 rue du Curé (tel. 9 30 07). 14 rooms. Free garage.

BOUR. Restaurant. *Janin,* 2 rte d'Arlon (tel. 3 03 78). Well worth the trip.

BOURSCHEID. The best hotels are at the beach, with the castle on the heights above. *Bel-Air* (M) (tel. 9 03 47), 10 rooms. *du Moulin* (M) (tel. 9 00 15), 20 rooms. *Week-End* (M) (tel. 9 00 20), 14 rooms. All offer fishing. In the hamlet proper, *St. Fiacre* (M), 4 rue Principale (tel. 9 00 23). Hunting in season. *Saint Laurent* (I), 27 rue Principale (tel. 9 00 10). 17 rooms; the largest.

CLERVAUX. 12th-century castle, bowls, minigolf, tennis. Has an embarrassingly wide choice for such a small place. *Claravallis* (E), 3 rue de la Gare (tel. 9 10 34), 28 rooms. TV; children's playground. *de l'Abbaye* (M), 80 Grand'Rue (tel. 9 10 49), 50 rooms. Fishing in season. *des Ardennes* (M), 22 Grand'Rue (tel. 9 22 54), 11 rooms. Terrace. *Central* (M), 9 place Princesse Maria-Theresa (tel. 9 11 05), 20 rooms. TV. *du Commerce* (M), 2 rue de Marnach (tel. 9 10 32), 45 rooms. TV; terrace. *International* (M), 10 Grand'Rue (tel. 9 10 67), 30 rooms. TV; fishing. *Koener* (M), 14 Grand'Rue (tel. 9 10 02), 25 rooms. *des Nations* (M), 29 rue de la Gare (tel. 9 10 18), 47 rooms. Equipped for the physicially limited. *du Parc* (M), 2 rue du Parc (tel. 9 10 68), 10 rooms. Intimate but all comforts.

At nearby **Reuler,** the *St. Hubert* (M), tel. 9 24 32. 27 rooms, welcomes families. Two public fishing ponds. *Les Nations* (M), 29 rue de la Gare (tel. 9 10 18).

CONSDORF. Good base for walking tours. *Mersch* (M), 1–3 rue de Luxembourg (tel. 7 90 35), 35 rooms, is best. *du Moulin* (M), rue du Moulin (tel. 7 90 02), 15 rooms. Welcomes children. *La Bonne Auberge* (I), Michelshof (tel. 7 90 63). Horseback riding.

Restaurant. *de la Gare* (I), 96 rue de Luxembourge (tel. 7 90 05).

DIEKIRCH. Cuisine is best at the *Hiertz* (M), 1 rue Clairefontaine (tel. 80 35 62), 7 rooms. *Kremer* (M), 4 ave. de la Gare (tel. 80 36 36), 35 rooms. Free garage. *du Parc* (M), 28 ave. de la Gare (tel. 80 34 72). 40 rooms. TV, terrace. *au Beau Séjour* (I), 12 Esplanade (tel. 80 34 03), 28 rooms. All amenities at good prices. *l'Europe* (I), 1 pl. de l'Etoile (tel. 80 34 01). Terrace.

Restaurants. *Aveirence* (I), 33 ave. de la Gare (tel. 80 33 60). *le Tivoli* (I), 53 ave. de la Gare (tel. 80 88 51).

ECHTERNACH. Over 30 hotels. *Bel-Air* (L), 1 rte. de Berdorf (tel. 72 93 83), 33 rooms, is the best. *Eden au Lac* (E), Nonnensees (tel. 72 82 83). 33 rooms. TV; playground. *Grand* (E), 27 rte. de Diekirch (tel. 72 96 72), 30 rooms. Top quality. *Ardennes* (M), 38 rue de la Gare (tel. 7 21 08). 35 rooms, good restaurant. *La Petite Marquise* (M), 18 place du Marché (tel. 7 23 82), 32 rooms. Terrace on the market place. *du Parc* (M), 18 rue Hoveleck/9 rue de l'Hôpital (tel. 72 94 81), 32 rooms, with indoor pool, but no restaurant. *Saint Hubert* (M), 21 rue de la Gare (tel. 7 23 06), 35 rooms. French cuisine. *Universel* (M), 40 rue de Luxembourg (tel. 72 99 91), 32 rooms. Garden terrace. Fishing and hunting in season. *du Commerce* (M), 16 place du Marché (tel. 7 23 01), 50 rooms. Free garage. *Aigle Noir* (I), rue de la Gare 54 (tel. 7 23 83). 23 rooms and restaurant with terrace.

Restaurants. Good restaurants at most of the bigger hotels Also *Parnass* (I), 7–8 place du Marché (tel. 72 94 83). *du Pont* (I), 34 rue du Pont (tel. 7 20 26).

EHNEN. A picturesque village, worth a lunch halt. *de la Moselle* (M), 131 rte. du Vin (tel. 7 60 22). 19 rooms. *Simmer* (E), 115 rte. de Moselle (tel. 7 60 30). 20 rooms. Famed for fish specialties such as *brochet* (pike) *à la mode de chez nous*. Both hotels have fine views over the Moselle.

ESCH-SUR-ALZETTE. Biggest industrial city (steel). The best hotels are small but comfortable. The *Acacia* (M), 10 rue de la Libération (tel. 54 10 61). 28 rooms. TV. *Auberge Royal* (M), 19 rue des Remparts (tel. 54 27 23). 4 rooms. Very quiet. *Le Carrefour* (I), 1 rue Victor Hugo (tel. 54 51 44). 19 rooms. Equipped for the physically limited. *Mercure* (I), 12 rue de l'Alzette (tel. 54 11 33). 6 rooms. In town center. *de la Poste* (I), 107 rue de l'Alzette (tel. 5 35 04). 17 rooms. Family hotel.

Restaurants. *au Bec Fin* (M), 15 place N. Metz (tel. 54 23 55). Fish, game in season. *Giarrosto* (I), 72 blvd. J.F. Kennedy (tel. 54 13 53). Italian cuisine, reasonable prices.

ESCH-SUR-SÛRE. Dramatically situated castle. Fishing center. *des Ardennes* (M), 1 rue du Moulin (tel. 8 91 08). 26 rooms. Terrace. *Beau-Site* (M), 2 rue de Kaundorf (tel. 8 91 34). 18 rooms; on the riverbank. *du Moulin* (I), 6 rue du Moulin (tel. 8 96 87). Hunting in season.

ETTELBRUCK. Busy market center for farmers and good tourist spot. *Cames* (M), 45 rue Prince Henri (tel. 8 21 80). 17 rooms. No restaurant. At the *Central* (M), 25 rue de Bastogne (tel. 8 21 16), 23 rooms, you'll get excellent meals, a wonderful wine list, comfort, local atmosphere. *de Luxembourg* (M), 7–9 rue Prince Henri (tel. 8 22 89). 23 rooms. *Solis* (I), 58 rue de Bastogne (tel. 8 23 93). 15 rooms. Luxembourg and French cuisine.

Restaurant. *Um Stamminet* (I), 96 Grand'Rue (tel. 8 24 33). Hearty, local cuisine.

GAICHEL (EISCHEN). Good excursion center. *de la Gaichel* (L) (tel. 3 91 29). 13 rooms, fishing. *La Bonne Auberge* (M) (tel. 3 91 40). 15 rooms. Cuisine (E) in both is out of this world. Choose their specialties; at La Bonne Auberge, young wild boar in wine sauce (in season) and, at the de la Gaichel, a family-run establishment for well over a 100 years, try the lobster, crayfish and such delicacies as veal cooked with rhubarb.

GOEBELSMÜHLE. *Schroeder* (I), 9 rue de la Gare (tel. 9 01 57), 12 rooms.

GREVENMACHER. Great wine center. *de la Poste* (M), 28 rue de Trèves (tel. 7 51 36). 12 rooms. Garage. *Le Roi Dagobert* (M), 32 rue de Trèves (tel. 7 57 17). 18 rooms. Outstanding table; French chef, no frozen foods. *Govers* (I), 15 Grand 'Rue (tel. 7 51 37). 15 rooms. Central, but quiet.

Restaurants. Both *Belle-Vue* (I), rte. du Vin (tel. 7 56 14) and *Relais des Bateliers* (I), rte. du Vin (tel. 7 56 28) overlook the Moselle.

Grevenmacher is the home port of the day liner *Princess Marie-Astrid* (M), 32 rte. de Thionville (tel. 75 82 75). Phone for reservations and dine on board.

GRUNDHOF. On the Sûre. *Brimer* (E), (tel. 8 62 51). 24 rooms, miniature golf, badminton. *Ferring* (M), 4 rte. de Beaufort (tel. 8 60 15). 27 rooms. TV; free garage. Good restaurant.

HALLER. *Hallerbach* (M), 2 rue des Romains (tel. 8 61 51). 18 rooms; serves superb meals in this ideal spot for walking. Near the Hallerbach rock formations. TV. Indoor pool, tennis.

KAUTENBACH. Another tucked-away hamlet from which to ramble through the hills. *Huberty* (I), Maison 21 (tel. 9 65 51). 10 rooms. Children's playground. *Hatz* (I), Maison 24 (tel. 9 65 61). 11 rooms. Garden.

LAROCHETTE. Dominated by romantic old castle, *du Château* (M), 1 rue de Medernach (tel. 8 70 09). 45 rooms. View of church and hills from terrace. *de la Poste* (M), 11 place Bleiche (tel. 8 70 06). 30 rooms. Very quiet. *Résidence* (M), 14 rue de Medernach (tel. 8 73 91). 20 rooms. Horseback riding.

MERSCH. *Marisca* (M), 1 rue de Colmar-Berg (tel. 32 84 56). 17 rooms. TV. Terrace. Garage. *Au Bon Accueil* (I), 34 route de Luxembourg (tel. 3 22 76). 11 rooms. Terrace. Family cooking. *Sept Chateaux* (I), 3 rue d'Avlon (tel. 3 22 53). 6 rooms; restaurant.

MONDORF-LES-BAINS. The gambling casino and the traditional spa animate this resort. More than 20 hotels and pensions. Excellent swimming pools and play spaces for children. *Casino de Jeux de Luxembourg* (E), rue Th. Flammang (tel. 66 10 10), 32 rooms. Casino; gourmet dining. *Grand Chef* (E), 36 ave. des Bains (tel. 6 80 12). 46 rooms. TV. Outstanding meals. *Beau Séjour* (M), 3 ave. Dr. Klein (tel. 6 81 08). 15 rooms. TV. Terrace. *International* (M), 58 ave. Fr. Clement (tel. 6 70 73), 44 rooms. TV. *Welcome* (M), 4 ave. Marie-Adelaide (tel. 66 07 85), 18 rooms. *Windsor* (M), 71 ave. des Bains (tel. 6 72 03), 17 rooms. Terrace. *du Midi* (I), 13 ave. Fr. Clement (tel. 6 80 77), 19 rooms.
  Restaurants. Besides the big casino restaurant and the hotels, try *Chez Jeannot* (M), 1 rue de Remich (tel. 6 81 31). Excellent steaks.

MÜLLERTHAL. In the lovely valley of the Ernz Noire. *Les Cascades du Müllerthal* (L), 1 rue des Rochers (tel. 8 76 84). 58 rooms, offers swimming, sauna, physical therapy. *Central* (M), 1 rue de l'Ernz Noire (tel. 8 72 88). 16 rooms, open March through November.

REMICH. Pleasantly situated on the banks of the Moselle. *Saint Nicolas* (E), 31 Esplanade (tel. 69 83 33). 45 rooms, TV; playground; terrace. *des Ardennes* (M), 29 rue de la Gare (tel. 6 97 49), 14 rooms. Parking. *Beau-Séjour* (M), 30 quai de la Moselle (tel. 69 81 26), 10 rooms. TV; garage. *Esplanade* (M), 5 Esplanade (tel. 6 91 71), 17 rooms. Terrace. *des Vignes* (M), 29 rte. de Mondorf (tel. 6 90 28), 16 rooms. Horseback riding. *de la Poste* (I), 16 place du Marché (tel. 69 81 33), 10 rooms.
  Restaurants. *Belle Epoque* (M), 19 rue Macher (tel. 69 84 89). Dine well and watch the river. *Hostellerie des Pecheurs* (M), 13 rue de Stadtbredimus (tel. 69 80 67). Another attractive spot on the river, serving excellent fish specialties. Closed Mon.

STEINHEIM. Near Echternach. *Gruber* (M), 36 rte. d'Echternach (tel. 7 24 33). 22 rooms. Excellent cuisine. Tennis, playground.

STOLZEMBOURG. North of Vianden, with its once-proud castle overlooking the Our valley. *Teisen* (I), 5 rue Principale (tel. 8 42 90). 7 rooms, a small inn. Good fishing.

TROISVIERGES. *Auberge Lamy* (I), 51 rue d'Asselborn (tel. 9 80 41). 8 rooms, has a restaurant. If full, try the *Hornung* (I), 4 rue d'Asselborn (tel. 9 82 26), 10 rooms, or the *Orion* (I), 26 rue de la Gare (tel. 9 80 18), 10 rooms.

VIANDEN. Ancestral castle of the Orange-Nassau dynasty. Chairlift. Fishing in season. *Berg en Dal* (M), 3 rue de la Gare (tel. 8 41 27). 46 rooms. Playground; terrace; garage. *du Château* (M), 74 Grand'Rue (tel. 8 45 74). 27 rooms. Playground; terrace. *Heintz* (M), 55 Grand'Rue (tel. 8 41 55). 30 rooms and a villa for overflow. The best hotel. *Nugget Gulch* (M), 2 rue de Bettel (tel. 8 42 66), a motel. *Oranienburg* (M), 126 Grand'Rue (tel. 8 41 53). 36 rooms. Free garage.
    Restaurants. The *Veiner Stuff* (E), 26 Rue de la Gare (tel. 8 41 74) has adjoining *Veiner Stiffchen* (I) for snacks. *Hostellerie Trinitaires* (M), in the Hotel Heintz. Atmospheric.

WASSERBILLIG. *Hengen* (I), 2 Grand'Rue (tel. 7 40 68). 29 rooms, warm and welcoming.
    Restaurant. *La Frégate* (M), Esplanade (tel. 7 41 57). Pleasantly situated near the Moselle, makes a good halt for an excellent meal.

WELSCHEID. Northwest of Ettelbruck, it's worth the trip to eat at *Reuter's* (M), 2 rue de la Wark (tel. 8 29 17), 9 rooms.

WILTZ. Be sure to make reservations at Festival time. *du Commerce* (M), 9 rue des Tondeurs (tel. 9 62 20). 13 rooms. Central. *du Vieux Château* (M), 1 Grand'Rue (tel. 9 60 18), 13 rooms. Terrace. *Beau Sejour* (I), 21 rue du X Septembre (tel. 9 62 50). 56 rooms.
    Restaurants. *des Ardennes* (M), 61 Grand 'Rue (tel. 9 61 52) and *Belle-Vue* (I), 5–7 rue de la Fontaine (tel. 9 60 62) are dependable.

YOUTH HOSTELS. Plentiful and rewarding, for they are usually near ancient fortresses and castles. You'll find them at Clervaux, Echternach, Hollenfels. Luxembourg City, Vianden, among other places. **Luxembourg Y.H.A.,** 18 place d'Armes, Luxembourg, and **Gîtes d'Etapes Luxembourgeois** (Catholic network catering to groups), 23 blvd. du Prince Henri, Luxembourg (tel. 2 36 98) are two sources for further information.

SPORTS. Among the many sports possible in Luxembourg, **fishing** is perhaps the most rewarding, with fast streams and well-stocked rivers—notably with trout (almost everywhere), grayling, perch and dace. You need a Government permit and a permit from the owner of the fishing rights which, in many cases, is your hotel. As fishing-regulations are complex and very strict, fishermen are requested to apply for detailed information to the Administration des Eaux et Forêts, P.O. Box 411, Luxembourg.
    The District Commissioners also issue 5-day **hunting** (shooting) permits on request, but the application must be franked by the owner of the hunting rights for the area. The Luxembourg **golf course,** 6 km. (4 miles) from the city, has

become extremely popular with visitors these last few years. The 18-hole course, more challenging than most found on the Continent, is 6,800 m (7,400 yards) long. The well-run clubhouse has become a social center. Those who like **horseback riding** can apply to the Fédération Luxembourgeoise de Sports Equestres, 9 rue du Fort Elisabeth, Luxembourg City. Riding tours through the country can be arranged. Most tourist centers have **tennis** courts. There are **bicycle** trails in the Diekirch, Echternach, Vianden, Reisdorf and other areas. Space allowing, bicycles can be carried on trains (20 fr.L.) but not on buses.

The Grand Duchy has many rivers suitable for small craft or canoes. The broadest and the safest for **canoeing** is the Moselle. The Wiltz is of a more capricious type and requires continuous attention, as does the Clerve. The Our, with its wooded gorges, is the wildest, but most rewarding is the Sûre, for its length and for the thrills it offers. Addresses to write for further information on the above, all in Luxembourg City: Fédération Luxembourgeoise de Canoë et de Kayak, 6 rue de Pulvermuhle, Luxembourg.

Walking Tours: Enthusiasts will find the wooded and hilly regions a real paradise. Excellent, well-marked footpaths take you along attractive country-side without causing undue fatigue. The *Guides Auto-Pédestres* show how best to combine motoring and hiking. *Circuits Trains-Pédestres* gives you comparable advice for the railways. A combined book *Auto-Trains-Pédestres* is on sale. The Fédération Luxembourgeoise des Marches Populaires, 176 rue de Rollinger-grund, Luxembourg (tel. 44 93 02), can give you much good advice and aid.

Best walking tours: Seven Castles track—from Steinfort through Gaichel to Mersch: Victor Hugo track—Ettelbruck to Vianden, via Brandenbourg: Charles Mathieu track—Esch-sur-Sûre to Vianden: Moselle track—Wasserbillig to Stromberg. Circuit of the Lake of the upper Sûre.

MUSEUMS AND PLACES OF INTEREST. Museums and archeological and historical sites abound in Luxembourg. Access to, or participation in, archeological digs can be arranged through the State Museums, Luxembourg City. Admission charges to museums range up to 120 fr.L., although many are free. There are special prices and arrangements for groups; check with the ONT. To many of the castles which are not on this list admission is free; others ask 20–60 fr.L. There are wine cellars to visit all along the Moselle. Admission costs 35–60 fr.L., including wine tasting.

BECH KLEINMACHER. A Possen, Sandtegass (tel. 69 82 33). Folklore and winegrowing museum, in old house. Open daily in season from 2 to 7, except Mon. Adults 50 fr.L.

CLERVAUX. Abbey of St. Maurice and St. Maur (tel. 910 27). Dioramas of monastical life. Open 9 to 8.

Château. *The Family of Man* photographs by Edward Steichen and 22 models of Luxembourg's castles. Museum of the Battle of the Bulge. Open 10 to 5 in season. Adults 25 fr.L. each exhibit.

DIEKIRCH. Museum of the Battle of the Bulge. Open daily in season from 2 to 6. Admission 80 fr.L.

Roman Museum. Especially fine mosaics. Open daily in season from 9 to 12 and 2 to 6. Admission 15 fr.L.

Church. Dates from 5th century. Open daily in season from 10 to 12 and 3 to 5. No admission charge.

EHNEN. Musée du Vin (Wine Museum), tel. 7 60 26. Open daily in season, except Mon., 9.30 to 11.30, 2 to 5. Adults 50 fr.L., includes wine.

ETTELBRUCK. Patton Museum. The General and the Battle of the Bulge are the themes here. Open daily in season from 10 to 11.45 and 2 to 4.45. Admission charge 25 fr.L.

MERSCH. Roman Museum, rue des Romains. Ask for key at 1A rue des Romains (Mme. Bettendorf), or at the Hôtel de Ville. Admission free.

RUMELANGE. Musée National des Mines (Mining Museum). Follow the signs. A mining museum in a real mine gallery, with a ride in a mine car available. Open daily in season, 2 to 6; or tel. 56 54 71 for reservations. Adults 60 fr.L.

VIANDEN. Musée d'Art Rustique (Museum of Rural Art), 98 Grand'Rue (tel. 8 45 91). Very attractive setting for a collection of local crafts. Open daily 10 to 12, 2 to 6. Adults 45 fr.L.

    Victor Hugo House, Grand'Rue (tel. 8 42 57). House where Hugo lived while in exile in Luxembourg. Open in season 9.30 to 12, 2 to 6, except Wed. Adults 20 fr.L.

WASSERBILLIG. Aquarium, Promenade de la Sûre (tel. 74 81 46). Open in season from 10 to 11.30 and 2.30 to 6. Admission charge 40 fr.L.

SPAS AND CASINOS. Mondorf-les-Bains has modern installations fed by springs of hot thermal waters, discovered over a century ago and heavily mineralized. They are well known for the treatment of liver and other intestinal complaints and for all forms of rheumatism. The thermal establishment and a new center specializing in physical rehabilitation and breath education are open year-round. The gambling casino, daily concerts, tennis, boating, swimming and lovely walks complete the holidaymaker's activities.

USEFUL ADDRESSES. Local Tourist Offices: Beaufort, rue Gang (tel. 8 62 69); Berdorf, Hôtel de Ville (tel. 7 96 43); Clervaux, in the castle (tel. 9 20 72); Diekirch, pl. Guillaume (tel. 8 30 23); Esch-sur-Alzette, Hôtel de Ville (tel. 54 73 83); Echternach, Porte St. Willibrord (tel. 7 22 30); Ettelbruck, 13 Grand'Rue (tel. 8 20 68); Grevenmacher, 32 route de Thionville (tel. 75 82 75); Larochette, 2 place de la Gare (tel. 8 76 76); Mondorf-les-Bains, Casino (tel. 6 75 75); Vianden, Victor Hugo's House, 37 rue Gare (tel. 8 42 57), April to Nov.; Wiltz, Château (tel. 9 61 99).

TOURIST
VOCABULARY

TOURIST VOCABULARY

USEFUL EXPRESSIONS

English	French	Dutch-Flemish
Please	S'il vous plaît	Alstublieft
Thank you very much	Merci beaucoup	Dank U zeer
Good morning, sir	Bonjour, Monsieur	Dag, Mijnheer
Good evening, madame	Bonsoir, Madame	Goeden avond, Mevrouw
Good night	Bonne nuit	Goede nacht
Goodbye	Au revoir	Tot ziens
Excuse me	Excusez-moi	Pardon
I understand, I don't understand	Je comprends, je ne comprends pas	Dat begrijp ik, dat begrijp ik niet
Hunger, thirst	Faim, soif	Honger, dorst
Yes, no	Oui, non	Ja, neen
Yesterday, today, tomorrow	Hier, aujourd'hui, demain	Gisteren, vandaag, morgen
This evening, this morning	Ce soir, ce matin	Vanavond, vanmorgen,
How much?	Combien?	Hocvccl
Expensive, cheap	Cher, bon marché	Duur, goedkoop
Where? Where is? Where are?	Où? Où est? Où sont?	Waar? Waar is? Waar zijn?
Is this the right way to . . . ?	Est-ce bien la route de . . . ?	Is dit de goede weg naar . . . ?
Can you direct me to the nearest . . . ?	Pouvez-vous m'indiquer le plus proche . . . ?	Kunt U mij . . . dichtst bijzijnde wijzen?
doctor	médecin	de . . . dokter
hotel	hôtel	het . . . hotel
garage	garage	de . . . garage
post office	bureau de poste	het . . . postkantoor
police station	poste de police	het . . . politiebureau
telephone	téléphone	de . . . telefoon
To the left	A gauche	Links
To the right	A droite	Rechts
Bus or trolley stop	Arrêt	Bus/tramhalte
Entrance	Entrée	Ingang
Exit	Sortie	Uitgang
Admission free	Entrée libre	Vrije toegang
Open from . . . to . . .	Ouvert de . . . à . . .	Geopend van . . . tot . . .
No smoking	Défense de fumer	Verboden te roken
Gentlemen	Messieurs	Heren
Ladies	Dames	Dames

English	French	Dutch-Flemish
Town Hall	Hôtel de Ville	Raadhuis (Stadhuis)
Art Gallery	Musée d'Art	Schilderijenmuseum
Cathedral	Cathédrale	Kathedraal (domkerk)

RESTAURANTS AND DINING

English	French	Dutch-Flemish
Please give us the menu	Donnez-nous la carte s'il vous plaît	Mag ik het menu zien?
What do you recommend?	Qu'est-ce que vous recommandez?	Wat kunt U aanbevelen?
We will have the table d'hôte	Nous prendrons le prix-fixe	Wij nemen het menu
Please serve us as quickly as possible	Servez-nous aussi vite que possible	Bedien ons zo vlug mogelijk, alstublieft
Please give me the check (bill)	L'addition, s'il vous plaît	Ober, mag ik afrekenen
Have you included the tip?	Est-ce que le service est compris?	Service inclusief?
Waiter! Waitress!	Garçon! Mam'selle!	Garcon! Juffrouw!
Please give us some . . .	Servez-nous, s'il vous plaît	Geeft U ons wat . . .

Breakfast

English	French	Dutch-Flemish
Bread and butter	Du pain et du beurre	Brood en boter
Toast	Du pain blanc grillé	Geroosterd brood
buttered	beurré	warm gesmeerd
dry	sans beurre	zonder boter
Jam	Confiture	Confituur
Marmalade	Marmelade	Marmelade
Bacon and eggs	Oeufs au bacon	Eieren met spek
Fried eggs	Oeufs sur le plat	Spiegeleieren
Boiled eggs	Oeufs à la coque	Geokookt ei
soft-boiled	peu cuit	zachtegkookt
medium	mollet	halfzacht
hard-boiled	dur	hardgekookt

Meat and Poultry

English	French	Dutch-Flemish
Pork chop	Côtelette de porc	Varkenskotelet
Roast lamb	Rôti d'agneau	Gebraden lamsvlees
Roast mutton	Rôti de mouton	Gebraden schapenvlees
Roast veal	Rôti de veau	Gebraden kalfsvlees
Roast beef	Rosbif	Rosbief
Spring chicken	Poulet de grain	Piepkuiken
Chicken	Poulet	Kip
Duck	Canard	Eend
Wild Duck	Canard sauvage	Wilde Eend
Goose	Oie	Gans
Partridge	Perdreau	Patrijs

English	French	Dutch-Flemish
Rabbit	Lapin	Konijn
Hare	Lièvre	Haas

Seafood

English	French	Dutch-Flemish
Cod	Morue (Cabillaud)	Kabeljauw
Eel	Anguille	Paling
Flounder	Limande	Bot
Halibut	Flétan (Elbot)	Heilbot
Herring	Hareng	Haring
Mackerel	Maquereau	Makreel
Plaice	Plie	Schol
Salmon	Saumon	Zalm
Trout	Truite	Forel
Crab	Crabe	Krab
Crayfish	Ecrevisse	Rivierkreeft
Lobster	Homard	Kreeft
Oysters	Huitres	Oesters
Shrimp	Crevettes	Garnalen
Snails	Escargots	Slakken

Cooking Methods

English	French	Dutch-Flemish
Fried	Frit	Gebakken
Roasted	Rôti	Gebraden
Smoked	Fumé	Gerookt
Stewed	En ragoût, étuvé	Gestoofd
Rare	Saignant	Bleu
Medium	A point	Half gaar
Well done	Bien cuit	Goed gaar

Vegetables

English	French	Dutch-Flemish
Asparagus	Asperges	Asperges
Beans	Fèves	Bonen
String beans	Haricots verts	Snijbonen
Brussels sprouts	Choux de Bruxelles	Brusselse spruitjes
Cabbage	Chou	Kool
Carrots	Carottes	Wortelen (Pekens)
Cauliflower	Choux-fleur	Bloemkool
Cucumber	Concombre	Komkommer
Mushrooms	Champignons	Champignons
Onions	Oignons	Uien (Ajuin)
Peas	Petit pois	Erwten
Potatoes	Pommes de terre	Aardappelen
boiled	à l'eau	gekookte
fried	sautées	gabakken
French-fried	frites	frites
mashed	Purée de pommes de terre	aardappelpuree

English	French	Dutch-Flemish
Sauerkraut	Choucroute	Zuurkool
Spinach	Epinards	Spinazie
Tomatoes	Tomates	Tomate
Turnips	Navets	Koolraap

Fruit

Apple	Pomme	Appel
Cherries	Cerises	Kersen
Grapes	Raisins	Druiven
Lemon	Citron	Citroen
Orange	Orange	Sinaasappel (Appelcien)
Pears	Poires	Peren
Fruit salad	Macédoine de fruits	Vruchtensla

Beverages

A bottle of . . .	Une bouteille de . . .	Een fles . . .
A pot of . . .	Une théière, cafetière . . .	Eee potje . . .
A glass of . . .	Un verre de . . .	Een glas . . .
A cup of . . .	Une tasse de . . .	Een kop . . .
Water	Eau	Water
Iced water	Eau glacée	IJswater
Mineraal water	Eau minérale	Mineralwater
Milk	Lait	Melk
Coffee	Café	Koffie
Coffee with hot milk	Café au lait	Koffie met warme melk
Tea, iced tea	Thé, thé glacé	Thee, thé glacé
Hot chocolate	Chocolat chaud	Warme chocolade
Beer	Bière	Bier
Wine (red, white)	Vin (rouge, blanc)	Wijn (rode, witte)

Seasonings

Sugar	Sucre	Suiker
Salt	Sel	Zout
Pepper	Poivre	Peper
Mustard	Moutarde	Mosterd

AT THE HOTEL

Can you recommend a good hotel?	Pouvez-vous me recommander un bon hôtel?	Kunt U me een goed hotel aanbevelen?
Which is the best hotel?	Quel est le meilleur hôtel?	Wat is het beste hotel?
Have you anything cheaper?	Avez-vous quelque chose de meilleur marché?	Hebt U iets goedkoper?

English	French	Dutch-Flemish
What is the price, including breakfast?	Quel est le prix avec le petit déjeuner?	Wat is de prijs met ontbijt?
Does the price include service?	Le pris s'entend-il service compris?	Geldt de prijs inclusief bediening?
At what time is . . .	A quelle heure . . .	Hoe laat is hier . . .
breakfast	le petit déjeuner	het ontbijt
lunch	le déjeuner	het middageten
dinner?	le dîner?	het avondeten?
Please wake me at . . . o'clock	Je voudrais être réveillé à . . . heures	Ik wil graag om . . . uur gewekt worden
I want this dry-cleaned	Envoyez cela au nettoyage	Kunt U dit laten stomen? (. . . droog-kuisen?)
I want these clothes washed	Envoyez ces vêtements à la lessive	Wilt U alstublieft deze kleren in de was doen
I would like to have a . . .	Je voudrais avoir	Ik zou . . . willen hebben
single room	Une chambre à un lit	Een eenpersoonskamer
double room with	Une chambre	Een kamer met
twin beds	à deux lits	twee bedden
double bed	avec un lit à deux	een tweepersoonsbed
with bath	personnels	met bad
avec salle de bain		
Another pillow	Encore un oreiller	Nog een kussen
Another blanket	Encore une couverture	Nog een deken
Soap, towel	Savon, serviette	Zeep, handdoek
Coathangers	Cintres	Klerenhangers

TRAVELING BY TRAIN

English	French	Dutch-Flemish
Timetable	Horaire	Dienstregeling
Through train	Train direct	Doorgaande trein
Slow train	Train omnibus	Stoptrein (Omnibus trein)
Fast train	Train rapide	Sneltrein
Express train	Train exprès	Exprestrein
Weekdays only	En semaine seulement	Alleen op werkdagen
Sundays and holidays only	Seulement les dimanches et jours fériés	Alleen op Zon- en feestdagen
Return ticket	Billet aller-retour	Retour
One-way-ticket	Billet aller	Enkele reis
Fare	Prix du billet	Prijs van het reiskaartje
Compartment	Compartiment	Coupé
Dining car	Wagon-restaurant	Restauratiewagen
Sleeping compartment	Compartiment de wagon-lit	Slaapcoupé
First class	Première classe	Eerste klas
Second class	Seconde classe	Tweede klas
Connection	Correspondance	Aansluiting

English	French	Dutch-Flemish
Delay	Retard	Vertraging
All aboard	En voiture	Instappen

AT THE POST OFFICE

Air mail	Par avion	Luchtpost
Ordinary mail	Comme lettre ordinaire	Gewone post
Special delivery	Comme exprès	Express
Cable	Télégramme	Telegram
Stamp	Timbre	Postzegel
Registered	Recommandée	Aangetekend
Insured	Valeur déclarée	Verzekerd

DAYS OF THE WEEK

Monday	Lundi	Maandag
Tuesday	Mardi	Dinsdag
Wednesday	Mercredi	Woensdag
Thursday	Jeudi	Donderdag
Friday	Vendredi	Vrijdag
Saturday	Samedi	Zaterdag
Sunday	Dimanche	Zondag

NUMERALS

The answers to many of the questions you ask will be given in numbers, hence you need to know what they sound like. Here they are, with approximate pronunciations following in parentheses:

one	un, une (ung, een)	een (ayn)
two	deux (duhh)	twee (tvay)
three	trois (trwah)	drie (dree)
four	quatre (kahtre)	vier (feer)
five	cinq (sank)	vifj (fife)
six	six (seess)	zes (zess)
seven	sept (set)	zeven (zayfen)
eight	huit (weet)	acht (aght)
nine	neuf (nuff)	negen (nayhgen)
ten	dix (deess)	tien (teen)
eleven	onze (onz)	elf (elf)
twelve	douze (dewze)	twaalf (tvahlf)
thirteen	treize (trayz)	dertien (dairteen)
fourteen	quatorze (katorz)	veertien (fairteen)
fifteen	quinze (canz)	vijftien (fifeteen)
sixteen	seize (sayz)	zestien (zessteen)
seventeen	dix-sept (deess-set)	zeventien (zayfenteen)
eighteen	dix-huit (deess-weet)	achttien (aghteen)
nineteen	dix-neuf (deez-nuf)	negentien (nayhgenteen)
twenty	vingt (vang)	twintig (tvintuhk)
twenty-one	vingt et un (vantay-ung)	een en twintig (ayn en tvintuhk)

English	French	Dutch-Flemish
twenty-two	vingt-deux (van-duhh)	twee en twintig (tvay en tvintuhk)
thirty	trente (trahnt)	dertig (dairtuhk)
forty	quarante (kahrante)	veertig (fairtuhk)
fifty	cinquante (sankahnt)	vijftig (fifetuhk)
sixty	soixante (swahsahnt)	zestig (zesstuhk)
seventy	* septante (septahnt)	zeventig (zayfentuhk)
eighty	quatre-vingt (kahtr-vang)	tachtig (tahgtuhk)
ninety	* nonante (nunahnt)	negentig (naygentuhk)
one hundred	cent (sahnt)	honderd (hondairt)
one hundred and ten	cent dix (sahnt dees)	honderd tien (hondairt teen)
two hundred	deux cents (dur sahnt)	tweehonderd (tvay hondairt)
one thousand	mille (meal)	duizend (doyzent)

* Belgicisms. In France, 70 and 90 are, respectively, soixante-dix (swahsahnt-deess) and quatre-vingt-dix (kahtr-van-deess).

Index

The letter H indicates hotels. The letter R indicates restaurants.

LUXEMBOURG

FODOR'S TRAVEL GUIDES

Here is a complete list of Fodor's Travel Guides, available in current editions; most are also available in a British edition published by Hodder & Stoughton.

U.S. GUIDES

Alaska
American Cities (Great Travel Values)
Arizona including the Grand Canyon
Atlantic City & the New Jersey Shore
Boston
California
Cape Cod & the Islands of Martha's Vineyard & Nantucket
Carolinas & the Georgia Coast
Chesapeake
Chicago
Colorado
Dallas/Fort Worth
Disney World & the Orlando Area (Fun in)
Far West
Florida
Fort Worth (see Dallas)
Galveston (see Houston)
Georgia (see Carolinas)
Grand Canyon (see Arizona)
Greater Miami & the Gold Coast
Hawaii
Hawaii (Great Travel Values)
Houston & Galveston
I-10: California to Florida
I-55: Chicago to New Orleans
I-75: Michigan to Florida
I-80: San Francisco to New York
I-95: Maine to Miami
Jamestown (see Williamsburg)
Las Vegas including Reno & Lake Tahoe (Fun in)
Los Angeles & Nearby Attractions
Martha's Vineyard (see Cape Cod)
Maui (Fun in)
Nantucket (see Cape Cod)
New England
New Jersey (see Atlantic City)
New Mexico
New Orleans
New Orleans (Fun in)
New York City
New York City (Fun in)
New York State
Orlando (see Disney World)
Pacific North Coast
Philadelphia
Reno (see Las Vegas)
Rockies
San Diego & Nearby Attractions
San Francisco (Fun in)
San Francisco plus Marin County & the Wine Country
The South
Texas
U.S.A.
Virgin Islands (U.S. & British)
Virginia
Waikiki (Fun in)
Washington, D.C.
Williamsburg, Jamestown & Yorktown

FOREIGN GUIDES

Acapulco (see Mexico City)
Acapulco (Fun in)
Amsterdam
Australia, New Zealand & the South Pacific
Austria
The Bahamas
The Bahamas (Fun in)
Barbados (Fun in)
Beijing, Guangzhou & Shanghai
Belgium & Luxembourg
Bermuda
Brazil
Britain (Great Travel Values)
Canada
Canada (Great Travel Values)
Canada's Maritime Provinces plus Newfoundland & Labrador
Cancún, Cozumel, Mérida & the Yucatán
Caribbean
Caribbean (Great Travel Values)
Central America
Copenhagen (see Stockholm)
Cozumel (see Cancún)
Eastern Europe
Egypt
Europe
Europe (Budget)
France
France (Great Travel Values)
Germany: East & West
Germany (Great Travel Values)
Great Britain
Greece
Guangzhou (see Beijing)
Helsinki (see Stockholm)
Holland
Hong Kong & Macau
Hungary
India, Nepal & Sri Lanka
Ireland
Israel
Italy
Italy (Great Travel Values)
Jamaica (Fun in)
Japan
Japan (Great Travel Values)
Jordan & the Holy Land
Kenya
Korea
Labrador (see Canada's Maritime Provinces)
Lisbon
Loire Valley
London
London (Fun in)
London (Great Travel Values)
Luxembourg (see Belgium)
Macau (see Hong Kong)
Madrid
Mazatlan (see Mexico's Baja)
Mexico
Mexico (Great Travel Values)
Mexico City & Acapulco
Mexico's Baja & Puerto Vallarta, Mazatlan, Manzanillo, Copper Canyon
Montreal (Fun in)
Munich
Nepal (see India)
New Zealand
Newfoundland (see Canada's Maritime Provinces)
1936 . . . on the Continent
North Africa
Oslo (see Stockholm)
Paris
Paris (Fun in)
People's Republic of China
Portugal
Province of Quebec
Puerto Vallarta (see Mexico's Baja)
Reykjavik (see Stockholm)
Rio (Fun in)
The Riviera (Fun on)
Rome
St. Martin/St. Maarten (Fun in)
Scandinavia
Scotland
Shanghai (see Beijing)
Singapore
South America
South Pacific
Southeast Asia
Soviet Union
Spain
Spain (Great Travel Values)
Sri Lanka (see India)
Stockholm, Copenhagen, Oslo, Helsinki & Reykjavik
Sweden
Switzerland
Sydney
Tokyo
Toronto
Turkey
Vienna
Yucatán (see Cancún)
Yugoslavia

SPECIAL-INTEREST GUIDES

Bed & Breakfast Guide: North America
Royalty Watching
Selected Hotels of Europe
Selected Resorts and Hotels of the U.S.
Ski Resorts of North America
Views to Dine by around the World

WITHDRAWN

AVAILABLE AT YOUR LOCAL BOOKST...
PUBLICATIONS, INC., 201 EAST 50...